THE HEBREW REPUBLIC

THE HEBREW REPUBLIC

Carlo Sigonio

With an Introduction by
Guido Bartolucci

Translated and Annotated by
Peter Wyetzner

SHALEM PRESS

JERUSALEM AND NEW YORK

Carlo Sigonio (1520/24-1584), Italian historian, taught at the San Marco School in Venice and at the Universities of Padua and Bologna. He wrote several works on Roman and Greek history, focusing especially on political institutions, and on the history of Italy in the Middle Ages. His book on the Hebrew Republic was one of the first analyses of the political and religious institutions of the Ancient State of Israel and one of the most read works on this topic in Europe.

Shalem Press, 13 Yehoshua Bin-Nun Street, Jerusalem
Copyright © 2010 by the Shalem Center

Cover design: Erica Halivni

ISBN 978-965-7052-48-8

Printed in Israel

∞ The paper used in this publication meets the minimum requirements of the American National Standard for Information Sciences—Permanence of Paper for Printed Library Materials, ANSI Z39.48-1992

CONTENTS

BOOK III Sacred Days

BOOK IV   Sacred Rites

BOOK V   Sacred People

INTRODUCTION

IN 1582, CARLO SIGONIO, a historian of Greek and Roman antiquity, published *De republica Hebraeorum* (*The Hebrew Republic*), on the institutions of the ancient state of Israel.[1] The book was initially published in Bologna, the second city of the papal states, and was reprinted several times, becoming the most famous work on its topic in all of early modern Europe.[2] The cultural and historical context of Sigonio's work has posed something of a problem for scholars seeking to recover its meaning and historical significance: while the study of the Hebrew polity and its employment as a model for politics was not uncommon in Calvinist countries, Sigonio was writing in a Catholic environment and dedicated his book to the pope. Furthermore, like some of his Calvinist contemporaries, Sigonio presented the Hebrew state as a possible model for the separation of powers between the religious and secular realms, which would effectively neutralize the papacy's secular authority.

The implications of Sigonio's work for contemporary political studies have not been given sufficient consideration by scholars. Sigonio is usually characterized as an objective historian and a champion of antiquarianism, and his book on the polity of the ancient Hebrews has been seen as a collection of source texts devoid of meaningful ideas that could be applied to his own context. Yet, as we shall see, the matter is far more complicated. To determine the meaning of Sigonio's work in its time, one must take into account a wide array of issues, including his relationship with the archbishop of Bologna, his interest in historiography, his knowledge of contemporary European political debates, and his long-running quarrel with the Catholic censors. Ultimately, Sigonio will be shown to have had mixed motivations, writing at some times for political purposes and at others out of a commitment to objective history. In this respect, he was no different from his contemporaries researching the ancient Hebrew state, in Italy or abroad.[3]

One reason scholarship has failed to see Sigonio as part of the greater phenomenon of *Respublica Hebraeorum* study in early modern Europe has to do with how scholars have accounted for the increased interest in the ancient

Jewish polity during the period.[4] Some have identified the primary stimu-
lus as the study and dissemination of the fourth book of Josephus Flavius'
Jewish Antiquities during the second half of the sixteenth century. Others
have pointed to the progressive "secularization" of biblical history, which
permitted scientific analysis of the Jewish political model.[5] This model then
became—as classical political models had been for some time—a means of
legitimizing specific political positions (although "secular" here is something
of a misnomer, since the model was used in religious debates).[6]

This assessment that the "secularization" of Bible study is fundamental
to the political study and use of scripture has resulted in modern-day historians', with few exceptions, concentrating on the seventeenth and eighteenth
centuries and studying works published in countries such as England and the
Netherlands. The concurrence of political strife, advanced Bible study, and a
ruling Calvinism (in all its variations) explained the presence of works devoted
to the Hebrew republic.[7] Accordingly, scholars have focused on the works of
Cunaeus, Grotius, Selden, and Harrington, disregarding the founders of this
genre, such as Bonaventure Corneille Bertram and Carlo Sigonio (authors of
De politia Iudaica [1574] and *De republica Hebraeorum* [1582], respectively),
since their works were deemed to be of less political relevance.[8]

A more careful analysis may show that Bertram, a sixteenth-century
Calvinist theologian and Hebraist, could also be included in the aforementioned group.[9] But Sigonio is different: an eminent historian of Greco-Roman antiquities and professor at the *Studio* (or university) in the papal city
of Bologna, he resists the mold scholars have constructed to account for
political Hebraism. His omission is particularly problematic when we consider that of all the works on the polity of the ancient Hebrews published
in early modern Europe, Sigonio's was the most frequently cited. In fact, all
subsequent authors even remotely interested in Jewish political institutions
referred to the work of our Modenese historian. Nonetheless, *The Hebrew
Republic* has been considered "mere erudition," dismissed as a curiosity, or
viewed as the product of the political-religious agenda of Sigonio's patron,
Cardinal Gabriele Paleotti. In other words, Sigonio's work has always been
isolated from others in its genre and from both the Italian and broader European cultural context in which he lived.[10]

CARLO SIGONIO IN CULTURAL AND
POLITICAL CONTEXT

Carlo Sigonio was born in Modena (ca. 1520–1524) and moved, over the course of his life, between the most important cultural centers of northern Italy.[11] His cultural gestation took place in Modena, where his teachers included Francesco Porto and Ludovico Castelvetro, and where he replaced Porto as Greek lector. He taught at the St. Marco school in Venice between 1552 and 1559, then in Padua until 1563, when he moved to Bologna to hold the chair of humanities at the *Studio*. From the beginning, Sigonio divided his interests between Greek and Roman antiquities and Aristotle's *Rhetoric*. In the first field of research, he concentrated on different magistracies throughout Roman history and later on Livy's history of the Roman republic. He also analyzed Roman law and the history of Athenian institutions.[12] As for his other field of investigation, Sigonio had lectured on Aristotle's *Rhetoric* while teaching at St. Marco and had published a translation of it.[13] During this period, Sigonio developed some of his cardinal ideas, which ultimately shaped all his activity as a historian.

Venice

In Venice, Sigonio wrote *Oratio de laudibus historiae*, which is enormously helpful in understanding his historical method within the cultural context of his time. In this work, Sigonio finds history to be the noblest of the humanities, writing that those who overlook the passage of time and past events cannot really be considered men; they are rather like inexperienced boys unable to distinguish one thing from another. Grammarians, rhetoricians, poets, and philosophers must resort to the art of history in order to truly understand their own disciplines,[14] since history—the analysis of particulars with the aim of reaching universals—lies at the foundation of every science.[15] After further explaining how grammar, rhetoric, and philosophy are indebted to history, he adds that this discipline is of capital importance in understanding civil institutions. Philosophers who wrote on the state had to investigate and compare the different kinds of constitutions and determine which forms survived, which degenerated, and which turned into tyranny.[16] Sigonio ends the *Oratio* with the remark that philosophers draw their conclusions not by means of the secrets of their discipline but rather by direct observation of

the history of the particular states whose description they find in the works
of the ancients.[17]

The *Oratio* addresses—in embryonic form—two fundamental issues that
illuminate the subsequent scholarship of our author. The first is his method
of historical inquiry, whereby universal conclusions are reached by analyzing and comparing particulars. This approach had its foundations in Italian
humanism and had been employed, for example, by Guillaume Postel in his
study of languages and religions. During the second half of the sixteenth
century, it became a cornerstone of the new historiography, whose most
prominent exponent was none other than Jean Bodin. The second issue is
Sigonio's defense of the study of history. He argues that historical research
should be regarded not just as a "cult of antiquities" but as an effort to reconstruct the evolution of certain foundations of human society, particularly
those of juridical and civil institutions. Humanism had attacked traditions
using philology. Sigonio considers himself part of this historical-philological
trend and applies it with full force.

Sigonio's library held several French works, namely Bauduin's *De institutione historiae universae et eius cum iurisprudentia coniunctione*; the works
of Hotman, among them the *Francogallia*; and probably Bodin's *Methodus*
(*Method for the Easy Comprehension of History*).[18] His reflections on the ancient
states of Rome and Athens belong to the same Venetian period in which he
wrote the *Oratio* and developed his historical form in the greater European
context. Already in his lectures on Aristotle's *Rhetoric*, where he lauds the
mixed-constitution model of Cicero's *Scipio*, Sigonio reveals his predilection
for the form of the Venetian republic that hosted him and which for his au-
dience was formed mainly by the ruling class of the Lagoon republic.[19] His
praise for the mixed model of government accorded with the Aristotelian
concept of the six types of state.

A similar dependence on Aristotle can be found in one of Sigonio's most
important works, *De Antiquo Iure Civium Romanorum*, where he analyzes
the Roman state from its origin to the end of the republican period.[20] The
first of several ideas on which Sigonio dwells is Aristotle's analysis identifying
the three just forms of government (monarchy, aristocracy, and democracy)
and the three corrupt ones (tyranny, oligarchy, and ochlocracy). He adds
that what distinguishes the two groups is not the number of people taking
part in the administration of the state but rather the purpose they set for
themselves: the rulers of just forms always govern for the sake of the common good, whereas the rulers of degenerate forms govern in pursuit of their
own interests.[21] Interestingly, Sigonio offers an additional type of government:

the *respublica temperata*, which combines all three just forms and which he considers the best.[22]

Bologna

Sigonio's time in Bologna, where he taught from 1563 until his death in 1584, was a turning point in his career. This period was characterized by a shift in his interests, which had heretofore centered on history from the late Roman empire until medieval Italy. Paolo Prodi has dwelt on Sigonio's collaboration with Gabriele Paleotti, archbishop of Bologna from 1566, during this period, pointing out that Sigonio became the instrument of Paleotti's attempt at cultural and religious reform.[23] But there was life in the papal city of Bologna beyond the presence of Paleotti and his ecclesiastical policy, which sought to reform the Church according to the principles of the Council of Trent. The city was also imbued with strong political tensions between the central government of Rome, on the one hand, and the Bolognese aristocracy, with its aspirations of autonomy, on the other.

Sigonio was torn between these two positions. While he collaborated with the bishop, being involved in 1569 in the reformation of the liturgical office of St. Petronius, he also showed interest in the history of Bologna and in its longstanding autonomous tradition, and the city's senate even asked him to write on the subject.[24] In the resulting tract, when he described events closer to his own time—particularly the birth and development of the Roman Church—Sigonio was forced to step into the contemporary historiographical debate and take a stand in the controversy between Catholics and Protestants. At this point he had to deal with a conflict between his historical-philological method and the Church's need to legitimize its positions against attacks originating in transalpine Europe.

Beginning in 1569, Sigonio became a target of ecclesiastical censorship. The first criticisms were directed at his *Historia Bononiensis* and accused him of doubting the privilege granted to Theodosius and of questioning the veracity of other historical documents, to the detriment of the Church of Rome.[25]

Sigonio's works following this period reflect a continuous conflict between Rome, represented by Cardinal Sirleto, and Bologna, home of Sigonio's greatest advocate, Paleotti. *De regno Italiae* is another work which was to cause numerous problems for its author. In a memorandum written in 1569, Sigonio states that he was asked to write a history of Bologna, adding that he intends to extend his research to other Italian cities, particularly in Lombardy and Romagna.[26] This is the basis of Sigonio's history of the Italian peninsula, especially its northern part, from the Lombard invasion to the defeat of Holy Roman Emperor Frederick I at the hands of the Italian *communes*.[27] While Sigonio describes these events in the style of a chronicle, he allows himself some digressions of particular interest for our discussion because they touch upon the connection between the Holy Roman Empire and the papacy. Sigonio claims that the communes ultimately owe their freedom not to the papacy but to the empire. Furthermore, he states that the pope, who represented spiritual authority, held no political power over the communes in his land, as everything secular was the domain of the empire.[28] This work encountered papal censorship, and Sigonio was compelled to modify some sections considerably.

Sigonio's next work, *De occidentali Imperio*, which covered the centuries from Diocletian to Justinian (284–565 CE), was also very controversial, especially regarding the "Donation of Constantine,"[29] which the author considered a forgery. The Church (specifically Cardinal Sirleto) considered the "Donation" authentic and requested that it be integrated into Sigonio's work. The dispute ended when Sigonio yielded to the Church, which permitted the publication of the work in 1578.

The year 1578 marked an improvement in Sigonio's relations with the papal court, though it was not to last: Gregory XIII, elected in 1574, decided to avail himself of Sigonio's erudition and summoned him to Rome to entrust him with the task of composing a history of the Church that would confute the Protestant work *Centuriae magdeburgenses*. Once again, however, Sigonio's research and his conception of the proper role of history clashed with the polemical spirit that drove the actions of the Holy See. Although Sigonio devoted himself fully to this project, producing the first three books in a short time, the reaction of the Holy See was so negative that publication was interrupted at Book 14, and the rest of the work remained in manuscript until the eighteenth century, when Argelati edited it as part of Sigonio's *Opera Omnia*.[30] The authorities objected that Sigonio's history neither faulted the Protestants nor defended the Roman Church. This clearly emerges from the censor's reports on Sigonio's works: the author is accused of using language inappropriate for the narration of the history of the Church and of failing to condemn the heresies of antiquity, which, according to the Church, only anticipated new ones. Sigonio responded to this criticism by stating his priorities and explaining that the integrity of his philological method did not allow him to describe the past with the polemical language of the present.[31]

Despite Sigonio's conflict with the Holy See, Paleotti—who was engaged in the cultural reform of church institutions and popular religious sentiments in Bologna and of Christians in general—commissioned him to prepare an annotated edition of Sulpicius Severus' *Historia Sacra* (published in 1581) with the aim of providing the clergy with a tool for the study of biblical history.[32] As we shall see, it is here that Prodi identifies the origins of Sigonio's *De republica Hebraeorum*. This book on the ancient state of the Jews was to be Sigonio's last historical work.

Sigonio would die two years later, in 1584, devastated by the scandal surrounding the publication of his edition of the *Consolatio*, a work supposedly written by Cicero but considered by many to be a fabrication. Some scholars had accused Sigonio of writing the book himself, and therefore he spent the last years of his life defending its authenticity.[33] After Sigonio's death, his works were no longer published in Italy, as the friction he had encountered with the ecclesiastical censors had impugned his reputation as a historian, in particular of late-ancient Italy and of the Jewish state. His works did, however, continue to be very successful in the rest of Europe.

THE COMPOSITION OF 'DE REPUBLICA HEBRAEORUM'

Prodi's Hypothesis

What motivated Sigonio, hitherto concerned with classical topics, to study the Hebrew polity? As mentioned, Prodi connected the genesis of *De republica Hebraeorum* to Sigonio's work on Severus' *Historia Sacra*. A dedicatory letter to Paleotti, included in Sigonio's edition of the latter, demonstrates the Bolognese bishop's and Sigonio's shared interest in a history of Christianity that treated the people of the Old and New Testaments as part of one continuous history of salvation, which began with Adam's first sin and would end with Christ's salvation.[34] Prodi's explanation *seems* plausible, because Sigonio's previous research cannot be reconciled with his choice to pursue an analysis of Jewish institutions unless we take into account the intervention of Paleotti.

Verifying any hypothesis regarding the reasons Sigonio wrote *De republica Hebraeorum* is complicated by the conspicuous absence of correspondence documenting its composition. Whereas Sigonio's method of writing was usually characterized by continuous dialogue with colleagues and constant requests for information from them, in this case there is no trace of the process by which he collected material or progressed in his work. Strangest of all, we find no reference to this work in Sigonio's letters to his dearest friends, such as Pinelli, with whom he discussed his research at length. This seems to leave no option but to accept the hypothesis that the work ultimately originated in the dialogue between Paleotti and Sigonio on the history of the Church and its continuity with the Old Testament. Additional evidence supporting this theory can be found in the dedicatory letter to Gregory XIII placed at the beginning of *De republica Hebraeorum*, in which Sigonio declares the ancient state of the Jews an appropriate model for the Roman Catholic Church, as this state exemplifies the Augustinian idea of a City of Man and a City of God. Sigonio adds that the pope himself gave him the idea of writing this work when he asked him to compile a history of the Church.[35] Thus Sigonio seems to imply that all the works he wrote between 1578 and 1582 (*Historia ecclesiastica*, the commentary on Severus, and *De republica Hebraeorum*) were part of the same concept.[36]

Connections to Thinkers Elsewhere in Europe

Sigonio's claim in the dedicatory letter that the pope inspired the project would make sense if not for the following quotation from Corneille Bertram, a French theologian who taught Hebrew in Geneva, in the introduction to his *De politia Iudaica*:

> And so, while we both were waiting until someone who would deal with these things would appear, behold Sigonio, a very learned man and one of extraordinary skill in Roman and Greek history, promised a specific treatment of this topic.[37]

De politia Iudaica was published in 1574, four years before Gregory XIII would entrust Sigonio with writing the history of the Church. Therefore both Sigonio's version of events (according to which the idea of *De republica Hebraeorum* came about as a consequence of this invitation in 1578) as well as the hypothesis suggested by Prodi (according to which the inspiration for writing the book began with Paleotti's commission to write a commentary on *Historia Sacra* in 1581) are untenable.

How should we date this statement by Sigonio to which Bertram refers? On the basis of Bertram's dedicatory letter to Bèze, where he reconstructs how he began thinking in 1561 about writing on the ancient state of the Jews, we could say he came into contact with Sigonio around the time of the first publication of his *De politia Iudaica*. Here is the evidence: in the second edition of Bertram's text, in 1580, he amends the sentence, which originally stated that Sigonio had "promised" (*pollicetur*) to write a work on Jewish institutions, to read that he "seemed to promise" (*polliceri visus est*), apparently because a few years later Bertram no longer believed his colleague actually intended to write it.[38]

The second problem posed by the quotation is how Bertram became aware of Sigonio's intention to write about the ancient state of the Jews. Once again the answer is problematic, because we have no statements of this kind in the works written before 1574 or in his letters. One possible connection could be through Henri Estienne, the French printer and eminent Hellenist who lived in Geneva and was in contact with Sigonio. The association between the two dated back a long time, presumably to 1555, when they visited Bessarione's library in Venice.[39] We also have a letter from Sigonio to Estienne dated 1563, written while Sigonio was in Padua and about to move to Bologna. This is the only known correspondence between the two, and it testifies to a certain familiarity and a frequent enough exchange of information, demonstrated by the fact that Sigonio updates Estienne on his research.[40]

Still, all this amounts to rather weak evidence considering that we have no indication that Estienne and Bertram were ever in contact. At best, it shows a part of the network built by Sigonio within the Republic of Letters. By overemphasizing Sigonio's collaboration with Paleotti, Prodi dismisses the possibility that Sigonio's involvement in other cultural settings could have spurred his interest in the Hebrew polity and the fact that the cultural life of Bologna cannot be reduced to the politics of its bishop.

Insofar as Sigonio's involvement in other environments is concerned, it is worth considering his strong ties with German scholars, and in particular with the renowned Joannes Caselius, who between 1563 and 1566 lived in Italy, where he met Sigonio. Numerous letters indicate that this relationship continued in the following years; Sigonio even hosted Caselius' students in his house in Bologna.[41]

Sigonio's scholarly reputation also reached France: Bodin quotes him often, criticizing some of his positions; Bauduin refers to his works on Roman law already in 1561. The polemics on the curiate law[42] saw Sigonio opposing Grouchy, which reinforced his image in transalpine Europe. Similarly, from the correspondence between Dupuy and Pinelli, we learn of the success Sigonio's works enjoyed all over Europe, drawing the attention of Parisian printers and even of Wechel in Frankfurt.[43]

In this respect it is useful to note the history surrounding the text of *De regno Italiae*. This work was published in Venice in 1574 after being harshly attacked both by the Church of Rome and by the government of Venice, which objected to the way the city was portrayed. From the Pinelli-Dupuy correspondence, we learn how Sigonio (thanks to Pinelli) made his way into the European book market.[44] Together with a letter dated March 18, 1575,

Pinelli sent Dupuy a non-censored copy of *De regno Italiae*.[45] Dupuy's reply
to Pinelli on March 25 clarifies Sigonio's editorial strategy, confirming that
the text would have three editions: in Venice; in Frankfurt, published by
Wechel; and in Lausanne (actually Basel), published by Pietro Perna.[46] The
three versions have yet to be compared, but from the different sources we can
gather that Sigonio had very good connections in the European intellectual
community, in particular on account of Pinelli.[47]

Bologna as a Cosmopolitan Environment

Just as Sigonio was not interested exclusively in Bologna, having works from
other European cities in his library and seeking to publish abroad, so the
cultural world of Bologna was not monopolized by Paleotti. It was permeated
by different trends, particularly concerning the rule of the city and republican virtues. The tension between the local government of Bologna and the
State of the Church was very high at all levels, as Angela De Benedictis has
shown, and resulted in a trend toward republican writing, typified by Camillo
Paleotti's *De republica Bononiensi*.[48]

  This republicanism affected the Bolognese Printing Society, of which
Sigonio was the scholarly director, and it should be placed within the context
of the life of the city and its citizens' pride in their form of government. This
trend is evident not only in the publication of Sigonio's history of Bologna,
promoted by the city's senate, but also by the emblem chosen by the Printing
Society, which portrayed Felsina (the female anthropomorphization of the
city of Bologna) holding a cornucopia in her left hand and a flag bearing the
motto "*Libertas*" in her right. Another cultural icon of Bologna was Ulisse
Aldrovandi, a famous naturalist who was close to Cardinal Paleotti and at
the same time involved in the great European debates and in particular in
discussing the origins of culture and the genealogy of peoples. In unpublished
works such as *Bibliologia* and *Theatrum biblicum naturale*, Aldrovandi makes a
series of characteristic assertions that the Jews were the founders of all human
knowledge. According to this line of reasoning, philosophy, physics, and even
politics were invented by the Jews, and other cultures (including the Greeks)
had copied from them. These works should be placed within the European and
Italian context of the book and compared in particular to contemporaneous
chronologies of ancient peoples and their *prisca sapientia*.[49]

  However little detail it contains, the passage cited from the introduction
to Bertram's *De politia Iudaica* is crucial for recovering the factors that led
Sigonio to compose his own work and for constructing an alternative to

Prodi's hypothesis that will place *De republica Hebraeorum* in the context of the political debates of its time.

THE CONTENT OF 'DE REPUBLICA HEBRAEORUM'

As mentioned, *De republica Hebraeorum* was dedicated to Pope Gregory XIII and is divided into seven books. In the first book, in the chapters on the history of Jewish religious and civil institutions, Sigonio lays out a precise structure for the rest of the text, to which he later refers at various points in his discussion. After introducing the history of the Jewish people, Sigonio dwells upon the focal point of the Hebrew republic: the law given by God to Moses. Sigonio claims it is possible to delineate the representation of every institution according to a scheme that distinguishes the proper precepts for religious jurisdiction from the laws designed to regulate the civil order. Accordingly, the remaining six books are divided into two sections: one concerning religious institutions, and the other, civil.

The first section (Books II–V) contains an antiquarian analysis. The description of the sacrifices, the priests, the calendar, and the holy places is mostly a dry list of citations, without comment, from sources ranging from the Bible through the church fathers, ancient Jewish authors such as Josephus Flavius and Philo of Alexandria, and the Talmud and other rabbinical texts cited through secondary sources.

The second section contains a strictly political reading of the ancient Hebrew polity. Here Sigonio elaborates a view which diverges both from pre-Bodin political thought, which ignored the Hebrew model, as well as from precedents set by Bodin and Bertram, who advocated monarchic and mixed-constitutional readings of the Hebrew polity, respectively. This "aristocratic" view would become common in writings of subsequent thinkers.[50]

Sigonio finds the distinction between the religious and civil authorities in the Israelite polity to be grounded in Mosaic law, and hence chapter 4 of Book I, "The Law Given by God to the Israelites," is key to understanding the work in its entirety. Sigonio imposes a two-part structure on Mosaic law and further divides each part into two. The resulting four-part structure breaks with medieval tradition,[51] which viewed ancient Jewish law as composed of three kinds of precepts: moral, ceremonial, and judicial. For Christian theologians, first among them Aquinas, only the first part (pertaining to moral precepts) remained valid for Christians, while the other two applied solely to Jewish history.

Sigonio takes a different approach. He begins his construct of Jewish law with the two commandments of loving God and loving one's neighbor, claiming they represent the categories of religious life and civil life, respectively. These categories cover between them all of Jewish law. Sigonio then differentiates between two types of commandments that regulate religious life—mandates and precepts—and between two types of commandments that rule the civil sphere: *iudicia* and *iustificationes*. The first two categories include norms of ritual and religious organization, and the last two are strictly juridical (being, in effect, the God-given tools by which humanity condemns the guilty and acquits the innocent).

This four-part scheme sheds light on Sigonio's controversial views on the validity of the Ten Commandments and the book of Deuteronomy. Although Sigonio concurred with Catholic consensus on the Ten Commandments, seeing them as an elaboration of the first two principles (love of God and love of man), on the book of Deuteronomy he parted ways with the Church, seeing it as a development and interpretation of the Decalogue.

This has two important implications that help us understand the intentions of our author and his vision of the Jewish state:

The first concerns the structure of the law, which makes it relevant politically-juridically and not just theologically. Jewish law and its commentaries then became relevant and comparable to the secular legacy of Greece and Rome. It almost seems as if Sigonio is referring to the same conception of the history of law that dominated the European debate in those years and was attempting to reconstruct a genealogy of the various ancient juridical traditions, placing the Jewish model at the top of the hierarchy dictated by chronology.[52]

The second, which is actually more important for understanding the contribution of the Jewish state, concerns the result that this division of the law produces in the distribution of powers within the state itself. The theoretical separation between the religious and civil spheres also requires a practical separation between the investment of religious authority and civil authority in the hands of individuals. In other words, those in charge of the administration of religious matters (the priestly class) could not intervene in the administration of the state, particularly the activities of the court. The pontiff could preside over the Sanhedrin (when it acted as a court of law) only if the crime to be judged was of a religious nature.[53]

One is consequently led to question the sincerity of Sigonio's recommendation, in his dedication to the pope, that the Hebrew republic serve as a model for the Church of Rome, because an application of the separation of powers identified in the Hebrew model would effectively cause the Church to forfeit its secular authority. Sigonio must have recognized the political ramifications of such a doctrine for Rome, since the separation of religious and secular powers dominated the debates in Europe among all confessions.

This distinction between religious and civil jurisdiction was a central point of debate in the Calvinist world. I do not have enough space here to discuss the development of this idea, but it is important to emphasize that the issue was analyzed in much the same way by one Calvinist author whom we have already mentioned: Corneille Bertram. In several places in his *De politia Iudaica* (published eight years before Sigonio's own study of Hebrew polity), he discusses the difference between these two jurisdictions and identifies its origin in a parallel distinction between the two purposes of law. At the beginning of the first chapter, for instance, Bertram presents his general conception of law, maintaining that good laws always have a double task: (1) to direct man's *pietas* to God; (2) to articulate the duties that tie every man to his neighbor. Bertram makes this division of the law the basis of a double policy administered by two different groups of magistrates, one ecclesiastical and one civil.[54]

Although it is possible to find parallels between Bertram's and Sigonio's works, Bertram did not use the same four-part scheme described by Sigonio. This, together with the fact that we have no evidence that Sigonio had read the work of Bertram, forces us to seek another explanation for their similarities.

Jonathan Ziskind has maintained that Sigonio's scheme might correspond to the Hebrew division into *mitzvot, hukim, mishpatim,* and *dinim*.[55] I do not accept this thesis for two reasons. First of all, this Hebrew typology of law was absent from the Jewish sources studied by Sigonio. Second, Sigonio's use of specific Greek terms in his analysis might be traced to Suidas' lexicon, the *Suda*; this is a possibility that I have examined elsewhere.[56] Nevertheless, one can find a connection between the Hebrew typology referred to by Ziskind, Sigonio's four-part scheme, and Bertram in a work published in 1575 entitled *Thesaurus linguae sanctae*. This Hebrew-Latin dictionary was originally written by Sante Pagnini, one of the most important Italian Hebraists of the sixteenth century, and published in 1529, seven years before his death.[57] Pagnini's dictionary was reedited in 1575 by Bertram. In his preparation of the new edition he also used the material of Antoine Chevalier (d. 1572) and Jean Mercier (d. 1570).[58] In the *Thesaurus*, Bertram adds to the entries written by Pagnini, distinguishing the various additions by printing them in italics and adding a letter at the end, referring to the author of the note: M for Mercier and C for Chevalier (Bertram's own comments were apparently included with those of Chevalier). While the first edition of 1575 included the names of the three editors on the title page, the second one, published in 1577, included just the name of Mercier, probably because he was the only author formally considered to be Catholic.[59] The additions concern not only linguistic and grammatical questions, but also problems of Calvinist theology. Thus, even with the changes to the title page, the *Thesaurus* in its "Calvinist" form was added to the Roman *Index librorum prohibitorum* in 1593 (nine years after Sigonio's death).[60] Despite the unorthodox status of this book, which would ultimately lead to its prohibition, a copy of the 1577 edition had been in the private library of Ulisse Aldrovandi, a close friend of Sigonio, who would share his books with friends in Bologna; it is therefore possible that Sigonio had been exposed to the book.[61]

The analysis of Hebrew law is discussed in different entries of the dictionary. The first relevant definition is in the entry for *hok*, a word that Mercier translates into Latin as *statutum*. Mercier identifies this term with the ceremonies related to religion and the worship of God, such as circumcision, sacrifices, and holidays. He also makes a distinction between two different sets of commands: *hukim*, or *hukot*, on the one hand, and *mishpatim* on the other, the latter meaning "political judgments" (*iudicia*) and laws that concern the administration of society.[62] Under the entry *mitzva* Mercier gives its meaning as "precept" (*praeceptum*): a compulsion of the individual to observe some matter. Later on, in reference to a passage from Nehemiah, Mercier also states that *mitzvot* (here referred to as *mandata*) are general in nature, whereas *hukim* refer to specific rites and ceremonies.[63]

This first distinction presented by Mercier within the religious sphere can be compared to the first part of Sigonio's scheme, but it is necessary to clarify some points of terminology. Sigonio uses Latin terms rather than the Hebrew terms defined by Mercier: *mandata* and *praecepta* as opposed to *mitzvot* and *hukim*. Nonetheless the meaning given to each of the two parts of the law by the two authors is similar. Mercier's *mitzvot* and Sigonio's *mandata* have the broad applicability of general precepts of divine command and prohibition; in other words, they have a "universal" meaning. Mercier's *hukim* and Sigonio's *praecepta*, by contrast, both correspond to specific ceremonies and to the different manners in which man is to worship God.[64]

The same correspondence can be found in the sphere of civil law. In his gloss added to the entry on *mishpat*, Mercier explains that this term refers to the magistrate's power and, in particular, his power of judgment over particular kinds of cases.[65] In the *Thesaurus*, in the entry on *tzedaka*, one finds a specific analysis of civil power that is the work not only of Mercier but also of Chevalier and probably of Bertram. In the course of this entry the authors distinguish between "judgment" (*mishpat*), which refers to "the punishment of guilty men and criminals," and "justice" (*tzedaka*), which means "to defend good people from the offenses of evil people." The authors explain that both concepts fall under the jurisdiction of the court. Nonetheless they add a particular nuance to these terms, shifting their sense from the juridical field to the theological one. They do this by maintaining that *mishpat* corresponds to the preaching of the law that requires people to avoid evil and to respect the commandments of God. *Tzedaka*, on the other hand, correlates with the gospel that teaches us to have faith in God's mercy as guaranteed in Christ.[66] Following Calvinist theology, the authors transfer the division of Jewish law to the domain of religion, linking it to their idea of justification *ex sola fide*.

This analysis, which we have ascribed to all three authors, corresponds to parallel concepts developed by Sigonio. Nonetheless, the Calvinist editors of the dictionary suggest an analogy between civil and theological justice, while, at the end of his examination, Sigonio stresses the fact that his definition of justification is not considered from a religious point of view. It is as though Sigonio wanted to distance himself from both his source and the debate, raging at the time between various Christian confessions, concerning the significance of justification.[67]

Even if the structure of Sigonio's scheme is derived from Pagnini's *Thesaurus*, the Greek vocabulary that he uses and its correspondence with the Hebrew terminology present another problem. Sigonio probably made use of another dictionary that he had in his library, namely, the *Dictionarium trilingue*, edited by Sebastian Münster in 1530. In this work we find not definitions of words, but rather the correspondence of terms in three languages: Greek, Latin, and Hebrew. If we look at the four Latin words used by Sigonio in defining Hebrew law, we find a correspondence with the same Greek terminology that he uses, as well as with the parallel Hebrew terms defined in the *Thesaurus*. Concerning the first part of the law, *mandatum* is translated into Greek as *entolma*, *entolē*, *ephetmē*, and *prostagma*, and into Hebrew as *mitzva*;[68] *praeceptum* is translated into several Greek words, including *prostagma*, and into Hebrew as *mitzva* and *hok*,[69] while *cerimoniae* is translated into Greek as *prostagmata* and into Hebrew as *hukim*, *hukot*.[70] For the civil part of the law, *iudicium* is translated into the Greek *krisis*, *krima*, and into the Hebrew *mishpat* and *din*.[71] There is no *iustificatio* in the *Dictionarium*, but there are two related terms: (1) *Iustitia*, which is translated into Greek as *dikaiosunē* and into Hebrew as *tzedek*, *tzedaka*; and (2) *Iustifico*, which is translated into the Greek *dikaiō* and into the Hebrew verb *hitzdik*.[72] The correspondence of the different words in Latin, Greek, and Hebrew shows how Sigonio worked. He founded his research on Greek sources such as Josephus, Philo, and in particular the Greek translation of the Bible. For this task, Sigonio needed a Greek vocabulary for his analysis of the law, but the meaning behind these words was taken from Hebrew sources, and in particular from the *Thesaurus* of Pagnini, Mercier, Bertram, and Chevalier. Since Sigonio did not know Hebrew, one of his friends probably helped him to distinguish the different Hebrew words and to combine them with Latin and Greek terminology. For example, his friend Ulisse Aldrovandi had studied Hebrew in Bologna as a youngster and may have helped him.

Sigonio's scheme, then, makes use of a combination of sources that were deeply influenced by Calvinist literature. Even though he tried to distance himself from the most evident dangers of the Calvinist authors (for example, concerning the definition of "justification"), there is no doubt that Sigonio had looked to these authors as a model for his work and that he had used them for his own political aims.

The political significance of Sigonio's work becomes most evident when we analyze the pages of this book devoted to the birth and development of the Jewish state. In this discussion, Sigonio distances himself from the nuances of his earlier writings on ancient institutions, and he seems to modify his language in light of the contemporary European political discourse. His thoughts on the Hebrew state are summarized in the fifth chapter of the first book, where he outlines its history, particularly with respect to the transition from aristocracy to monarchy.

Aristocracy Versus Monarchy

First of all, Sigonio distinguishes between the relevant forms of state based on who holds the authority: a few individuals or just one.[73] In this context, he considers two kinds of constitutions: one based on law, and the other on the will of one person. The aristocracy was founded on the initial will of God (manifested in laws), but following the rejection of his will (i.e. the rejection of the laws),[74] God granted by concession a second constitution in the form of a monarchy.[75] Thus, from Moses to Samuel, the Hebrew state was an aristocracy, and from Saul up to the destruction of the Second Temple, it was a monarchy.[76]

Starting from this identification of the form of a state with the number of its rulers, Sigonio develops a theoretical approach profoundly different from that in his earlier works. First, he abandons the scheme of the mixed constitution in favor of simpler forms. Second, he analyzes the two forms of state without ascribing a moral quality to either of them (unlike his analysis of the differences between monarchy and tyranny, for example). Rather, he evaluates them based on their dependence on the law. Aristocracy is a positive model because it rules within legal parameters; monarchy, on the other hand, being the arbitrary rule of one person, departs from God's precepts. Unlike in his other works, Sigonio articulates a very clear contradistinction between aristocracy and monarchy, the latter intended as an institution free of any law (*rex legibus solutus*). Gone is his openness to the mixed constitution, which was so important in his Venetian years. Rather, as we shall see, he resorts to the kind of terminology that was becoming more and more prominent in the political thought of the second half of the sixteenth century, particularly in the writings of authors such as Bodin.[77]

Sigonio identifies a key transition period between the rule of Joshua and that of the judges, noting that no central power united the Jews of this era, but nonetheless authority was aristocratic.[78] In this case Sigonio highlights the important role played by inferior magistracies, represented by the heads of the cities and tribes. The institutional role of local government dominated contemporary European debate and was often connected to the study of Jewish institutions. Bertram in particular had pointed out that the "*respublica sancta*" did not disappear after Joshua, despite the absence of a leader, because of the rule of local authorities.[79] Sigonio writes in the same vein, insisting on the role of these officers in the structure of the state, as we shall see.[80]

Sigonio's analysis of the subsequent period of the judges identifies the aristocracy as the administrative authority (as opposed to the holder of power) of the republic. While the judges acquired authority and ruled the state, the law was enforced as before, and power remained in the hands of God.[81]

The reference to God as the holder of power in the republic might be misconstrued as an allusion to a passage from the second book of *Against Apion*, where Josephus praises the constitution of the ancient Jewish state because of its uniqueness and difference from all the Aristotelian models. Since the Jewish constitution was ruled by God, Josephus coined a term to define it: *theocracy*. But this analysis could not have satisfied Sigonio, who preferred to place the Hebrew republic within the Aristotelian scheme, presenting it as the most ancient model worthy of imitation. Consequently, he adopted the idea that the republic of the Jews was an aristocracy from Josephus' *Jewish Antiquities*.[82]

Returning to the evolution of political institutions, Sigonio writes that when the Jews asked Samuel for a king like every other nation, they effectively renounced God's rule over them, and the law consequently lost its value.[83] Monarchy was rule without law. Sigonio emphasizes the difference between aristocracy and monarchy, praising the former to the detriment of the latter.

For this purpose, he cites a passage in which Aristotle emphasizes the superiority of the rule of law over the rule of man. This statement was the cornerstone of many treatises that found aristocratic government to be the best model for the state. Here is the passage, as quoted by Sigonio:

> *Qui legem vult imperare, Deum vult imperare, qui regem, idest hominem, belvam. Quod non semper ratione sed plerunque cupiditate ducatur.*[84]

> He who would have the law govern would have God govern; He who would have a king govern would have a beast govern, because man is led not always by reason, but frequently by his desires.[85]

Sigonio slightly altered this passage by inserting the word *regem* (king), though perhaps in so doing he clarified rather than distorted Aristotle's intended meaning. Whereas the original text speaks only of *man's* role in ruling the state, Sigonio's version refers to the specific role of the king. However faithful this alteration of Aristotle's text was to its author's intentions, it is very strange that a scholar like Sigonio, who takes great care in the accurate citation of his sources, could make such a mistake. Furthermore, the inventories of his library mention at least four commentaries on Aristotle's *Politics*, among them that of Vettori, who was a friend of Sigonio's and devoted part of his analysis to this passage in particular and its variations in different manuscripts. Perhaps Sigonio simply misremembered the passage. But this explanation does little more than confirm that he was more interested in interpreting the statement than in faithfully reproducing it. His interpretation attributes to the passage aristocratic and anti-monarchic meanings that other commentators of the time vehemently denied.[86]

Sigonio also introduces another factor, independent of Aristotle. In his attempt to demonstrate the arbitrary rule of the king, he quotes the famous passage from First Samuel 8, where Samuel describes for the Jewish people the right (*ius*) a king would be able to exercise in his dealings with them. The interpretation of this passage was one of the strongest points of anti-monarchic polemics. Bodin (as a pro-monarchist) had taken pains to invalidate this point by understanding the Hebrew term *mishpat* ("right," translated into Latin as *ius* and into Greek as *dikaiōma*) as "custom" and "behavior" (*mores*). Once again Sigonio relies on the tools employed by contemporary opponents of royal absolutism.

The final aspect of Sigonio's political analysis of the Hebrew republic is his treatment of what he perceives as its tri-leveled structure. He states that the republic is composed of three concentric circles, the first encompassing the entire state, the second encompassing the tribes, and the third encompassing the cities of each tribe.[87] The first, all-encompassing level operated from whichever location God had chosen at any given point for the religious rites (i.e. wherever the ark of the covenant was, ultimately Jerusalem). It included the main institutions of the republic: the supreme magistrate (the judge or king), the great senate, and the main court of law.[88] Each tribe had its own leader, who was also the head of the lesser leaders of the different families.[89] Likewise, every city had its own senate, magistracies, and civil and criminal courts.[90] This three-tiered structure was one of Sigonio's most important contributions to the study of the Hebrew polity, particularly with respect to the analysis of the court system.[91]

Sigonio and the Censors

To fully understand the innovations of Sigonio's text and the problems it posed, it is useful to look at the reaction of the ecclesiastical censors. This reaction indicates the threat that the Church of Rome recognized in the political analysis of the ancient state of the Jews. As we have said, Sigonio claims the Jewish commonwealth experienced two types of state: the first aristocratic, where God and the law ruled through the magistrates; and the second monarchic, where the king held power according to his will, ignoring God and the law. We should first look at the censors' reactions to the identification of the Jewish commonwealth as an aristocracy.

Sigonio's analysis connects his concept of aristocracy with the Aristotelian conception of the best government as the rule of law and reason as opposed to the rule of one person (i.e. the monarch). Sigonio had already used this definition in his commentary on Sulpicius Severus' *Historia Sacra* in 1581. There he wrote that a free people does not accept rule according to the will of one person; such a people accepts only the rule of law.[92] Sulpicius' text, as quoted by Sigonio, can be translated as follows:

> The people have desired the kings (something detested by all free peoples), showing a clear and evident example of insanity; they have preferred to exchange liberty for slavery.[93]

Sigonio's commentary reads:

> Sulpicius was amazed that the Hebrews should prefer kings to judges, because the republic of the judges was defined as free, while the monarchic one was defined as a state of slavery. And he ascribes to the masses a natural preference for new things that are not in the scriptures. Free

peoples fight the institution of kings, because a free people obeys laws (that is, is obedient to reason), and a people that submits to a king obeys a will (that is, the caprice of one man, who is usually vicious). So the man who prefers a king instead of liberty is insane.[94]

The censor quite understandably attacked this reading of Sulpicius, stating that while the passage could be interpreted in different ways, Sigonio had given it an exclusively anti-monarchic cast, justifying contemporaneous rebellions against regal authority.[95] Sigonio equivocates in his response. Rather than watering down his argument, he incorporates nuances that strengthen it. He connects the Aristotelian passage defining the best state as the government of the best men with the passage from First Samuel describing the right of the king (*ius regis*) in terms of a series of acts against the people, carried out by a monarch above any kind of law.[96]

But Sigonio's argument seems disconnected from the biblical narrative. On other occasions, he had justified his non-traditionalism as a literal reading of the sources, describing events as they historically happened and not as they *should* have happened in theory. In this case, however, Sigonio is very clearly expounding a principle found in Aristotle as if it were confirmed by the holy scripture.

The censor's criticism regarding the *Historia Sacra* is arranged differently from the other three censorial texts addressed to Sigonio. Whereas the other three were arranged in the form of statements by the censor and responses from Sigonio, here the initial statement by the censor is followed by a response from Sigonio, then an additional retort from the censor. In the interchange on the subject of aristocracy, the censor begins by stating that if this is a discussion about norms, then one should look to Catholic doctrine, not to Aristotle.[97] The censor then interprets the aforementioned passage from Aristotle as referring to tyrants instead of kings. According to the censor, whereas the tyrant rules according to caprice, the king follows reason.[98] Here the censor links Sigonio to such anti-monarchists as the Scotsman George Buchanan. Passages in the commentary on the *Historia Sacra* are traced (perhaps even correctly) to Buchanan's oration on the Scottish right of freedom, *De Iure apud Scotos*.[99] The censor raises additional objections to other anti-tyrannical statements that portrayed the king as the enemy of freedom, since these positions were clearly opposed to the pro-monarchical stance of the Church. Furthermore he criticizes Sigonio for interpreting the passage from the book of Samuel with the aim of showing how the holy scripture rejected royal power.[100]

Let us suspend, for the moment, these considerations regarding the censorship of the commentary on *Historia Sacra* and turn instead to the Church's response to *De republica Hebraeorum*. As stated, Sigonio had described the original Jewish state as an aristocracy ruled by law as opposed to a monarchy ruled by the will of an individual. First, the Church took issue with his reliance upon the authority of Josephus in defining the Israelite form of government, since it would have been more appropriate for Sigonio to have based himself on scripture. Second, he was accused of espousing theories similar to those of heretics such as Calvin and Buchanan. The censor points out that this sin is all the more grave, since he had already been admonished for the same.[101]

The censor continues analyzing the controversial passages of *De republica Hebraeorum* in more detail, emphasizing that the king cannot rule if he is not subject to the laws, since in Deuteronomy 17 God established limits on regal authority, and in the same way (as Sigonio also mentions) the monarchs themselves had been elected by God. It is because of divine intervention, according to the censor, that the Jewish model of state is unique and cannot be compared to the other forms of government. In this model it is God who rules the republic, in accordance with his will.[102] It seems that the Church is attempting to deny the political value of the Hebrew model of state; probably the censor is thinking not only of Sigonio's work but of other treatises composed throughout Europe in that period which tried to legitimize non-monarchic models, basing themselves on the Mosaic histories.[103]

The censor also objects to Sigonio's anti-monarchic interpretation of First Samuel 8:7, where God tells Samuel that the people "have not rejected you but have rejected me." Rather than God's rejecting the idea of monarchy, the censor holds that this verse reflects the departure of the priestly class from the government of the state.[104] Similarly he interprets the Aristotelian distinction between the rule of law and the rule of kings as anti-tyrannical, not anti-monarchical.[105]

Sigonio's response is long and highly nuanced. He begins by simply rejecting the censor's most defamatory accusation: that he was influenced by the political ideas of Protestant heretics. Next, he claims that he chose his definition of monarchic form to stress its differences from the aristocratic one (though this assertion does not satisfactorily address the interpretive objections of the censor). He then tries to demonstrate to the censor that his reading refers not only to the passage in Samuel but also to the pro-monarchical passage in Deuteronomy 17.[106] Indeed, Sigonio uses this second source in Book VII, in the chapter devoted to kings, but he quotes it together with a paraphrase of Josephus Flavius—without commenting on it—and in

effect cites Samuel only to argue (as he does in all other contexts) that the
rule of monarchy was arbitrary.

After quoting a long passage from *De republica Hebraeorum*, Sigonio
reasserts that his work is orthodox in yet another respect: he presents the
Jewish monarchy in a negative way, because in the history of the people of
Israel the rule of the judges proved itself superior to that of the kings.[107]
To support this contention, Sigonio quotes passages from Thomas Aquinas,
although he ignores this author's mixed model, perhaps because he identifies only the two simple forms of aristocracy and monarchy in the Hebrew
republic. Nonetheless, he attaches great importance to Aquinas' interpretation
of the power of kings.[108] Sigonio uses Aquinas to argue that the episode of
the first Jewish king described in the book of Samuel, not only was negative,
but was inextricably connected to the treachery of the Jewish people, which
was consequently given a king as a punishment by God. Aquinas then draws
on the Aristotelian argument that virtuous individuals are extremely rare and
that therefore monarchy easily degenerates into tyranny.[109]

There is more to Sigonio's defense, but what we have described thus far
is sufficient for our purposes and can enhance our understanding of the
political thought of *De republica Hebraeorum*. Sigonio defends a concept of
kingship whereby a king rules not through laws but according to his will,
arguing that the distinction is not between legitimate and illegitimate monarchy, or between monarchy and tyranny, but between an aristocracy bound
by law and a king free of all legal limitations. It is no mistake that the censor
mentions people such as the constitutionalist Buchanan, since the rejection
of absolutism made use of the same analytical schemes. Even the reference
to Thomas Aquinas does not dispel suspicion of unorthodoxy, since Aquinas'
writings on tyranny and the right of resistance were also employed in the
constitutionalist literature.[110]

Connections to Other European Thinkers

It is particularly appropriate to place *De republica Hebraeorum* in the context
of the political discourse in the rest of Europe. One cannot explain Sigonio's
profound interest in the political application of the Hebrew model without
considering his influences from the other side of the Alps. In Sigonio's earlier works, the comparison of the histories of different peoples as a way to
understand the essence of political institutions had driven him to accurately
compare the distinctive elements of the various ancient and modern experiences—Roman, Greek, and Venetian. Similarly, in his work on the state of

the Jews, Sigonio establishes some parallels between different political institutions—for instance, between the Jewish criminal trial and the Venetian one.[111] Nonetheless, the commonalities with his previous efforts are not so numerous that they could be regarded as one, unified study of antiquity.

As we have seen, Prodi's attempt to place Sigonio's interest in the Jewish people within a religious-cultural project promoted by Cardinal Paleotti is contradicted by the peculiarly political characteristics of De republica Hebraeorum. For instance, with respect to Jewish law, Sigonio provides a scheme that deviates from the traditional Catholic understanding. His separation between ritual and civil law is more reminiscent of Calvinist thought, particularly the work of Bertram. Indeed, it is conspicuous that within a few years, two works were published on the Hebrew state which were based on a similar analysis of Mosaic law, describing it as a model in which the religious sphere was separated from the civil.

The significance attached by Sigonio to the different parts of the law, in particular the civil part, recalls the preoccupation of many scholars with Mosaic law in those years. These scholars built not only comparative schemata incorporating the different juridical experiences but also a genealogy of legal systems, which placed Jewish law at the top of the hierarchy. This interpretative scheme sheds new light on the history of Jewish institutions, which became progressively more accepted as a model and an instrument of legitimization for specific political agendas. Thus, whereas the history of Israel had for centuries been excluded from studies of political thought and relegated to theological and controversialist arenas, from the fifteenth century onward it acquired an increasingly important role within European culture in political science as well as in other fields. This transition was justified not only by the rediscovery of the biblical sources, which from Valla to Erasmus had been characteristic of the Reformation, but also by the Italian Renaissance ideology of prisca theologia and its reverence for ancient texts. In line with this development, Sigonio praises the Hebrew republic in his dedicatory letter to Gregory XIII not only because of its divine origin, but also because it was the most ancient of states. We do not wish to imply that Sigonio was part of the prisca theologia phenomenon, but it is certainly important to note that his colleague Ulisse Aldrovandi, whose library Sigonio used to complete his work, took part in the debate on the origins of human culture.[112]

Perhaps most significant, the censors viewed Sigonio within the greater European context, since in their attack on De republica Hebraeorum they placed it alongside the anti-monarchic literature of the period. The comparison is understandable; Bertram, for instance, identified in the Jewish tradition all the elements of Huguenot, anti-monarchic thinking: the key role played by the representatives of the people gathered in the assembly of the States-General, who hold supreme administrative authority; the people's power of election or dismissal of the king; and the importance of the provincial and civic magistracies in the administration of the state.[113] To these one must add the decisive role of the concept of contract, which aimed at uniting the king, the people, and God. The right of resistance to tyranny was grounded in these principles, and tyranny was defined as disregard for them. Resistance to tyranny became a hallmark of Huguenot political thought following the increasingly violent repression of Protestants in late-sixteenth-century France.[114]

Sigonio also lived in an environment rife with republican tensions, with the Bolognese magistracies' coming into open conflict with the institutions of the Church in Rome. Angela De Benedictis has shown that between 1588 and 1589 all the motifs of the European political-juridical debate had been introduced into this conflict, including all those aspects of the right-of-resistance literature that were inspired by examples in Jewish history.[115] Sigonio had contributed to this discussion both in the *Historia Bononiensis* and in *De regno Italiae*, but with *De republica Hebraeorum* he went even further in advocating republican ideas.

Sigonio's analysis relates to the crucial problems discussed in Europe at the time: the role of the law; the rule of the aristocracy as opposed to the abusive rule of the king; the prerogatives of the assembly in electing the magistrates and the monarch; and, most of all, the three-part scheme of the republic, which entrusts the provincial and civic magistracies with the task of administrating parts of the state. The last point leads inevitably to contemporary Huguenot thought and to Hotman in particular, who had praised this role of the local offices as the backbone of the entire kingdom in his *Francogallia*.[116]

Sigonio's scheme of the three concentric circles enjoyed great popularity in the political literature of the seventeenth century. Both Althusius and Grotius adopted his model, and Grotius, particularly in *De republica emendanda*, makes an analogy between Sigonio's *respublica Iudaica* and the United Provinces.[117]

Another nuanced aspect of Sigonio's tract is its discussion of the concept of power. Sigonio introduces the subject by claiming that the structure of the state is determined by the attribution of supreme power to an authority (*principatum*).[118] This definition is very different from that used by Sigonio for the Roman and Athenian republics. In these two cases, there was full conformity with Aristotelian definitions, most importantly in the distinction between just constitutions and degenerate ones, which Sigonio ignores in relation to the Jewish state. This definition seems to refer to Bodin's claim in the *Methodus* that the state is defined by its ruler. Bodin added that the form of the state depends not on the moral qualities of the holder of power but rather on the description of the ruling authority.[119] This analysis is connected to the rejection of any reference to a mixed form of government. If sovereign power (*imperium*) is thus characterized, it cannot be divided between multiple authorities. Rather, it must reside only with one who is prepared, if necessary, to delegate some prerogatives to other bodies of the state. On this principle Bodin bases his distinction between form of state and form of government: if in the form of state no partition is possible, in the administration of the state several entities can take part.

We have seen how Sigonio initially (in his Venetian years) idealized mixed government. He had praised the Roman republic of Scipio described by Cicero, comparing it to the rule of the *Serenissima* (the Venetian state).[120] In the case of the Jewish state, he rejects mixed government in favor of simple constitutions. For example, while discussing the functions of the popular assembly, he hastens to add that even if the people assist in the management of the state, the senate (in an aristocracy) and the king (in a monarchy) are the ones who actually hold the power.[121]

Another connection between Bodin and Sigonio can be seen in their analyses of the role of the king. For Bodin, one of the most important characteristics of the supreme power was the right of life and death, unbound by any law and in the hands of the sovereign.[122] In describing the Jewish judicial system, Sigonio identifies in the sovereign power one of the main points that differentiated judges from kings in the Bible: during the period of the judges, the right of life and death was limited by law; during the period of the kings, however, it rested on the discretion of the king's will.[123]

Sigonio's work plays an important role in the development of these themes in subsequent European political thought. The deeply Aristotelian framework that characterizes his thinking on the institutions of Israel made them intelligible to European thinkers and thus participated in the process by which the content of Jewish history penetrated European political culture. Earlier Christian Hebraists had perhaps already begun translating Hebrew legal texts into Latin juridical-political terminology, but by discussing the Hebrew model within an Aristotelian framework, Sigonio goes one step further and places it on a par with the Greco-Roman tradition, or even in some cases above it, because of its antiquity and holiness. This encounter between classical tradition and the divine Hebrew republic posed a problem for the absolutist literature, which was forced to view the Jewish model as a danger to traditional balances. As we have seen, the censor's replies to Sigonio had already attempted to limit the political significance of the Jewish republic, anticipating the reaction of seventeenth-century German thought, in which the scholar Herman Conring, in his *De republica Hebraeorum*, would claim absolute incompatibility between Jewish political history and the Aristotelian model. Conring's approach typified the "dejudaization" of European culture, which gradually expelled Judaism from every form of knowledge, relegating it to the theological and polemical space from which it had emerged at the beginning of the fifteenth century.[124]

SIGONIO'S JEWISH SOURCES

We will now look at the last aspect of Sigonio's work that will be useful in better understanding the significance of his analysis: his use of Jewish sources. In *De republica Hebraeorum* we find several references to the Talmud and other post-biblical texts, such as *Sefer Hakabbala* by Abraham ibn Daud Ha-levi. Most of these quotations are found in the parts of the work devoted to religion, whereas only two references are included in the last two books. In these last two citations, Sigonio refers not only to rabbinic texts but also to the secondary source of his information. Both quotations concern the court system and the role of the Sanhedrin as a judicial body, and they are taken from the *Opus de arcanis catholicae veritatis*, an anti-Jewish polemical work written by Pietro Galatino in 1518.[125] Sigonio's use of Galatino is of little significance in the development of his political thought. Sigonio uses him only partially, ignoring altogether, for instance, Galatino's talmudic distinction between the twenty-three-member and three-member law courts, which had drawn the attention of his predecessors, such as Bodin and Bertram.[126] For Sigonio's purposes, the Jewish political model had to be understood exclusively through the categories of classical political thought, which would have been impossible if he had referred to the juridical tradition of the Talmud.

In the first five books of *De republica Hebraeorum* we do find other passages quoting Jewish sources. Among them are the depiction of Ezra's recodification of the law, a description of Kabbala, a quotation from *Sefer Hakabbala*, and, above all, an unusual description of the Second Temple.[127] Sigonio did not own any of the original sources, nor could he have read them, since he did not know Hebrew. The only accessible text Sigonio could rely on for trustworthy translations of these Jewish sources was the *Chronographia* by Gilbert Génébrard, a teacher of Hebrew at the College of France.[128]

Génébrard's chronology is divided into four books, extending from the creation of the world to the end of the sixteenth century. In the first part, on Jewish history, we find all the same information included in Sigonio's book. It is noteworthy that Génébrard was the Latin translator of *Sefer Hakabbala* and *Seder Olam* (a classic Jewish chronology) as well as part of Maimonides' *Mishneh Torah* (in particular, the section on the Messiah). As an example of the relationship between Sigonio's and Génébrard's texts, let us examine our author's definition of Kabbala:

> But the things Moses taught orally he first communicated to Joshua, and then Joshua to the elders, the elders to the prophets, and the prophets to the scribes. In the later scholarship of the Hebrews, these traditions are called *cabala historica*.

This distinction between written and oral law and, more importantly, the definition of *cabala historica* could not be found in the Christian Kabbalistic tradition of the time. The source could, however, be found in two different passages of Génébrard's work:

> Joshua was instructed by Moses on the meaning of the law and divine right... He conveyed it to the seventy elders, who directly conveyed it to the prophets, and the prophets conveyed it to the sages, i.e. the scribes and the Pharisees. The rabbis prided themselves on having received from them their own knowledge. In *Pirkei Avot* 1, the rabbis called this *Cabala* or oral law.[129]

This first part derives, as Génébrard says, from the mishnaic tractate *Avot*, and it is followed by a more precise explanation of the concept of Kabbala. Whereas Reuchlin and Pico had defined the Kabbalistic tradition as a science (*ars*), Génébrard repeats this definition sarcastically, referring to the content of Kabbala as insignificant trivia (*nugae*). Instead he offers a different definition:

> This is not the *Cabala* exalted by the learned fathers, which is one part historical and one part what is called *tora b'al peh*, i.e. oral law... In effect it is the simple interpretation of the written law and contains the simple traditions of the synagogue, the customs, and the explanations of the ritual of the forefathers. Sometimes the Talmud, doctrinal homilies, responsa, etc., contain fragments of this tradition, but we will discuss this elsewhere.[130]

It is clear that Sigonio was also using this passage in his reference to *cabala historica* as oral law and the interpretative tradition of the written law.

Apart from secondary sources, Sigonio uses the Bible, the Septuagint translation, Josephus Flavius, Philo, and a few others. His aim was most likely to give his work scholarly legitimacy despite his lack of direct access to the sources, but this information does not play a decisive role in his analysis. As in other works of the period on the same subject, he intends to build a "scientifically" valid model, and for this purpose the Jewish sources were not important. Sigonio tries to place the history of Jewish political institutions within the context of a well-defined intellectual tradition (in which Jewish sources had no place), influenced primarily by the struggles and hopes of his time.

Thus the Hebrew republic is used by Sigonio to legitimize, on account of its antiquity and holiness, a political model where the religious and civil spheres are clearly separated and the aristocracy rules through the law. In this framework, the inferior magistracies of the tribes and cities play an important role. These issues were very controversial, both between the different European confessions and within each one. The debate in which Sigonio participates transformed life in countries such as France and the Netherlands, where brutal wars erupted from conflicts both religious and political. The discussion would continue in Grotius' Holland and Althusius' Germany, with these thinkers' relying on the Sigonian model as an important contribution to the development of their works.

Guido Bartolucci
Bologna, Italy

NOTES

I would like to thank Aleida Paudice and Gadi Weber for their help in translating this introduction from Italian into English.

1. Carlo Sigonio, *De republica Hebraeorum libri VII* (Bologna: Ioannem Rossium, 1582) (hereinafter *DRH*).

2. By the end of the eighteenth century, there were at least twelve editions of Sigonio's *De republica Hebraeorum*. For a complete list, see William McCuaig, *Carlo Sigonio: The Changing World of the Late Renaissance* (Princeton: Princeton University Press, 1989), pp. 347–355.

3. François Laplanche, "L'Érudition Chrétienne Aux XVIe et XVIIe Siècles et l'État des Hébreux," in Groupe de Recherches Spinozistes, *L'Écriture Sainte au temps de Spinoza et dans le système spinoziste* (Paris: Presses de l'Université de Paris Sorbonne, 1992), pp. 133–147; C.R. Ligota, "Histoire à fondement théologique: la République des Hébreux," in Groupe de Recherches Spinozistes, *L'Écriture Sainte*, pp. 149–167; Frank E. Manuel, *The Broken Staff: Judaism Through Christian Eyes* (Cambridge, Mass.: Harvard University Press, 1992); B. Roussel, "Connaissance et interprétation du Judaisme antique: des biblistes chrétien de la seconde moitié du XVIe siècle," in C. Grell and F. Laplanche, eds., *La république des lettres et l'histoire du Judaisme antique, XVIe-XVIIIe siècles* (Paris: Presses de l'Université de Paris Sorbonne, 1992), pp. 21–50; Lea Campos Boralevi, "Introduction," in Petrus Cunaeus, *De republica Hebraeorum*, ed. Campos Boralevi (Florence: Centro Editoriale Toscano, 1996), pp. i–lv; Arthur Eyffinger, "Introduction," in Petrus Cunaeus, *The Hebrew Republic*, trans. Peter Wyetzner (Jerusalem: Shalem Press, 2006). For a history of the *Respublica Hebraeorum* as a political model, see I.V. Comparato and E. Pii, eds., *Dalle "repubbliche" elzeviriane alle ideologie del '900* (Florence: Olschki, 1997), pp. 17–33; Jonathan R. Ziskind, "Cornelius Bertram and Carlo Sigonio: Christian Hebraism's First Political Scientists," *Journal of Ecumenical Studies* 37 (2000), pp. 381–400; L. Campos Boralevi and D. Quaglioni, eds., *Politeia Biblica*, in *Il Pensiero Politico* 35:3 (2002); Yaakov Deutsch, "A View of the Jewish Religion: Conceptions of Jewish Practice and Ritual in Early Modern Europe," *Archiv für Religionsgeschichte* 3 (2001), pp. 273–295. In Israeli scholarship as well, this discussion has led to an emphasis on the diffusion of the idea of the Hebrew republic in the early modern period, with studies focusing on the role played by Jewish culture in the ideas of republicanism. Cf. Fania Oz-Salzberger, "The Jewish Roots of Western Freedom," *Azure* 13 (Summer 2002), pp. 88–132.

4. See note 7 below.

5. On the first aspect, see Ligota, "Histoire à fondement théologique," pp. 149–167. On the second, see Manuel, *Broken Staff*.

6. In truth, neither of these constitutes a complete explanation. Probably one reason political thinkers turned to the Hebrew model was the concept of *prisca theologia*, which ranked the validity of different traditions according to their antiquity, thus placing the Hebrew tradition at the top of the hierarchy, since it was considered

most ancient. In a similar vein, the second half of the fifteenth century saw the discovery and translation into Latin of works by ancient authorities who claimed that the Greek philosophical disciplines had been imported from the Hebrew tradition. Whereas earlier, the Hebrew model had been considered irrelevant, since it lacked fields comparable to those of the classical tradition (specifically ethics, rhetoric, and philosophy in general), now it could be viewed as the authentic origin of those fields and thus more relevant than anything else.

7. A compendium of all these works is provided by the Israeli scholar Kalman Neuman, who sees in Christian Hebraism at the end of the sixteenth century the context in which a biblical antiquarianism emerged that allowed a political interpretation of the text. See Kalman Neuman, "Political Hebraism and the Early Modern 'Respublica Hebraeorum': On Defining the Field," *Hebraic Political Studies* 1:1 (Fall 2005), pp. 57–70.

Valerio Marchetti offers another explanation. Starting from the reaction to this phenomenon in seventeenth- and eighteenth-century Germany, Marchetti extended his research to other fields as well, pointing out that the attack was directed not only at the Jewish political model but also at an entire philosophical movement accused of "judaizing" European culture beginning in the fifteenth century. A study of the dissertations of Protestant pastors during the same period reveals the delegitimization not only of the existence of a Jewish political model, but also of those arguments that claimed the dependence of Aristotle and Pythagoras on Judaism, and that had in general represented the principles of *prisca theologia* and of the "judaization" of European culture in the fifteenth century. See Valerio Marchetti, "An Pythagoras proselytus factus sit," *Dimensioni e problemi della ricerca storica* 2 (1996), pp. 111–121; V. Marchetti, "Aristoteles utrum fuerit iudaeus. Sulla degiudaizzazione della filosofia europea in età moderna," in Bruna Bocchini Camaiani and Anna Scattigno, eds., *Anima e Paura. Studi in onore di Michele Ranchetti* (Macerata, Italy: Quodlibet, 1998), pp. 249–266; V. Marchetti, "Sulla degiudaizzazione della politica. In margine alla relazione di Horst Dreitzel," in A.E. Baldini, ed., *Aristotelismo Politico e ragion di stato: Atti del convegno internazionale di Torino 11–12 Febbraio 1993* (Florence: Olschki, 1995), pp. 349–358; V. Marchetti, "Il teologo Johann Franz Budde (1667–1729) e la filosofia ebraica," in Mauro Perani, ed., *L'interculturalità dell'ebraismo* (Ravenna, Italy: Longo Editore, 2004), pp. 299–314.

8. This is the standard perception of Sigonio's work: "It is not always evident that the motivation for the work is other than pure scholarship. Sigonio was first and foremost an antiquarian and historian. His attempt to describe the political system of the Hebrews after writing descriptions of the systems of the Romans and the Athenians seems to reflect the same academic interest." Neuman, "Political Hebraism," p. 66. This definition suggests that the study of antiquity is detached from time and space and from reality in general. On the contrary, as evidenced by the presence of Sigonio's work within the context of the French discussion of Roman institutions, this kind of study constituted the basis for the elaboration of political ideas in the framework of contemporary historical events.

9. See Guido Bartolucci, *La repubblica ebraica di Carlo Sigonio: modelli politici dell'età moderna* (Florence: Olschki, 2007).

10. On the first point, see E. Cochrane, *Historians and Historiography in the Italian Renaissance* (Chicago and London: University of Chicago Press, 1981), p. 441. On the second, see Paolo Prodi, *Il Cardinale Gabriele Paleotti, 1522-1597*, 2 vols. (Rome: Edizioni di Storia e Letteratura, 1959-1967); P. Prodi, "Storia sacra e controriforma. Nota sulle censure al commento di Carlo Sigonio a Sulpicio Severo," *Annali dell'Istituto storico italo-germanico in Trento* 3 (1977), pp. 75-104. In the latter work, examining the censorship of Sigonio's commentary on *Historia Sacra*, Paolo Prodi connects it with *De republica Hebraeorum*. See also P. Prodi, "Cultura ebraica e mondo intellettuale Bolognase; 'Heri Dicebamus...,'" in Mauro Perani, ed., *La cultura ebraica a Bologna tra medioevo e rinascimento. Atti del convegno internazionale, Bologna, 9 aprile 2000* (Florence: Giuntina, 2002), p. 10: "*Il disegno dello storico e del vescovo che lo sosteneva era molto piu' ambizioso come progetto di costruzione di una storia della chiesa innestata nella storia del popolo ebraico e nell'Antica Alleanza perché servisse come base della formazione cristiana dei giovani.*"

11. The main sources for Sigonio's biography are L.A. Muratori, "Vita Caroli Sigonii," in C. Sigonio, *Opera omnia edita et inedita* (Milan: in aedibus Palatinis, 1732-1737), vol. 1, pp. i-xx; G. Tiraboschi, *Biblioteca Modenese* (Modena, Italy: Società Tipografica, 1781-1786), vol. 5, pp. 76-119; L. Simeoni, "Documenti sulla vita e la biblioteca di Carlo Sigonio," *Studi e Memorie della storia e dell'Università di Bologna*, vol. 11 (1933), pp. 183-262; McCuaig, *Carlo Sigonio*, pp. 3-95.

12. Cf. C. Sigonius, *De antiquo iure civium Romanorum* (Venice: Iordanum Zilettum, 1560); C. Sigonio, *De antiquo iure Italiae* (Venice: Iordanum Zilettum, 1560); T. Livius, *Historiarum ab Urbe condita libri*, cum commento C. Sigonii (Venice: Paulum Manutium, 1555); C. Sigonius, *De republica Atheniensium* (Bologna: Ioannem Rossium, 1564). For Sigonio's bibliography, see McCuaig, *Carlo Sigonio*, pp. 346-356.

13. Aristoteles, *De arte rhetorica (Carolo Sigonio interprete)* (Venice: ex officina Stellae Iordani Ziletti, 1565). On Sigonio's lecture on this work, see *MS gamma* 6.18 (Bergamo, Italy: Biblioteca civica Angelo Mai). This manuscript contains the transcription of Sigonio's lectures on the first book of Aristotle's *Rhetoric* at the St. Marco school during the years 1553-1554. For the description and content of the manuscript, see McCuaig, *Carlo Sigonio*, pp. 19-23. I am indebted to Dr. W. McCuaig for giving me his copy of the text. It must be noted that Sigonio's literary interest continued during the period of his lectures in Padua on the *Poetics* and is reflected in the composition of *De dialogo* (an analysis of the concept of mimesis). Torquato Tasso was one of Sigonio's students in these years and quotes his teacher in the introduction to the *Rinaldo*. See C. Sigonius, *De dialogo liber* (Venice: Iordanum Zilettum, 1562). For the lectures on the *Poetics*, see W. McCuaig, "Carlo Sigonio's Lectures on Aristotle's *Poetics*," *Quaderni per la storia dell'Università di Padova* 16 (1983), pp. 43-69. On the relationship between Tasso and Sigonio, see McCuaig, *Carlo Sigonio*, pp. 50-53 and the bibliography there.

14. C. Sigonius, *Oratio de laudibus historiae* (Venice: Ioannem Zilettum, 1560), p. 38r: "*Etenim, si omnem nostram scientiam, tum demum vere scientiam esse dicimus, cum causas in universum, cur aliquid ita sit, videmur posse reddere. Universa autem omnia non nisi singulis rebus ante perceptis ac diuturno studio collectis continentur.*

Quis scientiam hanc, sine veterum notatione temporum ac sine priscorum observatione hominum, aut sibi, aut aliis videbitur esse adeptus?"

15. Cf. R. Orestano, *Introduzione allo studio del diritto romano* (Bologna: Il Mulino, 1987), pp. 634–637. Compare the text quoted from Sigonio above with the following passage from the *Methodus*: "*Quamobrem utile visum mihi est, ad eam quam instituo methodum, philosophorum ac historicorum de republica disputationes inter se, et maiorum imperia cum nostris comparare, ut omnibus inter se collatis, universa rerumpublicarum historia planius intelligatur.*" J. Bodin, *Methodus ad facilem historiarum cognitionem*, in Bodin, *Oeuvres philosophiques*, ed. and trans. P. Mesnard (Paris: Presses Universitaires de France, 1951), pp. 106–269; passage quoted from p. 231.

16. Sigonius, *Oratio*, p. 41r: "*Etenim quis est, qui suam egregie capessere rempublicam possit, cum genus ipsius reipublicae cum causas salutis, atque interitus ignoret? Aut quis est, qui optime civitati suae possit consulere, si neque maiorum leges, neque mores aut instituta percalleat? Quid porro aliud continent scripti a philosophis de republica libri, nisi multa esse rerumpublicarum genera, eaque inter se facile commisceri, causas esse quasdam, quibus illae conserventur, hae pervertantur, consilia vero alia ad libertatis, alia ad tirannidis diuturnitatem?*"

17. Ibid., p. 40v: "*Quae si ita sunt, ea certe non ex arcana magis ista philosophorum scientia, quam ex aperta diversarum observatione rerumpublicarum, unde fere illa etiam admirabilia philosophorum praecepta sumpta sunt, eruere poterit, qui vetera annalium monumenta perlustraverit.*"

18. The question of Sigonio's library was addressed only in 1933 by Simeoni, who published Sigonio's will, which included a list of his books. No one has addressed this list's inclusion of French legal texts such as those cited above. McCuaig has discovered another very informative list of texts, commissioned by Giacomo Boncompagni, who was once in possession of Sigonio's property. The French legal references on this list are:

1. "Balduini, *Istitutuz Historia*, in 4°, Venetiis," which corresponds to F. Balduinus, *De institutione historiae universae et eius cum iurisprudentia coniunctione*. This work was never actually published in Venice, but there is no question that it was among the books owned by Sigonio.

2. "Bald., *De iure civili*, in 8°, Basilea," which corresponds to F. Balduinus, *Ad leges de iure civili, Voconiam, Falcidiam, Iuliam Papiam Poppaeam, Rhodiam, Aquiliam* (Basel: per Joannem Oporinum, 1559), 8°.

3. "Balduini, *Catechesis*, in 8°, Lion," which is F. Balduinus, *Iuris civilis catechesis ex... praelectionibus* (Basel: Ioannes Oporinus, 1557), 8°.

We also find references to Hotman: "Othoman, *Franc. Gul*, in 8°, Lion," and "Othoman, *De optim. Gener*, in 8°, Lion," which probably correspond to F. Hotomanus, *Francogallia. Libellus statum veteris Reipublicæ Gallicæ, tum deinde à Francis occupatæ, describens. Editio secunda* (Coloniae: ex officina Hieronymi Bertulphi, 1574), 8°; and F. Hotomanus, *De optimo genere iuris interpretandi* (Leiden: Antonium Gryphium, 1566), 8°, respectively.

There is a final reference, probably the most controversial but also the most striking: "Bondini, *Historia*, in 8°, Basilea," which probably corresponds to J. Bodin, *Methodus ad facilem historiarum cognitionem* (Basel: ex Petri Pernae officina, 1576). Cf. Città del Vaticano, Archivio vaticano, Fondo Boncompagni, Armadio i, mazzo q, *Nota di tutti i libri acquistati dalla eredità del celebre letterato Carlo Sigonio dal duca Giacomo Boncompagni Seniore*, cc. 11. The quotations come from fols. 4v, 7v, 11v, 11v, and 8r, respectively. On the history of Sigonio's library, see Simeoni, "Documenti"; and P. Pirri, "Gregorio XIII e l'eredità della biblioteca di Carlo Sigonio," in Carlo Bestetti, ed., *Studi Di Storia Dell'Arte Bibliologia Ed Erudizione In Onore Di Alfredo Petrucci* (Milan and Rome: Edizioni d'Arte, 1969), pp. 89–96.

19. McCuaig, *Carlo Sigonio*, pp. 19–24.

20. On the analysis of Sigonio's study of Roman institutions, see McCuaig, *Carlo Sigonio*, pp. 96–250.

21. C. Sigonius, *De antiquo iure populi romani libri undecim* (Bologna: Societatem Typografiae Bononiensis, 1574), p. 3: "*Qui autem praecepta nobis adhuc de republica reliquerunt, ii fere in eo universi consentiunt, ut tres rectas esse respublicas statuant et tres contra depravatas. In bonis regem numerant, optimates et populum, in vitiosis tyrannum paucorum factionem et plebem. Bonas autem vocant respublicas, cum sive a rege sive ab optimatibus, sive a populo bene ac iuste atque ad totius civitatis utilitatem accomodate res ipsa publica administratur; pravas vero, in quibus sive tyranni sive, paucorum, sive plebis libidine atque utilitate omnia diriguntur.*"

22. Sigonius, *De antiquo iure populi romani*, p. 3: "*Ut autem rectas illas, quas dixi, vocarunt, sic quae ex illis rectis esset temperata atque confusa, multi optimam esse arbitrati sunt.*" In his other work on ancient institutions, *De republica Atheniensium*, Sigonio uses the same Aristotelian categories: The Greek city was built in two stages—first, a kingdom, and second, a popular government.

23. Prodi, *Il Cardinale Gabriele Paleotti*, vol. 2, pp. 215–268.

24. Ibid., p. 246. On the *Historia Bononiensis* and the conflict with Rome, see in particular G. Fasoli, "Appunti sulla *Historia Bononiensis* ed altre opere di Carlo Sigonio (1522–1584)," in G. Fasoli, *Scritti di Storia Medievale* (Bologna: Patron, 1974), pp. 683–710; C. Bastia, "*Per una ricostruzione della genesi e delle vicende censorie dell'*Historia Bononiensis *di Carlo Sigonio*," *Schede Umanistiche* 2 (1993), pp. 99–113.

25. See Prodi, *Il Cardinale Gabriele Paleotti*, vol. 2, pp. 252–253.

26. Bologna, Archivio Isolani, MS F 31 3, f. 14v–16v.

27. The *communes* were part of a new kind of political institution that emerged in Italy in the twelfth and thirteenth centuries and revived the forms and ethos of the city-states of antiquity. They were characterized by a secular government in which officers were elected, and they had de facto independence under the nominal overlordship of emperor, pope, king, etc.

28. C. Sigonius, *De regno Italiae* (Frankfurt: apud heredes Andreae Wecheli, 1591), p. 177: "*Et sane, quanquam Italia a rege, eodemque imperatore et a romano pontifice*

tenebatur, non eadem tamen erat in utroque auctoritas. Pontifex Romam Ravennamque et ditiones reliquas tenebat auctoritate magis quam imperio, quod civitates pontificem, ut reipublicae principem, regem vero, ut summum dominum intuerentur, atque ei tributa, obsequiaque quae dixi, praeberent. Et pontificis vires in sacris detestationibus versabantur, quas christiani reges tum maxime exhorruerunt, imperatoris in armis et expeditionibus, quibus ipsi etiam pontifices cedere saepe compulsi sunt." See McCuaig, *Carlo Sigonio,* pp. 84–85, 280–282.

29. The "Donation of Constantine" was a famous document probably written in the late eighth century in Rome and listing grants made to Pope Sylvester I by Emperor Constantine I. Because it represented the foundation of the secular power of the Church of Rome, the debate on its authenticity was crucial. Even though in the fifteenth century both Lorenzo Valla and Nicholas of Cusa had proven it a forgery, this document was again the subject of a dispute between the Catholic Church and the Reformation movement in the sixteenth century. The latter, seeking to undermine the Church's secular authority, followed Valla and maintained that it was a forgery.

30. Sigonio, *Opera,* vol. 4, pp. xvi–318.

31. Sigonio's last four works (*De regno Italiae, De occidentali Imperio,* the commentary on the *Historia Sacra* of Sulpicius Severus, and *De republica Hebraeorum*) were attacked by Rome, as demonstrated by the censorship texts. The most numerous are those written against *De republica Hebraeorum,* which contain more than ninety objections. A first edition of these texts was included by Argelati in the sixth volume of Sigonio's *Opera Omnia* (see Sigonius, *Opera,* vol. 6, pars tertia, coll. 1067–1234). Dr. W. McCuaig has completed a critical edition of these texts, which I'm currently editing with the authorization of McCuaig and the University of Toronto's Center for Reform and Renaissance Studies. McCuaig has corrected Argelati's version and filled in the gaps. The following response by Sigonio indicates his conflict with the censors: "*Ad extremum censor obiicit Sigonio crimen omissionis et ait: debuisse loqui de Concilio Tridentino contra omnes haereses celebrato; quod primatus S. Petri sit de iure divino; quod fides illa sola sit Catholica quam Romana Ecclesia tenet ac docet; quod standum sit sanctis conciliis, sacris canonibus et Ecclesiae mandatis; debuisse agere de doctrina septem Ecclesiae sacramentorum, de merito bonorum operum, carpere haereticos huius temporis et eorum haereses confutare. Cui respondetur: haec omissa esse, quia ad historiam Sulpicii non pertinebant, quae finitur anno Christi 400 et Sigonio propositum tantum habuit illustrare acta Hebraeorum ab Adam usque ad Christum et nihil praeterea. Pro pueris autem non desunt libri qui talia doceant, ut catechismus Romanus et libelli de doctrina Christiana, qui in scholis leguntur.*" Sigonius, *Opera,* vol. 6, pars tertia, col. 1162. As can be seen, Sigonio refuses to use history as a polemical tool in the conflict between Catholics and Protestants. He views his work as independent of theological considerations.

32. Sulpicius Severus, *Sacrae Historiae libri ii,* In eosdem Caroli Sigonii Commentarius (Bologna: Societatem Typographiae Bononiensis, 1581).

33. See McCuaig, *Carlo Sigonio,* pp. 291–326.

34. *"...ad extremum vero sacrae etiam historiae lectionem in eadem auditoria inducere, a quibus adhuc tamquam perpetuo quodam damnata exilio abfuerat, voluit, non quidem, ut profanarum inde rerum cognitionem eiiceret, quam robustioribus tradi convenire putavit, sed ut prima cognoscendae vetustatis initia a Deo sumenda esse iis, qui ad sapientiae, et pietatis professionem ingrederentur, ostenderet... Quamobrem recte prudentia vestra, breviarium eius aliquod ex immenso illo utriusque Testamenti corpore conquisivit, quo studiosa iuventus omnia ab Adam usque ad Christum, idest a peccato ad salutem in ipsius Dei populo gesta quasi in unam tabulam conlata conspicere; et cum duos B. Severi Sulpicii libros in hoc genere distincte, atque ornate admodum scriptos probavit, tum ad tollendum exquisitioris interpretationis hominibus occupatis laborem, eosdem etiam expositione illustrari aliqua voluit."* Severus, *Sacrae Historiae*, p. 3v. On the commentary on this passage and on Prodi's thesis, see Prodi, "Storia sacra e controriforma," pp. 80-81.

35. *DRH*, pp. *2v-*3r. Cf. this edition, pp. 3-4.

36. See p. viii of this letter.

37. *"Itaque dum uterque nostrum expectamus quoad aliquis exoriretur qui haec pertractaret, ecce Sigonio vir doctissimus et historiae romanae iuxta ac graecae peritissimus peculiarem eius argumenti disputationem pollicetur."* B.C. Bertram, *De politia Iudaica* (Geneva: E. Vignon, 1574), p. 8. On the Calvinist theologian Corneille Bertram (1531-1594), see *Dictionnaire de Biographie Française*, s.v. "Bertram, Bonaventure Corneille"; Laplanche, "L'Érudition Chrétienne," pp. 133-147; A. de Montet, ed., *Dictionnaire biografique des Genevois et des vaudois, qui se sont distingués dans leurs pays ou à l'étrager pour leurs talents, leurs actions, leurs oeuvres littéraires ou artistiques etc.* (Lausanne, 1877), vol. 1, pp. 48-49.

38. On Bertram's text, see Ziskind, "Cornelius Bertram and Carlo Sigonio"; S. Rauschenbach, "*De republica Hebraeorum* Geschichtsschreibung zwischen 'hebraica veritas' und Utopie," *Zeitschrift für Neuere Rechtsgeschichte* XXVI:1-2 (2004), pp. 9-35; Bartolucci, *La repubblica ebraica di Carlo Sigonio*, pp. 45-65.

39. J. Kecskeméti, B. Boudou, and H. Cazes, *La France des Humanistes. Henri II Estienne, éditeur et écrivain* (Turnhout, Belgium: Brepols, 2003), p. 17: "*Meministine Carole, vir charissime, quum anno superiore tecum Venetiis bibliothecam Bessarionis una cum duobus Venetiis patriciis ingrederer, quis a nobis habitus fuerit sermo?*" The dedication to Sigonio is in the following edition: *Ex Ctesia, Agatharchide, Memnone excerptae historiae, Appiani Iberia. Item, De gestis Annibalis. Omnia nunc primum edita. Cum Henrici Stephani castigationibus* (Paris: ex officina Henrici Stephani Parisiensis typographi, 1556).

40. Sigonio's letter is found in J.Ph. Krebs, *Carlo Sigonio einer der grössten Humanisten des sechszehnten Jahrhunderts* (Frankfurt am Main: Druk und Verlag von Heinrich Ludwig Brönner, 1840), pp. 29-30. In the appendix, the author includes some letters written to and by Sigonio, including the one by Estienne and those by Jacob Gorski, Joannes Caselius, Paolo Sacrati, and Josephus Castalio. This is the full text: "*Accepi libellum a te perelegantem eum, in quo tu summo studio veterum fragmenta poetarum quasi aliquas ex foeda tempestate tabulas collegisti. In quo eodem nescio*

iudiciine, an amoris erga me tui magnitudinem sim potius admiratus, iudicii, quod ex ea re litterarum ad me mittendarum occasionem quaesiveris, cuius me magnopere studium delectaret. Amoris, quod me eiusmodi munere ad simile erga te obeundum litterarum officium, quod me eiusmodi munere ad simile erga te obeundum litterarum officium, quod tibi gratissimum fore significas, provocaris. Ego vero cum librum ipsum valde probavi, tum causam, quae te ad eum mittendum impulit, multo magis, neque enim illustri, mihi crede, tua erga me benevolentia ad voluptatem quidquam suavius, neque iis, quae a diligentia ingenioque tuo proficiscuntur, ad usum accomodatius aliquid potest contingere. Itaque doleo in primis, me tandiu Xenophontis illius tui Graeci Latinique iucundissimuo fructu carere, quem te ad me mississe binis iam litteris repetis. Neque vero ego solus hoc conficior desiderio, sed familiares mei omnes, qui his dediti studiis sunt, ita te tuosque labores amant, ut nullamrem vehementius cupiant. Quam ob rem scire avemus omnes, quae ex officina tua, praeter ea quae nunc ad te descripta mittimus, industriae tuae monumenta prodierint, ut ea sibi quisque cognita comparare possimus. Ego, quod de me quaeris, his diebus de republica Atheniensium magnum sane opus institueram, eo consilio, ut aliquando Atheniensium res non minus quam Romanorum mea ornatae ac illustratae industria posteris proderentur. Sed me praeter quotidianas occupationes multa iam e medio cursu revocarunt. Proxime vero quid a Bononiensibus honestis praemiis in Academiam suam accitus, eo iam prope totus animo incumbebam. Ubi si quid inciderit, quod ad tua commoda pertinere intellexero, noli putare, me amicitiae nostrae, cuius memoria apud me sanctissime custoditur, ullo unquam tempore defuturum. Vale. Patavio. Kal. Quintil. 1563." On Henri Estienne, see *Henri Estienne, Cahiers V. L. Saulnier* 5 (1988), especially O. Reverdin, "Henri Estienne a Genève," pp. 21–42; A.A. Renouard, *Annales de l'mprimerie des Estienne ou histoire de la famille des Estienne et de ses éditions* (Paris, 1843). Estienne had edited Hebrew works such as Antoine Chevalier's grammar text in 1566 and was professor of Hebrew at Geneva, preceding Bertram.

41. A history of Sigonio's relations with the German academic community has not yet been written. In particular, no one has dealt with Caselius' key role in disseminating Sigonio's works. At least five letters inform us of this encounter and its importance. Some appear in I. Caselius, *Epistolae bonae frugis plenae, quarum paucae antehac editae fuerunt, pleraeque iam primum lucem aspiciunt* (Hamburg: Typis Iacobi Rebenlini, 1641), pp. 24–27, 146–148.

42. See McCuaig, *Carlo Sigonio*, pp. 56, 197–225.

43. Cf. G.V. Pinelli and C. Dupuy, *Une correspondance entre deux humanistes,* ed. A.M. Raugei (Florence: Olschki, 2001), vol. 1, p. 162: "*Le facteur d'André Vechel m'a dit, que son maistre imprimeroit volontier les oeuvres d'icelui Sigonio de l'antiquité Romaine, sur l'édition derniere de Boulongne.*" On Wechel's press, see E.J.W. Evans, *The Wechel Presses: Humanism and Calvinism in Central Europe 1572-1627* (Oxford: Past and Present Society, 1975). On the relationship between Wechel and Sigonio's works, see McCuaig, *Carlo Sigonio*, pp. 74–75. In 1583, Wechel also printed the second edition of *De republica Hebraeorum*.

44. On the history of this work, see Pinelli and Dupuy, *Une correspondance,* pp. 132, 133, 157.

45. Pinelli and Dupuy, *Une correspondance*, p. 157: "*Nell'historia del Sigonio fecero un gran rumore, ma senza proposito, poiche non è stata punto mutata da quel di prima, quanto à Vinitiani, per un altro principe sì* [Pinelli refers to the pope], *del quale v'informerà un giorno il suddetto Luyeres* [i.e. François Pithou]. *Basta che V.S. ha l'esemplare, che non è stato mutato, et questo per gratia del libraro, ch'è mio amico.*"

46. Pinelli and Dupuy, *Une correspondance*, p. 162: "*Nous avons à ceste fois l'histoire du Seigneur Sigonio, et on m'a dit qu'il y en aura de trois impression diverses à la foire, à-sçavoir de Venise, de Francfort et de Lausanne à l'instance de Jac. Dupuis.*" C. Sigonio, *Historiarum de regno Italiae libri quindecim* (Basel: ex officina Petri Pernae, 1575); C. Sigonio, *Historiarum de regno Italiae libri quindecim* (Frankfurt am Main: ex officina typographica Andrae Wecheli, 1575).

47. Pinelli was also acquainted with another scholar who played a key role in kindling interest in the ancient state of the Jews: the jurist François Roaldès. In the introduction to *De politia Iudaica*, Bertram notes that the first person to suggest that he study the "twofold jurisdiction" of the Jewish state was Roaldès, his teacher in Cahors. See Bertram, *De politia Iudaica*, p. 7: "*Tertius et decimus agitur annus, Vir Clarissime, quum Franciscus Rhoaldus, iurisconsultus legum romanarum totiusque antiquitatis consultissimus, Cadurci meam in discutienda iudaica politia, eiusque duplici iurisdictione operam efflagitavit.*" On Roaldès' life (d. 1598), see E.L. de La Mothe-Langon, ed., *Biographie Toulousaine, ou Dictionaire historique des personnages qui... se sont rendus célèbres dans la ville de Toulouse ou qui ont contribué à son illustration* (Paris, 1823), vol. 2, p. 1823; Nicolas-Toussaint Le Moyne Des Essarts, *Les Siècles littéraires de la France* (Paris, 1880–1881), vol. 6; F. Roaldès, *Discours de la Vigne*, ed. Hilippe Tamizey de Larroque (Bordeaux: imprimerie G. Gounouilhou, 1886). Roaldès came to Italy in 1579 and met several Italian scholars, among them Pietro Vettori, Sigonio, Girolamo Mercuriale, Fulvio Orsini, and Gian Vincenzo Pinelli in particular. (These meetings are listed in a letter from Roaldès to Pierre Pithou. Cf. Roaldès, *Discours de la Vigne*, pp. 79–80.) Pinelli had heard about Roaldès before his arrival in Italy, and Pinelli's library contained the manuscript of one of Roaldès' juridical works. (Milan, Biblioteca Ambrosiana, MS B 143 sup. Franciscus Roaldesius, *Methodus ad ius universale* [1570]. On first reading, the work seems to contain no reference to Jewish law.)

48. On the debate in Bologna, see A. De Benedictis, *Repubblica per contratto. Bologna: una città europea nello Stato della Chiesa* (Bologna: Il Mulino, 1995). Two copies of the work (F 55, 124, which represents the "draft," and E 50.2, which is one of the definitive copies) are in the Archivio Isolani in Bologna. For a discussion of this work, see Prodi, *Il Cardinale Gabriele Paleotti*, vol. 2, pp. 47–50; and De Benedictis, *Repubblica per contratto*, p. 249.

49. Cf. Prodi, *Il Cardinale Gabriele Paleotti*, vol. 2, p. 202; P. Prodi, "Vecchi appunti e nuove riflessioni su Carlo Sigonio," in M. Firpo, ed., *Nunc alia tempora, alii mores. Storici e storia in età postridentina (Atti del Convegno internazionale, Torino, 24–27 settembre 2003)* (Florence: Olschki, 2005), pp. 291–310, esp. pp. 304–305. The *Bibliologia* is preserved in Bologna's Biblioteca Universitaria, MS Aldrovandi 83, 2 voll. Cf. A. Adversi, "Ulisse Aldrovandi Bibliofilo, bibliografo e bibliologo del Cinquecento,"

Annali della scuola speciale per archivisti e bibliotecari dell'università di Roma VIII:1–2 (1968), pp. 85–181. This work, which among other things reflects on Jewish culture, has not yet been studied. We encounter, for example, a chapter on "Della dottrina degli Hebrei che è di tre sorti" (fols. 535–537), in which Aldrovandi discusses the Jewish Kabbala and its meaning. The chapter on "Che il Misna et il Thalmud è una medesima cosa" (fols. 537–539) is also interesting, especially where Aldrovandi writes (fol. 539): *"Thalmud è il medesimo che dottrina, la quale contiene tutti i commenta et constitutioni de gli antichi, et l'historie di certi tempi; opera veramente piena non solo di sapienza divina et naturale, ma politica et regale, come chiaramente testifica il dottissimo Galatino nel suo primo libro De Archanis Catholicae veritatis."* Just as Bodin had used the etymology of Hebrew words to support his political thesis, so Aldrovandi writes (fol. 444): *"Questa santa et divina lingua non solo è attinta a fare conoscere le cose divine, ma ancora per conseguire le scienze humane. Perciochè chi considererà diligentemente la vista delle parole et saprà la forza della lor etimologia farà più progresso in la cognitione delle cose naturali che se egli havesse a memoria tutta la dottrina d'Aristotele."* The *Theatrum* can be found in Bologna's Biblioteca Universitario, MS 54, 2 voll, fol. 4r: *"Quamvis Tales, ut testatur Cicero, primus natura rerum disputasse dicatur, scire tamen oportet eum diu post Mosen fuisse. Floruit enim eo tempore quo Ezechias Iudeis et Numa Pompilius Romanis praesidebat... Etiam vetustissimi Graeci prophetis hebraeis sunt iuniores"*; fol. 4v: *"Quicquid gentiles dogmatum atque mysteriorum posteris reliquerunt id omne ab Hebraeis praesertim a Mosis divinissimi vatis voluminibus sacris suffurati sunt, quod Clemens Alexandrinus, Atticus Platonicus, Eusebius et Aristobulus aperte testatur."*

50. See note 49 above.

51. See Thomas Aquinas, *Summa Theologiae*, Ia2ae, q. 99, 1–6. On the meaning of the Decalogue in the Catholic tradition, see *Dictionnaire de théologie catholique*, s.v. "Décalogue."

52. It is important to bear in mind the following passage, where Sigonio describes the judicial role of issuing acquittals and condemnations: *"Iudicii porro in lege praescripta hoc sit exemplum: 'Nocturnum furem occidito'; iustificationis: 'Diuturnum dimittito.' Item iudicii: 'Qui prudens hominem occiderit, capite poenas luet,' iustificationis: 'Qui imprudens, rite exulerit.'"* It is useful to place it side by side with a work published in France in 1574, which compares the same biblical passage with the Roman juridical tradition: *"Quod si duodecim tabularum: 'nocturnum furem quoquo modo, diurnum autem si se audeat telo defendere, interfici iubent,' scitote, iuris consulti, quia Moyses prius hoc statuit, sicut lectio manifestat. Moyses dicit: 'Si perfodiens nocte parietem inventus fuerit fur et percusserit eum alius et mortuus fuerit hic, non est homicida is qui percusserit eum. Si autem sol ortus fuerit super eum, reus est mortis percussor: et ipse morietur.' Paulus libro sententiarum v ad legem Corneliam De sicariis et veneficis: 'Si quis furem nocturnum vel diurnum qui cum se telo defenderet occiderit, hac quidem lege non tenetur, sed melius fecerit, qui eum conprehensum transmittendum ad praesidem magistratibus obtulerit.'"* P. Pithoeus, *Collatio legum Mosaicarum et Romanarum*, in P. and F. Pithoeus, eds., *Observationes ad Codicem et Novellas Iustiniani Imperatoris* (Paris: e typographia regia, 1689), p. 33. Petrus Pithou, a French jurist and disciple of Cujas, published an edition of this anonymous work that was written around the

fourth century and systematically compares the laws found in the Old Testament with those described by ancient jurists in order to find similarities. On the early modern tradition of interpretation of Mosaic law, see Bartolucci, *La repubblica ebraica di Carlo Sigonio*, pp. 177–184.

53. *DRH*, p. 257: "*Advocarunt vero hoc concilium aut rex aut pontifex, prout crimen delatum aut civitatem attigit aut religionem.*" Cf. this edition, p. 250.

54. "*Legum omnium bonarum, sive sint scriptae, sive non scriptae, duplex est scopus: aut enim hominis erga Deum pietatem respiciunt, aut hominum inter se officia describunt. Hinc duplex nascitur politiae genus, quarum unam quae ad pietatem refertur, divinam, alteram quae hominum inter se officia continet, humanam merito vocemus. Nos tamen ex commune loquendi more illam quidem ecclesiasticam istam vero civilem appelabimus.*" Bertram, *De politia Iudaica*, pp. 9–10. The same scheme is also found in other Calvinist works, such as Theodore de Bèze's *Du droit des magistrats* and the *Vindiciae contra tyrannos*. See Bartolucci, *La repubblica ebraica di Carlo Sigonio*, pp. 48–54. See also T. Maruyama, *The Ecclesiology of Theodore Beza: The Reform of the True Church* (Geneva: Droz, 1978), pp. 228–242.

55. Ziskind, "Cornelius Bertram and Carlo Sigonio," p. 390.

56. See Bartolucci, *La repubblica ebraica di Carlo Sigonio*, pp. 86–99.

57. S. Pagninus, *Thesaurus Linguae Sanctae, sic enim inscribere placuit Lexicon hoc Hebraicum* (Lyon: Sebastianus Gryphius Germanus, 1529). On the life and works of Sante Pagnini, see T.M. Centi, "L'attività letteraria di Santi Pagnini (1470–1536) nel campo delle scienze bibliche," *Archivium Fratrum Praedicatorum* 15 (1945), pp. 5–51.

58. For the history of the revised edition of the *Thesaurus*, see F. Roudaut, ed., *Jean (c. 1525–1570) et Josia (c. 1560–1626) Mercier. L'amour de la philologie à la Renaissance et au début de l'âge classique (Actes du Colloque d'Uzès 2 et 3 mars 2001)* (Paris: Honorè Champion éditeur, 2006), pp. 81, 102–103. It is not known whether the *Thesaurus* was already finished before the death of Chevalier and Mercier, or whether Bertram used manuscript materials left by the two other authors. S. Pagninus, *Thesaurus linguae sanctae, sive, Lexicon Hebraicum,... auctore Sancte Pagnino... nunc demum... auctum et recognitum opera Ioannis Merceri, Antonii Cevallerii et B. Cornelii Bertrami* (Lyon: Bartholomaeum Vincentium, 1575).

59. Pagninus, *Thesaurus linguae sanctae, sive, Lexicon Hebraicum,... auctore Sancte Pagnino... nunc demum cum doctissimis quibusque hebraeorum scriptis quam accuratissime collatum, ex iisdem auctum ac recognitum, opera Ioannis Merceri, quondam in Hebraicis apud Parisios professoris regii, et aliorum doctorum virorum...* (Lyon: Bartholomaeum Vincentium, 1577). But in the edition of 1577 the names of Bertram and Chevalier are included in the Imperial privilegium for the edition, and in a letter to the reader written by Bertram before the index. Pagninus, *Thesaurus*, p. *viiiv: "*Diplomate Maximiliani II, Romanorum imperatoris semper augusti, cautum est Bartolomaeo Vincentio et Antonio Gryphio nequis in universis ditionibus ipsius Cesarae maiestatis, locis atque civitatibus tam sacro romano imperio, quam caeteris regnis, dominiis et provinciis eius mediate vel immediate subiectis, nisi ipsorum Bartholomaei*

Vincentii et Antonii Gryphii, aut haeredum utriusque permissu, hunc thesaurum linguae sanctae a Pagnino olim collectum, et superioribus annis opera Ioannis Merceri, Antonii Cevalleri et B. Cornelii Bertrami auctum ac recognitum, vel quicquam eorum quae illi in hanc eius editionem contulerunt, excudere ante decennium, a die qua finita fuerit computandum: vel ea quae excusa fuerint exemplaria vendere atque distribuere publice vel occulte aut quovis alio praetextu, ausit. Alioqui sibi praeter amissionem librorum, mulctam decem marcharum auri puri, irrogatam esse sciat, imperiali fisco et ipsis Bartholomaeo Vincentio et Antonio Gryphio, veleorum haeredibus, aut ab illis mandatum habentibus, ex aequo persolvenda." For Mercier's religious beliefs, see Roudaut, *Jean et Josia Mercier,* pp. 23–42.

60. See J.M. De Bujanda, *Index des livres interdits,* 10 vols. (Scherbrooke-Geneva: Centre d'Étude de la Renaissance-Librarie Droz, 1985–1996).

61. See M.C. Bacchi, "Ulisse Aldrovandi e la sua biblioteca," in *L'Archiginnasio* 100 (2005), pp. 256–366. The first page of all the books owned by Aldrovandi states: *Ulissi Aldrovandi et amicorum* (owned by Ulisse Aldrovandi and friends), which testifies to Aldrovandi's habit of sharing his books. The main part of Aldrovandi's library is in the University Library of Bologna. The location of the *Thesaurus* is A.M. P. IV 10.

62. Pagninus, *Thesaurus,* pp. 783–784: "*Kimchi inquit quia scribendum datur Ius hominis quod habet in socium, vel quod ipsi convenit ut illo accipiat, idcirco vocari 'hoq.' Sic et id quod tanquam pro decreto et statuto habetur, et est cuique ordinarium, demensum, dicitur hoc nomine, quasi formam, aut normam, ritumve, aut ordinationem constitutam, praescriptam et certam dicas, seu Constitutionem, constitutum. Statuta in Scriptura masc. 'huqim' vel foemin. 'huqot' dicuntur Ritus et cerimoniae aliquid referentes et repraesentes: quorum, ut Hebraei inquiunt, magna ex parte ratio ignoratur. Differt autem a 'mishpat,' cum quo saepe iunctum videas, quod per iudicia ritus politici intelligantur et constitutiones quae ad societatem tuendam pertinent: Statuta vero sint cerimoniae ad religionem et Dei cultum pertinentes, ab ipso institutae, ut circumcisio, sacrificia, feriae et id genus. M.*"

63. Ibid., col. 2312: "*Et nomen 'mitzwa' praeceptum, iussus, iussio, mandatum, quod adstringit ad rem aliquam observandam... Nechemia 9, 13: 'tovim wemitzwot,' 'et praecepta bona'. 'Tovim' non refertur ad 'mitzwot,' alioqui dicendum fuerat 'tovot,' sed ad 'chuqim' quod praeesserat, vel certe ad totum complexum 'chuqim umitzwot,' statuta et mandata. Mandata sunt generalia, statuta sunt ritus et ceremonia. M.*"

64. *DRH,* p. 18: "*Nunc venio ad singularum harum vocum explicationem. Mandata, quae graecus interpres 'entolas' vertit, verba fuisse videntur, quibus Deus iussit aut prohibuit aliquid fieri, quod praecipue se ipsum attingeret. Praecepta, quae ille 'prostagmata' vertit, quibus rationem, qua id fieret, ordinavit. Nam in illa voce 'prostagma' ordinatio quaedam insita est. Unde pro ea aliquando latinus interpres caeremonias edidit, neque enim solum iussit Deus, ut se supra omnia colerent, sed etiam sui colendi ritum demonstravit, nempe cum de tabernaculo, sacrificiis, diebus festis, sacerdotibus et eorum officiis tradidit.*" Cf. this edition, pp. 21–22.

65. Pagninus, *Thesaurus,* pp. 3085–3086: "*Varie sumitur, ut hic habes nos latius explicabimus. Pro officio, seu functione et administratione publica, id est Magistratu.*

Pressius pro legitima et iusta causarum cognitione et diiudicatione, quae iure fit in ea administratione, quae duo parum inter se discrepant, pro Causa iudiciali, pro Iure quod quis in re quapiam habet, et potestate pro interrogatione de rebus quae in iudicio venire solent in controversiam."

66. Ibid., p. 2302: *"Haec duo nomina, iudicii, hoc est 'mishpat,' et 'tzedeqa,' hoc est Iustitiae, passim in scriptura videas simul iungi. Iudicii nomine ea iuris pars intelligitur, qua nocentes et facinorosi puniuntur, iustitiae vero, qua boni defenduntur ab iniuria malorum utrunque est ex officio iudicis. Utrunque fecit Salomon in iudicio mulierum, de puero vivo concertantium. Sic Iehu in occidendis falsis prophetis etc. Ita et nos civiliter iubemur iudicium et iustitiam facere: id est, iusta iustificare et iniusta damnare. Theologice et spiritaliter iudicium ad Legis praedicationem referri potest, quae iubet malum vitare et Dei servare mandata, iustitia vero ad Evangelium, quod nos docet Dei misericordiae in Christo promissae fidere. Et quidam huc referunt illud dictum, 'Declina a malo et fac bonum.' (M.C.)"*

67. *DRH*, p. 19: *"Neque vero haec caelestis illa iustificatio est, de qua post in Evangelio disseretur, qua, ut theologi loquuntur: 'per inhaerentem nobis Dei gratiam vere formaliterque iusti sumus,' sed iudicialis atque terrena. Id ita esse probatur ex ipso verbo 'dikaiō,' quod iidem in veteri testamento usurpavere pro 'iustifico,' idest 'iustum et innocentem pronuncio.'"* Cf. this edition, p. 22.

68. *Dictionarium*, p. 130.

69. Ibid., p. 166.

70. Ibid., p. 34.

71. Ibid., p. 119.

72. Ibid., p. 120.

73. *DRH*, p. 257: *"Ceterum cum de forma reipublicae quaeritur, nihil aliud quaeritur, nisi penes quem principatum summa rerum fuerit constituta."* Cf. this edition, p. 26.

74. See note 80.

75. *DRH*, p. 23: *"Sequitur, ut de forma reipublicae disseram, quam Deus aut superiore lege praescripsit, aut post induci, neglecta lege, permisit."* Cf. this edition, p. 26.

76. Ibid., pp. 23–24: *"Haec vero apud Hebraeos primum penes optimates posita fuit, deinde penes reges, quorum principatuum illum aristocratiam, hoc regnum graeci vocant. aristocratia fuit sub Moyse, Iosue, senioribus et Iudicibus, regnum sub regibus."* Cf. this edition, pp. 26–27.

77. See note 119.

78. *DRH*, p. 27: *"Fuit tamen interim aliquando interregnum. Quod significatur in libro Iudicum, cum scribitur: 'erat Israel sine regibus et quisque faciebat, quod rectum videbatur' [Judges 17:16]. Innuens, non tribus singulas, aut civitates suis principibus vacavisse, sed universam duodecim tribuum rempublicam summis praesidibus et tutoribus caruisse."* Cf. this edition, p. 29.

79. "*Conciderat nimirum maxima ex parte facies illa elegantissima sanctae reipubli-cae quae emicuerat temporibus Mosis et Iosuae, ita tamen ut non prorsus extincta esset, remanserunt enim in unaquaque civitate sui iudices et seniores, nimirum Chiliarchi, Centuriones etc.*" Bertram, *De politia Iudaica*, p. 55. This idea recalls the praise of the government of the citizens and provincials, which was a major aspect of Hotman's treatment. He stated that the original form of the government of the Gauls consisted of the magistracies in the individual cities and provinces. On the relationship between Bertram and the Huguenot literature of his time, see Bartolucci, *La repubblica ebraica di Carlo Sigonio*, pp. 45–65.

80. Bodin also emphasized this passage of Jewish history. In the *Methodus* he maintained that the Jewish state was an aristocracy, while in *Six Books of the Commonweal* he wrote that God himself governed the people, sending prophets as his representatives. See Bartolucci, *La repubblica ebraica di Carlo Sigonio*, pp. 40–41.

81. *DRH*, pp. 24–25: "*Iudicibus inde rerum potientibus eodem modo aristocratia fuit, siquidem illis principatum administrantibus et lex, ut ante valuit, et Deus ipse imperium tenuit.*" Cf. this edition, p. 27.

82. Ibid., p. 25: "*Hoc autem ita esse, probatur etiam ex Iosepho, qui libro iiii Antiquitatum legem Dei ad hunc locum pertinentem explicuit, sic loquentem faciens Moysem: 'Aristocratia et vita, quae ex ea degitur, res optima est, nec vos capiat desiderium alterius reipublicae sed hanc amate leges habentes dominas, ex iis omnia facientes, satis enim est, ut Deus praesit. Quod si regis cupiditas vos incesserit, is ex eadem gente sit.'*" Cf. this edition, p. 27.

83. Ibid.: "*Hanc vero aristocratiam, in qua lex potissimum cum Deo dominata est, regnum ipsum excepit. Regnum autem appelarunt imperium summum unius hominis non ex lege, sed ex arbitrio imperantis, quem a Samuele Iudice postularunt his verbis VIII primi Regum: 'Constitue nobis regem ut iudicet nos, ut universae habent nationes'* [1 Samuel 8:5]. *Quod ut ille audivit, subito Deum, quid opus esset facto, consuluit, qui ita respondit: 'Audi vocem populi in omnibus quae loquuntur tibi non enim te abiecerunt, sed me, ne regnem super eos'* [verse 7]. *Et addit: 'Verumtamen contestare eos et praedic eis ius regis, qui regnaturus est super eos'* [verse 9]. *Significavit enim aperte, Iudicibus rerum summam ex lege habentibus regnasse Deum super Hebraeos, quia lex dominata esset, imperio vero ad regem gentium more translato, Deum non regnaturum, cum non penes legem, sed penes voluntatem unius hominis summa rerum esset futura.*" Cf. this edition, p. 27.

84. Ibid.: "*Probe etenim, ut optime dixit Aristoteles in Politicis: 'Qui legem vult imperare, Deum vult imperare, qui regem, idest hominem, belvam. Quod non semper ratione sed plerunque cupiditate ducatur'* [Aristotle *Politics* 1287a28–33]. *Hoc autem arbitrarium regis imperium expressit Deus, cum addidit: 'Filios et filias et praedia et servos vobis auferet, et greges vestros addecimabit et vos eritis ei servi. Neque clamantes audiemini a Deo'* [1 Samuel 8:11–18]." Cf. this edition, p. 27.

85. Cf. Harris Rackham's translation, in Aristotle *Politics* (Cambridge, Mass.: Harvard University Press, 1977), par. 3.16.

86. Regarding the problem of the manuscript tradition and its impact on early modern political thought, see Bartolucci, *La repubblica ebraica di Carlo Sigonio*, pp. 165–177.

87. *DRH*, p. 27: "*Est porro illud quoque tenendum, rempublicam Hebraeorum quodammodo tripartitam fuisse: una enim fuit, quae universum populum, idest XII tribus, complexa est; altera, quae singulas ipsius populi tribus; tertia, quae singulas singularum tribuum civitates.*" Cf. this edition, p. 29.

88. Ibid., p. 27: "*Primae reipublicae sedes in ea collocata urbe fuit, quam Deus religionis causa sibi ascivit. Ibi enim summus magistratus, summus senatus iudiciumque consedit.*" Cf. this edition, p. 29.

89. Ibid., p. 27: "*Secunda respublica praefectum unum habuit, qui princeps tribus dictus est, itemque alios, qui familiarum principes nominati sunt, qui tamen omnes summo principi, penes quem tota erat respublica, paruerunt.*" Cf. this edition, p. 29.

90. Ibid., pp. 27–28: "*Tertia vero hoc modo constituta fuit. Unaquaeque civitas suum habuit senatum, qui de rebus ad ipsam precipue pertinentibus decerneret et causas privatas capitalesque cognosceret et suos magistratus, qui senatum haberent et iudicia exercerent.*" Cf. this edition, p. 29.

91. Vittorio Conti has shown how this scheme inspired not only Grotius' *De republica Emendanda* but also Althusius' *Politica*. Sigonio's scheme succeeded partly because its Jewish "federalism" suited the institutions of the countries in which these authors lived. The Calvinist commentator Johannes Nicolaus notes: "*Tripartitum tale Imperium ad hunc usque diem viget. E. g. in Belgio foederato ubi 1. Est status generalis qui curat generalia harum regionum. 2. Quaelibet provincia proprias habet suas leges propriisque rectoribus paret. Et 3. Uniuscuiusque provinciae civitas rursus suas peculiares leges habet. Sic etiam rex Angliae tria quasi tenet regna: Angliae, Scotiae et Hyberniae, quae singula sua habent parlamenta et dividuntur in varios comitatus, regiones et urbes, quae singulae propriis gaudent et legibus et institutis.*" Cf. Sigonio, *De republica Hebraeorum* (Leiden: Cornelium Boutestein, 1701), p. 90. On the influence on Grotius and Althusius, see Conti, *Consociatio civitatum* (Firenze: Centro Editoriale Toscano, 1997), pp. 116–119; and Guido Bartolucci, "The Influence of Carlo Sigonio's 'De Republica Hebraeorum' on Hugo Grotius' 'De Republica Emendanda,'" *Hebraic Political Studies* 2:2 (Spring 2007), pp. 193–210.

92. Severus, *Sacrae Historiae*, p. 141. The reference is to 1 Samuel 8, in which the Jewish people, dissatisfied with Samuel's sons, requests a king.

93. Ibid. "*Regium nomen (cunctis liberis populis invisum) populus desiderabant, planeque non sine exemplo amentiae praeoptabat libertatem servitio mutare.*"

94. Ibid. "*Miratur autem Sulpicius, Hebraeos reges Iudicibus praetulisse, cum in republica Iudicum libertatis esset species, in regia servitutis, idque naturae vulgi nova semper optantis tribuit, quorum nihil est in scriptura... Liberi autem populi aversantur reges, quia liberi populi obediunt legibus, idest rationi, qui vero parent regi, obediunt voluntati, idest libidini unius plerumque pravi. Quare amens est, qui regem libertati anteponit.*"

95. Sigonius, *Opera*, vol. 6, pars tertia, col. 1147: "*Quod Sulpicius dixit de regibus potest multis modis excusari, sed quae dixit expositor nullo pacto. Is enim liberam vivendi rationem non solum regum regimini et monarchiae anteponit, sed tamquam impiam et a ratione alienam damnat, tacite confirmans hoc pacto pravitatem illorum, qui hodie contra suos reges bella gerunt, atque ut libere vivant ab eorum obedientia defecerunt.*"

96. Ibid., coll. 1147–1148: "*Censor autem inquit Sigonium favere haereticis et damnare monarchiam tamquam impiam et a ratione alienam et tacite favere eis, qui bella hodie faciunt regibus suis. Cui respondetur: rationem quam reddidit Sigonio esse Aristotelis in III Politicorum, ubi ostendit melius esse imperare legem, quam unum et congruit cum scriptura sacra, ubi in primo Regum [8, 11] Samuel iussu Dei ad populum regem postulantem dixit: 'hoc erit ius regis, qui imperaturus est vobis, filios vestros tollet et ponet in curribus suis, facietque sibi equites,' reliqua gravia quibus deterrere conatur a rege petendo, tamquam gravi futuro.*"

97. Ibid., col. 1148: "*At ubi ratio postulat ut ponat quae ad bonos mores, ad Catholicam doctrinam et usum in Ecclesia Romana receptum faciunt, facere debuisset. Nam quid nobis cum Aristotelis sententia hoc tempore?*"

98. Ibid.: "*Nec respondet Sigonius crimini, quod obiicitur, sed alio rem transfert, ut auctoritate Aristotelis monarchiam impugnare velle videatur, in qua re primum confundit regem cum tyranno, quod nec philosophia nec religio patitur. Ita enim dicit 'obediunt voluntati, idest libidini unius plerumque pravi.' Rex vero ratione, tyrannus libidine gubernat.*"

99. Ibid.: "*Buchananus haereticus in 'Dialogo de iure Regni Scotiae' similibus fere argumentis persuasit populo, ut se in libertatem vendicarent, reges eiicerent, et deperditam popularem libertatem quasi postliminio revocarent.*" The censor is very well acquainted with Buchanan's work. The Scottish author had in fact written: "*ut recte ac vere mihi dixisse videatur Aristoteles, qui legi pareat, eum Deo et legi parere, qui regi, homini et belvae.*" Cf. G. Buchanan, *De iure regni apud Scotos dialogus*, in Buchanan, *Rerum Scoticarum historia* (Edinburgh: Ad exemplar Alexandri Arbuthneti editum, 1600), p. 16v.

100. Sigonius, *Opera*, vol. 6, pars tertia, col. 1148: "*Praeterea cum locum 1 Regum adducat Sigonius in suam sententiam, vereor ne cum Buchanano sentiat, qui eodem argumento Saulem tyrannum fuisse contendit, quod falsum est. Nam tametsi in 1 Regum Samuel ita dixit, ut populum averteret a petendo rege, non tamen proinde regum dominatus improbatur a scriptura. Sed vult Sigonius pertinaciter confirmare quod dixit hoc tempore etiam ad pueros instituendos, quasi mos, qui iamdiu in Ecclesia Dei est, a summis pontificibus approbatus et constitutus creandi reges et imperatores, scripturae contradicat.*"

101. Ibid., col. 1193: "*Cum totus liber Iudicum usque ad finem tractet propositam ab ipso historiam, et aliis in locis scriptura petere posset, male ad confirmandam rem propositam citat Josephum lib. 4 'Antiquitatum,' cum melius et verius in sacris litteris habeantur. Quae vero eadem pagina dicit de regibus falsa omnino sunt, et a Calvino et Buchanano hereticis excogitata, ut ius regni delerent et civitates optimis legibus institutas*

everterent, sed in hac re auctor graviter peccavit, quod cum iam alias de hoc errore maxima cum caritate admonitus fuerit, non modo non resipuit, sed etiam vehementius et pertinacius animum obfirmavit."

102. Ibid.: *"Semper enim Deus illius populi legislator, rector et gubernator fuit, cum lex quid agendum esset perscriberet et illi arbitratu suo non regerent, sed Dei mandatis et iussis moverentur. Lex enim erat regiminis regula et norma, quae neque ad hos, neque ad illos transferri poterat, cum ex unius Dei voluntate penderet, quod sane ad formam alicuius reipublicae traduci non potest, cum illae gubernentur iudicio eorum qui praesunt et ad illorum arbitrium pro variis rerum eventibus immutentur. Haec quidem a Deo sui regiminis habet regulam, cum iudices et reges iuxta praescriptam formam gubernassent, sacerdotes vero legis interpretes extitissent."*

103. It is no accident that the same argument, that the Jewish state was a theocracy and therefore not comparable with the Aristotelian models, was used in 1648 by Conring to defend the German princedoms against the republics of the radical Calvinists. See Marchetti, "Sulla degiudaizzazione della politica." See note 7 above.

104. Sigonius, *Opera*, vol. 6, pars tertia, col. 1194: *"Quamobrem Dominus ut populum a regis postulatione deterreret, durum et difficile regum dominatum futurum esse proponebat, ut homines ab ea cogitatione ad aliam meliorem praestantioremque traduceret. Neque enim Dominus ideo regnum improbat quasi non esset ab eo, per quem reges regnant et legum conditores iura decernunt, constitutum, sed quia melius a sacerdotibus quam a regibus gubernanda erat respublica... Quare cum dicat Dominus i Regum: 'me et non vobis abiecerunt,' non significat legem Domini a regibus omnino contemptam, aut in iudicando neglectam fuisse, ita ut non penes legem sed suo arbitratu populum gubernare eis liberum fuerit (absurda enim haec sunt, ut voluit auctor) sed quia sacerdotes et Levitae qui proxime ad Deum accedunt, a reipublicae gubernatione eieci erant, eis eiectis Deus imperio exclusum et se iniuria affectum conqueritur."*

105. Ibid.: *"Nam cum citet auctor locum Aristotelis his verbis: 'Deinceps disputandum est de rege qui sua voluntate gerit,' non videt de tyranno potius quam de rege disputare? Plenum enim regnum proxime ad tyrannicum accedere videtur."*

106. Ibid.: *"Diluamus modo atrocem censuram, qua pene Calvinianus et alter Brutus factus est Sigonius. Principio praemittendum arbitror, verba quae cavillandi ansam censori obtulerunt, ea potissimum de causa fuisse a Sigonius prolata ut paucis exprimeret discrimen praecipuum inter regiminis formam quae sub iudicibus obtinuerat, ab ea quae sub regibus inducta est, moderantibus scilicet iudicibus legem dominatam esse cum Deo, at in regum principatu hominis voluntatem dominium tenuisse, non vero ut regium ius regiamque dominationem quod Calvinus, Buchananus, aliique faciunt sectarii convelleret."*

107. Ibid., col. 1196: *"Ex hisce prolixis contextibus apparet quod initio dixeram, proposuisse videlicet sibi Sigonium lectoribus aperire discrimen inter iudicum dominationem et regum, non vero animum habuisse auctoritatem regiumque ius veluti illegitimum atque iniquum damnandi, quod sectarii perverse moliuntur. Hac enim re ne ullum quidem verbum Sigonius protulit. Id unum adversus regium principatum colligi posse videtur, scilicet praestantiorem regio Iudaeorum dominatu iudicum aristocratiam fuisse."*

108. Ibid.: "*Verum hoc iure negari non posse mihi videor. Atque ut omittam modo scripturae testimonia quae id evincunt, placet hic S. Thomae auctoritatem usurpare, ex pr. 2, qu. 105, art. 1 in corpore, ita docentis: 'Unde optima ordinatio principum est in aliqua civitate vel regno, in qua unus praeficitur secundum virtutem, qui omnibus praesit et sub ipso sunt aliqui principantes secundum virtutem. Et tamen talis principatus ad omnes pertinet, tum quia ex omnibus eligi possunt, tum quia ab omnibus eliguntur. Talis enim est optima politia bene comista ex regno, in quantum unus praeest, et aristocratia, in quantum multi principantur secundum virtutem, et ex democratia, id est potestate populi, in quantum ex popularibus possunt eligi principes et ad populum pertinet electio principum. Et hoc fuit institutum secundum legem divinam. Nam Moyses et eius successores gubernabant populum quasi singulariter omnibus principantes, quod est quaedam species regni.'*" Cf. Thomas Aquinas, *Summa Theologiae*, 2, q. 105, art. 1.

109. Sigonius, *Opera*, vol. 6, pars tertia, col. 1198: "*Haec S. Thomas, qui praeterea cum sibi obiecisset optimam esse civitatis vel populi ordinationem, ut per regem gubernetur, ac propterea non debuisse Deum Iudaeis permittere ut sibi regem quando vellent constituerent, sed ab ipso Deo ab exordiis Iudaicae reipublicae oportuisse constitui, haec respondit, quae satis innuunt priorem Hebraeorum sub Iudicibus dominatum, quem in corpore articuli absolute dixerat, regio postmodum inducto fuisse perfectiorem: 'Ad secundum dicendum (sunt verba S. Thomae) quod regnum est optimum regimen populi si non corrumpatur, sed propter magnam potestatem, quae regi conceditur, de facili regimen degenerat in tyrannidem, nisi sit perfecta virtus eius, cui talis potestas conceditur... perfecta autem virtus in paucis invenitur, et praecipue Iudaei crudeles erant, et ad avaritiam proni, per quae vitia maxime homines in tyrannidem decidunt. Et ideo Dominus a principio eis regem non instituit cum plena potestate, sed iudicem et gubernatorem in eorum custodia, sed postea regem ad petitionem populi quasi indignatus concessit, ut patet per hoc quod dixit ad Samuelem...: "Non te abiecerunt sed me, ne regnem super eos."'*"

110. Some years ago, Diego Quaglioni did much to clarify the importance of the exegesis of 1 Samuel 8 in the history of the juridical interpretation of the role of the king from Augustine to Bodin. In his analysis, Quaglioni reconstructs an interpretative trend that extends from Thomas to Tolomeo da Lucca (who completed Aquinas' *De regimine principum*) to Bartolo da Sassoferrato. See D. Quaglioni, "L'iniquo diritto: 'Regimen regis' e 'ius regis' nell'esegesi di i Sam. 8, 11–17 e negli 'specula principum' del tardo Medioevo," in A. De Benedictis, ed., *Specula Principum* (Frankfurt am Main: Vittorio Klostermann, 1999), pp. 209–242.

According to this line of reasoning, we can understand how Aquinas' interpretation of the biblical right of kings as an unjust "right of tyrants" greatly influenced the late medieval juridical literature through its crystallization in *De regimine principum*. In this work Tolomeo da Lucca, using the passage from Samuel as a starting point, concluded that when God appointed a king, he had wanted to support the idea that for the people a *regimen politicum*, like that of the judges, was superior to a monarchy. See Quaglioni, "L'iniquo diritto," p. 223. Such a dichotomy was taken up by Bartolo in *De regimine civitatis*, and it was reinterpreted when the liberty of the Italian cities was jeopardized by the ascent of the *seigniories* (nobility). Against the backdrop of this conflict, Bartolo interpreted the passage from Samuel as indicating the inferiority of monarchic rule relative to rule by judges, the latter being a desirable model and one praised by God (adding in this context a passage from Book 3 of Aristotle's *Politics*). Quaglioni, "L'iniquo diritto," pp. 226–227. Bartolo da Sassoferrato, *De regimine civitatis*, ii, pp. 191–230, cited in D. Quaglioni, *Politica e diritto nel Trecento italiano* (Florence: Olschki, 1983), p. 157: "*Et per istos iudices Deus rexit populum Iudaeorum per multa tempora.*" It is thus clear how the medieval political-juridical literature influenced early modern political literature.

111. *DRH*, pp. 305–306: "*Fuere ergo tribuni, centuriones, quinquagenarii et decani magistratus, qui inter cetera ipsorum munera iudicibus praepositi causas ad eos introduxerunt et fortasse etiam docuerunt, quod hodie quoque Venetiis faciunt, quos Advocatores Communis dicunt.*" Cf. this edition, p. 293.

112. See note 52 above.

113. S. Testoni Binetti, *Il pensiero politico ugonotto: Dallo studio della storia all'idea di contratto (1572–1574)* (Florence: Centro Editoriale Toscano, 2002).

114. On August 24, 1572, during the festivities celebrating the marriage of Henry of Navarre to Marguerite of Valois, the Catholics massacred the Huguenots in Paris and other French towns.

115. De Benedictis, *Repubblica per contratto*, pp. 275–276: "*erano stati messi in campo… tutti i motivi del dibattito politico-giuridico in corso nell'Europa di quello scorcio di secolo. Sovranità popolare, 'imperium,' consenso, 'police' e giustizia, ruolo dei magistrati, irrevocabilità di capitolazioni e patti.*" Camillo Paleotti's writing of a tract entitled *De republica Bononiensi* during these years demonstrates the Bolognese cultural interest in republican questions. See note 51 above.

116. F. Hotman, *Francogallia*, Latin text by Ralph E. Giesey, trans. J.H.M. Salmon (Cambridge: Cambridge University Press, 1972), pp. 302–304.

117. See note 95 above.

118. *DRH*, p. 23: "*Ceterum, cum de forma reipublicae quaeritur, nihil aliud quaeritur, nisi penes quem principatum summa rerum fuerit constituta.*" Cf. this edition, p. 26.

119. Bodin, *Methodus*, p. 177: "*Prius igitur in omni republica intuendum est, quis imperium magistratibus dare et adimere, quis leges iubere aut abrogare possit, utrum unus, an minor pars civium, an maior. Hoc percepto, facile intellligitur qualis sit reipublicae status. Nihil enim quartum esse, ac ne cogitari quidem potest. Neque enim virtus aut vitium efficit reipublicae varietatem, sive enim princeps iniustus sit, sive probus, monarchia tamen est.*"

120. Cf. McCuaig, *Carlo Sigonio*, pp. 19–23.

121. *DRH*, p. 241: "*Quoniam vero respublica Hebraeorum omnino popularis non fuit, verum aut optimatium, aut regia, ut supra dictum est, propterea populus haud magnas admodum in illa opes habuit, cum in aristocratia Senatus, in regno rex prevaluerit.*" Cf. this edition, p. 234.

122. Bodin, *Methodus*, p. 177: "*Multo magis ad summum imperium pertinet, leges iubere ac tollere, bellum indicere ac finire, extremum ius provocare, vitae denique ac praemiorum potestatem habere.*"

123. *DRH*, pp. 279–280, 281: "*Ius vero necis liberum haudquaquam habuerunt, quia in omnibus legem sequuti sunt. Qua deinde soluti reges fuerunt... Atque omnino vitae, necisque potetstatem arbitrariam habuit et quodammodo superior legibus fuit.*" Cf. this edition, p. 272.

124. Cf. Marchetti, "Sulla degiudaizzazione della politica."

125. On Petrus Galatinus, cf. A. Kleinhans, "De vita et operibus Petri Galatini O.F.M. scientiarum biblicarum cultoris (c. 1460–1540)," *Antonianum* 1 (1926), pp. 145–179, 327–356; F. Secret, *Les Kabbalistes Chrétiens de la Renaissance* (Paris: Dunod, 1984), pp. 99–105; A. Morisi, "Galatino et la kabbale chrétienne," in Morisi, *Cahiers de l'Hermétisme. Kabbalistes Chrétiens* (Paris: Albin Michel, 1979), pp. 213–231; Cesare Vasoli, "Giorgio Benigno Salviati, Pietro Galatino e la edizione di Ortona (1518) del *De Arcanis Catholicae Veritatis*," in Vasoli, *Filosofia e religione nella cultura del Rinasciemnto* (Naples: Guida editori, 1988), pp. 183–209; C. Vasoli, "L'Apochalypsis nova: Giorgio Benigno, Pietro Galatino e Guillaume Postel," in C. Vasoli, *Filosofia e religione*, pp. 211–229; A. Paladini, *Il De Arcanis di Pietro Galatino, Traditio giudaica e nuove istanze filologiche* (Galatina: Congedo, 2004).

126. Both Bodin and Bertram had referred to the distinction between the two kinds of Jewish tribunals. Their analysis represents an important link between Bodin's *Methodus* and Bertram's work. Bertram, *De politia Iudaica*, pp. 79–80: "*Denique si unquam locum habuit politia illa magistratuum et iudicum quam Talmudistae nostri tradunt, profecto ad huius temporis progressum referenda est. Tradunt videlicet supremum Hebraeorum senatum, nimirum septuaginta, gladii seu morte plectendi potestatem, quam habebant in causis maioribus (quales erant, de Tribu, de summo sacerdote, de Pseudopropheta, et de Maiestate). Viginti tribus viris capitalibus, qui* דיני נפשות, *id est, iudicia capitalia tractabant, comunicasse, septem viros iudices* דיני ממנות, *id est, pecuniarum et bonorum in singulis urbibus constitutos; quarum tres (fortasse duo Levitae praefecti et unus ex loci iudicibus) iudicia instituerunt, quinque de prima provocatione cognoscerent, septem de secunda decernerent. Praeterea decem iudices rerum venalium, quasi aediles creatos fuisse, quorum unus ex sacerdotali genere esset, quinetiam receptos arbitros tres, quorum uterque litigator unum eligebat, electi duo tertium optabant. Atque de his fusissime in Talmud ad tractatum de Synedriis, et apud Maymonem in lib. De perplexis.*" Bodin, *Methodus*, pp. 219–220: "*Moses vero Maymo lib. III perplexorum cap. postremo scribit, gladii potestatem habuisse senatum. ab eodem senatu xxiii viros capitales, qui* דיני נפשות *id est animarum iudices et septem viros iudices pecuniarum ac bonorum, id est,* דיני ממנות *in singulis urbibus constitutos, quorum tres iudicia instituebant, quinque primam appellationem disceptabant, septem de secunda provocatione decernebant. Praeterea decem iudices rerum venalium quasi aediles creabantur, quorum unus erat sacerdos. Ad haec arbitri recepti tres, quorum uterque litigator unum eligebat, electi duo tertium optabant. Quae omnia in Pandectis Hebraeorum, titulo Sanedrim cap. I. II. III copiose explicantur.*" See Bartolucci, *La repubblica ebraica di Carlo Sigonio*, pp. 62–63.

127. The confusion of the Jewish oral law and even the Talmud with Kabbala was commonplace in the tradition of Christian Kabbala that developed in the Renaissance and that served as sources for Génébrard and Sigonio.

128. Gilbert Génébrard (1537–1597) was a professor of Hebrew at the Collège de France from 1569. His contribution to the study of the Hebrew language and the translation of Hebrew texts, such as *Seder Olam* and *Sefer Hakabbala*, was great. For a complete bibliography, see *Encyclopaedia Judaica* (1971), s.v. "Génébrard, Gilbert." Sigonio had Génébrard's work in his library. Cf. Città del Vaticano, Archivio vaticano, Fondo Boncompagni, Armadio i, mazzo q, *Nota di tutti i libri acquistati dalla eredità del celebre letterato Carlo Sigonio dal duca Giacomo Boncompagni Seniore*, cc. 11: c. 3r.

129. Gilbert Génébrard, *Chronographiae libri quatuor* (Paris: Martinum Iuvenem, 1580), p. 37: "*Edoctus est Iosue a Mose legis iurisque divinae intelligentia… Eam docet seniores septuaginta, qui per ordinem eam communicarunt cum prophetis et prophetae cum sapientibus, id est scribis et pharisaeis, a quibus rabbini se suam sapientiam accepisse gloriantur. Pirke Aboth i. hoc vocant Cabala, sive legem ore acceptam.*"

130. Ibid., p. 169: "*Neque enim ea est Cabala ab eruditis patribus laudata, quae partim historica est, partim* תורה שבעל פה *nominatur, id est lex ore precepta… Haec enim legis scriptae pura est interpres, et simplices Synagogae traditiones, consuetudines, ritus maiorum explanationes continet, quarum fragmenta nonnumquam suppeditant Talmud, doctrina 'derasim,' quaestiones etc. sed de hoc alias.*"

THE HEBREW REPUBLIC

DEDICATION

To the Most Blessed Father, Pope Gregory the Thirteenth

MOST BLESSED FATHER, everyone who has devoted his concerns and his thoughts to the welfare and advantage of mankind is worthy of the greatest praise; and it is above all those men who have been driven to establish states, to enact legislation, and to bind their peoples with the ties of religion and duty, who have earned from all of us enormous respect and gratitude. We should therefore take note that throughout recorded history, it is this drive that has made exceptional men struggle with all their might, and the love of this praise that more than anything else has spurred them on. After all, in most cases it was men of outstanding wisdom and learning who either established new states or devoted themselves to the administration of existing ones, or at least thought to leave behind them the laws by which those states could be most effectively governed. As a result, these men have won so much respect and regard that to this day people celebrate their memory in the noblest terms. And yet no one who has written about them has any doubts that their efforts would have been even more useful to the human race, and held in even greater esteem by subsequent generations, had they understood that the very thing that they themselves had tried to represent as the talents and efforts of human beings came in fact from a unique source—the particular care and wisdom of the highest God. Had they done so, they would have directed their energies, whether in forming a new state or in administering an existing one, to the contemplation of that one law which he had set down. For it is clear from their works that neither Solon nor Lycurgus nor Charondas nor Plato, nor any of the others who taught their peoples law and custom, had any knowledge of the Hebrew republic; this despite the fact that it was not only the oldest but the most distinguished of them all. Of course, it was vividly described by the deliberate word of the living God himself, and marvelous accouterments for the proper disposition of life were carefully examined and handed down to us, and assistance given for the interpretation of the sacred text.[1] I myself realized this four years ago, when, at the command of Your Holiness, I undertook to examine the history of the Church, and to elaborate upon it where necessary.[2] While I was still devoting my careful attention to this project, more out of eagerness to carry out your commission than out of any hopes that I might actually finish it, I made a start of publishing the results, beginning with the part that seemed to me the obvious starting point for this work: that is, I undertook to describe at length and as best I could the Hebrew republic, which others have neglected. Since it had a great influence on the form of the Christian Church, and since it faithfully represented the character of the blessed life that will be lived in the celestial city, it seemed a fitting start for the ecclesiastical history which I intend to compose. Once I had declared my intentions to the most illustrious Cardinal Paleotti, our bishop,[3] and to other great men known for their uncommon discretion and piety, I reaped the greatest reward my labors could have earned—they were ratified by the most convincing testimony possible, the opinion of these men. This made me all the more determined to get to the end quickly, and I decided that I had to dedicate the work to the august name of Your Holiness, someone who not only considers the republic that I am describing to be the first among the nations, but reserves for it his highest praises, because he is wonderfully zealous in the cause of restoring the ancient Church. For (leaving aside his unparalleled efforts to recover its traditional authority) he has established the various seminaries in order to relieve the hardships of impoverished and displaced nations, and provided them with large endowments; he has reined in the months and days (which have been running away with themselves) and fixed the days of festivals (which were going awry) by means of a cleverly applied correction; he has revised, restored, and explained the rulings of previous popes, which human neglect had allowed to become somewhat garbled; and (last but not least) he has decreed that the Holy Bible be restored to its original, unsullied form. For this reason I beseech Your Holiness, as I should, with a most heartfelt prayer that he may, as I hope, receive my work with a cheerful countenance, as being in keeping with his own efforts.[4] It was, after all, produced under his absolute and universal authority, in order to pique the interest of those who get their nourishment from the sacred texts; and it is being published by a man who for many years has been entirely devoted to your name and your family. May God, for the sake of expanding his Church, bless all your plans and actions; and may he grant you a life long enough to achieve this purpose.

Bologna, August 22, 1582

BOOK I

The Form of the Republic

PREFACE

I PROPOSE in this book to examine the ancient republic of the Hebrews that was established by God long ago, and that is contained within the deepest recesses of the holy scripture; and, once I have discovered it, to somehow bring it into the light as a record for future generations. For this topic is, as everyone will admit, both a wonderful field of study in its own right, and so useful for understanding the holy books that anyone could be forgiven for wondering why none of the ancients ever stayed awake nights working on it. After all, it is generally agreed that the latter were men of exceptional ability and learning and were driven by an unbelievable eagerness to explain matters of theology. I wish that I too had seen this some time ago, for I would not have put my energy and industry to the test with any other kind of research. In fact, this work is incumbent upon anyone who would both use his time efficiently and show some regard for his own salvation. But in truth, it seemed best to submit to God's will; and he has, I think, reserved my declining years for the most sacred undertaking of all. And now that I am advanced in age, and my ability to stay up late is diminishing with each passing day, he wants to show me what I did not consider as a young man who was driven to write—that is, which people it was that God chose for himself, the kind of republic he set up, and the laws he gave it. For my intention in this book is, as I have said, to dig out from the sacred texts and expose to the light of day the character of the Hebrew rites and their priests; the structure of the councils, the courts, and the magistrates; and every aspect of the training they received for both war and peace. As a young man years ago, I did the same for the Athenians and the Romans, bringing to light the secrets of their laws, customs, states, and republics, which had been hidden away in their various books. But I now realize, after considerable efforts to achieve excellence in my writing, that just as the works of the Greeks and Romans have supplied me with a generous abundance of words for use in my own work, so they have also furnished me with powerful tools for recreating the ancient world even after the passage of so many years. On the other hand, the works of the

Hebrews show little of the ornament of rhetoric; but even though they do not demonstrate the same literary elegance as the works of the classical authors, they are of value to us because of the holiness of their mysteries. Even if I cling, as I ought, tightly to the heels of the ancient Latin translator,[1] I will often have to employ the kinds of expressions that might understandably offend the elegant and refined tastes of many of my readers. But when the matter at stake is important, and especially when it is absolutely necessary, I think that any attempt I might make deserves respect, and that even if I may lack the means to perfect this work I should not be faulted for trying. So let us agree to the proposition that God himself has been summoned to our aid, he who told his prophet: *Blessed are they who keep my testimonies and seek me with a whole heart.*[2] For the only testimony of God is Christ himself, his son, who is the end of all Hebrew history. To him refer, by way of certain hidden mysteries, all the commandments of the law, all the visions of the prophets, and all the actions of the Hebrews.[3] Here is Moses, who showed men the true God and his true law. Here is Joshua, who conquered the enemies of the Hebrews and distributed to them the heavenly land of Canaan. Here is David, who built heavenly Jerusalem, which God had reserved for himself from the beginning. Here is Solomon, who prepared the heavenly Temple—a temple which, I say, was not built by human hands[4]—for those selfsame believers. And here, finally, is that king who gave both the Jews and his converts an equal share, in heaven, in the republic whose rough copy God handed down to Moses on earth. For just as in the terrestrial republic King David judged the people of Israel alongside the twelve chiefs of the tribes, so in the celestial kingdom Jesus the king, with his twelve apostles, will judge the faithful. Since, moreover, I have divided my discussion into two parts, "Religion" and "The State," I would like to make it clearer by prefacing my explanation of these topics with a description of the ancient origin of the Hebrews. This will be followed by a discussion of the history of the law that was handed down to them, the republic that they established, and the state that was chosen for this system of government. After all, as I have already explained to the person who would read about those ancient times, it will make his labors much more useful and productive if he can acquire some understanding of the deeds performed by the Hebrews, and drawn from their sacred histories, before he applies himself to learning about these matters. I too devoted myself as best I could to this duty, in that work in which I explained the *Sacred History* of the blessed Sulpicius Severus.[5]

CHAPTER 1

The Hebrew People

SINCE THIS PEOPLE did in fact bear three names—Hebrews, Israelites, and finally Jews[6]—and since it periodically adopted new homes and new governments, circumstances clearly require us to consider before anything else who this people was, what it was like, and what caused the changes in its character. So first of all, it is generally agreed that since the beginnings of mankind it has produced, as it were, four branches, or offshoots. The holy scripture calls these *geneseis*, that is, generations: the first of these extended from Adam, the first man, to Noah; the second from Noah to Abraham; the third from Abraham to David; and the fourth from David to Christ, of whom I have already spoken. In the second age the Hebrews appeared, in the third the Israelites, and in the fourth the Jews. In fact the Hebrews were the most ancient nation in all of recorded history: in the second age they reached Assyria,[7] which appears so often in the earliest writings of the gentiles. And although among the first generations of mankind some people were naturally disposed to worship the one true God, and others the images of false gods, the Hebrew race was among those who recognized God of their own accord; and knowing him, they worshiped him. It was for this reason that in the years that followed, God loved this people so much that not only did he reveal himself especially to them, but in the end it was his will that from them his son Jesus Christ would be born for the salvation of the human race. Although all this takes up many volumes of the holy scripture, I would like to summarize it here only briefly.

Adam, then, was the first man created by God and was therefore the first to perceive him as his creator; so he was also the first man to doom himself and all his descendants by transgressing God's command. Above all he had three sons: Cain, Abel, and Seth. Of these, Cain took away his brother Abel's life and abandoned God completely; he fathered impious descendants who adopted many false gods. This is why the scripture did not take any notice of him—it wanted to focus solely on the lineage of Christ the savior, which was going to produce him from a family of pious men. Seth, on the other hand, knew God just as his father did, and so did most of his descendants. It is for this reason that scripture has described them to the very last, including those to whom God was going to reveal himself, and from whom he was going to send salvation to fallen mankind. These were Adam's descendants: Seth, Enosh, Cain, Mahalalel, Jared, Enoch, Methuselah, Lamech, and Noah. But in the time of Noah, when pious men—descended from Seth though they may have been—had married the daughters of godless men (who were obviously the offspring of Cain) and had greatly increased the wickedness that had already been brought into the world, God became enraged by their criminal acts and decided to punish the human race, and he sent a flood which covered the entire earth and wiped out all of humanity, both men and women. The only ones spared were Noah, who was a just man, and his family; he was saved by the ark he had constructed at God's command. Now Noah had three sons: Shem, Ham, and Japhet. And just as the descendants of Shem (though not all of them) continued the worship of God begun by their ancestor, the offspring of Ham and Japhet fell completely away from it. This is why scripture mentions only the line of Shem, which lived in the second age; that is, Shem, Arpachshad, Shelah, Eber, Peleg, Reu, Serug (who abandoned God and is said to have been the first to make images of the gods), Nahor, and Terah, who was equally devoted to the impiety practiced by his father and grandfather. It was these descendants who first bore the name "Hebrew," for after the flood, when the ark had come to rest in the mountains of Armenia, Noah and his sons Shem, Ham, and Japhet came to live in the east. According to the Hebrews' calculations, this was on our side of the Tigris, the region which later on was generally called Assyria. Shem fathered Arpachshad, who crossed the Tigris and settled in Chaldea (as St. Jerome has also confirmed). Some scholars are therefore of the opinion that it was the people who crossed over with Arpachshad—and who were obviously his children and grandchildren—who were first called "Hebrews," because they crossed the river. For among the Hebrews, "Eber" means "across." This explains Genesis 10: *Shem was the father of all the sons of Eber*, that is, of all those who crossed over the river. Then the descendants of Ham and Japhet also decided to settle in other lands; and when they had withdrawn into Chaldea in the time of Eber (who was the son of Shelah and the grandson of Arpachshad) and settled the plain of Shinar (this was before they gave it up), they decided at the initiative of Nimrod the grandson of Ham to build as a monument to their glory a city with a tower tall enough to reach heaven. At that time the earth was, as the scripture says, *of one lip*—that is, everyone spoke the same language, which they had gotten from Adam himself. But God was put off by their disgusting arrogance and inflicted such a diversity of languages upon them that they could not understand each other's instructions. So because the glory for which they had struggled yielded only confusion—which is the meaning of "babel"—the tower, the city, and the region came to be called "Babel," "Babylonis," and "Babylonia"; while Eber, who had had nothing to do with building the tower, kept his original language, which the Hebrews of the line of Shem had used. This is why St. Augustine, in his book *The City of God*, claimed that the Hebrews were named entirely after this Eber. Certainly Abraham, who was sixth in line from Eber, is called "Hebrew" in chapter 14.[8] Then, after they had divided the lands among them, Eber remained in Chaldea and in the east. The descendants of Japhet, on the other hand, took possession of the west, and those of Ham the areas in between. Indeed, the origins of the Hebrews and the beginnings of their nation (which are just as true as they are ancient) are described in the first ten chapters of Genesis. Moreover, while Terah, the son of Nahor and the great-great-grandson of Peleg, was still passing his days in Chaldea, living in Ur and worshiping its gods (whose images had been set up by his grandfather Serug), he went with his son Abraham and his grandson Lot to Mesopotamia, the region between the Tigris and Euphrates rivers, and settled in the city of Haran.

From this time begins the story of the Hebrews, which is both ancient and holy. It is chiefly concerned with Abraham, who was the starting point of the nations and their exploits.[9] For once Terah had died, Abraham received the word of God, and, encouraged by the promise of great things, he crossed the Euphrates and the Jordan with Lot, his brother's son, and entered the land of Canaan, which was later given the name "Judea." He lived in the town of Shechem, in the region that was later called Samaria. But God had made Abraham promises, and he repeated them very often. *Get thee... unto a land that I will show thee* (here he showed him Canaan), *and I will make of thee a great nation, and I will bless thee and make thy name great; and thou shalt be a blessing, and I will bless them that bless thee and curse him that curseth thee, and in thee shall all families of the earth be blessed.*[10] Abraham was actually made three promises: first, the land of Canaan, which his offspring would possess in power and glory, i.e. the nation of the Israelites according to the flesh; and all the nations according to faith. (All our sources say continually that "offspring" refers to Jesus Christ, who would arise from Abraham's line after many centuries, and who is called his son.) And later on, when Abraham lamented that he had not been given any children and would have to appoint his servant as his heir (for his wife, Sarah, was barren), God said: *Look now toward heaven, and tell the stars, if thou be able to number them... so shall thy seed be.*[11] And in another verse he repeats the same promise, that he is going to multiply his seed like the sand of the sea. Then from his maid

Hagar Abraham fathered Ishmael, and from Sarah, his wife, he fathered Isaac. From these, two peoples emerged: the Ishmaelites, who abandoned God, and the Hebrews, who retained their ancestral religion. Then Isaac had two sons, Esau (whom God also called Edom) and Jacob (whom he also called Israel). From Edom came the Idumean people, which was estranged from God, and from Israel the Israelites, who preserved their ancient awareness of him. It is about them in particular that I wish to speak.

CHAPTER 2

The Israelite People and Their Twelve Tribes

IN ANY CASE, God loved Israel himself above all others and fulfilled for him his promises to his grandfather Abraham. In fact he fathered twelve sons, that is, six from Leah (Reuben, Simon, Levi, Judah, Issachar, and Zebulon); then two from his maid Bilhah (Dan and Naphtali); then the same number from his other maid Zilpah (Gad and Asher); then finally, from his second wife, Rachel, Joseph and Benjamin. Then the ten brothers sold Joseph to Egyptian merchants without their father's knowledge. They were insanely jealous because their father cared more for Joseph than for any of them, and his reputation for wisdom outshone their own. The merchants handed him over to Potiphar, the king's overseer. Moreover, Joseph came to the king's attention because of his uncommon skill at interpreting dreams, and the king then awarded him the highest honors and put him completely in charge of the grain supply. This happened when the country began to suffer seven years of severe grain shortages, which Joseph himself had foreseen. Jacob was forced by this shortage to send his ten sons to Egypt to buy grain; he had heard that there, because of Joseph's prudence, grain had been stockpiled for many years so as to alleviate the hardships of the Egyptians. Since Joseph recognized his brothers but they did not recognize him, at first he played various tricks on them; then he revealed himself and restored them, trembling with fear, to his brotherly favor and love, and he directed them to bring back his father and all the rest of his family. For, as he explained, the land would continue to be afflicted with barrenness for many years to come. So these were the circumstances under which Jacob left the land of Canaan, where he had lived as a stranger, and with the seventy members of his family he went off to Egypt, where he was received with great honors by his son Joseph and lived a number of years. When finally he reached the end of his life, he adopted Joseph's two sons, Manasseh and Ephraim, added them to his own twelve sons, and rewarded them with his sacred blessing.

Once Jacob had left this world behind, Joseph assumed the leadership of his family, and after some years he too went the way of all flesh. His eleven brothers and his two sons stayed in Egypt, and just as God had promised they produced an enormous number of descendants, who took the name "Israelites" after Jacob (who was called "Israel"). And as this people increased in size, it divided into thirteen parts, called tribes, corresponding to the thirteen leaders of the family: Reuben, Simon, Levi, Judah, Issachar, Zebulon, Dan, Naphtali, Gad, Asher, Benjamin, Manasseh, and Ephraim (who also gave their names to tribes). And when, after Joseph's death, the Israelites in Egypt were placed by a new king under a degrading and unbearable servitude, God was moved by pity for their lot to fulfill his earlier promises. He revealed himself to Moses the grandson of Levi out of a burning bush, while he was grazing his sheep in the deserts of Arabia, and he commanded him to lead the Israelites out of Egypt and bring them into the land of Canaan, which he had set aside long before as their proper home for all time. God would, he said, be at Moses' side and serve as a constant source of assistance. So Moses obeyed God's command, and with the help of his brother, Aaron, he visited various plagues upon the king of Egypt, who was trying with all his might to keep him from leaving, and he escaped from Egypt at the head of six hundred thousand people. Then, once he had gotten away from a band of Egyptians who were pursuing him, he crossed the Red Sea with God's help and traversed the desert of Arabia by the long route he had planned; and there, in accordance with God's will, he kept the people (who were understandably resistant) for forty years. It was there, in the first year, that God again revealed himself to Moses, summoned him to Mount Horeb, in the Sinai Desert, gave him the law inscribed on two stone tablets, and ordered the Israelites to keep it forever. In fact, it contained the entire plan of the republic which he wanted them to adopt. Moses, moreover, announced all God's commands to the people, and they pledged themselves to listen to his word. Then in the fortieth year, on the plains of Moab by the Jordan River, Moses made a general survey of the laws and collected them in a book which he called Deuteronomy. And before his death a short while later, he bequeathed the leadership of the Israelites to Joshua the son of Nun from the tribe of Ephraim.

Eventually Joshua crossed the Jordan, took possession of the land of Canaan, and defeated its thirty-one kings; and he conquered almost the entire region inhabited by the Amorites, the Canaanites, the Girgashites, the Hittites, the Hivvites, the Jebusites, and the Perizites. When this was done, he distributed the land to the twelve tribes as God commanded, partly through lots and partly according to his own discretion.[12] The area across the Jordan which Moses had acquired in battle and assigned to the Reubenites, the Gadites, and half of the Manassites was confirmed as their possession. Then

Judah, Ephraim, and the other half of Manasseh were assigned part of the area between the Jordan and the sea. The rest was divided into seven equal portions, for which the remaining tribes (Simon, Benjamin, Dan, Issachar, Zebulon, Naphtali, and Asher) drew lots. While Judah's territories were close to Arabia, Naphtali and Asher bordered on Syria; and the length of the entire province stretched from Dan to Beersheba (the former was next to Syria, the latter to Arabia). Moreover, God had ordered Levi, the thirteenth tribe, to be excluded from the drawing of lots. Though they did not receive any of the land, they were granted priesthoods, first fruits, tithes, offerings, and sacrifices. There were also six cities of refuge—the first in Naphtali, the second in Ephraim, the third in Judah, and the rest across the Jordan in Reuben, Gad, and Manasseh. To these God permitted to flee those men who had committed unintentional murder. To these six were then added another nine, distributed throughout the tribes. The Levites lived in forty-three towns together with the lands surrounding them, on which they could raise their own animals. So it is written in Joshua.[13] They did not, therefore, constitute their own tribe, but were enrolled in the tribes within whose territory they lived. Thus it is written in the first chapter of Numbers: *Only thou shalt not number the tribe of Levi, neither take the sum of them among the children of Israel.*[14] And in Judges 17: *And there was a young man out of Bethlehem Judah of the family of Judah, who was a Levite, and he sojourned there. And the man departed out of the city from Bethlehem to sojourn where he could find a place; and he came to Mount Ephraim, to the house of Micah, as he journeyed. And Micah said unto him, Whence comest thou? And he said unto him, I am a Levite of Bethlehem Judah, and I go to sojourn where I may find a place.*[15] There was also a law that no young woman who was an heir could marry outside of her own tribe and family, as it says in the last chapter of Numbers in the actual Hebrew:[16] *And every daughter who possesseth an inheritance in any tribe of the children of Israel shall be wife unto one of the family of the tribe of her father, that the children of Israel may enjoy every man the inheritance of his fathers.*[17] For this reason, the holy interpreters of the gospel have decided that since the Virgin Mary was an heir, she married Joseph, who was from the same tribe and family, and that this is why St. Matthew and St. Luke list the ancestors of Joseph rather than those of Mary, as though they were one and the same. The Levites, however, were exempted from this law—from the very start they had enjoyed the right to marry with all the other tribes. Thus it is written in chapter 19 of Judges: *a... Levite sojourning on the side of Mount Ephraim, who took to him a concubine out of Bethlehem Judah.*[18] And according to Second Chronicles 22, Jehoiada, a high priest from the tribe of Levi, married Jehoshabeath the sister of Ahaziah the king of Judah.[19] This is the reason St. Luke recorded that St. Elizabeth, who was one of the daughters of Aaron and therefore a Levite, was a relation of the Virgin Mary, who was from the tribe of Judah; and there is no need to suggest, as a number of scholars have proposed, that Mary was in fact from the tribe of Levi. For if this were true, the consequence would be that Christ was descended not from Judah and the line of David but from the flesh of Levi, in the face of every testimony of the sacred scriptures.

Once all these tribes had been securely settled in Canaan, they set up the republic that God had commanded. At first they lived under judges, then under kings: Saul the Benjaminite; David the Judean, who placed his capital in Jerusalem, a city of Judah; and David's son Solomon, who founded the Temple in Jerusalem. At that time the kingdom of the Israelites was the most glorious in the world, just as God had once promised would happen. And these are the tribes whose republic I am going to describe.

CHAPTER 3

The Judean, Ephraimite, and Samaritan Peoples

AFTER SOLOMON DIED, two of the tribes—Judah and Benjamin—recognized his son Rehoboam as their king and set up the kingdom of the Judeans. The other ten joined with Jeroboam the son of Nebat, of the tribe of Ephraim, founding the kingdom of the Ephraimites, or Israel. Thus Jeremiah 7: *...I have cast out all your brethren, even the whole seed of Ephraim,*[20] that is, the ten tribes of Israel. (Hosea, too, often says "Ephraim" and "Judah" instead of "Ephraimites" and "Judeans.") But since relations between Judah and Benjamin were very close, scripture regards the two as one single tribe, and together they are called "Judeans" (as I will show later on). And in this way the republic was reduced to the Judeans alone.

Once they had split into two states, there were violent disputes between the Judeans and the Ephraimites, and terrible hatreds flared. For Jeroboam steered the ten tribes away from the service of God and toward the worship of idols, out of fear that if his people were to go every year to the Jerusalem Temple, they might for some reason conspire to desert him. Once he had perpetrated this criminal act, the Levites abandoned their towns within the territory of the ten tribes and joined the tribe of Judah and Benjamin. And having thus become close neighbors of the Jerusalem Temple, they took even better care of the sacred rites which God had entrusted to them (just as we are told by Second Chronicles 11).[21] Moreover, the Judeans often fought battles with those tribes, and during the reign of Ahaz they claimed for themselves the Israelite region of Galilee, whose inhabitants Tiglat-Pileser, the king of Assyria, had expelled and deported to Assyria during the reign of Pekah (Second Kings 15 and 16). Not long afterward, God decreed that the rest of the Ephraimites, who had devoted themselves to such great impiety, should be defeated in battle and transported to Assyria by King Shalmaneser, during the reign of Hosea.[22]

Their now empty territory was, however, subsequently filled up with men from Babylon, Cuthah, Ava, Hamath, and Sepharvaim, who had been transported there; and since the latter occupied a city in the tribe of Ephraim called Samaria, after which the whole area was also named Samaria, they were called Samaritans. Now, these men were constantly being devoured by lions because they continued to honor the pagan gods of their fathers; and once they learned that this was happening because they were not worshiping the God of the Judeans or observing his law, they sought the king's permission to summon a priest from Assyria to teach them the law of God. And yet, they maintained alongside the true God the cult of their own gods. For this reason, Second Kings 17 says about them: *They feared the Lord and served their own gods, after the manner of the nations whom they carried away from thence. Unto this day they do after the former manners: they fear not the Lord, neither do they after their statutes, or after their ordinances, or after the law and commandment which the Lord commanded the children of Jacob, whom he named Israel; with whom the Lord had made a covenant and charged them, saying, Ye shall not fear other gods, nor bow yourselves to them, nor serve them, nor sacrifice to them. But the Lord, who brought you up out of the land of Egypt... Howbeit they did not hearken, but they did after their former manner. So these nations feared the Lord and served their graven images, both their children and their children's children; as did their fathers, so do they unto this day.*[23]

Then, after several years had passed, the Judean kings too were conquered, by Nebuchadnezzar the Babylonian; the city of Jerusalem and the Temple were burned, and the Judeans were transported to Babylonia and lost their republic.[24] But after seventy years, the Israelites or Ephraimites remained in Assyria, while the Judeans returned to their homeland, just as it says in the first chapter of Hosea: *...I will no more have mercy upon the house of Israel; but I will utterly take them away. But I will have mercy upon the house of Judah and will save them by the Lord their God...*[25] And then Cyrus the king of the Persians[26] laid up supplies and began to restore the Temple and the city. The Samaritans, however, kept the Judeans from being able to finish the work at that time (which inflamed the Judeans' hatred of them). Then, when Darius king of the Persians[27] came to power, the Judeans not only finished the Temple despite the resistance of the Samaritans, they also forced them to give back the Galilee (which they had acquired during the exile), and they began to recover their republic (as Josephus tells us in his book).[28] Then, after many years, the course of events arrived at the last Darius, who was defeated by Alexander the Great. During the latter's reign, they tried to force Manasseh the brother of the high priest Jaddua to divorce (in accordance with the law) his foreign-born wife, namely the daughter of Sanballat the Samaritan, the prefect of King Darius. So Manasseh took refuge with his father-in-law, who promised that he would make him high priest.[29] But when Alexander won, he showered the Jews with wonderful honors and exalted their religion. So once Sanballat agreed to go over to Alexander, he was given permission to build a temple much like the one in Jerusalem, on the highest mountain in Samaria (which is called Gerizim). And he placed in charge of it his own son-in-law Manasseh, whom he had appointed high priest. From then on the Samaritans grew arrogant, and, thinking they had been made the equal of the Jews, they declared themselves to be the descendants of Joseph the father of Ephraim, that is, to be real Ephraimites; and they said that they were worshipers of God no less than the Jews. They were also in the habit of welcoming with open arms people who fled to them after having been convicted by the Jews of various crimes. Then, several years later, the Jews were persecuted by the Syrian king Antiochus Epiphanes, who abolished their law and their sacred rites.[30] Since these practices were being punished by death, the Samaritans grew terrified and insisted that they worshiped not God but gods, that they were not Israelites but rather Sidonians, and that they were going to dedicate their own temple to the Cretan Zeus. In this way they escaped the imminent anger of a heavily armed king. Once they had survived that era, both the Jews and the Samaritans began to prosper again, so much so that they sometimes fought armed battles. The Samaritans were finally conquered by John Hyrcanus the Jewish king, who deprived them of their temple and made them subjects of the Jews. It was moreover a constant source of rancor to the Jews that whenever they traveled to and from their own province of Galilee, they always had to cross through territory of the Samaritans, who were hostile to their sacred rites. Though both peoples were roused to revolt a number of times, in the end they yielded to the power of the Romans. All this comes from Ezra and Josephus.

CHAPTER 4

The Law Given by God to the Israelites[31]

NOW THAT I HAVE set forth the information necessary for understanding the people whom I am going to discuss, I return to the law which God gave this people, and which contained the republic I am going to describe. This law, which was given by God through Moses, contained two categories in particular: the religious life, and a civil education. The rationale behind these principles is contained above all in two commands, the worship of God and affection for one's neighbor. Hence the following: *And thou shalt love the Lord thy God with all thine heart, and thy neighbor as thyself.*[32] In fact, these principles were expanded into ten. Three of them dealt with God: that we should worship only one God, that we should not use his name in vain, and that we should observe the Sabbath (for on that day God himself rested from his labors). Moreover, it is often repeated: *Ye shall not fear other gods, nor bow yourselves to them... nor sacrifice to them. But the Lord, who brought you up out of the land of Egypt...*[33] The next seven principles saw to it that parents would be respected; that there would be no murder, theft, or adultery; that no one would give false testimony; and that no one would desire another man's wife or his property. The laws were inscribed on two stone tablets; but then these ten were explained more fully and productively, and the whole was reduced to four commands alone—two of these are called commands and precepts, and two of them statutes and judgments.[34] The first two relate to God, and the second two to one's fellow man; and each one consists of many parts.[35] These I will discuss later on, as well as what each of them was and where they originated;[36] though first I will mention some passages of the law in which these terms are reiterated, apparently because they are integral to it. Exodus 15: *...God made for them a statute and an ordinance... and said, If thou wilt diligently hearken to the voice of the Lord thy God... and wilt give ear to his commandments, and keep all his statutes.*[37] Exodus 21:[38] *do my statutes, and keep my judgments.* Exodus 26:[39] *If ye walk in my statutes, and keep my commandments...* And at the end of the book: *These are the statutes and judgments and laws, which the Lord made between*

him and the children of Israel at Mount Sinai by the hand of Moses.[40] Then
at the end of Numbers: *These are the commandments and the judgments,
which the Lord commanded by the hand of Moses unto the children of Israel
in the plains of Moab...*[41] This is why Moses repeats in the fourth chapter of
Deuteronomy: *And the Lord commanded me... to teach you statutes and judgments...*[42] Likewise: *Behold, I have taught you statutes and judgments, even as
the Lord my God commanded me...*[43] Finally, it concludes: *And this is the law
which Moses set before the children of Israel. These are the testimonies, and the
statutes, and the judgments, which Moses spake unto the children of Israel...*[44]
And in chapter 6: *Now these are the commandments, the statutes, and the
judgments, which the Lord your God commanded to teach you.*[45] And this is
in fact the way these terms are used in the law. Then those who came later
on spoke in the same way about following the law, as in Joshua 24: *he set
them a statute and an ordinance.*[46] And in the second chapter of First Kings,
David said to Solomon: *Act to keep his statutes, and his commandments, and
his judgments, and his testimonies, as it is written in the law of Moses...*[47] And
in Second Kings 17: *...and keep the commandments and the statutes, according
to all the law which* God commanded you.[48] And in Second Chronicles 19:
*Jehoshaphat set of the Levites, and of the priests... for the judgment of... law
and commandment, statutes and judgments.*[49] And in chapter 24:[50] King Josiah
*made a covenant before the Lord, to walk after the Lord and to keep his com-
mandments and his testimonies and his statutes, with all his heart.* Of course,
David repeats many times in Psalm 118 that he had observed, or neglected,
or wished to learn what was contained in the law, namely, the commands,
precepts, statutes, judgments, and testimonies of God; as when he says: *Thou
hast commanded us to keep thy precepts diligently... O that my ways were directed to keep thy statutes... I have rejoiced in the way of thy testimonies... I
will delight myself in thy statutes... Thy testimonies also are my delight and my
counselors... Make me to understand the way of thy precepts.*[51] And in Psalm
17: *For all his judgments were before me, and I did not put away his statutes
from me.*[52] And Psalm 104: *That they might observe his statutes and keep his
laws.*[53] And Psalm 147: *He showeth his word unto Jacob, his statutes and his
judgments unto Israel.*[54] And in Nehemiah 10: They made *an oath, to walk
in God's law... and to observe and do all the commandments of the Lord our
Lord, and his judgments and his statutes.*[55] And Ezekiel 44: *...they shall stand
in judgment; and they shall judge it according to my judgments: and they shall
keep my laws and my statutes in all mine assemblies.*[56]

　　Let it suffice that I have brought these few examples from among the
many to be found in the Old Testament. It is now time for me to explain
each of these terms. Commands, which the Greek translator calls *entolai,*

appear to have been the expressions with which God required or prohibited something that had a particular bearing on himself. Precepts, which
in Greek are *prostagmata*, have been provided with reasons why they were
commanded; for the term *prostagma* implies some kind of provision. This is
why the Latin translator sometimes renders "precepts" as *caeremoniae*.[57] For
God not only commanded that he must be revered beyond all others, but he
also explained the rites through which this reverence was to be expressed,
namely when he told them about the tabernacle, the sacrifices, the festival
days, the priests, and their duties. And in fact, these two categories have to do
with God, while the statutes and the judgments have to do with one's fellow
man. For the statutes—which the Greeks translate as *dikaiōmata*—were the
commands through which God taught us how we should judge our fellow
man's innocence, and whom we should consider, and pronounce, guiltless
and righteous.[58] This is the point of Psalm 7: *...judge me, O Lord, according
to my righteousness, and according to mine integrity that is in me.*[59] This is
not, however, that heavenly justification that was discussed later on in the
Gospels, and by means of which (as the theologians say) *we are made truly
and formally righteous through God's grace, which clings to us*; rather, it is the
product of an earthbound court. We may draw this conclusion from the term
dikaiō itself, which is used in the Old Testament for "justify," i.e. "pronounce
righteous and innocent." As in Exodus 23, in the very law which deals with
justification: Do not *justify the wicked*; that is, do not absolve them (in Greek,
ou dikaiōseis). Hence Isaiah: *Woe unto them... who justify the wicked for reward.*[60] And in the second chapter of Leviticus:[61] *Ye shall have one manner of
law, as well for the stranger as for one of your own country* (in Greek, *dikaiōsis
mia*); that is, you shall acquit the foreigner no less than the citizen. And in
Deuteronomy 25: *If there be a controversy between men, and they come unto
judgment, that the judges may judge them; then they shall justify the righteous
and condemn the wicked*[62] (in Greek, *dikaiosōsi*). And Proverbs 17: *He that
justifieth the wicked, and he that condemneth the just, even they both are an
abomination to the Lord.*[63] And in Matthew 12: *For by thy words thou shalt
be justified, and by thy words thou shalt be condemned.*[64] God also ordered
judgments, through which he showed us just how to reach a verdict of guilt,
and whom we should consider—and pronounce—guilty and unjust. For they
used the term *krinein*, "to judge," to mean "to condemn," as in Genesis 15:
...that nation, whom they shall serve, will I judge.[65] And in Second Chronicles
36:[66] The Ammonites *cast us out of thy possession, which thou hast given us
to inherit. O our God, wilt thou not judge them?* (That is, *not condemn them.*)
In the fourth chapter of St. John:[67] *...I came not to judge the world, but to
save the world.* And in chapter 7: *Doth our law judge any man, before it hear*

him, and know what he doeth?[68] Accordingly, let this serve as an example of a judgment prescribed by the law: *One who steals at night should be killed*; and this, of a statute: *If during the day, he should be released.*[69] Likewise, a judgment would be: *One who has killed a man intentionally should pay with his life*; and a statute: *One who has killed unintentionally should be duly exiled.*[70] In fact, the testimonies which I have mentioned many times above were the words with which God himself bore witness that he would bestow the various blessings associated with this life on those who had kept the commands, precepts, statutes, and judgments which he handed down in the law; while those who did not he would afflict with evils. Hence Jeremiah says in chapter 9:[71] Neither do they hearken *unto thy commandments and thy testimonies, wherewith thou didst testify against them.* And in Second Kings 17: *And they rejected* God's *statutes, and his covenant that he had made with their fathers, and his testimonies which he had testified against them...*[72] In fact, a good example of these testimonies is Exodus 19: *Now therefore, if ye will obey my voice indeed, and keep my covenant, then ye shall be a peculiar treasure unto me above all people: for all the earth is mine, and ye shall be unto me a kingdom of priests and a holy nation.*[73] And Deuteronomy 11: *For if ye shall diligently keep all these commandments which I command you, to do them, to love the Lord your God, to walk in all his ways, and to cleave unto him; then will the Lord drive out all these nations from before you, and ye shall possess nations greater and mightier than yourselves.*[74] Then He promises many other benefits, and threatens many evils; these are called blessings and curses. In the Gospels, moreover, St. Luke uses these terms in the same way, in the first chapter: *And they were both righteous before God, walking in all the commandments and statutes of the Lord blameless.*[75] Which means, of course, that Zacharias and his wife had kept the law of God, in that they paid particular attention to its two parts, the commands and the statutes. (The first of these deals with God, and the second with one's fellow man.) Now these principles ought to apply to the whole of the law; so I decided to give them pride of place, because from these four terms (as though from the whole of the law) my entire argument about the republic can be derived. I will now return to the history of the law.

This law, then, was applied first by God to the two stone tablets, and then by Moses to the written text. Moreover, God ordered that this second set of laws be recited and learned by the kings, and that the high priest present it to the people on the Festival of Tabernacles. The first of these commands is written in Deuteronomy 17: *And it shall be, when* the king *sitteth upon the throne of his kingdom, that he shall write himself a copy of this law in a book out of that which is before the priests the Levites, and it shall be with him, and he shall read therein all the days of his life: that he may learn to fear the Lord his God, to keep all the words of this law and these statutes, to do them.*[76] The second is in Deuteronomy 31: *At the end of every seven years, in the solemnity of the year of release, in the Feast of Tabernacles, when all Israel is come to appear before the Lord thy God in the place which he shall choose, thou shalt read this law before all Israel in their hearing... that they may hear, and that they may learn, and fear the Lord your God, and observe to do all the words of this law.*[77] So for a long time after the Israelites set out for Canaan, they maintained this practice. Then, in the time of the kings, it was completely forgotten. When Jehoshaphat the king of Judea (a man who was graced with the most perfect piety) realized this, ...*he sent to his princes... to teach in the cities of Judah... and they taught the people* (as it is written in Second Chronicles 17).[78] But then this practice encountered such wickedness or neglect that even the written book of the law faded from the memory of the Jews; it was found by accident in the Temple, while the latter was being restored, and Hilkiah the high priest brought it to Josiah the king. When he read it, *he rent his clothes...* and said, *Great is the wrath of the Lord that is kindled against us, because our fathers have not hearkened unto the words of this book, to do according unto all that which is written concerning us.*[79] So he ordered that the book be recited to the people, and he pledged that he was going to observe it. Thus is it written in Second Kings 23: ...*and he made a covenant before the Lord, to walk after the Lord, and to keep his commandments and his testimonies and his statutes with all their heart and all their soul, to perform the words of this covenant that were written in this book. And all the people stood to the covenant.*[80] Then, a few years later, when the Jews were being led off to Babylon, the book of the law again disappeared; and when they returned to their homeland, Ezra, who was a scribe and a priest, either replaced the text (if it was lost) or restored it (if it was corrupted), putting it into the form in which we have it today. Then he himself wrote: ...*Ezra had prepared his heart to seek the law of the Lord, and to do it, and to teach in Israel statutes and judgments.*[81] And starting with Ezra, the scribes, who were the teachers of the law, spread throughout the republic, as I will show later on. Then these books were translated into Greek by seventy interpreters, at the order of Ptolemy Philadelphus the king of Egypt.[82] Then, some time later, Antiochus Epiphanes the king of Syria forced the Jews to abandon the law of God, and even to burn it. The source for this is in the First Book of Maccabees: *Moreover King Antiochus wrote to his whole kingdom that all should be one people, and every one should leave his laws... Yea, many also of the Israelites consented to his religion, and sacrificed unto idols, and profaned the Sabbath. For the king had sent letters by messengers unto Jerusalem and the cities of Judah that they should follow the strange laws of the land, and forbid burnt offerings, and sacrifice, and drink offerings, in the Temple; and that they should profane the Sabbaths and festival days, and pollute the sanctuary and holy people, set up altars, and groves, and chapels of idols, and sacrifice swine's flesh, and unclean beasts: That they should also leave their children uncircumcised, and make their souls abominable with all manner of uncleanness and profanation, to the end that they might forget the law, and change all the ordinances. And whosoever would not do according to the commandment of the king, he said, he should die.* And a little afterward: *...they built idol altars throughout the cities of Judah on every side; and burnt incense at the doors of their houses, and in the streets. And when they had rent in pieces the books of the law which they found, they burnt them with fire. And whosoever was found with any book of the testament, or if any committed to the law, the king's commandment was that they should put him to death.*[83] Judea suffered terribly under this evil for a little more than two years; then there arose Judah Maccabee, who took back the city and restored both the law and its teaching to their original state. During the reigns of his descendants the Hasmoneans, all kinds of sects were constantly emerging, such as the scribes, the Sadducees, and the Pharisees. The latter were mostly scribes, that is, teachers of the law, whose untraditional interpretations infected the people with meaningless misconceptions.[84] They were constantly criticized by Christ, who in his own declarations taught the truth, and also ridiculed quite frequently the Pharisees' absurd teachings. He brought us a new law, and in the New Testament he showed that he would give the men who listened to his words a home not in Canaan, but in heaven; and he announced that he had come not to destroy the law but to fulfill it.[85] This is correct; for though the law, for example, had prohibited murder, Christ forbade us not only to murder our brother but even to be angry with him. And though the law had banned adultery, Christ banned not only adultery but even casting lewd glances at a woman; and he adds: *...That except your righteousness shall exceed the righteousness of the scribes and Pharisees, ye shall in no case enter into the kingdom of heaven.*[86] Furthermore, everything implied by my argument[87] is also true of the law in general.

CHAPTER 5

The Form of the Israelite Republic

IT IS NOW TIME for me to discuss the structure of the republic that God either ordained in his earlier law or allowed to be introduced later on, once that law was forgotten.[88] But since the question at hand is the structure of the republic, we are essentially asking: in whose hands had the leadership of the state been placed? In fact, among the Hebrews it was under the control first of the optimates,[89] then of the kings. Government under the former is called by the Greeks "aristocracy," and under the latter "monarchy." The aristocracy existed under Moses, Joshua, the elders, and the judges, while the monarchy existed under the kings.

Moses was referring to the aristocracy under his leadership in Deuteronomy 13,[90] when he said: *Ye shall not do* in the land of Canaan *after all the things that we do here this day, every man whatsoever is right in his own eyes. For ye are not as yet come to the rest and to the inheritance, which the Lord your God giveth you.* Moses, in fact, handed over the entire government to a large group of men, men who were good and wise, so that some could look after the sacred matters, and others the profane ones. (And of the men responsible for sacred matters, one was the high priest and the rest were priests[91] and Levites. The latter handled profane matters: some devoted their time to giving counsel, and others to judgments, and many of them saw to civil or military education.) But Moses decided that none of them would have any choice about his duties, but that these would be imposed by law, and above all that they would carry out the judgments and statutes. This system continued to function in the time of Joshua and the judges in the land of Canaan, after its territories had been distributed. For God says to Joshua in chapter 1: *Only be thou strong and very courageous, that thou mayest observe to do according to all the law, which Moses my servant commanded thee: turn not from it to the right hand or to the left, that thou mayest prosper whithersoever thou goest.*[92] And afterward, when he gave the Israelites their orders, they answered: *...All that thou commandest us we will do, and whithersoever thou sendest us, we will go. According as we hearkened unto Moses in all things,* *so will we hearken unto thee...*[93] Then before Joshua died, he summoned the Israelites and repeated to them the words that God had said to him when he charged him to look after his law (chapter 33).[94] And the people promised that they were going to obey God's commands.

The government of the elders is referred to in the second chapter of Judges: *And the people served the Lord all the days of Joshua, and all the days of the elders who outlived Joshua, who had seen all the great works of the Lord, that he did for Israel.*[95] The same kind of aristocracy continued to exist while the judges were in power; that is, for as long as they administered the government the law kept its authority as before, and God himself was in command. And that this was so is also clear from Josephus, who explains in Book 4 of his *Antiquities* that this place[96] was ruled by the law of God. He has Moses say: *Aristocracy and the way of life that accompanies it are the best possible state of affairs; do not allow yourselves to be seized by the desire for some other form of state, but love this one, in which you have the laws as mistresses and do everything according to them. For it is enough that God is in charge. But if the desire for a king has overcome you, let him be one of your own nation.*[97]

But this kind of aristocracy, in which the law above all held power alongside God, was replaced by an actual monarchy. This was the term for the absolute rule of one man not according to the law, but according to the whim of the ruler. This was what they demanded of Samuel the judge, in this passage from First Samuel 8: *...now make us a king to judge us like all the nations.*[98] When Samuel heard this, he immediately asked God what he should do, and he answered: *...Hearken unto the voice of the people in all that they say unto thee: for they have not rejected thee, but they have rejected me, that I should not reign over them.*[99] He then added: *...howbeit yet protest solemnly unto them, and shew them the manner of the king that shall reign over them.*[100] Clearly this meant that as long as the judges ruled in accordance with the law, God himself had ruled over the Hebrews, since the law was in charge; but once power was transferred to a king in the manner of the gentiles, God was no longer king—the conduct of affairs was now going to be placed in the hands not of the law, but of one man's will.[101] This was a very accurate assessment, for as Aristotle put it best in his *Politics*:[102] *he who wants the law to rule, wants God to rule; and he who wants a king, that is, a man, wants a beast. Rule is not always accompanied by reason, but it is frequently governed by desire.* Moreover, God was also describing the arbitrariness of monarchic rule when he added: *He will take your sons... and... your daughters... and he will take your fields... and your menservants... and the tenth of your sheep: and ye shall be his servants... And ye shall cry out on*

that day... and the Lord will not hear you on that day.[103] Hence David said
in Psalm 2: *I have been appointed king by God upon the holy hill of Zion...
the Lord hath said unto me... Ask of me, and I shall give thee the heathen
for thine inheritance, and the uttermost parts of the earth for thy possession...
Thou shalt break them with a rod of iron; thou shalt dash them in pieces like
a potter's vessel.*[104] Moreover, these two sorts of monarchies—that is, the sort
where the king is bound by law, and the sort where he is not—have also been
remarked upon by Aristotle: he thought that the first was not really a proper
type of republic (though it is to be found in every state), but that the second
kind could properly be called a monarchy. For he says as follows: *Next we
must discuss the question of a king who governs everything according to his
will. For the so-called "king according to law" is not a distinct type of state,
because under all types of government there can be a permanent general, just
as in a democracy or an aristocracy; and many citizens may choose one man
to dominate their affairs.*[105] Aristotle is referring to what is called absolute
monarchy, in which the king runs everything according to his best judgment.
So the Hebrews, after they had settled in the land of Canaan, lived first
under judges, who ruled according to the laws, and then (like the gentiles)
under kings, who ruled as they saw fit. The first of these was Saul, and the
second was David. With him there began a hereditary kingship among the
Jews, which lasted until the time of Zedekiah, when he and his people were
led away captive to Babylon by King Nebuchadnezzar. But when the Jews
returned to their homeland after seventy years, their government returned
to its ideal state. At that time (as Josephus says in Book 11) the high priests,
who served as occasion demanded, acted as both priests and judges, until
Antiochus enslaved the people and the Levite family of the Hasmoneans
rose up. They governed all of the Jews' affairs first as princes, then as kings;
so the ancient practices were preserved.[106] When they died out, they were
succeeded by the kings from Ashkelon (though they might be better called
tyrants than kings), who were converts.[107] Of this family, Herod the Great,
son of Antipater, and his son Archelaus, and his grandson Agrippa ruled
in Judea; while Herod Antipas was a tetrarch in the Galilee, and two men
named Herod Agrippa were at various times kings in Chalcis. From the Romans, who ruled Judea at that time, they received the authority to appoint
whomever they wanted as high priest. In the end the Romans threw out
the Ashkelonites, conquered Judea, and saddled it with an administration
and taxes. But since the Jews had for the most part maintained their laws,
they laid claim to the sovereignty of their region and the right to look after
themselves. When they did finally rebel, the Romans burned down the city
and the Temple and practically snuffed out the entire nation.

Moreover, I would suggest that the government of the Hebrews was in a sense divided into three parts. The first was composed of the entire people, that is, the twelve tribes; the second, of the individual tribes themselves; and the third, of the individual towns within each of the tribes. The first seat of the republic was located in the city that God adopted as his own for reasons of religion. (Which city this was I will discuss later on.) He chose it because it was the seat of the highest magistrates, the highest senate, the people, and the court. Nevertheless, there were from time to time temporary lapses of authority. This is what Judges means when it says: *In those days there was no king in Israel, but every man did that which was right in his own eyes,*[108] meaning not that the individual tribes or cities lacked rulers, but that the entire state of twelve tribes was without high officials and guardians. The "second state" had one leader, who was called the head of the tribe, as well as others who were called the heads of families but were subordinate to the chief, who was in charge of the entire state.

The "third state" was organized as follows: each town had its own senate, which decided matters that were especially important to the community, judged private and capital cases, convened their own magistrates and senate, and ran the courts. The republic of the Hebrews, then, had a people,[109] a senate, judges, and magistrates. Hence in Joshua 23 it is written: *And Joshua called for all Israel, and for their elders, and for their heads, and for their judges, and for their officers.*[110] And wars waged beyond the boundaries of the nation at the public's expense and in the name of the people could be declared only by the king and the supreme senate, though the latter would be assisted by the individual chiefs of tribes and families and by the towns, as I will show below in the proper place.

CHAPTER 6

The Israelite Citizen and the Convert

NOW THAT I HAVE explained the structure of the Hebrew republic, it follows that I should describe the kind of citizens that belonged to it. Aristotle was of the opinion that different types of states produce different types of citizens, and that a citizen of the best kind of state has the power both to give advice and to render judgments. The same definition could also be applied to the Hebrew citizen, as it was ultimately taking part in both counsels and judgments that made one a citizen of the Hebrew state. After all, the sacred rites did not belong to everyone—they were the particular possession of the Levites. We should also point out that the Hebrew population was divided into two halves—the natives, called in Greek *autochthones*, and the foreigners, called *prosēlutoi*. This is the term "convert" used by the scholars who translated the sacred narratives into Latin. The natives included all those who were, as I said, descendants of Israel and underwent circumcision according to the law. God had commanded this of Abraham in Genesis 18,[111] as follows: *And he that is eight days old shall be circumcised among you... And the uncircumcised man child the flesh of whose foreskin is not circumcised, that soul shall be cut off from his people; he hath broken my covenant.* The converts, on the other hand, were foreigners who had been born among the gentiles but were converted from idol worship to the worship of God, and granted the privilege of circumcision. God orders them to be accepted like the native-born in Exodus 12, where he discusses the practice of the paschal lamb: *And when a stranger shall sojourn with thee, and will keep the passover to the Lord, let all his males be circumcised, and then let him come near and keep it; and he shall be as one that is born in the land: for no uncircumcised person shall eat thereof. One law shall be to him who is homeborn, and unto the stranger who sojourneth among you.*[112] This is the Latin version, but the Greek says more fittingly: *to him who is homeborn, and to the convert who has joined you.*[113] And in Leviticus 17: *...Whatsoever man there be of the house of Israel, or of the strangers which sojourn among you, who offereth a burnt offering or sacrifice, and bringeth it not unto the door of the tabernacle* *of the congregation, to offer it unto the Lord; even that man shall be cut off from among his people.*[114] And again:[115] *Ye shall have one manner of law for the citizen and for the stranger,* i.e. the convert. And just as gentiles could become Jews once they were circumcised, Genesis has the example of the Shechemites in the time of Jacob.[116] Likewise Achior in Judith 14: *Then Achior, seeing the power that the God of Israel had wrought, leaving the religion of the gentiles, he believed God, and circumcised the flesh of his foreskin, and was joined to the people of Israel, with all the succession of his kindred until this present day.*[117] Then King John Hyrcanus conquered the Idumeans and forced them to accept circumcision. This is why Herod the Idumean was a convert rather than a Jew of ancient descent, and since he had become king of the Jews even though he was a convert, he turned the high priesthood itself over to converts. Christ taught us how eager the Jews were to make converts, that is, to circumcise the gentiles, when he said to them (Matthew 13):[118] *...ye compass sea and land to make one convert, and when he is made, ye make him twofold more the child of hell than yourselves.* Hence in Second Chronicles 30: *And all the congregation of Judah, with the priests and the Levites, and all the congregation that came out of Israel, and the strangers who came out of the land of Israel, and who dwelt in Judah, rejoiced.*[119] And Ezekiel 14: *For every one of the house of Israel, or of the stranger who sojourneth in Israel, who separateth himself from me, and setteth up his idols in his heart...*[120] And the Acts of the Apostles 2: *...Jews and converts.*[121]

CHAPTER 7

The Capital City

NOW TO THE LOCALE in which this republic was established. It was a part of Greater Syria, whose length extended from Antiochene Syria[122] to Egypt, and whose width was from the Syrian Sea to Hollow Syria[123] and the other Arabia.[124] It was divided more or less down the middle by the River Jordan, which (as Pliny tells us)[125] flows from the spring Paneas and empties out, as soon as it has the chance to collect in a valley, into the lake that most people call Genesareth.[126] (In the gospel, though, it is called the swamp of Genesareth and the Sea of Tiberias.) From there it heads, with seeming reluctance, toward the loathsome Asphalt Lake (which is also called the Dead Sea), and there it is finally swallowed up, and its praiseworthy waters are mixed with the disease-ridden waters of the lake. In ancient times, as I have said, the holy books called the entire area Canaan or Cananea, at the time when Abraham was commanded by God to move there from Mesopotamia. In those days it was inhabited by seven nations: the Amorites, the Canaanites, the Girgashites, the Hittites, the Hivvites, the Jebusites, and the Perizites. (To these we might also add the Philistines, or Palestinians.) Then, after the offspring of Israel had conquered the land, they named it the land of Israel, and (as I said) they divided it into twelve parts, which they called tribes. On the other side of the Jordan were Reuben, Gad, and Manasseh; on this side were Judah, Benjamin, Simon, Ephraim, Dan, Asher, Issachar, Zebulon, and Naphtali. Then the ten tribes split off from the two, and after they were deported to Assyria, the various areas of the region on this side of the Jordan came to be known as Judea, Samaria, and Galilee (the inner regions); Palestine (on the coast); and Iturea, Trachonitis, and Chalcidica (across the Jordan). Judea was named after the tribe of Judah. Its most important towns were Jerusalem, Bethel, Jericho, Arimathea, Emmaus (or Nicopolis), Bethlehem, Hebron, Kirjath Jearim, and Eleutheropolis. Samaria was called after the city of that name, which King Omri founded on Mount Samaria in the tribe of Ephraim. Its towns were Shiloh, Shechem (or Sichar),[127] and Samaria. Galilee already had its name when the Israelites entered it. Its towns included Nazareth, Naim, Capernaum, Bethsaida (which was later called Julias), and Paneas (which was later called Tiberias). It had two parts: the Upper Galilee, which reached the Syrian Sea,[128] and the Lower, which reached the Tiberian. The most important cities of Palestine were Gath, Gaza, Azotus, Ekron, and Ashkelon. Since at that time the Judeans were the most powerful people there, the entire region was called Judea, though after Christ it was also called "Palestine" and "the Holy Land." So because (to return to the previous subject) the entire Israelite people was one joint republic of twelve tribes, they had to establish one place to which everyone could come from their tribes and towns to sacrifice to God, offer their first fruits, discuss their plans as one group, and conduct trials. This place would also serve as a seat for whoever was in charge of both sacred and profane affairs. In fact, God decided that it would be the place where he had chosen for his name to be called. This is what he says in the law found in Deuteronomy 12: *Ye shall not do so unto the Lord your God. But unto the place which the Lord your God shall choose out of all your tribes to put his name there, even unto his habitation shall ye seek, and thither thou shalt come. And thither ye shall bring your burnt offerings, and your sacrifices... Thou mayest not eat within thy gates the tithe of thy corn, or of thy wine, or of thy oil... But thou must eat them before the Lord thy God in the place which the Lord thy God shall choose...*[129] And chapter 17: *If there arise a matter... of controversy within thy gates, then shalt thou arise, and get thee up into the place which the Lord thy God shall choose,* so that you may call upon him.[130] Moreover, he chose those cities in which his tabernacle and his Temple stood. There were in fact two such places—Shiloh in Samaria and the territory of Ephraim,[131] and (once God had rejected this) Jerusalem in Judea and the territory of Judah. For Shiloh, we have the following sources. Once Joshua had been commanded by God to place the tabernacle and the ark in Shiloh, he also made it the seat of the religion and the state. Hence the facts reported in Joshua's narrative, chapter 22:[132] *And the whole congregation of the children of Israel assembled together at Shiloh and set up the tabernacle of the congregation there.* And also: *...the whole congregation of the children of Israel gathered themselves together at Shiloh, to go up to war against* those who were across the Jordan.[133] And Judges 21: *And the people came to the house of God in Shiloh, and abode there till even before God, and lifted up their voices, and wept sore.*[134] And a little later: *Then they said, Behold, there is a feast of the Lord in Shiloh yearly in a place which is on the north side of Bethel, on the east side of the highway that goeth up from Bethel to Shechem.*[135] Then God rejected Shiloh and chose Jerusalem and Mount Zion in the tribe of Judah, and ordained that his house and the entire state be moved there; and in time he even destroyed Shiloh. For it is written as follows in Jeremiah 7: *But go ye now unto my place which was in Shiloh, where I set my name at the first, and see what I did to it for the wickedness of my people Israel.*[136] And elsewhere: *Therefore will I do unto this house, which is called by my name... as I have done to Shiloh.*[137] God chose Jerusalem in the time of King David, for it was David who overcame the Jebusites, whom Judah and Benjamin had failed in their day to expel.[138] And he was the first to place the capital there at God's command, and to move the ark to Mount Zion. Scripture describes this in Second Chronicles 6, where God says: *Since the day that I brought forth my people out of the land of Egypt I chose no city among all the tribes of Israel to build a house in, that my name might be there; neither chose I any man to be a ruler over my people Israel. But I have chosen Jerusalem, that my name might be there...*[139] And in Second Kings 21: *...In this house, and in Jerusalem, which I have chosen out of all the tribes of Israel, will I put my name for ever.*[140] Hence Josephus expresses this law of God as follows: *There should be one holy city in the most beautiful and virtuous place in the land of Canaan, which God has chosen for it; and there should be one temple and one altar made of unhewn stones... And there should be no other temples or altars in any other cities; for God is one, and the people of the Hebrews is one... And they should gather in the Temple three times a year from all over the territory of the Hebrews, and give offerings to God from whatever they have, and entreat him for what they would like to have. And by meeting each other and feasting together, let them become friends; for it is fitting that they take note of one another, that they treat each other as fellow tribesmen, and that they share in the same pursuits.*[141] David hints at this in Psalm 77 when he says: *Moreover he refused the tabernacle of Joseph, and chose not the tribe of Ephraim, but chose the tribe of Judah, the mount Zion which he loved. And he built his sanctuary like high palaces* or *his holy place as though of unicorns.*[142] This means that God decided that the Temple should not be built in Shiloh in the tribe of Ephraim, and alongside the tabernacle of Joseph the father of Ephraim (who had received that land from his father without casting a lot [as it is written in Genesis 48][143] and was later buried in that city [Joshua 24]);[144] and that he wanted it to be built in Jerusalem, in the tribe of Judah. I believe that this is also the point of what the Samaritan woman says to Christ in the gospel of St. John: *Our fathers worshiped in this mountain;*[145] *and ye say that in Jerusalem is the place where men ought to worship.*[146] For by "fathers" she meant "Ephraimites," from whom the Samaritans claimed they were descended; and she says that they worshiped on Mount Ephraim, about which Joshua 20 says: *...Shechem in Mount Ephraim.*[147] This was during the time when the house of God was in Shiloh; while the Judeans claimed that honor for themselves and contended that the place of worship was in Judah rather than Ephraim, because it was in the city of Jerusalem. But David himself sang in Psalm 121 of how he had transferred the religion and the state to Jerusalem: *Jerusalem is built as a city that is compact together. Whither the tribes go up, the tribes of the Lord, unto the testimony of Israel, to give thanks unto the name of the Lord. For there are set thrones of judgment, the thrones of the house of David.*[148] This means that the tribes, i.e. the people, had gone up to Jerusalem—first to praise God, then to call for justice from the magistrates or the judges—at the time when the latter had built Jerusalem and formed it into a state.

But let me discuss in broader terms the character of Jerusalem. In the earliest times it was called Salem and was subject to King Melchizedek. Since he was a priest, he ran to meet Abraham and offer him bread and wine when the latter was returning from the war he had fought to free Lot from captivity (Genesis 14). The people who lived there were even then called Jebusites. Judah and Benjamin[149] did not succeed in removing them from the city until the time of David, so the city was situated in the territories of both tribes. For as it is written in Joshua 15, Judah could not expel the Jebusite inhabitants of Jerusalem,[150] while Moses' prophecy in Deuteronomy 33 has: *And of Benjamin he said, The beloved of the Lord shall dwell in safety by him; and the Lord shall cover him all the day long, and he shall dwell between his shoulders,*[151] predicting, then, that Benjamin was going to rest between the Lord's shoulders, because the Temple would be founded in that tribe. And Judges 18 adds that although Benjamin could not dislodge the Jebusites living in Jerusalem, it did settle among them.[152] From these sources we can see that Jerusalem, because of its size, was connected to both tribes. There are for the same reason scholars who propose that part of the Temple itself was in the tribe of Benjamin. The two tribes were, at any rate, treated as one and the same, because they were right next to each other and had a close relationship. The same thing happened later on, when the tribes split apart—Judah and Benjamin followed Rehoboam and took one name, Judah. David, then, was moved by the Holy Spirit to drive the Jebusites out of the city as soon as he became king (for God had chosen Jerusalem as the place where he, i.e. his Temple, would dwell), and he built it up and extended the reach of its walls. And there he built a fortress on one of the hills of Mount Zion overlooking the city, and walled it around; and he called it the city of David. It was there he moved his residence, along with the ark of the covenant. But later on, when he wanted to found the Temple on a different hill of Mount Zion called Moriah, God did not allow it, so he left this distinction to his son Solomon.

The latter carried out this work when he became king, and for the Temple's protection he built a fortress on a third hill of the same mountain (according to Josephus in *Jewish War*, Book 5, and *Jewish Antiquities*, Book 7).[153] Then during the reign of Rehoboam the son of Solomon, Shishak the king of Egypt conquered the city and carried off the royal treasuries; and when Hezekiah was king, Sennacherib the king of Assyria harassed the city with a bitter but unsuccessful siege. Then Nebuchadnezzar the king of Babylonia conquered it, after it had been recovered once by Jehoiakim, a second time by Jehoiachin, and a third time by Zedekiah.[154] He burned it, along with the Temple, and deported its people as captives to Babylonia. Then, after seventy years, the people was permitted to return by Cyrus, the king of Persia. The Temple was restored by Zerubabel, the city by Nehemiah, and the law by Ezra. Even the fortress on the third hill was rebuilt, not far from the Temple.[155] Then the city was plundered by Antiochus Epiphanes the king of Syria, the law was burned, and the Temple was defiled. But when, not long afterward, Judah the Hasmonean had won back all these things and launched a new effort to restore them, the state began to flourish. Until, that is, the shameful feud between two royal brothers, Hyrcanus and Aristobulus, allowed the Roman general Gnaeus Pompeius (who was fighting a war in Syria) to enter and occupy the country, though he spared the Temple.[156] A short while later Antigonus the son of Aristobulus recovered the state with the help of the Parthians;[157] but Herod the Ashkelonite, whom the Romans had declared king, took it away from Antigonus with the help of Gaius Sosius, the proconsul[158] of Syria.[159] Herod's descendants held it for a long time, until the Jews regained their power and rejected the good offices of the Romans. At that time Roman authority over the state was restored by Titus Caesar the son of the emperor Vespasian, and it was leveled to the ground and burned along with the Temple. Finally, after the rise of Christianity Hadrian rebuilt the city, though without the Temple, and called it Aelia.[160]

These are the aspects of the Hebrew republic which, in my opinion, deserved a general treatment. Now that our foundations have been laid down, we may proceed in good order to the remainder of our discussion.

BOOK II

Sacred Places

CHAPTER 1

Religion

NOW THAT I HAVE described the structure of the republic set before us, I should go on to describe its parts in the same order with which I began. And because the republic of the Hebrews had, as I said, both religious and civil life, I will pay particular attention to religion, and then to state. In fact, I will categorize according to this distinction the very legal terms whose meaning we need to define. The types of laws were, again, commands, precepts, statutes, and judgments. Of these the commands and precepts generally have to do with religion, and the statutes and judgments with state. But I have further divided religion (that is, the ways in which we revere God, codified into law and frequently reiterated) into four parts—sacred places, sacred days, sacred rites, and sacred people; for God wished to be worshiped in fixed locations, and paid special respect on fixed days, with fixed rites, and by fixed persons. I will therefore also see to it that each of these in turn receives individual attention.

CHAPTER 2

Sacred Places

THERE WERE MANY sacred places, that is, places where holiness dwelled on earth. First God established the tabernacle, and within it the holy of holies, the ark, and the altar. Then he called for the Temple to be built in Jerusalem in place of the tabernacle. But for a time he also allowed people to sacrifice to him outside the tabernacle and the Temple, beneath shady trees in the hills; they called these spots "high places."[1] Moreover, two more temples were later built in defiance of God's command, one in Samaria, the other in Egypt. But even in Jerusalem and in the provinces, they set up certain small gathering places called synagogues, and once the temples had been destroyed, these remained the only option. Given all this variety, it is abundantly clear that if we want to do complete justice to this part of the discussion, we must explain each of these institutions separately. So let me begin with the tabernacle.

The Tabernacle, the Holy of Holies, the Ark of the Covenant, the Altars, and Their Accouterments

THE TABERNACLE, which was also called the sanctuary, was as follows: Its structure was like that of the Temple but made of wood, and it could be put together, taken apart, and moved wherever one wished. Within it was an area set apart, by a curtain, called the sanctuary of the sanctuary or the holy of holies. It was there that the ark of the covenant was kept. This had a cover called the mercy seat and the oracle,[2] which was notable for the two cherubs spreading their wings above it, and for the gold altar on which incense was burned. Outside the curtain was a table with twelve sacred loaves called showbread, as well as a candelabrum with seven lamps, and a gold basin, and the gold altar for incense. Outside the tabernacle, on the other hand, was a bronze altar for burnt offerings and a bronze basin, as well as a courtyard and a covering.[3] God ordered Moses to make all of these things when he was on Mount Sinai. Exodus 25 says: *And let them make me a sanctuary, that I may dwell among them. According to all that I shew thee, after the pattern of the tabernacle, and the pattern of all the instruments thereof, even so shall ye make it.*[4] Then instructions are given for the ark and its decorations, as follows: *And they shall make an ark of shittimwood... And thou shalt overlay it with pure gold, within and without shalt thou overlay it, and shalt make upon it a crown of gold round about. And thou shalt cast four rings of gold for it, and put them in the four corners thereof; and two rings shall be in the one side of it, and two rings in the other side of it. And thou shalt make staves of shittimwood, and overlay them with gold. And thou shalt put the staves into the rings by the sides of the ark, that the ark may be borne with them. The staves shall be in the rings of the ark: they shall not be taken from it. And thou shalt put into the ark the testimony which I shall give thee. And thou shalt make a mercy seat of pure gold... And thou shalt make two cherubim of gold, of beaten work shalt thou make them, in the two ends of the oracle. And make one cherub on the one end, and the other cherub on the other end... And the cherubim shall stretch forth their wings on high, covering the oracle with their wings, and their faces shall look one to another; toward the mercy seat shall the faces of the cherubim be. And thou shalt put the mercy seat above upon the ark; and in the ark thou shalt put the testimony that I shall give thee.*[5] Then, in the following passage, it goes on to discuss the table and its implements: *Thou shalt also make a table of shittimwood... And thou shalt overlay it with the purest gold: and thou shalt make to it a golden ledge round about. And to the ledge itself a polished crown... and over the same another little golden crown...*[6] *Thou shalt prepare also dishes, and bowls, censers, and cups, wherein the libations are to be offered, of the purest gold. And thou shalt set upon the table showbread before me always. And thou shalt make a candlestick of pure gold; of beaten work shall the candlestick be made: its shaft, and its branches, its bowls, its knobs, and its flowers, shall be of the same... And thou shalt make the seven lamps thereof: and they shall light the lamps thereof, that they may give light over against it. And the tongs thereof, and the snuffdishes thereof, shall be of pure gold.*[7] After describing these things God ordered that a tabernacle be made of shittimwood, and that one part of it be holier than the other; this he called the holy of holies. He also specified the shape, dimensions, and decoration of this tabernacle. (Since this is the subject of a very long narrative, I would prefer not to re-peat it; it is enough that I point it out.) After he has finished with this dis-cussion, he adds the following about the curtain and the mercy seat: *And thou shalt make a veil of blue, and purple, and scarlet, and fine, twined linen of cunning work... And thou shalt hang up the veil under the taches, that thou mayest bring in thither within the veil the ark of the testimony: and the veil shall divide unto you between the holy place and the most holy. And thou shalt put the mercy seat upon the ark of the testimony in the most holy place. And thou shalt set the table without the veil, and the candlestick over against the table on the side of the tabernacle toward the south: and thou shalt put the table on the north side.*[8] Then he discusses the hanging, the altar of burnt offerings, and the courtyard: *And thou shalt make a hanging for the door of the tent, of blue, and purple, and scarlet, and fine, twined linen, wrought with needlework... And thou shalt make an altar of shittimwood... and thou shalt overlay it with brass. And thou shalt make its pans to receive its ashes, and its shovels, and its basins, and its fleshhooks, and its firepans: all the vessels thereof thou shalt make of brass. And thou shalt make for it a grate of network of brass... And thou shalt make the court of the tabernacle... with twenty pil-lars...*[9] Finally he concludes with the incense altar, the brass basin, and the incense: *And thou shalt command the children of Israel, that they bring thee pure oil olive beaten for the light, to cause the lamp to burn always. In the tabernacle of the congregation without the veil, which is before the testimony... And thou shalt make an altar to burn incense upon: of shittimwood shalt thou make it... And thou shalt overlay it with pure gold... And thou shalt put it before the veil that is by the ark of the testimony, before the mercy seat that is over the testimony... And Aaron shall burn thereon sweet incense... Thou shalt also make a laver of brass, and his foot also of brass, to wash withal: and thou shalt put it between the tabernacle of the congregation and the altar... Take thou also unto thee principal spices, of pure myrrh... and of sweet cinnamon... and of sweet calamus... And of cassia... and of oil olive... And thou shalt make it an oil of holy ointment... And thou shalt anoint the tabernacle of the congregation therewith, and the ark of the testimony, and the table* and everything... *Take unto thee sweet spices, stacte, and onycha, and galbanum; these sweet spices with pure frankincense: of each shall there be a like weight. And thou shalt make it a perfume... and put of it before the testimony in the tabernacle of the congregation, where I will meet with thee.*[10] These are the instructions contained in Exodus 25 through 30. Then in Leviticus 17, God commands all the sacrifices for the altar of burnt offerings at the entrance of the tabernacle: *What man soever there be of the house of Israel, who killeth an ox, or lamb, or goat, in the camp, or who killeth it out of the camp, and bringeth it not unto the door of the tabernacle of the congregation, to offer an offering unto the Lord before the tabernacle of the Lord; blood shall be imputed unto that man... Whatsoever man there be of the house of Israel, or of the strangers who sojourn among you, who offereth a burnt offering or sacrifice, and bringeth it not unto the door of the tabernacle of the congregation, to offer it unto the Lord; even that man shall be cut off from among his people.*[11] Moses wasted no time in carrying out all these tasks; and the Israelites contributed everything required of them with the greatest enthusiasm. This is in Exodus 37 and 38, where specific instructions are given for the gold and brass altars, namely the incense and burnt offering altars: *And he made the incense altar of shittimwood... and he overlaid it with pure gold... And he made the altar of burnt offering of shittimwood: five cubits was the length thereof, and five cubits the breadth thereof; it was foursquare; and three cubits the height thereof. And he made the horns thereof on the four corners of it; the horns thereof were of the same: and he overlaid it with brass. And he made all the vessels of the altar, the pots, and the shovels, and the basins, and the fleshhooks, and the firepans: all the vessels thereof made he of brass. And he made for the altar a brazen grate of network under the compass thereof beneath unto the midst of it. And he cast four rings for the four ends of the grate of brass, to be places for the staves. And he made the staves of shittimwood, and overlaid them with brass. And he put the staves into the rings on the sides of the altar, to bear it withal; he made the altar hollow with boards.*[12] Then chapter 40 concludes: *Thus did Moses: according to all that the Lord commanded him, so did he. And it came to pass in the first month in the second year, on the first day of the month, that the tabernacle was reared up. And Moses reared up the tabernacle, and fastened its sockets, and set up the boards thereof, and put in the bars thereof, and reared up its pillars. And he spread abroad the tent over the tabernacle, and put the covering of the tent above upon it... And he took and put the testimony into the ark, and set the staves on the ark, and put the mercy seat above upon the ark. And he brought the ark into the tabernacle, and set up the veil of the covering... And he put the table in the tent of the congregation, upon the side of the tabernacle northward, without the veil. And he set the bread in order upon it... And he put the candlestick in the tent of the congregation, over against the table, on the side of the tabernacle southward. And he lighted the lamps... And he put the golden altar in the tent of the congregation before the veil: And he burnt sweet incense thereon... And he set up the hanging at the door of the tabernacle. And he put the altar of burnt offering by the door of the tabernacle... And he set the laver between the tent of the congregation and the altar, and put water there... And Moses and Aaron and his sons washed their hands and their feet thereat: When they went into the tent of the congregation, and when they came near unto the altar... And he reared up the court round about the tabernacle and the altar, and set up the hanging of the court gate.*[13] We are told, moreover, in Deuteronomy 10 that Moses did in fact place the testimony in the ark: *And I turned myself and came down from the mount, and put the tables in the ark which I had made; and there they be, as the Lord commanded me.*[14] Besides all this there was a perpetual flame sent down by God from heaven to light the burnt offerings. This is described in Leviticus 6 (and I will discuss it in its proper place): *And the fire upon the altar shall be burning in it... and the priest shall burn wood on it every morning, and lay the burnt offering in order upon it; and he shall burn thereon the fat of the peace offerings.*[15] The tabernacle of testimony and the ark of the covenant (or of testimony or of testament) are so called because within them were preserved the tablets of the law, which contained the testimony, the testament, the pact, and the covenant that God had struck with them.[16] According to this covenant the people had to give God their adoration, and God had to take the people under his stewardship and watch over them with particular care. For in Exodus 19, God says: *...if ye will obey my voice indeed, and keep my covenant, then ye shall be a peculiar treasure unto me above all people.*[17] And in Leviticus 26: *If ye walk in my statutes... And I set my tabernacle among you:*

and my soul shall not abhor you. And I will walk among you, and will be your God, and ye shall be my people.[18]

This description of the tabernacle, the ark, the table, the altars, and the other objects has been written into the law. But they may also be found in chapter 9 of St. Paul's Letter to the Hebrews: *For there was a tabernacle made; the first, wherein was the candlestick, and the table, and the showbread; which is called the sanctuary. And after the second veil, the tabernacle which is called the holiest of all; which had the golden censer, and the ark of the covenant overlaid round about with gold, wherein was the golden pot that had manna, and Aaron's rod that budded, and the tables of the covenant; and over it the cherubim of glory shadowing the mercy seat.*[19] Then Paul states that this tabernacle, which was of this earth and made by human hands, was a copy of the heavenly and incorporeal tabernacle entered by Christ,[20] who was the source of a new testament. For later on they also called the law of Christ "testament," because he himself testified within it that he would offer eternal heavenly rewards to those who revered his law. The same point is made by St. Jerome in Letter 128:[21] *We read in Exodus of the tabernacle, the table, the candelabrum, the altar, the columns, the hangings, the scarlet, the linen, the violet, the purple, the various vessels of gold, silver, and bronze; the tabernacle divided into three parts, the twelve loaves placed on the table every day of the week, the seven lamps in the candelabrum, the altar set up for sacrifices and burnt offerings, the bowls, the cups, the censers, the saucers, the mortars, the pins, the red-dyed skins, the goathair, and the undecaying*[22] *wood. So many wonderful things are offered up in the tabernacle of God that no one could despair of receiving salvation. One person possesses the gold of the senses, another the silver of eloquence, a third a voice of bronze. The whole world is represented in the sacrament of the tabernacle. The first and second courtyards lie open to all, for water and earth have been given to all men; while entrance into the holy of holies, that is, into the sky and to heaven, is granted to very few. The twelve loaves signify the twelve months of the year, and the seven lamps the seven celestial bodies.* This is what Jerome has to say; I now return to the particulars of history.

This tabernacle which I have described was constructed in such a way that (as we are told in Numbers 4) it could be broken down into its parts and put back together again, and (just like the ark) carried wherever one wished. It was taken into the land of Canaan promised by God: Joshua led the people across the Jordan (which had been dried up), the priests and the Levites carrying the tabernacle and the ark on their shoulders, and they were placed in the camp at Gilgal. It was at this time that the fortifications of Jericho collapsed, after the Levites carried the ark around its walls (Joshua

4 and 5). After the victory both the tabernacle and the ark were brought to Shiloh, a town in the tribe of Ephraim, where Joshua kept his command. So it is reported in Joshua 18: *And the whole congregation of the children of Israel assembled together at Shiloh and set up the tabernacle of the congregation there.*[23] Afterward they stood at the entrance to the tabernacle while lots were cast for the distribution of the land; for in the following chapter it says: *These are the inheritances, which Eleazar the priest, and Joshua the son of Nun, and the heads of the fathers of the tribes of the children of Israel, divided for an inheritance by lot in Shiloh before the Lord, at the door of the tabernacle of the congregation.*[24] And once this was done, Shiloh became the site of the house of God and the dwelling place of the faith. In fact, later on they made it a practice to gather there three times a year and offer sacrifice, as it was the place God had chosen for himself; just as the law commanded in Exodus 23:[25] *Thrice in the year shall all your men children appear before the Lord God, the God of Israel. For I will cast out the nations before thee, and enlarge thy borders: neither shall any man desire thy land, when thou shalt go up to appear before the Lord thy God thrice in the year.* And so the ark remained in Shiloh throughout the rule of the judges; and it was there that the people gathered together to decide matters of religion. So in Judges 18 it says of the rulerless period between Samson and Eli: *And they set them up Micah's graven image, which he made, all the time that the house of God was in Shiloh.*[26] And in Judges 20: *And the children of Israel arose, and went up to the house of God, that is, to Shiloh.*[27] And then: *...all the people went up, and came unto the house of God in Shiloh.*[28] And a little after: *Then they said, Behold, there is a feast of the Lord in Shiloh yearly.*[29] Later on, when Eli the high priest was dispensing judgment in Israel, and the war with the Philistines was not going well, it was decided to take the ark itself into battle against the enemy, in hopes of scaring them out of their wits. But the battle turned out very badly—the ark fell into the hands of the enemy, and Eli's sons were killed. When he received the news, Eli, who was a decrepit old man, collapsed and died. As we are told in First Samuel 4: *...Let us fetch the ark of the covenant of the Lord out of Shiloh unto us, that, when it cometh among us, it may save us out of the hand of our enemies. So the people sent to Shiloh, that they might bring from there the ark of the covenant of the Lord of hosts, which dwelleth between the cherubim.*[30] Then it adds: And when the battle began *the ark of God was taken; and the two sons of Eli were slain.*[31] After that the Philistines brought the ark to Azotus, one of their towns, and set it up in the temple of Dagon. As a result the statue of Dagon fell to the ground, and the population of Azotus began to die from a great plague sent by God. So the ark was moved from Azotus to Gath; but when its people

began to die of the same plague, it was transferred to Ekron. When the
Ekronites, too, began to die it was decided that as seven months had passed,
the ark should be given back to the Israelites; and so it was placed on a new
wagon, and two cows were entrusted with carrying it back. The cows, moreover, showed no concern at all for the calves they had left behind,[32] and with
no driver to urge them on, they went straight down the road on their own,
until they reached the border of the Philistines and the Judeans. And there
they were sacrificed as a burnt offering by the Judeans who lived in Beth
Shemesh. However, some inhabitants of that city perished as well, because
they had looked into the ark of the Lord; so they sent messengers to Kirjath
Jearim, to ask its citizens to take the ark. The latter set out and brought it
back with them, to the house of Abinadab in Giveah, a town of Benjamin;[33]
and they appointed his son Eleazar to look after it (First Samuel 5–7). Then
when Saul was king the tabernacle was brought, without the ark, to the town
of Nob in the tribe of Benjamin, where Achimelech was high priest (First
Samuel 21).[34] Later on, in the time of David, it was brought to the town of
Gibeon (also in Benjamin), as in First Chronicles 1:[35] ...*at Gibeon; for there
was the tabernacle of the congregation of God, which Moses the servant of the
Lord had made in the wilderness.* And chapter 16: David appointed *Zadok
the priest, and his brethren the priests, before the tabernacle of the Lord in
the high place that was at Gibeon, to offer burnt offerings unto the Lord upon
the altar of the burnt offering continually, morning and evening, and to do
according to all that is written in the law of the Lord, which he commanded
Israel.*[36] And chapter 21: *For the tabernacle of the Lord, which Moses made
in the wilderness, and the altar of the burnt offering, were at that season in
the high place at Gibeon.*[37] Then King David took the ark from the house of
Abinadab so that he could bring it to Jerusalem, or to Zion, his city; but he
was disheartened to find that Uzza had been suddenly struck dead when he
tried to keep the ark from falling off the wagon during its journey; so he
placed it in the home of Obed-edom of Gath. And after he heard that God
had blessed Obed and all his affairs, he made a new tabernacle for the ark
and took it, after three months, from Obed's house to his city. It arrived to
general acclaim and approval, and David put it in its place within the tabernacle which he himself had pitched for it. This means that the tabernacle
that Moses had made was still in Gibeon in the time of Solomon, for so we
are told in First Chronicles 2:[38] *So Solomon, and all the congregation with
him, went to the high place that was at Gibeon; for there was the tabernacle
of the congregation of God, which Moses the servant of the Lord had made in
the wilderness. But the ark of God had David brought up from Kirjath Jearim
to the place which David had prepared for it; for he had pitched a tent for it*

at Jerusalem. Nor is there any further mention of this original tabernacle in the sacred scriptures.

Then Solomon completed the Temple, and after setting up the sanctuary, he brought the ark and the tabernacle of David there from the city of David, along with all the vessels for the sanctuary which were in that tabernacle. It says in First Kings and in First Chronicles:[39] *And the priests brought in the ark of the covenant of the Lord unto his place, into the oracle of the house, to the most holy place, even under the wings of the cherubim. For the cherubim spread forth their two wings over the place of the ark, and the cherubim covered the ark and the staves thereof above... There was nothing in the ark save the two tables of stone, which Moses put there at Horeb, when the Lord made a covenant with the children of Israel, when they came out of the land of Egypt.* After that the ark was with the tabernacle of David in the Temple, until the latter was burned by the Babylonians. In the chaos that ensued, the eternal flame for the burnt offerings was hidden along with the tabernacle, the ark, and the incense altar. The story was told by the Jews of Jerusalem in a letter they sent to the Egyptian Jews, in Second Maccabees: *For when our fathers were led into Persia, the priests... took the fire of the altar privily, and hid it in a hollow place of a pit without water, where they kept it sure, so that the place was unknown to all men.*[40] And then: At the same time Jeremiah *the prophet, being warned of God, commanded the tabernacle and the ark to go with him, as he went forth into the mountain, where Moses climbed up, and saw the heritage of God. And when Jeremiah came thither, he found a hollow cave, wherein he laid the tabernacle, and the ark, and the altar of incense, and so stopped the door. And some of those that followed him came to mark the way, but they could not find it. Which when Jeremiah perceived, he blamed them, saying, As for that place, it shall be unknown until the time that God gather his people again together, and receive them unto mercy. Then shall the Lord show them these things, and the glory of the Lord shall appear, and the cloud also, as it was showed under Moses.*[41] Though after returning to their homeland the Jews did build a second temple, they did not find the fire, the ark, or the tabernacle. The letter written by the Jews has this to say about the fire: *Now after many years, when it pleased God, Nehemiah, being sent from the king of Persia, did send of the posterity of those priests that had hid it to the fire: but when they told us they found no fire, but thick water; then commanded he them to draw it up, and to bring it; and when the sacrifices were laid on, Nehemiah commanded the priests to sprinkle the wood and the things laid thereupon with the water. When this was done, and the time came that the sun shone, which afore was hidden in the cloud, there was a great fire kindled, so that every man marveled... Now when the sacrifice was consumed,*

Nehemiah commanded the water that was left to be poured on the great stones. When this was done, there was kindled a flame: but it was consumed by the light that shined from the altar.[42] In fact, the talmudists claim that neither the ark nor the tabernacle was ever found, and that their place in the sanctuary was filled by a stone that was three inches high and topped by a censer. But the other ancient ornaments of the tabernacle—the implements for the altar and the table—were replaced as circumstances dictated[43] and were kept until the final days of the Temple.

CHAPTER 4

The "High Places"

NOW THAT I HAVE described the tabernacle, it is time to discuss the "high places." These were high hills where they offered sacrifices under leafy trees, a practice that was against God's law but which he nevertheless tolerated. In fact, the first time God banned these places was in Deuteronomy 12: *Ye shall utterly destroy all the places, wherein the nations which ye shall possess served their gods, upon the high mountains, and upon the hills, and under every green tree. And ye shall overthrow their altars, and break their pillars, and burn their groves with fire; and ye shall hew down the graven images of their gods, and destroy the names of them out of that place. Ye shall not do so unto the Lord your God.*[44] And yet, in the time of the judges, he permitted sacrifices at those places. In fact, Gideon was the first to do this under an oak tree, according to Judges 6: *...he brought it out unto him under the oak and presented it.*[45] St. Augustine says the following about this institution in his commentary on Judges:[46] *Rather than forbidding it, God upheld his people's custom of making offerings outside his tabernacle—not to foreign gods, but to their own Lord God—and he even heard the prayers of these suppliants.* This practice persisted until the age of the kings, since the Temple had not yet been built. As in First Samuel 9, in the reign of Saul: *...he came today to the city; for there is a sacrifice of the people today in the high place.*[47] And in the second chapter of First Chronicles:[48] *Solomon... went to the high place that was at Gibeon; for there was the tabernacle of the congregation of God, which Moses... had made in the wilderness.* And in the third chapter of First Kings: *Only the people sacrificed in high places, because there was no house built unto the name of the Lord, until those days. And Solomon loved the Lord... only he sacrificed and burnt incense in high places. And the king went to Gibeon to sacrifice there; for that was the great high place...*[49] Even after the Temple was built, they did not abandon the "high places." Jeroboam the king of Israel rejected God and set up shrines there, and following his example, the other kings of Israel worshiped foreign gods there.[50] As it says in the seventeenth chapter of Second Kings: *...and they built them high places in all their cities... And they set them up images and groves in every high hill, and under every green tree. And there they burnt incense in all the high places, as did the heathen whom the Lord carried away before them.*[51] This is why God allowed Shalmaneser the king of Assyria to lead King Hosea and all his people away as captives, and to bring their state to an end. Of course, Rehoboam the king of Judah was no more conscientious about preserving the pure and complete worship of God. In fact, with his blessing the Judeans *built them high places, and images, and groves, on every high hill, and under every green tree.*[52] Nor did his descendants, the kings Asa and Jehoshaphat, remove them, exceptionally pious though they were. As it is written in First Kings 12:[53] Jehoshaphat did *that which was right in the eyes of the Lord: nevertheless the high places were not taken away; for the people offered and burnt incense yet in the high places.* After him the kings Amaziah, Azariah, and Ahaz were just as fond of the "high places," for it is written of Ahaz: *And he sacrificed and burnt incense in the high places, and on the hills, and under every green tree.*[54] Then King Hezekiah scattered these cults, though his son Manasseh restored them. About him it is written: *For he built up again the high places which Hezekiah his father had destroyed; and he reared up altars for Baal, and made a grove, as did Ahab king of Israel...*[55] Finally, Josiah hunted down and destroyed every kind of practice associated with the "high places." In chapter twenty-four of Second Chronicles,[56] it is reported about him as follows: *...he began to purge Judah and Jerusalem from the high places, and the groves, and the carved images, and the molten images.* And in Second Kings 23: *And he put down the idolatrous priests, whom the kings of Judah had ordained to burn incense in the high places in the cities of Judah... and defiled the high places where the priests had burned incense, from Geba to Beersheba... Nevertheless the priests of the high places came not up to the altar of the Lord in Jerusalem, but they did eat of the unleavened bread among their brethren... And the high places that were before Jerusalem... which Solomon the king of Israel had built* for idols, *did the king defile... Moreover the altar that was at Bethel, and the high place which Jeroboam... had made, both that altar and the high place he brake down, and burned the high place... and burned the grove... And all the houses also of the high places that were in the cities of Samaria, which the kings of Israel had made to provoke the Lord to anger, Josiah took away...*[57] St. Augustine therefore says about Josiah: *There are kings mentioned, among whose praiseworthy actions was that they did not destroy the "high places," where the people used to sacrifice contrary to God's law. And the one who did destroy them is lauded with even greater praise.*[58] And that was the end of the "high places."

CHAPTER 5

The Jerusalem Temple

AFTER THE TABERNACLE, the Temple was built. God gave notice from the very beginning that this was what he wanted done, in Deuteronomy 12: *You shall not sacrifice to the Lord your God upon the high hills, but unto the place which the Lord your God shall choose out of all your tribes to put his name there, even unto his habitation shall ye seek, and thither thou shalt come; and thither ye shall bring your burnt offerings, and your sacrifices, and your tithes, and heave offerings of your hand, and your vows, and your freewill offerings, and the firstlings of your herds and of your flocks.*[59] And farther on: *Take heed to thyself that thou offer not thy burnt offerings in every place that thou seest, but in the place which the Lord shall choose in one of thy tribes, there thou shalt offer thy burnt offerings, and there thou shalt do all that I command thee.*[60] Then King David had the idea of building a temple to God, once he had defeated all his enemies everywhere and brought peace to his entire realm, and before he handed over the throne to his son Solomon. He shared his plans with Nathan the prophet, insisting that it was shameful that he himself should live in a house of cedar while the ark of God was sheltered by hides. Though Nathan had approved of this plan, he came back and told David that it was God's will that he should not do it—God had reserved that honor for his son Solomon. We have David's words in chapter twenty-eight of First Chronicles: *…Hear me, my brethren, and my people: As for me, I had in mine heart to build a house of rest for the ark of the covenant of the Lord, and for the footstool of our God, and had made ready for the building; but God said unto me, Thou shalt not build a house for my name, because thou hast been a man of war, and hast shed blood. Howbeit the Lord God of Israel chose me before all the house of my father to be king over Israel for ever.*[61] And later: *Solomon thy son, he shall build my house and my courts; for I have chosen him to be my son, and I will be his father.*[62] And in Second Samuel 7: *Thus saith the Lord, Shalt thou build me a house for me to dwell in? Whereas I have not dwelt in any house since the time that I brought up the children of Israel out of Egypt, even to this day, but have walked in a tent and in a* *tabernacle.*[63] And likewise: *And when thy days be fulfilled, and thou shalt sleep with thy fathers, I will set up thy seed after thee... and I will establish his kingdom. He shall build a house for my name...*[64] Then David, following the instructions of the prophet Gad, bought a tract on Mount Zion called Moriah from Araunah the Jebusite, so that he could be delivered from a plague; and there he built an altar, and made burnt offerings and peace offerings, and so appeased God.[65] Then David summoned his son Solomon before his death, when all the financial arrangements for constructing the Temple had been made,[66] and said to him: *My son, as for me, it was in my mind to build a house unto the name of the Lord my God; but the word of the Lord came to me, saying, Thou hast shed blood abundantly, and hast made great wars: thou shalt not build a house unto my name, because thou hast shed much blood upon the earth in my sight. Behold, a son shall be born to thee, who shall be a man of rest; and I will give him rest from all his enemies round about: for his name shall be Solomon, and I will give peace and quietness unto Israel in his days. He shall build a house for my name... Now, my son, the Lord be with thee; and prosper thou, and build the house of the Lord thy God...*[67] He also ordered all the chiefs of Israel to help the person he had chosen as king. This is found mostly in First Kings and First Chronicles.[68] Then Solomon began to build the Temple in the fourth year of his reign, on Mount Moriah, that is, on the other hill of Mount Zion, which his father had marked out for him on the site he had bought from Araunah the Jebusite. What is more, he finished the work within seven years. The Temple's size, shape, and magnificence, which outstripped those of any other building, are described in both books at great length.[69] It therefore does not seem worth the effort to repeat those passages here. After the Bible has thoroughly described the construction of the Temple, it adds a description of its ornaments and instruments, which were the same as those in the tabernacle (First Kings 7): *And the oracle he prepared in the house within, to set there the ark of the covenant of the Lord... And he made a porch before the Temple... And Solomon made all the vessels that pertained unto the house of the Lord: the altar of gold, and the table of gold, whereupon the showbread was, and the candlesticks of pure gold, five on the right side, and five on the left, before the oracle, with the flowers, and the lamps, and the tongs of gold, and the bowls, and the snuffers, and the basins, and the spoons, and the censers of pure gold; and the hinges of gold, both for the doors of the inner house, the most holy place, and for the doors of the house, to wit, of the Temple... And Solomon brought in the things which David his father had dedicated; even the silver, and the gold, and the vessels, did he put among the treasures of the house of the Lord.*[70] Likewise in the third and fourth chapters of First

Chronicles: *And in the most holy house he made two cherubim... And he made the veil of blue, and purple, and crimson, and fine linen, and wrought cherubim thereon... Moreover... an altar of brass... a molten sea... ten lavers... ten candlesticks of gold... a hundred basins of gold... all the vessels that were for the house of God, the golden altar also, and the tables whereon the showbread was set; the candlesticks with their lamps... And the snuffers, and the basins, and the spoons, and the censers, of pure gold...*[71] We are told that after all this was done, David's tabernacle and the ark of Moses were moved to the holy of holies in the Temple with great pomp. This is what it says in Kings: *And all the elders of Israel came, and the priests took up the ark. And they brought up the ark of the Lord out of the city of David, which is Zion, and the tabernacle of the congregation, and all the holy vessels that were in the tabernacle... And the priests brought in the ark of the covenant of the Lord unto his place, into the oracle of the house, to the most holy place, even under the wings of the cherubim. For the cherubim spread forth their two wings over the place of the ark, and the cherubim covered the ark and the staves thereof above... There was nothing in the ark save the two tables of stone, which Moses put there at Horeb, when the Lord made a covenant with the children of Israel, when they came out of the land of Egypt...*[72] When all this was finished, the king blessed the people and poured out his prayers to God for the Temple (I will not include these prayers because of their length).[73] And after he had made sacrifice, *he dedicated the house of the Lord. And he hallowed the middle of the court that was before the house of the Lord; for there he offered burnt offerings, and meat offerings, and the fat of the peace offerings; because the brazen altar that was before the Lord was too little to receive the burnt offerings, and meat offerings, and the fat of the peace offerings... Then the Lord appeared to Solomon... And said unto him, I have heard thy prayer and thy supplication... I have hallowed this house, which thou hast built, to put my name there for ever... And if thou wilt walk before me, as David thy father walked, in integrity of heart, and in uprightness, to do according to all that I have commanded thee... Then I will establish the throne of thy kingdom upon Israel for ever... But if ye shall at all turn from following me, ye or your children... but go and serve other gods, and worship them; then will I cut off Israel out of the land which I have given them; and this house, which I have hallowed for my name, will I cast out of my sight...*[74] It also adds that three times a year, Solomon made burnt offerings and peace offerings on the altar that he had built for the Lord, and burned incense before the Lord[75] (we will see later on that this refers to Passover, Pentecost, and Tabernacles).

After Solomon's death, Jeroboam the son of Nebat, from the tribe of Ephraim, lured to his side ten of the tribes, and seized a territory from

Solomon's son Rehoboam, which he called Israel. Because he feared the day would come when his people, taken with longing for the Temple in Jerusalem, would abandon him, he himself abandoned God, and after turning the entire people from their ancestral worship of God to the cult of idolatry, he sanctified two calves—one in Bethel and the other in Dan—and built altars there (as we are told in First Kings 12).[76] All the rest of the kings of Israel who followed after him were zealously loyal to this godless cult. This is why God permitted Shalmaneser the king of Assyria to carry off King Hosea and all his people as captives.

For the same reason[77] the kings of Judah did not treat the Temple with all the reverence it deserved. In fact, even a queen, Athaliah or Gotholia[78] by name, defiled it with her unflagging wickedness.[79] But since her successor, her grandson Joash, had been raised by the high priest Jehoiada to fear God, when he found out what she had done he ordered the Temple to be restored.[80] And so the legally required money was collected from the Judeans, and Joash set up a treasury (about which I will have more to say later) to fund the restorations, and had the work carried out. This is described in Kings and Chronicles.[81] Then things reached such a pitch of madness that the sacred rites of the Temple were forgotten, and King Ahaz defiled even the Temple itself, and its vessels.[82] This is why Hezekiah later said to the people: Your *fathers... have turned away their faces from the habitation of the Lord... Also they have shut up the doors of the porch, and put out the lamps, and have not burned incense nor offered burnt offerings in the holy place unto the God of Israel...*[83] And he ordered as follows: that they should cleanse *all the house of the Lord, and... the vessels, which King Ahaz in his reign did cast away in his transgression.*[84] After him came Josiah, who again restored the Temple.[85] About him we are told in Kings: *And let them... who have the oversight of the house of the Lord give it to the doers of the work which is in the house of the Lord, to repair the breaches of the house.*[86] But only a few years later, the Temple and the city were burned down by Nebuchadnezzar, and the Jews left and went to Babylon. And as Hosea says in chapter 2, for seventy years they were without sacrifices, the altar, the ephod,[87] and the teraphim.[88] Once they had served out this term, Cyrus the king of Persia allowed them to return to their ancestral land; and Joshua the high priest and Zerubabel the chief built an altar on the soil of Jerusalem so that they could make burnt offerings. Then they laid the foundations of a new temple. But they were soon blocked by their enemies the Samaritans, and by order of King Cambyses[89] they were forced to discontinue the work. It was therefore after slightly less than forty-six years, when Darius the son of Hytaspes had given his approval, that they were able to complete and dedicate the building (as we are told in Ezra 4–6). The talmudists say that this second Temple, which Ezekiel describes at great length, was in many respects inferior to the first. First of all, it lacked a divine presence to give responses at the mercy seat (a practice I will describe in its proper place); second, there was no holy spirit, as this had stopped inspiring the prophets (the last was Malachi, in the time of Darius); third, there was no sacred fire, as it had been found solidified into water; fourth, there were no longer any stones on the high priest's breastplate, which the priests had examined to reveal hidden secrets; and fifth, there was no ark, no mercy seat, and neither of the cherubs that were attached to the ark, and which (as I said above) the talmudists claim had not been recovered. Then, after some years, dominion over the Jews went from the Egyptian kings to the Syrian ones, and Antiochus Epiphanes the Syrian king came to Jerusalem from Egypt at the request of the sons of Tobias, whom Onias the high priest had conspired to banish from the city. *And he entered proudly into the sanctuary, and took away the golden altar, and the candlestick of light, and all the vessels thereof, and the table of the showbread, and the pouring vessels, and the vials, and the censers of gold, and the veil, and the crown, and the golden ornaments that were before the Temple, all of which he pulled off. And after two years fully expired the king... set up the abomination of desolation upon the altar...*[90] That is, as Josephus reports, he dedicated it to Zeus Olympius, and once he had murdered Onias he made Alcimus high priest, even though he did not come from the high priestly line (this is in First Maccabees).[91] But two years later there appeared Judah the Hasmonean, surnamed Maccabee, the prince of the Jews. He took back the city and cleansed the Temple, and removing the abomination[92] he restored everything to its original state. For as it is written there, after he had expelled the enemy he said: *Behold, our enemies are discomfited: let us go up to cleanse and dedicate the sanctuary. Upon this all the host assembled themselves together, and went up into Mount Zion. And they saw the sanctuary desolate, and the altar profaned, and the gates burned up... Then Judah appointed certain men to fight against those who were in the fortress, until he had cleansed the sanctuary. So he chose priests of blameless conversation, such as had pleasure in the law, who cleansed the sanctuary, and bore out the defiled stones into an unclean place. And when as they consulted what to do with the altar of burnt offerings, which was profaned, they thought it best to pull it down, lest it should be a reproach to them, because the heathen had defiled it; wherefore they pulled it down, and laid up the stones in the mountain of the Temple in a convenient place, until there should come a prophet to show what should be done with them. Then they took whole stones according to the law, and built a new altar according to the former; and made up the sanctuary, and the things that were within the Temple, and hallowed the courts. They made also new holy vessels, and into the Temple they brought the candlestick, and the altar of burnt offerings, and of incense, and the table. And upon the altar they burned incense, and the lamps that were upon the candlestick they lighted, that they might give light in the Temple. Furthermore they set the loaves upon the table, and spread out the veils, and finished all the works which they had begun to make. Now on the five and twentieth day of the ninth month, which is called the month of Kislev... they rose up betimes in the morning, and offered sacrifice according to the law upon the new altar of burnt offerings, which they had made. Look, at what time and what day the heathen had profaned it, even in that was it dedicated with songs... And so they kept the Dedication of the Altar eight days and offered burnt offerings with gladness, and sacrificed the sacrifice of deliverance and praise... Moreover Judah and his brethren with the whole congregation of Israel ordained, that the days of the Dedication of the Altar should be kept in their season from year to year by the space of eight days, from the five and twentieth day of the month of Kislev, with mirth and gladness. At that time also they built up the mount Zion with high walls and strong towers round about, lest the gentiles should come and tread it down as they had done before. And they set there a garrison to keep it...*[93] Finally, King Herod wanted to rebuild the Temple and raise it higher, so he spoke to the Jews and explained the reasons for his plan as follows: *You know that this Temple was built by our fathers after they returned from Babylonia. And though it falls sixty cubits short of the height of Solomon's building, no one would fault our ancestors' piety, since it was not their fault that their Temple was shorter—Cyrus and Darius the son of Hytaspes decided the building's dimensions. Since the Jews were subjected first to these kings and their successors, and then to the Macedonians, they had no opportunity to adjust the Temple's measurements to those of its predecessor.*[94] Then Herod added that he wanted to set right a work that had never been finished, and offer it whole to God. So he prepared everything necessary for so enormous a project, and after demolishing the Temple he placed a new foundation on the original one, and raised the Temple upon it. It was a hundred cubits long and as many wide, and its height was one hundred and twenty. Then Josephus, the author of this account, goes on to describe the magnificence of the project in great detail, in Book 7 of his *Antiquities*;[95] and later on in a different passage he describes the site of a fortified tower: *A rocky hill rose a short distance from the eastern side of the city, which sloped down above the fortress that King Solomon had long before, with his God-given foresight, taken the trouble to surround with a wall; this began from the lower parts of the city, and was surrounded by a deep valley... at the north* side was a tall tower that the Hasmonean kings had constructed before Herod and called Bar, so that they could store there the priestly garments that the high priest would wear when the need arose. Herod kept these garments, but when he died they came under Roman control until the time of Tiberius Caesar. Tiberius returned them during Vitellius' term as proconsul of Syria, because when the latter visited Jerusalem he was warmly welcomed by its people... Herod fortified this tower in order to help guard the Temple, and as a compliment to his friend, the Triumvir[96] Mark Antony, he called it Antonia... the city lay before the Temple like a theater,[97] and there was a deep valley surrounding the whole area to the south... These projects took Herod one year and five months to finish. In the eighth year of his reign, the dedication of the Temple was celebrated amid great joy, on the same day as Herod's birthday. So Josephus says in Book 15.[98] There are, however, some scholars who think that Herod did not rebuild the Temple, but only enlarged it while preserving the original structure, and that Josephus had his facts wrong. After all, when after Herod's death the Jews heard Jesus say Destroy this Temple, and in three days I will raise it up,[99] they answered: Forty and six years was this Temple in building.[100] These scholars insist that the Jews would never have said this if Herod had in fact built that Temple in two years. Their statement is instead appropriate to the temple which Zerubabel began in the time of Cyrus and finished in the sixth year of Darius, forty-six years later. I cannot agree with the opinion of these scholars, because I don't believe that Josephus could have been so brazen as to write what he did about something that was so well known, and could be refuted by the testimony of many men who were still alive in his day.[101] For Josephus did not live very long after the government of Augustus Caesar,[102] under whom Herod built the Temple, or that of Tiberius,[103] who was emperor when the Jews made this statement.[104] But the Jews wanted to contradict Christ; and since they knew that it had taken Solomon seven years to build the first Temple, Zerubabel forty-six years to build the second, and Herod a bit more than a year to build the third, they failed to mention the first and third buildings, since these were not as helpful to their cause, and mentioned only the second. After all, three days are much less compared with forty-six years than they are compared with only one.[105]

When Christ died the veil in the Temple tore from top to bottom. Then Caligula[106] converted the Jews' synagogues to the worship of his own self, and decorated them with his statues;[107] and the Temple, which had thus far been inviolate, he dedicated in his own name. It seems, then, that the statement which the Jews had unwisely made before Pilate—that they had no king but Caesar[108]—had quite rightly redounded on their heads. (This is what Josephus writes.)[109] In the end, the Jews rebelled and caused a war while Vespasian was emperor; Titus Caesar conquered the city, and (whether accidentally or by design) he burned down the Temple on the very same date it had once been set afire by the Babylonians. Josephus records the details of this disaster at great length.[110] Then the emperor Hadrian[111] put down the Jews when they again rebelled, captured the city, leveled it to the ground, and burned to ashes what was left of the Temple. The divine words of Jesus Christ, who had said that one day not a single stone in Jerusalem would rest on top of another, were finally fulfilled.[112] But Hadrian buried the Temple of the Lord because he wanted to do away with the faith,[113] and he dedicated on its site another temple to Venus. This is what Eusebius writes.[114] St. Paulinus[115] accordingly wrote to Severus:[116] *In the very spot where our Savior was born and cried his infant tears, the infamous rites of Venus were shrieking the laments of those who pretended to serve her with their obscene cries of mourning.*[117] And Severus writes in his history: *Hadrian thought he could thwart the Christian faith by ruining the place it came from, and he set up the images of demons in the Temple and the place of Our Lord's passion.*[118] This, moreover, was the idol that Daniel (in chapter 9) called the "abomination of desolation": *and there shall be in the Temple the abomination of desolation; and the desolation shall continue even to the consummation, and to the end.*[119] For this passage has nothing to do with the desolation of Epiphanes.

CHAPTER 6

The Samaritan Temple

THERE WAS ANOTHER temple, in Samaria. As we have already said, Manasseh the brother of Jaddua the high priest fled to his father-in-law Sanballat, the prefect of Darius king of Persia, rather than be forced by the law to divorce his foreign wife, and begged for his help. So Sanballat, afraid he might be robbed of a son-in-law of such noble blood, persuaded him to abandon the Jews. When Alexander the Great emerged victorious, Sanballat received his permission to build a temple on the highest mountain of Samaria, Mount Gerizim, and there he installed Manasseh as high priest of the Samaritans. This people, as I have already said, had come from Assyria and adopted the law of God while continuing to worship their old idols, and it was this that made them hateful to the Jews. Their building was called the "temple of the transgressors."[120] From then on there was a bitter dispute between the Jews and the Samaritans over where it was that God should be revered: since the law declared that he should be worshiped only in the one place he had selected, and since he had first chosen Shiloh, in the tribe and on the mountain of Ephraim, and then rejected it in favor of Jerusalem and Mount Zion in the tribe of Judah, the Samaritans (who possessed Mount Ephraim) claimed that the glory belonged to them, because the name of the Lord was first invoked in Shiloh. The Jews, on the other hand, appropriated this honor for themselves, since God had gone on to place Zion ahead of Shiloh. Though this is what David wrote,[121] the Samaritans themselves did not accept it, for they acknowledged only the five books of Moses. When the two peoples came to debate this point before King Ptolemy Philometor,[122] he ruled in favor of the Jews, as Josephus reports in Book 13.[123] In fact, when later on Antiochus Epiphanes came storming into Judea, the Samaritans themselves offered no objections to his dedicating their temple to the Zeus of Strangers.[124] But in the end, John Hyrcanus the king of the Jews subjected Samaria to Jewish authority and completely destroyed its temple, two hundred years after it was built (as Josephus tells us in the same passage).[125] Then the Samaritan woman[126] touched on this old debate a number of years later, when she spoke with Christ the Jew[127] (according to John 4): *Our fathers worshiped in this mountain; and ye say that in Jerusalem is the place where men ought to worship.* Christ *saith unto her, Woman, believe me, the hour cometh, when ye shall neither in this mountain, nor yet at Jerusalem, worship the Father.*[128]

CHAPTER 7

The Egyptian Temple

THE THIRD JEWISH temple was built in Egypt by Onias. In the time of
Antiochus Epiphanes a sedition broke out in Jerusalem, and Onias, the son
of that high priest Onias whom Epiphanes had murdered, fled the city and
presented himself to Ptolemy, who was the king of Egypt and no friend of
Epiphanes. There Onias was given a plot of land in the district of Heliopolis,
where he founded a city much like Jerusalem, and built a temple. And there
he served as high priest to the Jews who had been exiled from the city because
of the sedition, and so withdrew to Egypt.[129] But at the same time that Titus
Caesar set fire to the Jerusalem Temple, the Egyptian one was ordered shut
by Paulinus the proconsul of Egypt; so that three hundred and thirty years
after it had been founded, there remained not a trace of its sacred rites (as
Josephus tells us in the seventh book of his *War*).[130] There is a letter from
the Jews of Jerusalem to the Egyptian Jews, asking them to celebrate the
Festival of the Dedication of their Temple[131] along with their other holidays.
The letter is in Second Maccabees 1,[132] and it is well worth a look.

CHAPTER 8

Synagogues

SO FAR WE HAVE discussed the Temple, or rather the temples. We should therefore go on to deal with the synagogues; for even though they were not temples, they had certain things in common with them. The synagogue, however, was not of ancient origin, as it is never mentioned in the narratives of Judges and Kings. But if the reader is willing to entertain a conjecture which would help us to understand how old it is, I would propose that synagogues were first built during the Babylonian exile, so that people who had no temple in which to pray or study could have some other place similar to it, where they could gather to perform these kinds of functions. I would also suggest that the rest of the diaspora Jews living in Asia,[133] Egypt, and Europe[134] did the same thing. It was, accordingly, the regions without a temple where the practice of building synagogues was most common. When, moreover, the Jews returned from Babylonia and rebuilt the Jerusalem Temple, they also continued to use synagogues, which had become an established custom. So the Jews of Jerusalem heard the law in the Temple, and the provincials heard it in the synagogues whenever they came to town. At any rate, we know from the writings of the Hebrews that in its final years Jerusalem contained four hundred and eighty synagogues, where Jews gathered from every part of the world.[135] So Jerusalem had synagogues for the foreigners, and the Temple for its own citizens, while in the rest of Judea, the Galilee, and the other regions where Jews lived after the exile, there were also synagogues for the locals, who found it difficult to get to Jerusalem. Chapter 6 of Acts takes particular notice of one of the Jerusalem synagogues: *Then there arose certain of the synagogue, which is called the synagogue of the Libertines, and Cyrenians, and Alexandrians, and of them of Cilicia and of Asia, disputing with Stephen.*[136] These were all Jews, but they lived in the provinces. It was their practice, when they came to Jerusalem to do business, to gather not at the Temple, but at the synagogue which they had organized for themselves. Likewise in John 18: *...I ever taught in the synagogue, and in the Temple,* *whither the Jews always resort.*[137] As for the other synagogues, there is Acts 15: *For Moses of old time hath in every city them who preach him, being read in the synagogues every Sabbath day.*[138] (By "Moses" he means "his books.") And in chapter 9: *And* Paul... *desired of* the high priest *letters to Damascus to the synagogues, that if he found any of this way, whether they were men or women, he might bring them bound unto Jerusalem.*[139] There is a great deal of evidence in the Gospels and in Acts about the synagogues of the Galilee visited by Christ, and those of Asia visited by St. Paul. We will examine this later on when we discuss the scribes. These synagogues were sometimes built by private individuals, and even by gentiles who wanted to do pious deeds, as for example the synagogue built in Capernaum by the Roman centurion in Luke 7; about this the Jews said: *...he is worthy that you should heal his servant; for he loveth our nation, and he hath built us a synagogue.*[140] And just as in the Temple the priests and the high priests were in charge, so in the synagogues it was the scribes and their chief, who was called the chief of the synagogue, or *archisynagogus*. The Jews considered it the greatest source of shame to be barred from the synagogue, that is, from the community that gathered together to learn. Thus it is written in John 9: *These words spake his parents, because they feared the Jews; for the Jews had agreed already that if any man did confess that he was Christ, he should be put out of the synagogue.*[141] And in John 12: *Nevertheless among the chief rulers also many believed in him; but because of the Pharisees they did not confess him, lest they be put out of the synagogue...*[142] While in those very same places the scribes, who loved their honors, sat in the most important seats. Christ faulted them for this, because he wanted to undermine their excessive pride.[143] I will add a great deal more about the scribes' duties in these synagogues in the appropriate place, where I will also say more about the synagogues themselves; but I wanted to say something about them here in order to show how they differed from the Temple. The proof of this is that they survived even after the Temple was destroyed, and they still exist today. This is why the church of the Christians has been contrasted with the synagogue of the Jews.[144]

BOOK III

Sacred Days

CHAPTER 1

The Hebrew Calendar

SINCE I HAVE DISCUSSED sacred places, it follows that, just as I proposed, I should now consider sacred days. But in order to explain my argument as clearly as possible, I should first discuss the entire system of years and months which the Hebrews used. It is, accordingly, more or less generally agreed among the commentators that the Hebrews had a lunar calendar of twelve months and 354 days, and that it had two aspects: one they called "natural" and "common," and the other "civil" and "sacred." The natural calendar started at the beginning of the world, just before the autumnal equinox, which was, they believed, the moment God created the world. On the other hand, God gave the Hebrews their civil calendar before they left Egypt, just before the vernal equinox.[1] (The natural calendar started after the produce was stored away, the civil before the harvest began.) Because, moreover, they wanted the lunar calendar to be solar as well, that is, to be completed in the time it takes the sun to traverse the zodiac (a course of 365¼ days), they had to insert an additional 11¼ days.[2]

The figure of twelve months is confirmed by First Kings 4: *And Solomon had twelve officers over all Israel, who provided victuals for the king and his household: each man his month in a year made provision.*[3] And in Daniel 4: *At the end of twelve months he walked in the palace of the kingdom of Babylon.*[4] And in Esther 3: *In the first month, that is, the month of Nisan... they cast... the lot... to the twelfth month, that is, the month of Adar.*[5]

On the other hand, we learn about the natural year beginning in September[6] from chapter 23 of Exodus: You will keep the festival *which is in the end of the year, when thou hast gathered in thy labors out of the field.*[7] And in Exodus 34: *And thou shalt observe the Feast of Weeks, of the first fruits of the wheat harvest, and the feast of ingathering at the year's end.*[8] Moreover, just as the ancient and natural calendar began with the seventh month, so (as we will see later on) did the seventh year and the fiftieth year.[9] For that matter, the Aramaic translation of the Bible[10] renders First Kings 8 as follows: *They gathered before Solomon on the festival in the month of Strong Men,*[11] *which they used to call the first month but is now called the seventh month.*[12] And Josephus reports in Book 1 of his *Antiquities* that Noah's flood began in the second month of the year, which the Macedonians call Dios and the Hebrews Marheshvan, and which corresponds to the Roman October.[13]

On the other hand, God ordered the establishment of the sacred calendar in Egypt, in Exodus chapter 12: *This month shall be unto you the beginning of months: it shall be the first month of the year to you.*[14] But later on this month is called (in chapter 33)[15] *the month of new corn* and in chapter 34 *the month of the springtime.*[16] This is why everyone agrees that all these were in fact the same month, i.e. March.

Though the law does not contain any provisions about adjusting the calendar, the commentators suggest that it would have been necessary in order to preserve the order of the months, which always began from the new moon;[17] and of Passover, which was supposed to fall on the fourteenth day of the month, a little before the harvest; and of Tabernacles, which God ordered to be celebrated when the vintage had been completed.[18] In fact the Hebrews inserted those extra days every second and fourth year[19] after the twelfth month, which is called Adar. They call this thirteenth month V'adar, "another Adar" so to speak; it alternates between twenty-two and twenty-three days, in order to take account of the quarter day.[20]

CHAPTER 2

The Months

EACH MONTH WAS begun from the new moon. Before the Babylonian exile they were called by their number, according to whether they were first, second, or third, all the way to twelve. But as the commentators say, shortly after the Jews returned from Babylon they bestowed on the months the following names: Nisan, Ziv or Iyar, Sivan, Tammuz, Av, Elul, Ethanim[21] or Tishri, Bul or Marheshvan, Kislev, Tebet, Shebat, and Adar; these correspond to March, April, June, July, August, September, October, November, December, January, and February. Of these months some were thirty days long, and the others twenty-nine; the first were called full, and the second empty.[22] According to this reckoning the year contained 354 days. Evidence for the first system of names may be found at the beginning of Exodus 40:[23] *In the fourteenth day of the first month at evening is the Lord's Passover.* And in Numbers 9: *The fourteenth day of the second month at even they shall keep it...*[24] And in First Chronicles 27: *Over the first course for the first month was Jashobeam... And over the course of the second month was Dodai... The third captain of the host for the third month was Benaiah... The fourth captain for the fourth month was Asahel... The fifth captain for the fifth month was Shamhuth... The sixth captain for the sixth month was Ira...*[25] And so on until twelve.

On the names subsequently given to the months, we have the fifth chapter of the Third Book of Esdras:[26] *the second year of his reign, in the month of Nisan, which is the first month.*[27] The third chapter of Esther: *In the first month, that is, the month of Nisan...* The first chapter of Baruch: *the tenth day of the month of Sivan.*[28] The sixth chapter of Second Esdras: *on the twentieth day of the month of Elul.* Zechariah 7: *...in the fourth day of the ninth month, even in Kislev.*[29] And the first chapter: *Upon the four and twentieth day of the eleventh month, which is the month of Shebat.*[30] And in First Maccabees 16: *...in the eleventh month, called Shebat.*[31] Esther 16:[32] *the twelfth month, that is, the month of Adar.*[33] The sixth chapter of First Kings: *In the fourth year was the foundation of the house of the Lord laid, in the month of Ziv; and in the eleventh year, in the month of Bul, which is the eighth month, was the house* *finished...*[34] And chapter 8: *And all the men of Israel assembled themselves... at the feast in the month of Ethanim, which is the seventh month.*[35] The rest were named as the commentators have demonstrated; but since they were lunar months, they did not always respond to the Roman system; instead they often ran over from one month to the next.

CHAPTER 3

The Weeks

EACH MONTH WAS divided into units of seven days, or weeks; and every seventh day was called Sabbath, that is, rest, because it was on that day that God rested after six days of labor. It was for the same reason that the week was also called a Sabbath, as in Second Chronicles 33:[36] *which were accustomed to succeed one another every week.*[37] And in Luke 18: *I fast twice in the Sabbath,*[38] that is, in the week. This is why they said it was the first, or one, or another of the Sabbath, instead of saying the first and second day of the week. As in Mark 16: *And very early in the morning the first day of the Sabbaths...;*[39] and then: *risen early the first day of the Sabbath...*[40] And St. Matthew: *In the end of the Sabbath, as it began to dawn toward the first day of the Sabbath...*[41] that is, in the evening of the following day, which was the first of the week, or on the evening preceding the first day of the week. And Acts 20: *And upon the first day of the Sabbath, when the disciples came together to break bread...*[42] It is, moreover, the first or one day of the Sabbath that Christians call the "Lord's day"; this is mentioned in the Apocalypse of St. John: *I was in the Spirit on the Lord's day...*[43] This is why in later times St. Jerome said in his letter against Vigilius:[44] *St. Paul makes it a rule... that, on the first day of the week, that is, on the Lord's day, contributions should be made by every one which should be sent up to Jerusalem.* We learn the same thing from the First Letter to the Corinthians 16:[45] *Upon the first day of the Sabbath let every one of you lay by him in store...*

CHAPTER 4

The Profane Days

THEY ALSO CALLED the days "moons," so that "first and second moon" and "first and second day" were interchangeable. As in the first chapter of the Third Book of Esdras: *And Josiah... offered the passover the fourteenth moon of the first month,*[46] instead of *the fourteenth day*. And both summer and winter days had twelve hours, and the nights just as many, though they were not all of the same length.[47] Hence John 2:[48] *...Are there not twelve hours in the day?* Matthew 20 implies the same thing—it mentions the third hour, the sixth, the ninth, and finally the eleventh (which was apparently the end of the day).[49] Some of these days were profane,[50] and some were festivals. The profane days were those on which it was permissible to do work, and there were burnt offerings in the morning and in the evening. On festival days one was not allowed to work. The profane days were either at the beginnings of the months, which were called new moons, or interspersed throughout the weeks (I will deal with these in another chapter).

CHAPTER 5

The New Moons

GOD ACCORDINGLY DECLARED the beginning of each month sacred. (The Greeks called these days *neomeniae*, and the Romans *kalendae*.) They were sacred in that they were set apart by a special burnt offering, but they held no prohibition on doing work. It was commanded in Numbers 28: *And on the Kalends*, that is, on the beginnings of the months,[51] *ye shall offer a burnt offering unto the Lord; two young bullocks, and one ram, seven lambs of the first year without spot; and three tenth deals of flour for a meat offering, mingled with oil... unto one lamb;*[52] *for a burnt offering of a sweet savor, a sacrifice made by fire unto the Lord. And their drink offerings shall be half a hin of wine unto a bullock, and the third part of a hin unto a ram, and a fourth part of a hin unto a lamb: this is the burnt offering of every month throughout the months of the year.*[53] Josephus explains it this way: *At the beginning of the month they offer, in addition to the daily sacrifice, two bullocks, seven year-old lambs, a ram, and a kid to deflect the consequences of any sins that may have been committed inadvertently.*[54] Accordingly, it is written in Second Chronicles 2: *for the burnt offerings... on the new moons... This is an ordinance for ever to Israel.*[55] And in chapter 8: *Then Solomon offered burnt offerings unto the Lord on the altar of the Lord... Even after a certain rate every day, offering according to the commandment of Moses, on the Sabbaths, and on the new moons...*[56] And in the second chapter of Ezra:[57] *And afterward they offered the continual burnt offering of the new moons...* And in the first chapter of Isaiah: *Your new moons and your appointed feasts my soul hateth...*[58]

CHAPTER 6

The Individual Days

IT WAS IN ACCORDANCE with God's command that even the other days of the week were full of religious practices. For though the Hebrews naturally had to devote time to their work, they were nonetheless commanded by God to bring burnt offerings every day, in the morning and in the evening. As it is written in Exodus 29 and Numbers 28: ...*This is the offering made by fire which ye shall offer unto the Lord; two lambs of the first year without spot day by day, for a continual burnt offering. The one lamb shalt thou offer in the morning, and the other lamb shalt thou offer at even; and a tenth part of an ephah of flour for a meat offering, mingled with the fourth part of a hin of beaten oil. It is a continual burnt offering, which was ordained at Mount Sinai for a sweet savor, a sacrifice made by fire unto the Lord. And the drink offering thereof shall be the fourth part of a hin for the one lamb in the holy place... And the other lamb shalt thou offer at even: as the meat offering of the morning, and as the drink offering thereof, thou shalt offer it, a sacrifice made by fire, of a sweet savor unto the Lord.*[59] And in Leviticus 23: ...*to offer an offering made by fire unto the Lord, a burnt offering, and a meat offering, a sacrifice, and drink offerings, every thing upon its day.*[60] Josephus describes this law as follows: *The law instructs that a year-old lamb should be slaughtered every day at public expense, at the beginning of the day and at its end.*[61] Hence the second chapter of Second Chronicles: ...*for the burnt offerings morning and evening... This is an ordinance for ever to Israel.*[62]

CHAPTER 7

The Festival Days[63]

THE FESTIVALS WERE also called Sabbaths, as in Leviticus 19: *...and keep my Sabbaths.*[64] They were observed from evening to evening, as God went on to command in chapter 23: *...from even unto even, shall ye celebrate your Sabbath.*[65] Likewise: *...on the first day shall be a Sabbath, and on the eighth day shall be a Sabbath; that is, a rest.*[66] They observed these days not only by ceasing from their work, but by making sacrifice, and praying, and sometimes even by afflicting their souls, i.e. by fasting (as we will see later on). Some of these festivals were established by God, and some by men. God's festivals were: the Sabbath, Passover (including the Feast of Unleavened Bread), First Fruits (including Pentecost), the Festival of Horns, the Day of Atonement, Tabernacles (including the Assembly), the sabbatical year, and the fiftieth year. The festivals founded by men were the Dedication[67] and several other less important ones, which we will discuss in their place. Let us then deal with them one at a time.

CHAPTER 8

The Sabbath

GOD COMMANDED IN particular that the seventh day, called the Sabbath, be kept with the greatest reverence. In fact, the performance of work was so thoroughly forbidden on that day that the Hebrews would not even light fires for household use. The first source is Exodus 20: *Remember the Sabbath day, to keep it holy. Six days shalt thou labor, and do all thy work; but the seventh day is the Sabbath of the Lord thy God: in it thou shalt not do any work... For in six days the Lord made heaven and earth, the sea, and all that in them is, and rested the seventh day; wherefore the Lord blessed the Sabbath day, and hallowed it.*[68] And Exodus 35: *Ye shall kindle no fire throughout your habitations upon the Sabbath day.*[69] Then Leviticus 23: *Six days shall work be done; but the seventh day is the Sabbath of rest, a holy convocation; ye shall do no work therein...*[70] God did, however, order that sacrifices should be made on the Sabbath, and that the showbread should be replaced. On sacrifices, we have Numbers 28: *And on the Sabbath day two lambs of the first year without spot, and two tenth deals of flour for a meat offering, mingled with oil, and the drink offering thereof; this is the burnt offering of every Sabbath...*[71] On the showbread, Exodus chapter 24: *And thou shalt take fine flour, and bake twelve cakes thereof:... Every Sabbath he shall set it in order before the Lord continually, being taken from the children of Israel by an everlasting covenant.*[72] This is how Philo explains these matters in his book on sacrifices: *Some of the public sacrifices happen every day, and others on the seventh day, the new moon, the fasts, or the three special festival days. The law commands that every day two lambs are to be slaughtered, in the morning and in the evening, to give thanks for the benefits that God lavishes so generously on the human race—one for the daytime, and one for the night. On the seventh day this number is doubled in honor of eternity... because the seventh day is the birthday of the world... Twice every day incense is burned on the altar within the veil, at sunrise and sunset; this happens before the morning sacrifice and after the evening one... Moreover, it is on the seventh day that the loaves are placed on the sacred table... and along with the bread they put salt and incense.*[73]

CHAPTER 9

Passover and the Festival of Unleavened Bread

PARTICULAR HONOR WAS given to Passover. I will explain when it was established, the origin of its name, and the reason it is celebrated, first setting out the law itself, and then expanding upon it. Exodus 12: *This month shall be unto you the beginning of months: it shall be the first month of the year to you… In the tenth day of this month they shall take to them every man a lamb, according to the house of their fathers, a lamb for a house… Your lamb shall be without blemish, a male of the first year… from the goats:… on the fourteenth day of the same month, they… will kill it in the evening. And they shall take of the blood, and strike it on the two side posts and on the upper doorpost of the houses, wherein they shall eat it. And they shall eat the flesh in that night, roast with fire, and unleavened bread; and with bitter herbs they shall eat it. Eat not of it raw, nor sodden at all with water, but roast with fire… And thus shall ye eat it; with your loins girded, your shoes on your feet, and your staff in your hand; and ye shall eat it in haste: it is the Lord's Passover. For I will pass through the land of Egypt… And the blood shall be to you for a token upon the houses where ye are: and when I see the blood, I will pass over you, and the plague shall not be upon you to destroy you, when I smite the land of Egypt. And this day shall be unto you for a memorial; and ye shall keep it a feast to the Lord throughout your generations; ye shall keep it a feast by an ordinance for ever.*[74] Then it adds about the Festival of Unleavened Bread: *Seven days shall ye eat unleavened bread; even the first day ye shall put away leaven out of your houses: for whosoever eateth leavened bread from the first day until the seventh day, that soul shall be cut off from Israel. And on the first day there shall be a holy convocation, and on the seventh day there shall be a holy convocation to you; no manner of work shall be done on them, save that which every man must eat, that only may be done of you. And ye shall observe the Feast of Unleavened Bread… until the one and twentieth day of the month at even. Seven days shall there be no leaven found in your houses: for whosoever eateth that which is leavened, even that soul shall be cut off from the congregation of Israel, whether he be a stranger, or born in the land.*[75] And then: *And it shall come to pass, when ye be come to the land which the Lord will give you, according as he hath promised, that ye shall keep this service. And it shall come to pass, when your children shall say unto you, What mean ye by this service? That ye shall say, It is the sacrifice of the Lord's Passover, who passed over the houses of the children of Israel in Egypt, when he smote the Egyptians, and delivered our houses.*[76] Then Leviticus 23 repeats the same instructions about the Passover and the Festival of Unleavened Bread: *In the fourteenth day of the first month at even is the Lord's Passover... seven days ye must eat unleavened bread. On the first day ye shall have a holy convocation: ye shall do no servile work thereon. But ye shall offer an offering made by fire unto the Lord seven days: on the seventh day is a holy convocation; ye shall do no servile work therein.*[77] Likewise Deuteronomy 16: *Six days thou shalt eat unleavened bread: and on the seventh day shall be a solemn assembly to the Lord thy God: thou shalt do no work thereon.*[78]

Now that I have discussed the content of this law, I will offer an explanation of its meaning. I must therefore reiterate that before Moses the year began with the autumnal equinox in the month of September, but God ordered Moses that it should now begin from the month in which they left Egypt. At the time this was called "the first month," but later it was called Nisan, while the Romans called it March.[79] Within this month was the vernal equinox, which is why Exodus 13 calls it "the month of new grain": *This day came ye out in the month of new grain.*[80] And in Deuteronomy 12:[81] *Observe the month of new grain, and keep the Passover unto the Lord thy God...* So the reason it received this name is that in Egypt and Syria the grain begins to mature in the month of March. This is what Philo writes in Book 3 of the *Life of Moses*:[82] *Moses appointed as first that month which fell during the vernal equinox, unlike the leaders who gave this honor to one of the earlier months because they were oblivious to the benefits of nature.*[83] *For it is at the equinox that the grain necessary for our sustenance begins to mature, and the fruit of the tree, which has only recently appeared, starts to ripen before reaching maturity in the subsequent months. Of course, without wheat, barley, and the other grains we cannot live; while in many countries people can continue on for years without wine, oil, or the fruits of the trees. The fourteenth day of that month, at the very time when the moon is at its fullest, is the occasion for the public celebration of the Exodus, which in Aramaic is called* Pascha. *Unlike the rest of the year, when regular citizens bring sacrifices to the altar to be slaughtered by the priests, on this occasion the law orders that the entire nation participate, so that everyone will perform this sacrifice for himself, with his own hands.* Likewise in his book on the Ten Commandments: *In the ancestral language of the Hebrews it is called* Pascha; *at this time the entire people, every one by himself, offers sacrifice without waiting for the priests. Every year, on the one day set aside for this purpose, the law permits them to act as priests themselves. At that time a sheaf of grain is offered to give thanks for the fertility of the fields and the abundance of fruit.*[84]

So Passover, or Pascha, that is, the passing over of the Lord, was celebrated on the fourteenth moon, or the fourteenth day of the month of March in the evening, when each family slaughtered a lamb for itself and ate it roasted with unleavened bread. And the following day, that is the fifteenth, was called both Passover and the first day of the Festival of Unleavened Bread; and seven days after that, that is the twenty-first, was the seventh day of the Festival of Unleavened Bread, which was called the Gathering,[85] because they harvested and gathered up the produce of their lands. And since among the Hebrews festivals began in the evening, the celebration of Passover began on the fourteenth day and concluded on the fifteenth, which I have therefore called both Pascha and the Festival of Unleavened Bread. This is what St. Luke says: *Now the Feast of Unleavened Bread drew nigh, which is called the* Pascha.[86] Likewise: *Then came the Day of Unleavened Bread, when the* Pascha *must be killed.*[87] And St. Mark: *And the first day of Unleavened Bread, when they killed the* Pascha...[88] Here, in fact, the term *pascha* is used instead of "paschal lamb," as in the verse: *...For even Christ our passover is sacrificed for us.*[89]

A law was passed by the Sanhedrin (and preserved by the Hebrews in the book *Seder Olam*)[90] that Passover could not be celebrated on the second, fifth, or sixth day of the week, if it happened to fall on any of these.[91] If, then, the fifteenth day of the month should fall on the sixth day of the week, Passover was postponed until the following day, which was the Sabbath, just as they say happened in the year of Christ's Passion. But as many commentators believe, he himself celebrated the holiday on the evening of the fifth day, because he did not want to distance himself from God's law. The Jews, on the other hand, followed a new custom or a tradition of their ancestors[92] and kept it on the evening of the sixth, as a segue into the sanctity of the Sabbath.[93] Nor in fact did many of the commentators think there was any other way to reconcile St. John's description with those of the other gospels: while the latter report that Christ celebrated the Passover on the evening of the fifth day, John states that he was crucified on the *paraskeue*, that is, the preparations for Passover that took place the day before the festival.[94] In addition, the Jews said on the *paraskeue*, which was the sixth day, that they did not want to enter the office of the praetor[95] in case they might become impure and be unable to eat the paschal lamb.[96] This they were going to do not that morning but that evening, which would be joined to the coming Sabbath.

But, in fact, it was not only the first day of the Festival of Unleavened Bread that was called Pascha—so were all the rest. As in Acts 12: *...Then were the Days of Unleavened Bread. And when he had apprehended him, he put him in prison... intending after* Pascha *to bring him forth to the people.*[97]

We must, in addition, not allow it to go by unnoticed that according to God's command, Passover could not be observed anywhere but in the capital city of the nation. Deuteronomy 16: *Thou mayest not sacrifice the passover within any of thy gates, which the Lord thy God giveth thee; but at the place which the Lord thy God shall choose to place his name in...*[98] It was therefore the practice to celebrate it first at Shiloh, and then at Jerusalem.

In order to make these issues clearer, I have decided to attach here descriptions of the magnificent Passover celebrations that appear in the sacred literature. The first Passover, then, was celebrated by Joshua in the land of Canaan, as it is written in Joshua 5: *And the children of Israel encamped in Gilgal and kept the Passover on the fourteenth day of the month at even in the plains of Jericho. And they did eat of the old corn of the land on the morrow after the Passover, unleavened cakes, and parched corn in the selfsame day.*[99] The second celebration was during the reign of Hezekiah king of Judah, according to Second Chronicles 30: *For the king had taken counsel, and his princes, and all the congregation in Jerusalem, to keep the Passover in the second month. For they could not keep it at that time, because the priests had not sanctified themselves sufficiently, neither had the people gathered themselves together to Jerusalem.*[100] And later on: *And the children of Israel that were present at Jerusalem kept the Feast of Unleavened Bread seven days... offering peace offerings and making confession to the Lord God of their fathers. And the whole assembly took counsel to keep another seven days: and they kept another seven days with gladness... So there was great joy in Jerusalem: for since the time of Solomon the son of David king of Israel there was not the like in Jerusalem.*[101] The third time it was celebrated by King Josiah (Second Kings 23): *Surely there was not holden such a Passover from the days of the judges that judged Israel, nor in all the days of the kings of Israel, nor of the kings of Judah; but in the eighteenth year of King Josiah.*[102] Likewise in Second Chronicles 35[103] and the first chapter of Third Esdras.[104] The fourth time was after they returned from Babylonia, in Ezra chapter 6: *And the children of the captivity kept the Passover upon the fourteenth day of the first month... And kept the Feast of Unleavened Bread seven days with joy...*[105] So much for Passover and the Festival of Unleavened Bread.

CHAPTER 10

Pentecost, or the Festival of Weeks

THE NEXT FESTIVALS were First Fruits[106] and the Pentecost,[107] which were also called the Festival of Weeks.[108] I will discuss these festivals and the days on which they were celebrated according to the same system I used in the previous section: first I will reproduce the passages from the law, and then I will add short explanations of those passages. God commands the observance of the Day of First Fruits in Leviticus 23, as follows: ... *When ye be come into the land which I give unto you, and shall reap the harvest thereof, then ye shall bring a sheaf of the first fruits of your harvest unto the priest; and he shall wave the sheaf before the Lord, to be accepted for you: on the morrow after the Sabbath the priest shall wave it. And ye shall offer that day... a he lamb without blemish of the first year for a burnt offering unto the Lord. And the meat offering thereof shall be two tenth deals of fine flour mingled with oil, an offering made by fire unto the Lord for a sweet savor: and the drink offering thereof shall be of wine, the fourth part of a hin.*[109] After this passage he adds that the Pentecost should be celebrated seven weeks later, as follows: *And ye shall count unto you from the morrow after the Sabbath, from the day that ye brought the sheaf of the wave offering; seven Sabbaths shall be complete: Even unto the morrow after the seventh Sabbath shall ye number fifty days; and ye shall offer a new meat offering unto the Lord... two wave loaves of two tenth deals... seven lambs without blemish of the first year, and one young bullock, and two rams: they shall be for a burnt offering unto the Lord, with their meat offering, and their drink offerings, even an offering made by fire, of sweet savor unto the Lord. Then ye shall sacrifice one kid of the goats for a sin offering, and two lambs of the first year for a sacrifice of peace offerings.*[110] Likewise in Numbers 18[111] and Deuteronomy 16: *Seven weeks shalt thou number unto thee: begin to number the seven weeks from such time as thou beginnest to put the sickle to the corn. And thou shalt keep the Feast of Weeks unto the Lord thy God.*[112] Moreover, the second chapter of Leviticus tells us the procedure for offering first fruits: *And if thou offer a meat offering of thy first fruits unto the Lord, thou shalt offer for the meat offering of thy first fruits green ears of corn dried by the fire, even corn beaten out of full ears. And thou shalt put oil upon it, and lay frankincense thereon: it is a meat offering. And the priest shall burn the memorial of it, part of the beaten corn thereof, and part of the oil thereof, with all the frankincense thereof: it is an offering made by fire unto the Lord.*[113] Josephus explains this procedure in greater detail in the third book of his *Antiquities: On the second day of the Festival of Unleavened Bread, which is the sixteenth of the month of March, they eat part of the wheat they had harvested (which they do not touch until then). And because the reason is that they should first pay their respects to God, who had given them this bounty, they offer him the first fruits of their harvest as follows: once they have dried the sheaf of grain and crushed it, they expose the barley itself in order to grind it; they bring a tenth to the altar for God, and after throwing on a handful of it they leave the rest for the priest to use. The people then have permission to perform their harvests. Moreover, on the First Fruits they sacrifice a lamb as a burnt offering to God. When seven weeks have passed after this sacrifice (this equals forty-nine days), they present to God loaves made from two tenths of barley flour and yeast,*[114] *and two lambs for a sacrifice. And though they are offered to God alone, they are given to the priests to eat; the latter are not permitted to leave any of the meal over for the next day. They also give as a burnt offering three bullocks, two rams, fourteen lambs, and two goats as a sin offering.*[115]

If we put together all of this information, it is clear enough that on the sixteenth of March (which as we said was the second day of the Festival of Unleavened Bread), the sickle was first put to the barley, and a sheaf of the new wheat was chosen and offered to God so that the coming harvest would be blessed; and that this day was called First Fruits.[116] The harvest was completed forty-nine days later, and the very next day, the fiftieth, was the Festival of Pentecost (or *fiftieth*), which was celebrated on the sixth day of the month of Sivan (which corresponds to May). On that day the loaves of new wheat were offered to God. The Festival of Pentecost was also called the Festival of Weeks, because it was celebrated at the end of the weeks. Hence the statement in Second Maccabees 12: *They gave them thanks, desiring them to be friendly still unto them: and so they came to Jerusalem, the Feast of Weeks approaching. And after the feast, called Pentecost, they went forth against Gorgias...*[117] And in Acts 2: *And when the Day of Pentecost was fully come...*[118]

CHAPTER 11

The Festival of Horns

NEXT WAS THE DAY of the Horns, which was celebrated on the first day of the seventh month (which they call Tishri and we call September). These are God's instructions for its observance, in Leviticus 23: *In the seventh month, in the first day of the month, shall ye have a Sabbath, a memorial of blowing of trumpets, a holy convocation. Ye shall do no servile work therein: but ye shall offer an offering made by fire unto the Lord.*[119] As the commentators tell us, it was celebrated in remembrance either of the day that God, with a flourish of horns, gave the law to Moses on Mount Sinai; or of the day when Isaac was released because Abraham had found a ram caught by its horns.[120] In fact, this is alluded to in Psalm 80: *Blow up the trumpet in the new moon, in the time appointed, on our solemn feast day. For this was a statute for Israel...*;[121] as well as in the *ten commandments* of Philo: *the sacred new moon, on which the horn is sounded.*[122]

CHAPTER 12

The Festival of Atonement

THE FESTIVAL OF Atonement took place on the tenth day of the seventh month; it was also called the "Day of Fasting," because on that day the Hebrews were commanded by the law to afflict their souls, that is, to fast. God went on to give instructions about this day as follows, in Leviticus 23: *Also on the tenth day of this seventh month there shall be a Day of Atonement: it shall be a holy convocation unto you; and ye shall afflict your souls, and offer an offering made by fire unto the Lord. And ye shall do no work in that same day: for it is a Day of Atonement...* You will afflict your souls on the ninth day of the month. *For whatsoever soul it be that shall not be afflicted in that same day, he shall be cut off from among his people.*[123] God also commands about this same day as follows, in chapter 16: *...in the seventh month, on the tenth day of the month, ye shall afflict your souls, and do no work at all, whether it be one of your own country, or a stranger that sojourneth among you. For on that day shall the priest make an atonement for you, to cleanse you, that ye may be clean from all your sins before the Lord. It shall be a Sabbath of rest unto you, and ye shall afflict your souls, by a statute for ever. And the priest, whom he shall anoint... shall make an atonement for the holy sanctuary, and he shall make an atonement for the tabernacle of the congregation, and for the altar, and he shall make an atonement for the priests, and for all the people of the congregation. And this shall be an everlasting statute unto you, to make an atonement for the children of Israel for all their sins once a year.*[124] The same chapter also describes how this atonement for sins and for the tabernacle was carried out by sending a goat into the desert as a representative. Since this ritual was one of the high priest's duties, I will reserve it for my discussion of the high priest. The holiday is called the "Day of Fasting" in Jeremiah 36: *...read in the roll... the words of the Lord in the ears of the people in the Lord's house upon the fasting day.*[125] This is why Josephus writes in the sixth book of his *War:*[126] *It was the practice on the Day of Atonement for everyone to fast.*

CHAPTER 13

The Festivals of Gathering and Tabernacles

THE LAST HOLIDAY of the year was Tabernacles, which lasted for eight days. The first day was the fifteenth of December, and the eighth (which was on the twenty-second) was called the "gathering of fruits,"[127] to distinguish it from that other gathering which I have already discussed.[128] Leviticus 23 describes this day as follows: *…The fifteenth day of this seventh month shall be the Feast of Tabernacles for seven days unto the Lord. On the first day shall be a holy convocation… it is a solemn assembly; and ye shall do no servile work therein. Also in the fifteenth day of the seventh month, when ye have gathered in the fruit of the land, ye shall keep a feast unto the Lord seven days: on the first day shall be a Sabbath, and on the eighth day shall be a Sabbath. And ye shall take you on the first day the boughs of goodly trees, branches of palm trees. And ye shall keep it a feast unto the Lord seven days in the year… ye shall celebrate it in the seventh month. Ye shall dwell in booths seven days; all that are Israelites born shall dwell in booths; that your generations may know that I made the children of Israel to dwell in booths, when I brought them out of the land of Egypt.*[129] The same things are repeated in Numbers 29, with the addition of the offerings that were to be made on each day of the festival: *…on the first day…*[130] *ye shall offer a burnt offering for a sweet savor unto the Lord; one young bullock, one ram, and seven lambs of the first year without blemish. And on the fifteenth day… ye shall offer a burnt offering, a sacrifice made by fire… thirteen young bullocks… And on the second day ye shall offer twelve young bullocks, two rams, fourteen lambs of the first year without spot. And on the third day eleven bullocks, two rams, fourteen lambs of the first year without blemish… And on the fourth day ten bullocks, two rams, and fourteen lambs… And on the fifth day nine bullocks, two rams, and fourteen lambs… And on the sixth day eight bullocks, two rams, and fourteen lambs… And on the seventh day seven bullocks, two rams, and fourteen lambs… On the eighth day ye shall have a solemn assembly… one bullock, one ram, seven lambs of the first year without blemish. These things ye shall do unto the Lord in your set feasts, besides your vows, and your freewill offerings, for your burnt* *offerings, and for your meat offerings, and for your drink offerings, and for your peace offerings.*[131] And in Deuteronomy 16: *Thou shalt observe the Feast of Tabernacles seven days, after thou hast gathered in thy corn and thy wine; and thou shalt rejoice in thy feast...*[132]

Tabernacles, then, was a remembrance of the time when the people lived in the desert in tabernacles; and it coincided with the "gathering of fruits" in the autumn, at the end of the ancient or natural year. We learn this from Exodus 23: You will make... *the Feast of Ingathering, which is in the end of the year, when thou hast gathered in thy labors out of the field.*[133] And from Exodus 34: *And thou shalt observe... the Feast of Ingathering at the year's end.*[134] For the autumnal equinox means the end of the past natural year and the beginning of the new one, in the month of September. The eighth chapter of Jeremiah[135] describes the great joy with which this holiday was celebrated after the city was restored: *And they found written in the law which the Lord had commanded by Moses, that the children of Israel should dwell in booths in the feast of the seventh month; and that they should publish and proclaim in all their cities, and in Jerusalem, saying, Go forth unto the mount, and fetch olive branches, and pine branches, and myrtle branches, and palm branches, and branches of thick trees, to make booths, as it is written. So the people went forth, and brought them, and made themselves booths, every one upon the roof of his house, and in their courts, and in the courts of the house of God, and in the street of the water gate, and in the street of the gate of Ephraim. And all the congregation of them that were come again out of the captivity made booths, and sat under the booths: for since the days of Joshua the son of Nun unto that day had not the children of Israel done so. And there was very great gladness. Also... from the first day unto the last day, he read in the book of the law of God. And they kept the feast seven days; and on the eighth day was a solemn assembly, according unto the manner.* Josephus wrote a clear account of the observance of this holiday in the third book of his *Antiquities*, which I could not omit in good conscience: *On the fifteenth day of that month, when the season was turning towards winter, God ordered that every family should set up a tabernacle, in order to be spared the cold and for the sake of guarding the year.*[136] *And when they arrived in their homeland, they were to hold a festival for eight days in the city that they considered their capital because the Temple was there; and to make burnt offerings, and sacrifice to God, and make peace offerings. And they were to carry in their hands myrtle branches, and willows, and the heads of palms, and the boughs of Persian apples.*[137] *On the first day there was a burnt offering consisting of thirteen oxen, one or more lambs,*[138] *and two rams, plus a goat for the expiation of sins. Moreover, during the next six days the same number of lambs and rams, as well as a goat, were sacrificed, and one less bull was offered each day until the number reached seven; and on the eighth day they refrained from all sorts of work, and offered God a calf, and a ram, and seven lambs, and a goat for the expiation of sins.*[139] In Greek this festival is called *Scaenopegia,*[140] and we are told in the gospel that even Christ came to Jerusalem to celebrate it.[141]

The many festivals I have been describing can be reduced to three in particular—Passover, Pentecost, and Tabernacles.[142] It was on these occasions that, three times a year, all the men had to gather in Jerusalem from all over Judea to take part in the sacred rites. This was God's command in Exodus 23:[143] *Three times thou shalt keep a feast unto me in the year. Thou shalt keep the Feast of Unleavened Bread; thou shalt eat unleavened bread seven days, as I commanded thee, in the time appointed of the month of Abib... And the Feast of Harvest, the first fruits of thy labors, which thou hast sown in the field: and the Feast of Ingathering, which is in the end of the year, when thou hast gathered in thy labors out of the field.*[144] *Three times in a year shall all thy males appear before the Lord thy God in the place which he shall choose*; that is, as we said, *in the Feast of Unleavened Bread, and in the Feast of Weeks, and in the Feast of Tabernacles.* It therefore says in the eighth chapter of Second Chronicles:[145] *Then Solomon offered burnt offerings unto the Lord on the altar of the Lord, which he had built before the porch, even after a certain rate every day, offering according to the commandment of Moses, on the Sabbaths, and on the new moons, and on the solemn feasts, three times in the year, even in the Feast of Unleavened Bread, and in the Feast of Weeks, and in the Feast of Tabernacles.*

Since there were three "Sabbaths," or festivals, each year—Passover, Pentecost, and Tabernacles—which every man was supposed to attend, it would be sensible for us to ask which of these St. Luke in chapter 6 calls "the second first Sabbath," as follows: *And it came to pass on the second first Sabbath, that Jesus went through the corn fields; and his disciples plucked the ears of corn...*[146] It could not have been Passover, since on the fourteenth of March the grain had not yet ripened; and it could not have been Pentecost, because by the sixth of May the harvest was already finished. And even if it *were* one of these two, there is no reason why it should have been referred to as "the second first Sabbath." It is, moreover, universally agreed that it must have fallen between Passover and Pentecost, because only then was the harvest at its full. The commentators have come up with many ingenious explanations of this passage, but to men of learning none is more convincing or more fitting than the claim of St. John Chrysostom that it was the Sabbath, i.e. the seventh day, which fell on the new moon of April. It was, therefore, a double festival—both the seventh day and the new moon. Now, even this theory can be rejected: first, because it rests entirely on conjecture; second, because it offers no explanation as to why such a Sabbath should be called "the second first"; and third, because even though the new moon was a holy day, it was not a festival—work was performed on it. That is why such a day could not have been a double Sabbath. "So what do *you* think it means?" someone will ask. Well, with all due respect to anyone who may have written something different, I will offer my own explanation, not because I want to disprove anyone else's opinion, but in order to clarify my own as it now stands. The Hebrews did not always celebrate Passover in the first month, but occasionally in the second, as we know from Second Chronicles 30: *For the king had taken counsel, and his princes, and all the congregation in Jerusalem, to keep the Passover in the second month. For they could not keep it at that time, because the priests had not sanctified themselves sufficiently, neither had the people gathered themselves together to Jerusalem.*[147] So perhaps when they observed it in the second month they called it "the second first," meaning that they celebrated Passover in the second month even though it was supposed to be in the first. This is what the Greeks called *hysteron proteron*, i.e. "what comes after before," since they said afterward what they should have said first.[148] So Christ came for Passover in the first month, just before the harvest; and when it was not celebrated he returned in the second, which was already the middle of the harvest. This is why Mark chapter 2 says of the same incident: *And it came to pass again, that he went through the corn fields on the Sabbath day...*[149] The Greek is more explicit: *And it happened that he again made his way through the fields...* This must mean that *again* refers to Christ's going twice through the fields, and not to the Pharisees' slandering him on two occasions (which was Jansen's suggestion).[150] And if he did journey through the fields twice, it means he made an additional trip to Jerusalem for the Sabbath that was celebrated in the second month, when by chance it could not have been held in the first.

CHAPTER 14

The Seventh Year

THE SEVENTH YEAR (which was called the sabbatical year) is also relevant to this discussion, because during that year the land was allowed to rest from cultivation. The instructions for this practice are in Exodus 23: *And six years thou shalt sow thy land, and shalt gather in the fruits thereof; but the seventh year thou shalt let it rest and lie still; that the poor of thy people may eat: and what they leave the beasts of the field shall eat. In like manner thou shalt deal with thy vineyard, and with thy oliveyard.*[151] And Leviticus 25: *Speak unto the children of Israel, and say unto them, When ye come into the land which I give you, then shall the land keep a Sabbath unto the Lord. Six years thou shalt sow thy field, and six years thou shalt prune thy vineyard, and gather in the fruit thereof; but in the seventh year shall be a Sabbath of rest unto the land, a Sabbath for the Lord: thou shalt neither sow thy field, nor prune thy vineyard. That which groweth of its own accord of thy harvest thou shalt not reap, neither gather the grapes of thy vine undressed: for it is a year of rest unto the land. And the Sabbath of the land shall be meat for you...*[152] And shortly thereafter: *And if ye shall say, What shall we eat the seventh year? behold, we shall not sow, nor gather in our increase. Then I will command my blessing upon you in the sixth year, and it shall bring forth fruit for three years. And ye shall sow the eighth year, and eat yet of old fruit until the ninth year; until her fruits come in ye shall eat of the old store.*[153]

We are then taught, in Deuteronomy 15, about how there was also to be a release granted in the seventh year: *At the end of every seven years thou shalt make a release. And this is the manner of the release: Every creditor that lendeth ought unto his neighbor shall release it; he shall not exact it of his neighbor, nor of his brother... Of a foreigner thou mayest exact it again: but that which is thine with thy brother thine hand shall release; save when there shall be no poor among you... and thou shalt lend unto many nations, but thou shalt not borrow... Beware that there be not a thought in thy wicked heart, saying, The seventh year, the year of release, is at hand; and thine eye be evil against thy poor brother, and thou givest him nought... And if thy brother, a Hebrew man, or a Hebrew woman, be sold unto thee, and serve thee six years; then in the seventh year thou shalt let him go free from thee. And when thou sendest him out free from thee, thou shalt not let him go away empty: Thou shalt furnish him liberally out of thy flock, and out of thy floor, and out of thy winepress...*[154]

CHAPTER 15

The Fiftieth Year

THE FIFTIETH YEAR was also a sabbatical year: slaves were released from their bondage, and land that had been sold off returned to its original possessors. This is described in Leviticus 25, as follows: *And thou shalt number seven Sabbaths of years unto thee, seven times seven years; and the space of the seven Sabbaths of years shall be unto thee forty and nine years. Then shalt thou cause the trumpet of the Jubilee to sound on the tenth day of the seventh month, in the Day of Atonement shall ye make the trumpet sound throughout all your land. And ye shall hallow the fiftieth year, and proclaim liberty throughout all the land unto all the inhabitants thereof: it shall be a Jubilee unto you; and ye shall return every man unto his possession, and ye shall return every man unto his family. A Jubilee shall that fiftieth year be unto you... And if thou sell ought unto thy neighbor, or buyest ought of thy neighbor's hand, ye shall not oppress one another: According to the number of years after the Jubilee thou shalt buy of thy neighbor, and according unto the number of years of the fruits he shall sell unto thee. According to the multitude of years thou shalt increase the price thereof, and according to the fewness of years thou shalt diminish the price of it; for according to the number of the years of the fruits doth he sell unto thee.*[155] Hence in Numbers 36, people ask about whether the daughters of Zelophehad were to marry into the various other tribes, as follows: *And if they be married to any of the sons of the other tribes of the children of Israel, then shall their inheritance be taken from the inheritance of our fathers, and shall be put to the inheritance of the tribe whereunto they are received: so shall it be taken from the lot of our inheritance. And when the Jubilee of the children of Israel shall be, then shall their inheritance be put unto the inheritance of the tribe whereunto they are received: so shall their inheritance be taken away from the inheritance of the tribe of our fathers.*[156] God's response was to declare in a law: *Let them marry to whom they think best; only to the family of the tribe of their father shall they marry. So shall not the inheritance of the children of Israel remove from tribe to tribe...*[157] The fiftieth year was, moreover, called the Jubilee, because (as it is written earlier in the text) the

Levites called the people together and blew rams' horns, called in Hebrew *yovelim*,[158] to declare its arrival.[159] Hence Joshua chapter 6: *And seven priests shall bear before the ark seven trumpets, which are used in the Jubilee...*[160] And these were the celebrations established by God.

CHAPTER 16

The Dedication

THE HOLIDAYS ESTABLISHED by men, on the other hand, were (give or take a few) the Dedication; the festivals of Jephthah, Judith, and Esther; and some others later on as well. The Dedication was an annual celebration held in honor of the dedication of the Temple—as I said above, *enkainizein*[161] means "to consecrate" and "to dedicate"; this is why it was also used for the consecration of a king. There were, moreover, four dedications of the Jerusalem Temple, observed at different times of the year.[162] The first was for Solomon's Temple, in the seventh month. According to First Kings: *...so the king and all the children of Israel dedicated the house of the Lord... And at that time Solomon held a feast, and all Israel with him... even fourteen days.*[163] And in Second Chronicles 7: *Also at the same time Solomon kept the feast seven days... And in the eighth day they made a solemn assembly: for they kept the dedication of the altar seven days, and the feast seven days. And on the three and twentieth day of the seventh month he sent the people away into their tents...*[164]

The second dedication was for the Second Temple, that is the temple of Zerubabel, which was instituted by the Jews after they came back to their homeland; it was celebrated in the month of Adar, which corresponds to February. According to Ezra chapter 6: *And this house was finished on the third day of the month of Adar... and they... kept the dedication of this house of God with joy.*[165] Josephus, however, adds that this happened on the twenty-third of the month of Adar, shortly before the festival of Passover.[166]

The third dedication was not of the Temple but of the altar, since Judah Maccabee restored the altar for burnt offerings which King Antiochus had polluted; he dedicated it in the ninth month, i.e. November. According to First Maccabees: *And so they kept the Dedication of the Altar eight days... Moreover Judah and his brethren with the whole congregation of Israel ordained that the days of the Dedication of the Altar should be kept in their season from year to year by the space of eight days, from the five and twentieth day of the month of Kislev, with mirth and gladness.*[167] Hence the Jews of Jerusalem wrote to the

Egyptian Jews: *Therefore whereas we are now purposed to keep the purification of the Temple upon the five and twentieth day of the month of Kislev, we thought it necessary to certify you thereof, that ye also might keep it, as the Feast of Tabernacles, and of the fire, which was given us when Nehemiah offered sacrifice, after he had built the Temple and the altar.*[168] It was this dedication, observed in the winter, which St. John seems to have had in mind when he wrote: *And it was at Jerusalem the Feast of the Dedication, and it was winter. And Jesus walked in the Temple on Solomon's porch.*[169]

The fourth dedication was of the Temple built by Herod, which occurred on his birthday and was celebrated with great pomp (Josephus, Book 15).[170]

CHAPTER 17

The Other Festivals

BESIDES THESE FESTIVALS there were many others, which the Hebrews established as circumstances warranted; I will include them all in this chapter, and set them down in chronological order. The first of these, then, which was observed at the end of the year, was the lamentation of the daughter of Jephthah the judge of Israel, whom her father had offered up as a virgin sacrifice. For he had vowed to God that *if* he should *without fail deliver the children of Ammon into his hands, then it shall be, that whatsoever* should *cometh forth of the doors of his house to meet him... shall surely be the Lord's... and, behold, his daughter came out to meet him with timbrels and with dances: and she was his only child... and he did with her according to his vow which he had vowed...* [171] This is why it is written in Judges 11: *And it was a custom in Israel, that the daughters of Israel went yearly to lament the daughter of Jephthah the Gileadite four days in a year.* [172]

They also kept as a festival the day upon which was revived the heavenly fire they had found extinguished after the Babylonian exile. We are told about this in the letter that the Jews of Jerusalem wrote to the Egyptian Jews: *Therefore whereas we are now purposed to keep the purification of the Temple upon the five and twentieth day of the month of Kislev, we thought it necessary to certify you thereof, that ye also might keep it, as the Feast of Tabernacles, and of the fire, which was given us when Nehemiah offered sacrifice, after he had built the Temple and the altar.* [173] Then the story itself is told, as I have already reported it. [174] The Jews celebrate this day on the twentieth of Kislev (i.e. November), which Josephus called the Festival of Lights. [175]

There is also an account of the day on which Judith, a Hebrew widow, achieved victory over Holofernes the viceroy of the king of Assyria. We know that the Jews decreed this to be one of their festivals; because it is written in Judith chapter 16: *the day of the festivity of this victory is received by the Hebrews in the number of holy days, and is religiously observed by the Jews from that time until this day.*[176] It was celebrated by the Jews on the twenty-fifth of the month of Kislev.[177]

There was also the victory of Esther over Haman, who had planned to lead the Jews to the gallows; this was made a holiday by order of Esther's adviser Mordecai. We are told about the holiday in Esther chapter 9: *On the thirteenth day of the month of Adar; and on the fourteenth day of the same rested they, and made it a day of feasting and gladness. But the Jews that were at Shushan assembled together on the thirteenth day thereof, and on the fourteenth thereof; and on the fifteenth day of the same they rested, and made it a day of feasting and gladness. Therefore the Jews of the villages, that dwelt in the unwalled towns, made the fourteenth day of the month of Adar a day of gladness and feasting, and a good day, and of sending portions one to another. And Mordecai wrote these things, and sent letters unto all the Jews that were in all the provinces of the king Ahasuerus, both nigh and far, to establish this among them, that they should keep the fourteenth day of the month of Adar, and the fifteenth day of the same, yearly, as the days wherein the Jews rested from their enemies, and the month which was turned unto them from sorrow to joy, and from mourning into a good day: that they should make them days of feasting and joy, and of sending portions one to another, and gifts to the poor. And the Jews undertook to do as they had begun, and as Mordecai had written unto them; because Haman the son of Hammedatha, the Agagite, the enemy of all the Jews, had devised against the Jews to destroy them, and had cast Pur, that is, the lot, to consume them, and to destroy them; but when Esther came before the king, he commanded by letters that his wicked device, which he devised against the Jews, should return upon his own head, and that he and his sons should be hanged on the gallows. Wherefore they called these days Purim after the name of Pur...*[178] According to the end of Second Maccabees, this festival is also called the "Day of Mordecai": *And they ordained all with a common decree in no case to let that day pass without solemnity, but to celebrate the thirtieth day of the twelfth month, which in the Syrian tongue is called Adar, the day before Mordecai's Day.*[179]

Finally, they also observed the day on which they defeated Nicanor, the general of Demetrius the king of Syria. Josephus tells us about this in Book 12: *This victory took place on the fourteenth day of the month of Adar, and the Jews celebrate it every year as a festival day.*[180]

They also observed as a fast the third day of the month of Tishri (or September) because of the death of Gedaliah,[181] about whom we are told in Second Kings 25: *But it came to pass in the seventh month, that Ishmael... came, and ten men with him, and smote Gedaliah, that he died...*[182] In fact, they fasted not only on this day but on many others besides, as they continue to do to this day. But these fasts were their own doing, not God's; so I thought better of including them in this discussion.

CHAPTER 18

The Ancient Hebrew Calendar

NOW THAT I HAVE explained these matters, I would like to make the information I have provided here easier to retain by setting out as follows the order of the months, and of the sacred and secular days, which in Latin is called a calendar. This was its form:183

MARCH *First month, or Nisan.*   *Days: 30*

1	1	New moon	Daily sacrifice and new moon	
2	2		Daily sacrifice	
3	3		Daily sacrifice	
4	4		Daily sacrifice	
5	5		Daily sacrifice	
6	6		Daily sacrifice	
7	7	Sabbath	Daily sacrifice and Sabbath	Not even fires were lit.
8	8		Daily sacrifice	
9	9		Daily sacrifice	
10	10		Daily sacrifice	
11	11		Daily sacrifice	
12	12		Daily sacrifice	
13	13		Daily sacrifice	
14	14	Sabbath	Daily sacrifice and Sabbath	A lamb was slaughtered and eaten at evening, and no work was done.
15	15		Daily sacrifice	Passover. First day of the Festival of Unleavened Bread. No work was done. A holy day.

16	16	2nd day of Unleavened Bread	Daily sacrifice	A sheaf was offered as first fruits. The harvest began. Beginning of the seven weeks (49 days) set aside for the harvest.
17	17	3rd day of Unleavened Bread	Daily sacrifice	
18	18	4th day of Unleavened Bread	Daily sacrifice	
19	19	5th day of Unleavened Bread	Daily sacrifice	
20	20	6th day of Unleavened Bread	Daily sacrifice	
21	21	7th day of Unleavened Bread	Daily sacrifice	Gathering of produce. Last day of eating unleavened bread. This day was holier than the first of the holiday.
22	22		Daily sacrifice	1st week of the harvest.
23	23		Daily sacrifice	
24	24		Daily sacrifice	
25	25		Daily sacrifice	
26	26		Daily sacrifice	
27	27		Daily sacrifice	
28	28	Sabbath	Daily sacrifice and Sabbath	
29	29		Daily sacrifice	2nd week of the harvest.
30	30		Daily sacrifice	

APRIL *Second month, or Iyar.*   *Days: 29*

31	1	New moon	Daily sacrifice and new moon	
32	2		Daily sacrifice	
33	3		Daily sacrifice	
34	4		Daily sacrifice	
35	5	Sabbath	Daily sacrifice and Sabbath	

36	6		Daily sacrifice	3rd week of the harvest.
37	7		Daily sacrifice	
38	8		Daily sacrifice	
39	9		Daily sacrifice	
40	10		Daily sacrifice	
41	11		Daily sacrifice	
42	12	Sabbath	Daily sacrifice and Sabbath	
43	13		Daily sacrifice	4th week of the harvest.
44	14		Daily sacrifice	
45	15		Daily sacrifice	
46	16		Daily sacrifice	
47	17		Daily sacrifice	
48	18		Daily sacrifice	
49	19	Sabbath	Daily sacrifice and Sabbath	
50	20		Daily sacrifice	5th week of the harvest.
51	21		Daily sacrifice	
52	22		Daily sacrifice	
53	23		Daily sacrifice	Festival of purification of the tower by Simon the Prince.[184]
54	24		Daily sacrifice	
55	25		Daily sacrifice	
56	26	Sabbath	Daily sacrifice and Sabbath	
57	27		Daily sacrifice	6th week of the harvest.
58	28		Daily sacrifice	
59	29		Daily sacrifice	

MAY   *Third month, or Sivan.*   *Days: 30*

| 60 | 1 | New moon | Daily sacrifice and new moon | |
| 61 | 2 | | Daily sacrifice | |

62	3		Daily sacrifice	
63	4	Sabbath	Daily sacrifice and Sabbath	
64	5		Daily sacrifice	7th week of the harvest.
65	6		Daily sacrifice	Festival of Weeks, or Pentecost. Sacrifice of Weeks.
66	7		Daily sacrifice	
67	8		Daily sacrifice	
68	9		Daily sacrifice	
69	10		Daily sacrifice	
70	11	Sabbath	Daily sacrifice and Sabbath	
71	12		Daily sacrifice	
72	13		Daily sacrifice	
73	14		Daily sacrifice	
74	15		Daily sacrifice	
75	16		Daily sacrifice	
76	17		Daily sacrifice	
77	18	Sabbath	Daily sacrifice and Sabbath	
78	19		Daily sacrifice	
79	20		Daily sacrifice	
80	21		Daily sacrifice	
81	22		Daily sacrifice	
82	23		Daily sacrifice	
83	24		Daily sacrifice	
84	25	Sabbath	Daily sacrifice and Sabbath	
85	26		Daily sacrifice	
86	27		Daily sacrifice	
87	28		Daily sacrifice	
88	29		Daily sacrifice	
89	30		Daily sacrifice	

JUNE *Fourth month, or Tammuz.* *Days: 29*

90	1	New moon	Daily sacrifice and new moon	
91	2	Sabbath	Daily sacrifice and Sabbath	
92	3		Daily sacrifice	
93	4		Daily sacrifice	
94	5		Daily sacrifice	
95	6		Daily sacrifice	
96	7		Daily sacrifice	
97	8		Daily sacrifice	
98	9	Sabbath	Daily sacrifice and Sabbath	
99	10		Daily sacrifice	
100	11		Daily sacrifice	
101	12		Daily sacrifice	
102	13		Daily sacrifice	
103	14		Daily sacrifice	
104	15		Daily sacrifice	
105	16	Sabbath	Daily sacrifice and Sabbath	
106	17		Daily sacrifice	
107	18		Daily sacrifice	
108	19		Daily sacrifice	
109	20		Daily sacrifice	
110	21		Daily sacrifice	
111	22		Daily sacrifice	
112	23	Sabbath	Daily sacrifice and Sabbath	
113	24		Daily sacrifice	
114	25		Daily sacrifice	
115	26		Daily sacrifice	
116	27		Daily sacrifice	

| 117 | 28 | | Daily sacrifice | |
| 118 | 29 | | Daily sacrifice | |

JULY   *Fifth month, or Ab.*   *Days: 30*

119	1	New moon and Sabbath	Daily sacrifice, new moon, and Sabbath	
120	2		Daily sacrifice	
121	3		Daily sacrifice	
122	4		Daily sacrifice	
123	5		Daily sacrifice	
124	6		Daily sacrifice	
125	7		Daily sacrifice	
126	8	Sabbath	Daily sacrifice and Sabbath	
127	9		Daily sacrifice	
128	10		Daily sacrifice	
129	11		Daily sacrifice	
130	12		Daily sacrifice	
131	13		Daily sacrifice	
132	14		Daily sacrifice	
133	15	Sabbath	Daily sacrifice and Sabbath	
134	16		Daily sacrifice	
135	17		Daily sacrifice	
136	18		Daily sacrifice	
137	19		Daily sacrifice	
138	20		Daily sacrifice	
139	21		Daily sacrifice	
140	22	Sabbath	Daily sacrifice and Sabbath	
141	23		Daily sacrifice	
142	24		Daily sacrifice	

143	25		Daily sacrifice	
144	26		Daily sacrifice	
145	27		Daily sacrifice	
146	28		Daily sacrifice	
147	29	Sabbath	Daily sacrifice and Sabbath	
148	30		Daily sacrifice	

AUGUST   *Sixth month, or Elul.*   *Days: 29*

149	1	New moon	Daily sacrifice and new moon	
150	2		Daily sacrifice	
151	3		Daily sacrifice	
152	4		Daily sacrifice	
153	5		Daily sacrifice	
154	6	Sabbath	Daily sacrifice and Sabbath	
155	7		Daily sacrifice	
156	8		Daily sacrifice	
157	9		Daily sacrifice	
158	10		Daily sacrifice	
159	11		Daily sacrifice	
160	12		Daily sacrifice	
161	13	Sabbath	Daily sacrifice and Sabbath	
162	14		Daily sacrifice	
163	15		Daily sacrifice	
164	16		Daily sacrifice	
165	17		Daily sacrifice	
166	18		Daily sacrifice	
167	19		Daily sacrifice	
168	20	Sabbath	Daily sacrifice and Sabbath	

169	21		Daily sacrifice	
170	22		Daily sacrifice	
171	23		Daily sacrifice	
172	24		Daily sacrifice	
173	25		Daily sacrifice	
174	26		Daily sacrifice	
175	27	Sabbath	Daily sacrifice and Sabbath	
176	28		Daily sacrifice	
177	29		Daily sacrifice	

SEPTEMBER *Seventh month, or Tishri.*   *Days: 30*

178	1	New moon	Daily sacrifice and new moon	Festival of Horns. No work was done. Special burnt offering is given. From this date the Jews begin the year, believing the world was created then.
179	2		Daily sacrifice	
180	3		Daily sacrifice	Fast of Gedaliah.
181	4		Daily sacrifice	
182	5	Sabbath	Daily sacrifice and Sabbath	
183	6		Daily sacrifice	
184	7		Daily sacrifice	
185	8		Daily sacrifice	
186	9		Daily sacrifice	
187	10		Daily sacrifice	Day of Atonement, or of expiation through fasting. Declaration of the Jubilee in the seventh and fiftieth years. Special burnt offering given.
188	11		Daily sacrifice	
189	12	Sabbath	Daily sacrifice and Sabbath	
190	13		Daily sacrifice	
191	14		Daily sacrifice	

192	15	Gathering of produce. 1st day of Tabernacles or *Scaenopegia*	Daily sacrifice	No work was done. A festival day. Its own sacrifice.
193	16	2nd day of Tabernacles	Daily sacrifice and special	
194	17	3rd day of Tabernacles	Daily sacrifice and special	
195	18	4th day of Tabernacles	Daily sacrifice and special	
196	19	5th day of Tabernacles and Sabbath	Daily sacrifice and Sabbath and special	
197	20	6th day of Tabernacles	Daily sacrifice and special	
198	21	7th day of Tabernacles	Daily sacrifice and special	
199	22	8th day of Tabernacles	Daily sacrifice and special	No work was done. A festival day.
200	23		Daily sacrifice	Dedication of Solomon's Temple.
201	24		Daily sacrifice	
202	25		Daily sacrifice	
203	26	Sabbath	Daily sacrifice and Sabbath	
204	27		Daily sacrifice	
205	28		Daily sacrifice	
206	29		Daily sacrifice	
207	30		Daily sacrifice	

OCTOBER   *Eighth month, or Marheshvan.*   *Days: 29*

208	1	New moon	Daily sacrifice and new moon	
209	2		Daily sacrifice	
210	3	Sabbath	Daily sacrifice and Sabbath	

211	4		Daily sacrifice	
212	5		Daily sacrifice	
213	6		Daily sacrifice	
214	7		Daily sacrifice	
215	8		Daily sacrifice	
216	9		Daily sacrifice	
217	10	Sabbath	Daily sacrifice and Sabbath	
218	11 .		Daily sacrifice	
219	12		Daily sacrifice	
220	13	.	Daily sacrifice	
221	14		Daily sacrifice	
222	15		Daily sacrifice	
223	16		Daily sacrifice	
224	17	Sabbath	Daily sacrifice and Sabbath	
225	18		Daily sacrifice	
226	19		Daily sacrifice	
227	20		Daily sacrifice	
228	21		Daily sacrifice	
229	22		Daily sacrifice	
230	23		Daily sacrifice	
231	24	Sabbath	Daily sacrifice and Sabbath	
232	25		Daily sacrifice	
233	26		Daily sacrifice	
234	27		Daily sacrifice	
235	28		Daily sacrifice	
236	29		Daily sacrifice	

NOVEMBER   *Ninth month, or Kislev.*   *Days: 30*

237	1	New moon	Daily sacrifice and new moon	
238	2	Sabbath	Daily sacrifice and Sabbath	
239	3		Daily sacrifice	
240	4		Daily sacrifice	
241	5		Daily sacrifice	
242	6		Daily sacrifice	
243	7		Daily sacrifice	
244	8		Daily sacrifice	
245	9	Sabbath	Daily sacrifice and Sabbath	
246	10		Daily sacrifice	
247	11		Daily sacrifice	
248	12		Daily sacrifice	
249	13		Daily sacrifice	
250	14		Daily sacrifice	
251	15		Daily sacrifice	
252	16	Sabbath	Daily sacrifice and Sabbath	
253	17		Daily sacrifice	
254	18		Daily sacrifice	
255	19		Daily sacrifice	
256	20		Daily sacrifice	
257	21		Daily sacrifice	
258	22		Daily sacrifice	
259	23	Sabbath	Daily sacrifice and Sabbath	
260	24		Daily sacrifice	
261	25		Daily sacrifice	Purification of the Temple by Judah Maccabee, which is considered one of the dedications. Festival of the revival of the heavenly fire, called Lights. Festival of Judith.

262	26		Daily sacrifice	
263	27		Daily sacrifice	
264	28		Daily sacrifice	
265	29			
266	30	Sabbath	Daily sacrifice and Sabbath	

DECEMBER   *Tenth month, or Tebet.*   *Days: 29*

267	1	New moon	Daily sacrifice and new moon	
268	2		Daily sacrifice	
269	3		Daily sacrifice	
270	4		Daily sacrifice	
271	5		Daily sacrifice	
272	6		Daily sacrifice	
273	7	Sabbath	Daily sacrifice and Sabbath	
274	8		Daily sacrifice	
275	9		Daily sacrifice	
276	10		Daily sacrifice	The Jews fast in memory of the siege of Nebuchadnezzar.
277	11		Daily sacrifice	
278	12		Daily sacrifice	
279	13		Daily sacrifice	
280	14	Sabbath	Daily sacrifice and Sabbath	
281	15		Daily sacrifice	
282	16		Daily sacrifice	
283	17		Daily sacrifice	
284	18		Daily sacrifice	
285	19		Daily sacrifice	
286	20		Daily sacrifice	

287	21	Sabbath	Daily sacrifice and Sabbath	
288	22		Daily sacrifice	
289	23		Daily sacrifice	
290	24		Daily sacrifice	
291	25		Daily sacrifice	
292	26		Daily sacrifice	
293	27		Daily sacrifice	
294	28	Sabbath	Daily sacrifice and Sabbath	
295	29		Daily sacrifice	

JANUARY *Eleventh month, or Shebat.*   *Days: 30*

296	1	New moon	Daily sacrifice and new moon	
297	2		Daily sacrifice	
298	3		Daily sacrifice	
299	4		Daily sacrifice	
300	5		Daily sacrifice	
301	6	Sabbath	Daily sacrifice and Sabbath	
302	7		Daily sacrifice	
303	8		Daily sacrifice	
304	9		Daily sacrifice	
305	10		Daily sacrifice	
306	11		Daily sacrifice	
307	12		Daily sacrifice	
308	13	Sabbath	Daily sacrifice and Sabbath	
309	14		Daily sacrifice	
310	15		Daily sacrifice	
311	16		Daily sacrifice	
312	17		Daily sacrifice	

313	18		Daily sacrifice	
314	19		Daily sacrifice	
315	20	Sabbath	Daily sacrifice and Sabbath	
316	21		Daily sacrifice	
317	22		Daily sacrifice	
318	23		Daily sacrifice	
319	24		Daily sacrifice	
320	25		Daily sacrifice	
321	26		Daily sacrifice	
322	27	Sabbath	Daily sacrifice and Sabbath	
323	28		Daily sacrifice	
324	29		Daily sacrifice	
325	30		Daily sacrifice	

FEBRUARY *Twelfth month, or Adar.* *Days: 29*

326	1	New moon	Daily sacrifice and new moon	
327	2		Daily sacrifice	
328	3		Daily sacrifice	
329	4	Sabbath	Daily sacrifice and Sabbath	
330	5		Daily sacrifice	
331	6		Daily sacrifice	
332	7		Daily sacrifice	
333	8		Daily sacrifice	
334	9		Daily sacrifice	
335	10		Daily sacrifice	
336	11	Sabbath	Daily sacrifice and Sabbath	
337	12		Daily sacrifice	
338	13		Daily sacrifice	

339	14		Daily sacrifice	Festival of Judah Maccabee's victory over Nicanor. Fast of Esther. Festival of Mordecai, or minor festival of Lots.
340	15		Daily sacrifice	Major festival of Lots.
341	16		Daily sacrifice	
342	17		Daily sacrifice	
343	18	Sabbath	Daily sacrifice and Sabbath	
344	19		Daily sacrifice	
345	20		Daily sacrifice	
346	21		Daily sacrifice	
347	22		Daily sacrifice	
348	23		Daily sacrifice	Dedication of Zerubabel's Temple.
349	24		Daily sacrifice	
350	25	Sabbath	Daily sacrifice and Sabbath	
351	26		Daily sacrifice	
352	27		Daily sacrifice	
353	28		Daily sacrifice	
354	29		Daily sacrifice	

THE INTERCALARY MONTH OF ADAR *or Second February.*

In every second year they would insert 22 days, and in every fourth year 23 days. And thus the lunar year of 354 days was adjusted to the solar year of 365 days and four hours.[185] This thirteenth month is called V'adar.

BOOK IV

Sacred Rites

CHAPTER 1

Types of Sacred Rites

MARCUS CICERO—A MAN who was not only extremely eloquent, but very well educated in every field of knowledge—felt called upon to state, at the beginning of his investigations into the nature of the gods (which he wrote among gentiles ignorant of the heavenly truths), that everyone should play an active part in, learn about, and take note of what he ought to think about religion, piety, holiness, and rituals, and about temples, shrines, and solemn offerings.[1] So, needless to say, I who am living among Christians to whom the true faith of God has been revealed, have all the more pressing an obligation to do the same thing: to record, as I have promised, the history of the Hebrews' rites. After all, though this history is suffused with an exceptional degree of holiness, it is also wrapped in an incredible amount of obscurity, not to say a darkness like that of blackest night. It does contain most of the ancient ceremonies that God included in his law; but just as the light of the ancient Church clearly revealed what these ceremonies, which brought us our salvation, really meant beneath their grand façades, so now in our time we have forgotten and neglected them to the point that they are shrouded in an almost impenetrable blackness, and they demand of us more than a little zeal and effort if we are to make any sense of them. But with the scripture leading the way, and with my own hard work alongside it, I will do my best to dispel even so dense a fog.

The Hebrews, then, had many sacred rites, though among these they reserved a special place for the offerings, of which there were two kinds: one was called "sacrifices, offerings, and slaughtered animals"; and the other "gifts and donations." It seems that these two kinds of rites were offered for three reasons in particular: to honor the presence of God, who deserved every kind of respect; to obtain from him one's well-being and security; and to atone for and blot out one's sins. Hence this statement in the first chapter of Leviticus: *...of the herd, he shall offer a male without blemish... to make the Lord favorable to him.*[2] And in the eighth chapter of First Samuel:[3] *...I have sworn unto the house of Eli, that the iniquity of Eli's house shall not be purged* *with sacrifice nor offering for ever.* And in the eighth chapter of the Letter to the Hebrews: *For every high priest is ordained to offer gifts and sacrifices...*[4] And in the fifth: *For every high priest... is ordained... that he may offer both gifts and sacrifices for sins.*[5] But the gifts I will leave for later; for now I will deal with the sacrifices.

CHAPTER 2

Types of Sacrifices

THE TERM "SACRIFICE" was used not only when the priests offered an animal, but when they made something sacred to God, as when they slaughtered an animal and sprinkled its blood, when they threshed the grain,[6] when they fried flour mixed with oil in a pan, and when they burned incense. It is clear from these examples that an object was made holy to God primarily through blood or fire: through blood, as when an animal was slaughtered; and through fire, as when libations were cooked in an oven, a pan, or a griddle.[7] But the priests also used fire for the sacrifices, when they reduced either the fat or the entrails to ashes, or when they roasted the meat or boiled it in a pot for eating, or burned it in the flames. In Greek this was called *thusia*.[8] The pomp with which these rituals were performed was, moreover, so impressive that it was for the best that they ceased to be performed. For (as Origen[9] says in homily 23) who could gaze at the sanctuary, the altar, the priests performing their sacrifices, and the order with which everything was carried out, and not think that these were the most perfect rites with which the human race could ever worship God its creator? But let us give thanks for the arrival of Christ, who tore our eyes away from that kind of pageantry, and led our minds to the contemplation of heavenly and spiritual matters.

Moreover, God handed down to us six types of sacrifices in Leviticus: burnt offerings,[10] libations,[11] peace offerings,[12] sin offerings,[13] trespass offerings,[14] and the sacrifice of consecration.[15] Philo, the most learned man among both the Hebrews and the Greeks,[16] grouped the first five of these into three categories—burnt offerings, peace offerings, and sin offerings—which correspond to the three reasons I have already given for offering sacrifices. This is what Philo says in his book on sacrifices: *The lawgiver*[17] *reduced all the sacrifices to three categories: burnt offerings, peace offerings or safety offerings, and sin offerings.*[18] Philo then adds: *If anyone should like to discover the reasons those ancients used to make sacrifices, he will find three:*[19] *first, that the worship of God for its own sake is both honorable and necessary; and second, that by making sacrifice we gain two advantages—we obtain good things, and we are freed from bad ones. In the first category, which contains the honors offered to God alone, the law quite properly places the burnt offering... the entire animal is consumed, and our human lusts have nothing to gain. The law has also set apart another category of sacrifice... so that we should be able to obtain good things (this is called the peace offering) and to avoid bad ones (this is the sin offering). Thus the burnt offering belongs to God alone, to whom we must always show respect, even when we can expect nothing in return, while the other two kinds are tied to our own particular concerns: one asks for our well-being and for a turn toward the better, and the other for forgiveness for our sins and a cure for those offenses committed by the soul.*[20] Of these sacrifices, moreover, five were offered by the priest on behalf of individuals or the people, while the sixth was offered by the priests themselves as part of their consecration. The procedures and rituals for all these sacrifices were given by God in the law, where he also added some information about the sacrifice of purification, the sacrifice of expiation or propitiation, and the offering of incense. This is why my discussion of these issues will be organized as follows: first I will report what is written in the law about each of the various sacrifices; and then I will discuss whatever I have learned about them from outside the law.[21]

CHAPTER 3

Burnt Offerings

THE BURNT OFFERING, then, was a sacrifice in which (according to Philo) the entire offering was consumed by divine fire in order to honor and even propitiate God, as though sent in the smoke from earth up to heaven as a sweet savor to God.[22] For in all the other sacrifices, such as the peace offering, one part was burned (for example, the fat and the entrails), and another part was given to the priests along with the libations.[23] Origen tells us in his fifth homily that this sacrifice was also called *holocarpoma*, as if to say that all the fruits were being offered to God, for the burnt offering belonged to him alone.[24] The procedure of the burnt offering is reported in the first chapter of Leviticus, as follows: *...If any man of you bring an offering unto the Lord, ye shall bring your offering of the cattle, even of the herd, and of the flock. If his offering be a burnt sacrifice of the herd, let him offer a male without blemish: he shall offer it of his own voluntary will at the door of the tabernacle of the congregation before the Lord. And he shall put his hand upon the head of the burnt offering; and it shall be accepted for him to make atonement for him. And he shall kill the bullock before the Lord; and the priests, Aaron's sons, shall bring the blood, and sprinkle the blood round about upon the altar that is by the door of the tabernacle of the congregation. And he shall flay the burnt offering, and cut it into its pieces. And the sons of Aaron the priest shall put fire upon the altar, and lay the wood in order upon the fire; and the priests, Aaron's sons, shall lay the parts, the head, and the fat, in order upon the wood that is on the fire which is upon the altar; but its inwards and its legs shall he wash in water; and the priest shall burn all on the altar, to be a burnt sacrifice, an offering made by fire, of a sweet savor unto the Lord.*[25] In fact, God said to follow the same procedure whether a burnt offering was made with sheep, with goats, or with birds (though I would rather not copy entire pages of the law into my book). Then in the sixth chapter, the law of the burnt offering is given as follows: *...This is the law of the burnt offering: It is the burnt offering, because of the burning upon the altar all night unto the morning, and the fire of the altar shall be burning in it. And the priest shall* put on his linen garment, and his linen breeches shall he put upon his flesh, and take up the ashes which the fire hath consumed with the burnt offering on the altar, and he shall put them beside the altar. And he shall put off his garments, and put on other garments, and carry forth the ashes without the camp unto a clean place. And the fire upon the altar shall be burning in it; it shall not be put out; and the priest shall burn wood on it every morning, and lay the burnt offering in order upon it; and he shall burn thereon the fat of the peace offerings. The fire shall ever be burning upon the altar; it shall never go out.[26] So much for what God says; Philo explains it as follows: In the first place a male animal should be chosen for sacrifice from among the pure animals—a bullock, or a lamb, or a kid. The person who is offering it should wash his hands and place them upon the animal's head. Then a priest will take it from him, and after some of the others have caught up its blood in a bowl, he will sprinkle it around the altar. Then the hide will be flayed, the animal's limbs will be cut into pieces, and the intestines and the legs will be washed; and once the parts which had been cut up are reassembled, the entire animal will be placed on the fire of the altar.[27] Moreover, the fire mentioned in the law was that which afterward came down from heaven and snatched up the first offerings made by Aaron as high priest;[28] and since it was perpetual, the priests continued to use it to burn the sacrifices up until the Babylonian exile. So when Nadab and Abihu the sons of Aaron took each of them his censer, and put fire therein, and put incense thereon, and offered strange fire before the Lord, which he commanded them not. And there went out fire from the Lord, and devoured them… This is what is written in Leviticus chapter 7,[29] and it explains why St. Augustine wrote in regard to Psalm 65: the burnt offering is totally consumed, but by divine fire.[30] And Philo makes a brilliant comment about this fire in his Life of Moses: Regular fire was barred from the sacred altar as though it were contaminated, and instead another fire was sent down from the celestial ether in order to make a distinction between the sacred and the profane, the human and the divine. For it was fitting that the fire applied to the sacrifices should be of a purer character than that which was used for everyday purposes.[31] Though Philo used his intimate knowledge of God to present to us the secret reasons not only for this sacrifice but for the others as well, it is not my task to reproduce this knowledge here; it is enough for me to present the law of God without delving into his intentions when he wrote it.

CHAPTER 4

Libations

THE LIBATION, WHICH is properly called a "sacrifice," was made from grain (that is, from the purest flour and without any yeast), oil, and incense, and baked in an oven, a pan, or a griddle; or it was wheat toasted with fire.[32] Part of these offerings was burned, and part was given to the priests. The Bible then describes the method of performing such offerings, in the second chapter of Leviticus: *And when any will offer a meat offering unto the Lord, his offering shall be of fine flour; and he shall pour oil upon it, and put frank-incense thereon; and he shall bring it to Aaron's sons the priests; and he shall take thereout his handful of the flour thereof, and of the oil thereof, with all the frankincense thereof; and the priest shall burn the memorial of it upon the altar, to be an offering made by fire, of a sweet savor unto the Lord; and the remnant of the meat offering shall be Aaron's and his sons': it is a thing most holy of the offerings of the Lord made by fire. And if thou bring an oblation of a meat offering baked in the oven, it shall be unleavened cakes of fine flour mingled with oil, or unleavened wafers anointed with oil. And if thy oblation be a meat offering baked in a pan, it shall be of fine flour unleavened, mingled with oil. Thou shalt part it in pieces, and pour oil thereon: it is a meat offering. And if thy oblation be a meat offering baked in the griddle, it shall be made of fine flour with oil. And thou shalt bring the meat offering that is made of these things unto the Lord; and when it is presented unto the priest, he shall bring it unto the altar. And the priest shall take from the meat offering a memorial thereof, and shall burn it upon the altar; it is an offering made by fire, of a sweet savor unto the Lord. And that which is left of the meat offering shall be Aaron's and his sons'; it is a thing most holy of the offerings of the Lord made by fire. No meat offering, which ye shall bring unto the Lord, shall be made with leaven; for ye shall burn no leaven, nor any honey, in any offering of the Lord made by fire. As for the oblation of the first fruits, ye shall offer them unto the Lord; but they shall not be burnt on the altar for a sweet savor. And every oblation of thy meat offering shalt thou season with salt; neither shalt thou suffer the salt of the covenant of thy God to be lacking from thy meat offering; with all thine offerings thou shalt offer salt. And if thou offer a meat offering of thy first fruits unto the Lord, thou shalt offer for the meat offering of thy first fruits green ears of corn dried by the fire, even corn beaten out of full ears. And thou shalt put oil upon it, and lay frankincense thereon: it is a meat offering. And the priest shall burn the memorial of it, part of the beaten corn thereof, and part of the oil thereof, with all the frankincense thereof...*[33] Then the law of libations is described in chapter 6: *And this is the law of the meat offering: the sons of Aaron shall offer it before the Lord, before the altar. And he shall take of it his handful, of the flour of the meat offering, and of the oil thereof, and all the frankincense which is upon the meat offering, and shall burn it upon the altar for a sweet savor, even the memorial of it, unto the Lord. And the remainder thereof shall Aaron and his sons eat: with unleavened bread shall it be eaten in the holy place; in the court of the tabernacle of the congregation they shall eat it. It shall not be baked with leaven. I have given it unto them for their portion of my offerings made by fire; it is most holy, as is the sin offering, and as the trespass offering. All the males among the children of Aaron shall eat of it...*[34] Instructions for offering these libations also appear in chapter 15 of Numbers.[35]

CHAPTER 5

Peace Offerings

THE THIRD TYPE of sacrifice, which is the next one reported in Leviticus, is called in Latin *pacifica*,[36] *victimae pacificae*,[37] *hostia pacificorum*,[38] and *salutares hostiae*;[39] and in Greek *eirēnika*[40] *thusia eirēnikē*,[41] *sotērion*,[42] and *thusia eirēnik*.[43] Origen, moreover, says in his fifth homily that there were two types of peace offering—one was "for a vow,"[44] and the other "for praise."[45] It is clear, then, that this sacrifice was performed either to ask God for peace or well-being, or to praise and thank him once it had been granted. Moreover, in this sacrifice only the fat was burned, as a sweet savor to God, while the breast and the limbs went to the priests. The rest of the meat was eaten by the individuals who brought the sacrifice. The procedure for performing this offering is explained as follows in the third chapter of Leviticus: *And if his oblation be a sacrifice of peace offering, if he offer it of the herd; whether it be a male or female, he shall offer it without blemish before the Lord. And he shall lay his hand upon the head of his offering, and kill it at the door of the tabernacle of the congregation; and Aaron's sons the priests shall sprinkle the blood upon the altar round about. And he shall offer of the sacrifice of the peace offering an offering made by fire unto the Lord; the fat that covereth the inwards, and all the fat that is upon the inwards, and the two kidneys, and the fat that is on them, which is by the flanks, and the caul above the liver, with the kidneys, it shall he take away. And Aaron's sons shall burn it on the altar upon the burnt sacrifice, which is upon the wood that is on the fire; it is an offering made by fire, of a sweet savor unto the Lord.*[46] We are then instructed to use the same procedure when offering a lamb or a goat, and the following is added on the subject of the fat: *...and the sons of Aaron shall sprinkle the blood thereof* (i.e. of the goat) *upon the altar round about. And he shall offer thereof his offering, even an offering made by fire unto the Lord: the fat that covereth the inwards, and all the fat that is upon the inwards, and the two kidneys, and the fat that is upon them, which is by the flanks, and the caul above the liver, with the kidneys, it shall he take away. And the priest shall burn them upon the altar; it is the food of the offering* *made by fire for a sweet savor: all the fat is the Lord's. It shall be a perpetual statute for your generations throughout all your dwellings, that ye eat neither fat nor blood.*[47] Then the law is given in chapter 7: *And this is the law of the sacrifice of peace offerings, which he shall offer unto the Lord. If he offer it for a thanksgiving, then he shall offer with the sacrifice of thanksgiving unleavened cakes mingled with oil, and unleavened wafers anointed with oil, and cakes mingled with oil, of fine flour, fried. Besides the cakes, he shall offer for his offering leavened bread with the sacrifice of thanksgiving of his peace offerings. And of it he shall offer one out of the whole oblation for a heave offering*[48] *unto the Lord, and it shall be the priest's who sprinkleth the blood of the peace offerings. And the flesh of the sacrifice of his peace offerings for thanksgiving shall be eaten the same day that it is offered; he shall not leave any of it until the morning. But if the sacrifice of his offering be a vow, or a voluntary offering, it shall be eaten the same day that he offereth his sacrifice; and on the morrow also the remainder of it shall be eaten; but the remainder of the flesh of the sacrifice on the third day shall be burnt with fire. And if any of the flesh of the sacrifice of his peace offerings be eaten at all on the third day, it shall not be accepted, neither shall it be imputed unto him that offereth it: it shall be an abomination, and the soul that eateth of it shall bear his iniquity. And the flesh that toucheth any unclean thing shall not be eaten; it shall be burnt with fire; and as for the flesh, all that be clean shall eat thereof. But the soul who eateth of the flesh of the sacrifice of peace offerings, which pertain unto the Lord, having his uncleanness upon him, even that soul shall be cut off from his people. Moreover the soul that shall touch any unclean thing, as the uncleanness of man, or any unclean beast, or any abominable unclean thing, and eat of the flesh of the sacrifice of peace offerings, which pertain unto the Lord, even that soul shall be cut off from his people... Ye shall eat no manner of fat, of ox, or of sheep, or of goat. And the fat of the beast that dieth of itself, and the fat of that which is torn with beasts, may be used in any other use, but ye shall in no wise eat of it. For whosoever eateth the fat of the beast, of which men offer an offering made by fire unto the Lord, even the soul who eateth it shall be cut off from his people. Moreover ye shall eat no manner of blood, whether it be of fowl or of beast, in any of your dwellings. Whatsoever soul it be who eateth any manner of blood, even that soul shall be cut off from his people. He who offereth the sacrifice of his peace offerings unto the Lord shall bring his oblation unto the Lord of the sacrifice of his peace offerings. His own hands shall bring the offerings of the Lord made by fire, the fat with the breast, it shall he bring, that the breast may be waved for a wave offering*[49] *before the Lord. And the priest shall burn the fat upon the altar; but the breast shall be Aaron's and his sons'. And the right shoulder shall ye give unto the priest for a heave offering*[50] *of the sacrifices of your peace offerings. He among the sons of Aaron, who offereth the blood of the peace offerings, and the fat, shall have the right shoulder for his part.*[51] Likewise in chapter 10: *And the wave breast and heave shoulder shall ye eat in a clean place; thou, and thy sons, and thy daughters with thee: for they be thy due, and thy sons' due, which are given out of the sacrifices of peace offerings*[52] *of the children of Israel. The heave shoulder and the wave breast shall they bring with the offerings made by fire of the fat, to wave it for a wave offering before the Lord; and it shall be thine, and thy sons' with thee, by a statute for ever...*[53] Philo writes the following (which is absolutely correct) about this offering, in his book on sacrifices: *In the case of the peace offering it does not matter which sex the animal happens to be, but the following three parts are given to the priests: the fat, the lobe of the liver, and the two kidneys. The rest are given to serve as a banquet for the person making the offering... This type of offering may be eaten for only two days, so that nothing will remain on the third... For it is a sacrifice made for the well-being of two things, the body and the soul. Each of these is therefore given its own feast day... Because, moreover, there is no third thing for whose particular well-being we are asking, we have been prohibited from extending the banquet to a third day, so that if one should forget and leave something over, it would be considered an offense... The sacrifice called Praise belongs to the same category, and is performed in the following way: when a person has survived any sort of hardship, whether of his external circumstances or of his body, and has been enjoying a quiet and peaceful life... he must offer his thanks to God... and show his gratitude with hymns, praises, sacrifices, and other expressions of thankfulness, all of which are collectively called "praise." The law orders that this animal be eaten not over two days (like the other peace offering) but on the very same day, because people who have experienced God's unstinting blessings should waste no time in using this sacrifice to share them with others.*[54] And this is the command in Leviticus 12:[55] *And when ye will offer a sacrifice of thanksgiving unto the Lord, offer it at your own will. On the same day it shall be eaten up; ye shall leave none of it until the morrow...* When, therefore, David had escaped great danger, he gave thanks to God in Psalm 115, with the words: *What shall I render unto the Lord for all his benefits toward me? I will take the cup of salvation, and call upon the name of the Lord... I will offer to thee the sacrifice of thanksgiving, and will call upon the name of the Lord.*[56]

CHAPTER 6

Sin Offerings

THE FOURTH TYPE of sacrifice atoned for the sins of the priest,[57] the people, the prince,[58] and the private individual; we are told about it in the fourth chapter of Leviticus: *If the priest that is anointed do sin according to the sin of the people; then let him bring for his sin, which he hath sinned, a young bullock without blemish unto the Lord for a sin offering. And he shall bring the bullock unto the door of the tabernacle of the congregation before the Lord; and shall lay his hand upon the bullock's head, and kill the bullock before the Lord. And the priest that is anointed shall take of the bullock's blood, and bring it to the tabernacle of the congregation; and the priest shall dip his finger in the blood, and sprinkle of the blood seven times before the Lord, before the veil of the sanctuary. And the priest shall put some of the blood upon the horns of the altar of sweet incense before the Lord, which is in the tabernacle of the congregation; and shall pour all the blood of the bullock at the bottom of the altar of the burnt offering, which is at the door of the tabernacle of the congregation. And he shall take off from it all the fat of the bullock for the sin offering; the fat that covereth the inwards, and all the fat that is upon the inwards, and the two kidneys, and the fat that is upon them, which is by the flanks, and the caul above the liver, with the kidneys, it shall he take away, as it was taken off from the bullock of the sacrifice of peace offerings; and the priest shall burn them upon the altar of the burnt offering. And the skin of the bullock, and all his flesh, with his head, and with his legs, and his inwards, and his dung, even the whole bullock shall he carry forth without the camp unto a clean place, where the ashes are poured out, and burn him on the wood with fire; where the ashes are poured out shall he be burnt.*[59] After the procedure of the priest's sin offering has been set out, we are given the procedures for the sin offerings of the people, the prince, and the private individual when they have sinned unintentionally. Since these procedures differ very little from one another, I don't believe it is necessary to quote them here; I am content to point out where in the text these passages occur. The law governing sin offerings is recorded afterward, in chapter 6: *...This is the law of the sin* *offering: In the place where the burnt offering is killed shall the sin offering be killed before the Lord; it is most holy. The priest that offereth it for sin shall eat it; in the holy place shall it be eaten, in the court of the tabernacle of the congregation. Whatsoever shall touch the flesh thereof shall be holy; and when there is sprinkled of the blood thereof upon any garment, thou shalt wash that whereon it was sprinkled in the holy place. But the earthen vessel wherein it is sodden shall be broken; and if it be sodden in a brazen pot, it shall be both scoured, and rinsed in water. All the males among the priests shall eat thereof; it is most holy. And no sin offering, whereof any of the blood is brought into the tabernacle of the congregation to reconcile withal in the holy place, shall be eaten; it shall be burnt in the fire.*[60] We are then told in the same terms about the procedures and the laws governing the sin offerings given for withholding knowledge of the truth,[61] for impurity, for a mistake,[62] for an oath,[63] and for the misuse of sacred objects.[64]

CHAPTER 7

Trespass Offerings

THE FIFTH TYPE of sacrifice was for the expiation of trespasses. The passage I just quoted next contains a law about this rite: *If a soul sin, and commit a trespass against the Lord, and lie unto his neighbor in that which was delivered him to keep, or in fellowship, or in a thing taken away by violence, or hath deceived his neighbor; or have found that which was lost, and lieth concerning it, and sweareth falsely; in any of all these that a man doeth, sinning therein; then it shall be, because he hath sinned, and is guilty, that he shall restore that which he took violently away, or the thing which he hath deceitfully gotten, or that which was delivered him to keep, or the lost thing which he found, or all that about which he hath sworn falsely; he shall even restore it in the principal, and shall add the fifth part more thereto, and give it unto him to whom it appertaineth, in the day of his trespass offering. And he shall bring his trespass offering unto the Lord, a ram without blemish out of the flock, with thy estimation, for a trespass offering, unto the priest; and the priest shall make an atonement for him before the Lord; and it shall be forgiven him for any thing of all that he hath done in trespassing therein.*[65] There is also a law recorded in chapter 7: *Likewise this is the law of the trespass offering: it is most holy. In the place where they kill the burnt offering shall they kill the trespass offering; and the blood thereof shall he sprinkle round about upon the altar. And he shall offer of it all the fat thereof; the rump, and the fat that covereth the inwards, and the two kidneys, and the fat that is on them, which is by the flanks, and the caul that is above the liver, with the kidneys, it shall he take away; and the priest shall burn them upon the altar for an offering made by fire unto the Lord: it is a trespass offering. Every male among the priests shall eat thereof; it shall be eaten in the holy place; it is most holy. As the sin offering is, so is the trespass offering: there is one law for them; the priest who taketh atonement therewith shall have it. And the priest that offereth any man's burnt offering, even the priest shall have to himself the skin of the burnt offering which he hath offered. And all the meat offering that is baked in the oven, and all that is dressed in the griddle, and in the pan, shall be the priest's who offereth it.*

And every meat offering, mingled with oil, and dry, shall all the sons of Aaron have, one as much as another.[66]

This is what Philo writes about this kind of sacrifice, and it should shed some light on the topic: *The sacrifice called the sin offering varies according to both the persons who perform it and the animals that are sacrificed. The persons include the high priest, the people, the prince, and the private individual; while the animals include bullocks, kids, she-goats, and ewes. Cows are also offered by those who have sinned unintentionally, and by those who have sinned knowingly but had a change of heart and now condemn their own actions, and wish to put their lives on a better footing.*[67] *The sins of the high priest and the people are expiated by the same sacrifice, a bullock. In the case of the prince it is a smaller animal, but still a male, for he offers a goat; whereas private individuals offer an animal still smaller than that...*[68] And later on: *After the lawgiver wrote about unintentional sins, he moved on to sins which we acknowledge having committed willingly and intentionally. If, he says, a person has lied about a partnership, or a deposit, or a theft, or finding something that was lost, and has then agreed to take an oath in order to deflect suspicion from himself; but in the end his conscience has gotten the better of him and he has implicated himself for his perjuries and denials, confessed the truth, and sought forgiveness, then he deserves to be forgiven for his crime. After all, he has proven that his penitence is real not only in word but in deed: he returns whatever was deposited with him or which he found, or whatever he was using that belonged to someone else, and he adds a fifth of the object's value so as to compensate the person he has wronged.*[69] From these passages we can see that "sin" is the name for an act committed through ignorance, and "trespass" for one committed willingly and knowingly. And yet St. Augustine thought that a sin was the commission of evil, and a trespass the neglect of good; or that one was guilty of a sin if one was aware of it, and of a trespass if one was not.[70] What is more, he often claimed that both may be placed in the same category.[71]

Once God had handed down these commands, Aaron undertook to carry them out; and at God's behest he performed the sacrifices for his own sins and those of the people, and the burnt offerings, and the peace offerings. Then a fire came down from heaven and set them alight, as it is written in chapter 8.[72] (It will not trouble me to insert these passages as well, since they are especially well suited to clarifying the sacrificial process.) *Aaron therefore went unto the altar, and slew the calf of the sin offering, which was for himself. And the sons of Aaron brought the blood unto him; and he dipped his finger in the blood, and put it upon the horns of the altar, and poured out the blood at the bottom of the altar; but the fat, and the kidneys, and the caul above the liver of the sin offering, he burnt upon the altar... And the flesh and the hide he burnt with fire without the camp. And he slew the burnt offering; and Aaron's sons presented unto him the blood, which he sprinkled round about upon the altar. And they presented the burnt offering unto him, with the pieces thereof, and the head; and he burnt them upon the altar. And he did wash the inwards and the legs, and burnt them upon the burnt offering on the altar. And he brought the people's offering, and took the goat, which was the sin offering for the people, and slew it, and offered it for sin, as the first. And he brought the burnt offering, and offered it according to the manner. And he brought the meat offering, and took a handful thereof, and burnt it upon the altar, beside the burnt sacrifice of the morning. He slew also the bullock and the ram for a sacrifice of peace offerings, which was for the people; and Aaron's sons presented unto him the blood, which he sprinkled upon the altar round about, and the fat of the bullock and of the ram, the rump, and that which covereth the inwards, and the kidneys, and the caul above the liver; and they put the fat upon the breasts, and he burnt the fat upon the altar; and the breasts and the right shoulder Aaron waved for a wave offering before the Lord... And Aaron lifted up his hand toward the people, and blessed them, and came down from offering the sin offering, and the burnt offering, and peace offerings... And there came a fire out from before the Lord, and consumed upon the altar the burnt offering and the fat... And Nadab and Abihu, the sons of Aaron, took each of them his censer, and put fire therein, and put incense thereon, and offered strange fire before the Lord, which he commanded them not. And there went out fire from the Lord, and devoured them... And Moses spake unto Aaron, and unto Eleazar and unto Ithamar, his sons who were left, Take the meat offering that remaineth of the offerings of the Lord made by fire, and eat it without leaven beside the altar, for it is most holy; and ye shall eat it in the holy place, because it is thy due, and thy sons' due, of the sacrifices of the Lord made by fire; for so I am commanded. And the wave breast and heave shoulder shall ye eat in a clean place; thou, and thy sons, and thy daughters with thee: for they be thy due, and thy sons' due, which are given out of the sacrifices of peace offerings of the children of Israel. The heave shoulder and the wave breast shall they bring with the offerings made by fire of the fat, to wave it for a wave offering before the Lord; and it shall be thine, and thy sons' with thee, by a statute for ever; as the Lord hath commanded. And Moses diligently sought the goat of the sin offering, and, behold, it was burnt; and he was angry with Eleazar and Ithamar, the sons of Aaron who were left alive, saying, Wherefore have ye not eaten the sin offering in the holy place, seeing it is most holy, and God hath given it you to bear the iniquity of the congregation, to make atonement for them before the Lord? Behold, the blood of it was not brought in within the holy place; ye should indeed have eaten it in the holy place, as I commanded. And Aaron said unto Moses, Behold, this day have they offered their sin offering and their burnt offering before the Lord; and such things have befallen me: and if I had eaten the sin offering today,*[73] *should it have been accepted in the sight of the Lord? And when Moses heard that, he was content.*[74] This is what is written in the law about each of the sacrifices.

CHAPTER 8

More About All of the Offerings

NOW I WOULD like to go back and discuss all of the sacrifices at the same time, in order to explain the most puzzling of them all. But first I would like to mention the scheme according to which Josephus organizes these offerings; this will point up clearly the differences between them. Then I will cite a number of examples of sacrifices from the biblical narratives, in order to explain more clearly the rationale behind them all. This, then, is what Josephus writes: *There are two kinds of sacrifices, those offered by private individuals and those offered by the people; and they are performed in two different ways. Either the offering is burned whole (and for this reason is called a holocaust),[75] or it is used to discharge a debt of thanks, and served at a banquet for the sacrificers... The individual who makes a burnt offering sacrifices a bull, a lamb, and a kid, each a year old, though the bulls may be older. And all these burnt offerings are made with male animals. The priests then kill the offering and sprinkle the blood around the edge of the altar. Then they clean the carcass and dismember it, sprinkle it with salt, and place the whole on the altar, which has been laid with wood and set afire. They also clean the legs and the liver, and offer them (together with the fat) alongside the other sacrificers, though the priests keep the hide for themselves. And this was the burnt offering. In a thank offering, on the other hand, the sacrificers slaughter the very same animals, but mature ones older than a year; and males together with females. They kill the animals and pour out the blood on the altar; and they place upon it the kidneys, and the caul, and all the fat, together with the lobe of the liver and the rump of the lamb. But the breast and the right leg they give to the priests; and for two days they dine on the rest of the meat, but whatever is left over they burn. Moreover, the same procedure is followed for sin offering; though people who cannot afford larger animals offer two pigeons or turtledoves—one of these is used for a burnt offering to God, and the other is given to the priests to eat... When a person sins unintentionally, he offers a lamb and a female kid of the same age,[76] and the priest pours out the blood on the altar. But unlike the case of the thank offering, here he touches it to the corners; and they place on the altar the kidneys and the rest of the fat, along with the lobe of the liver. Moreover, the priests get both the hide and the meat, which they must eat in the Temple on the very same day; for the law does not allow it to be left over till the next. When, on the other hand, someone sins with full awareness but no one can prove his guilt, the law orders him to offer a ram; and the priests likewise eat its flesh in the Temple on the same day. And when a prince sins he offers the same kinds of sacrifices as a private individual; but he appeases God by offering a bull and a kid, both males.*[77] *The law also commands that the purest flour be added to both public and private sacrifices: for a lamb one issar,*[78] *for a ram two issars, and for an ox three. And this, mixed with oil, they sanctify upon the altar; for the sacrificers bring oil as well—for a cow half a hin, for a ram one-third, and for a lamb one-quarter. (The hin is an ancient Hebrew measure equal to two Attic choas.)*[79] *They offer wine according to the same measures.*[80] This is Josephus' account, from which emerges clearly the procedure for all the sacrifices—the burnt offering, the peace offering, and the sin offering; we can see in particular that to all the sacrifices were added libations, that is, the purest meal or flour.

Now, in order to corroborate this, I would like to assemble mentions of these sacrifices from all over the Bible. Joshua 8: *...and they offered on the altar burnt offerings unto the Lord, and sacrificed peace offerings.*[81] And 22: *That we have built us an altar to offer thereon burnt offering and meat offering, and to offer peace offerings thereon.*[82] Then in Judges 6: *And Gideon... made ready a kid, and unleavened cakes of an ephah of flour; the flesh he put in a basket, and he put the broth in a pot, and brought it out unto him under the oak, and presented it. And the angel of God said unto him, Take the flesh and the unleavened cakes, and lay them upon this rock, and pour out the broth. And he did so. Then the angel of the Lord put forth the end of the staff that was in his hand, and touched the flesh and the unleavened cakes; and there rose up fire out of the rock, and consumed the flesh and the unleavened cakes.*[83] Then in First Samuel: *And Samuel took a sucking lamb, and offered it for a burnt offering wholly unto the Lord; and Samuel cried unto the Lord for Israel, and the Lord heard him.*[84] And in chapter 10: *...I will come down unto thee, to offer burnt offerings, and to sacrifice sacrifices of peace offerings...*[85] And in chapter 13: *...Bring hither a burnt offering to me, and peace offerings...*[86] And likewise: *Therefore said I, The Philistines will come down now upon me to Gilgal, and I have not made supplication unto the Lord; I forced myself, therefore, and offered a burnt offering.*[87] And in Second Samuel 6: *...and David offered burnt offerings and peace offerings before the Lord.*[88] And First Kings 3: *And Solomon... offered up burnt offerings, and offered peace offerings...*[89] And chapter 9: *And three times a year did Solomon offer burnt offerings and*

peace offerings upon the altar which he built unto the Lord...[90] And in the
sixteenth chapter of Second Kings: *And* King Ahaz *burnt his burnt offering
and his meat offering, and poured his drink offering, and sprinkled the blood of
his peace offerings, upon the altar.*[91] And a little after: *...Upon the great altar
burn the morning burnt offering, and the evening meat offering, and the king's
burnt sacrifice, and his meat offering, with the burnt offering of all the people
of the land, and their meat offering, and their drink offerings; and sprinkle
upon it all the blood of the burnt offering, and all the blood of the sacrifice.*[92]
And Second Chronicles 29: *...come near and bring sacrifices and praises into
the house of the Lord.*[93] In Greek this is *anapherete thusias aineseos,* i.e. *offer
the sacrifices of praise.* And later on: *...and they did eat throughout the feast
seven days, offering peace offerings, and making confession to the Lord God.*[94]
But there is a much clearer description of these offerings in the passage in
Second Chronicles 29 where the burnt offering and sin offering are described
in stages: *And they brought seven bullocks, and seven rams, and seven lambs,
and seven he-goats, for a sin offering for the kingdom, and for the sanctuary,
and for Judah. And he commanded the priests the sons of Aaron to offer them
on the altar of the Lord. So they killed the bullocks, and the priests received the
blood, and sprinkled it on the altar; likewise, when they had killed the rams,
they sprinkled the blood upon the altar; they also killed the lambs, and they
sprinkled the blood upon the altar. And they brought forth the he-goats for the
sin offering before the king and the congregation; and they laid their hands
upon them; and the priests killed them, and they made reconciliation with
their blood upon the altar, to make an atonement for all Israel; for the king
commanded that the burnt offering and the sin offering be made for all Israel.*[95]
And then: *...And the congregation brought in sacrifices and thank offerings;
and as many as were of a free heart burnt offerings.*[96] And afterward: *And also
the burnt offerings were in abundance, with the fat of the peace offerings, and
the drink offerings for every burnt offering...*[97] Finally, in the sixth chapter of
Ezra: *And offered at the dedication of this house of God a hundred bullocks,
two hundred rams, four hundred lambs; and for a sin offering for all Israel,
twelve he-goats...*[98] And in the fourth chapter of First Maccabees: *...and offered burnt offerings with gladness, and sacrificed the sacrifice of deliverance
and praise.*[99] Though all these texts come from the biblical narratives,[100] the
prophets also mention the same sacrifices, for example, David in Psalm 39:
*Sacrifice and offering thou didst not desire... burnt offering and sin offering
hast thou not required.*[101] And in Ezekiel 45: *...he shall prepare the sin offering, and the meat offering, and the burnt offering, and the peace offerings, to
make reconciliation for the house of Israel.*[102] And in Proverbs 7: *I have peace
offerings with me; this day have I payed my vows.*[103]

Now, the terms *offering of justice* and *offering of praise* are often used metaphorically rather than literally[104]—that is, they mean not "blood sacrifice" but "work of charity and piety," what is called an "inner sacrifice." I should therefore explain the origins of this usage: The Hebrews were so eager to make blood sacrifices that they concerned themselves with them alone, and forgot about works of charity toward their neighbors and piety toward God (the first of which is called the offering of justice, and the second the offering of praise).[105] But as God wanted to correct them and make their duty clear to them, he gave them frequent notice that he did not care for burnt offerings and other animal sacrifices, but for offerings of justice and praise. That, in other words, they should show charity toward their neighbors and piety toward him, and he would rather receive the thanks of their souls than the blood of their sacrifices. On the subject of justice, there is the third chapter of Proverbs:[106] *To do justice and judgment is more acceptable to the Lord than sacrifice.* This means it is more pleasing to God that we keep his law—which contains two parts, justice and judgment—than that we offer him blood sacrifice. And in Psalm 39: *Sacrifice and offering thou didst not desire... burnt offering and sin offering hast thou not required.*[107] And the fourth Psalm: *Offer the sacrifices of righteousness, and put your trust in the Lord.*[108] Likewise Hosea: *For I desired mercy, and not sacrifice...*[109] The authors of the Gospels also taught that this was so. In the first chapter of St. James: *Pure religion and undefiled... is this, to visit the fatherless and widows in their affliction...*[110] Chapter 12 of St. Mark: *...and to love his neighbor as himself is more than all whole burnt offerings.*[111] In chapter 13 of St. Paul's Letter to the Hebrews: *But to do good and to communicate forget not: for with such sacrifices God is well pleased.*[112] On the other hand, on the offering of praise there is Psalm 49: first God says that he never asked men to give him animal sacrifice, since he has no need of cows; and then he says: *Offer unto God the sacrifice of praise...;*[113] that is, praise God. And Psalm 115: *I will offer to thee the sacrifice of thanksgiving, and will call upon the name of the Lord.*[114] And Psalm 116:[115] *And let them sacrifice the sacrifices of thanksgiving...* St. Paul also teaches us that this is so, in the same passage:[116] *...let us offer the sacrifice of praise to God continually, that is, the fruit of our lips giving thanks to his name.* For Hosea had said in chapter 14: *...Take away all iniquity, and receive us graciously; so will we render the calves of our lips.*[117]

CHAPTER 9

Thanksgivings

CONNECTED WITH THE offerings were thanksgivings. This was what they called the praises with which, during sacrifice, they extolled God's goodness and mercy; and which generally took the form: *O give thanks unto the Lord, for he is good; for his mercy endureth for ever.*[118] And to these words of praise they added the sounds of musical instruments, such as psalteries,[119] citharas, cymbals, and organs. (King David was the chief inspiration for this.) We have the following testimonies of these praises. In First Chronicles 23, on the burnt offering made in the time of David: *And to stand every morning to thank and praise the Lord, and likewise at even; and to offer all burnt sacrifices unto the Lord in the Sabbaths, in the new moons, and on the set feasts...*[120] And in the fifth chapter of Second Chronicles: *Also the Levites who were the singers... having cymbals and psalteries and harps... and with them a hundred and twenty priests sounding with trumpets. It came even to pass, as the trumpeters and singers were as one, to make one sound to be heard in praising and thanking the Lord; and when they lifted up their voice with the trumpets and cymbals and instruments of music, and praised the Lord, saying, For he is good; for his mercy endureth for ever...*[121] And in chapter 29: *...And when the burnt offering began, the song of the Lord began also with the trumpets, and with the instruments ordained by David king of Israel. And all the congregation worshiped, and the singers sang, and the trumpeters sounded; and all this continued until the burnt offering was finished.*[122] And chapter 30:[123] *And Hezekiah appointed the courses of the priests and the Levites... for burnt offerings and for peace offerings, to minister, and to give thanks, and to praise in the gates of the tents of the Lord.* And in the third chapter of Ezra: *And when the builders laid the foundation of the Temple of the Lord, they set the priests in their apparel with trumpets, and the Levites the sons of Asaph with cymbals, to praise the Lord, after the ordinance of David king of Israel. And they sang together by course in praising and giving thanks unto the Lord; because he is good, for his mercy endureth for ever...*[124] Hence we have in Psalm 101[125] as follows: *His work is praise and magnificence.* And in First Chronicles 16: *Glory and honor are* *in* the Lord's *presence...*[126] And in chapter 39 of Ecclesiasticus:[127] *...bless the Lord in his works. Magnify his name, and give glory to him with the voice of your lips...*[128] And chapter 9 of Ezra:[129] *Now therefore give confession and magnificence unto the Lord God of your fathers...* This "magnificence" seems to have been the same thing as "magnification," that is, an exceptional and magnificent sort of commendation which was more than just thanksgiving and praise. The Greek translation calls this *homologēsis* and *ainesis.*[130] Hence the phrase: *My soul doth magnify the Lord.*[131] I will return to thanksgivings later on, when I discuss the singers.

CHAPTER 10

The Consecration Offering

HAVING PRESENTED THESE sacrifices one after another, the law adds several more which were not performed by everyone but were particular to certain individuals; the first of these was called *consecration*, the second *purification*, and the third *expiation*. I shall deal with these one at a time.

The offering called *consecration* or *teleiōsis*[132] had only to do with the priests and was part of their consecration; they were bound to offer it both morning and evening on the day they were anointed (this was entirely different from the offering with which they were consecrated once they had been anointed, and which I will discuss when I come to the subject of the high priest). The consecration offering is commanded as follows in Leviticus 6 (which also deals with the above-mentioned sacrifices): *And the Lord spake unto Moses, saying, This is the offering of Aaron and of his sons, which they shall offer unto the Lord in the day when he is anointed; the tenth part of an ephah of fine flour for a meat offering perpetual, half of it in the morning, and half thereof at night. In a pan it shall be made with oil; and when it is baked, thou shalt bring it in; and the baked pieces of the meat offering shalt thou offer for a sweet savor unto the Lord. And the priest of his sons who is anointed in his stead shall offer it: it is a statute for ever unto the Lord; it shall be wholly burnt. For every meat offering for the priest shall be wholly burnt; it shall not be eaten.*[133] It is, moreover, clear that this was one of the six sacrifices I mentioned above, since the law in this passage concludes as follows: *This is the law of the burnt offering, of the meat offering, and of the sin offering, and of the trespass offering, and of the consecrations, and of the sacrifice of the peace offerings; which the Lord commanded Moses at Mount Sinai, in the day that He commanded the children of Israel to offer their oblations unto the Lord, in the wilderness of Sinai.*[134]

CHAPTER 11

The Purification Offering

NOW THE OFFERING I called "purification"[135] was brought for the impurity of a woman who had given birth, a leper, a man with a seminal discharge, and a menstruating woman, just as the expiation offering was brought to purify the sanctuary and the people when they were defiled.[136]

On the purification of the new mother it is written in Leviticus 12: ...*If a woman have conceived seed, and born a man child, then she shall be unclean seven days; according to the days of the separation for her infirmity shall she be unclean.*[137] *And in the eighth day the flesh of his foreskin shall be circumcised. And she shall then continue in the blood of her purifying three and thirty days; she shall touch no hallowed thing, nor come into the sanctuary, until the days of her purifying be fulfilled. But if she bear a maid child, then she shall be unclean two weeks, as in her separation;*[138] *and she shall continue in the blood of her purifying threescore and six days. And when the days of her purifying are fulfilled, for a son, or for a daughter, she shall bring a lamb of the first year for a burnt offering, and a young pigeon, or a turtledove, for a sin offering, unto the door of the tabernacle of the congregation, unto the priest; who shall offer it before the Lord, and make an atonement for her; and she shall be cleansed from the issue of her blood. This is the law for her who hath born a male or a female. And if she be not able to bring a lamb, then she shall bring two turtledoves, or two young pigeons; the one for the burnt offering, and the other for a sin offering: and the priest shall make an atonement for her, and she shall be clean.*[139] Hence St. Luke's remarks about the blessed Virgin: *And when the days of her purification according to the law of Moses were accomplished, they brought him to Jerusalem, to present him to the Lord (as it is written in the law of the Lord, Every male that openeth the womb shall be called holy to the Lord); and to offer a sacrifice according to that which is said in the law of the Lord, A pair of turtledoves, or two young pigeons.*[140]

Then we are told about the purification of the leper in chapters 13 and 14, but first we are taught that the leper is brought to the high priest or to the priests, who use their experience and judgment to decide whether or not the spot that has appeared on the man's body is leprous. (They had many kinds of evidence with which to reach this decision.)[141] Then the procedure of purification is described as follows: *This shall be the law of the leper in the day of his cleansing: He shall be brought unto the priest; and the priest shall go forth out of the camp; and the priest shall look, and, behold, if the plague of leprosy be healed in the leper; then shall the priest command to take for him who is to be cleansed two birds alive and clean, and cedar wood, and scarlet, and hyssop. And the priest shall command that one of the birds be killed in an earthen vessel over running water. As for the living bird, he shall take it, and the cedar wood, and the scarlet, and the hyssop, and shall dip them and the living bird in the blood of the bird that was killed over the running water. And he shall sprinkle upon him who is to be cleansed from the leprosy seven times, and shall pronounce him clean, and shall let the living bird loose into the open field.*[142] I will pass over the rest for the sake of brevity; I think in this particular case it is enough to point out where the passages are found.

The man with a seminal discharge is discussed in chapter 15. After describing the signs of his impurity, the text adds: *And when he who hath an issue is cleansed of his issue; then he shall number to himself seven days for his cleansing, and wash his clothes, and bathe his flesh in running water, and shall be clean. And on the eighth day he shall take to him two turtledoves, or two young pigeons, and come before the Lord unto the door of the tabernacle of the congregation, and give them unto the priest; and the priest shall offer them, the one for a sin offering, and the other for a burnt offering; and the priest shall make an atonement for him before the Lord for his issue.*[143] Then it teaches us about the menstruating woman as follows:[144] *And if a woman have an issue of her blood many days out of the time of her separation, or if it run beyond the time of her separation; all the days of the issue of her uncleanness shall be as the days of her separation: she shall be unclean. Every bed whereon she lieth all the days of her issue shall be unto her as the bed of her separation; and whatsoever she sitteth upon shall be unclean, as the uncleanness of her separation. And whosoever toucheth those things shall be unclean, and shall wash his clothes, and bathe himself in water, and be unclean until the even. But if she be cleansed of her issue, then she shall number to herself seven days, and after that she shall be clean. And on the eighth day she shall take unto her two turtles, or two young pigeons, and bring them unto the priest, to the door of the tabernacle of the congregation. And the priest shall offer the one for a sin offering, and the other for a burnt offering; and the priest shall make an atonement for her before the Lord for the issue of her uncleanness... This is the law of him who hath an issue, and of him whose seed goeth from him, and is defiled therewith; and of her who is sick of her flowers, and of him who hath an issue, of the man, and of the woman, and of him who lieth with her who is unclean.*[145]

CHAPTER 12

The Expiation Offering

AFTER THIS PASSAGE is added a description of the offering of expiation or propitiation. The Day of Expiation[146] was, as I have already said, one of the most important festivals of the year; it was observed with great pomp on the tenth day of September. This was when the high priest put on his priestly garments and entered the holy of holies; and while the entire people fasted, he performed a special sacrifice with which he cleansed the sanctuary of the people's impurities, its misdeeds, and its other sins. Chapter sixteen of Leviticus describes the offering in these words: *Speak unto Aaron... that he come not at all times into the holy place within the veil before the mercy seat, which is upon the ark; that he die not... Thus shall Aaron come into the holy place: with a young bullock for a sin offering, and a ram for a burnt offering. He shall put on the holy linen coat, and he shall have the linen breeches upon his flesh, and shall be girded with a linen girdle, and with the linen mitre shall he be attired... And he shall take of the congregation of the children of Israel two kids of the goats for a sin offering, and one ram for a burnt offering. And Aaron shall offer his bullock of the sin offering, which is for himself, and make an atonement for himself, and for his house. And he shall take the two goats, and present them before the Lord at the door of the tabernacle of the congregation. And Aaron shall cast lots upon the two goats; one lot for the Lord, and the other lot for the scapegoat. And Aaron shall bring the goat upon which the Lord's lot fell, and offer him for a sin offering. But the goat, on which the lot fell to be the scapegoat, shall be presented alive before the Lord, to make an atonement with him, and to let him go for a scapegoat into the wilderness. And Aaron shall bring the bullock of the sin offering, which is for himself, and shall make an atonement for himself... and shall kill the bullock of the sin offering which is for himself; and he shall take a censer full of burning coals of fire from off the altar before the Lord, and his hands full of sweet incense beaten small, and bring it within the veil. And he shall put the incense upon the fire before the Lord, that the cloud of the incense may cover the mercy seat that is upon the testimony, that he die not. And he shall take of the blood of the bullock, and sprinkle it with his finger upon the mercy seat eastward; and before the mercy seat shall he sprinkle of the blood with his finger seven times. Then shall he kill the goat of the sin offering, that is for the people, and bring his blood within the veil, and do with that blood as he did with the blood of the bullock, and sprinkle it upon the mercy seat, and before the mercy seat. And he shall make an atonement for the holy place, because of the uncleanness of the children of Israel, and because of their transgressions in all their sins... And there shall be no man in the tabernacle of the congregation when he goeth in to make an atonement in the holy place, until he come out, and have made an atonement for himself, and for his household, and for all the congregation of Israel. And he shall go out unto the altar that is before the Lord, and make an atonement for it; and shall take of the blood of the bullock, and of the blood of the goat, and put it upon the horns of the altar round about. And he shall sprinkle of the blood upon it with his finger seven times, and cleanse it, and hallow it from the uncleanness of the children of Israel. And when he hath made an end of reconciling the holy place, and the tabernacle of the congregation, and the altar, he shall bring the live goat. And Aaron shall lay both his hands upon the head of the live goat, and confess over him all the iniquities of the children of Israel, and all their transgressions in all their sins, putting them upon the head of the goat, and shall send him away by the hand of a fit man into the wilderness. And the goat shall bear upon him all their iniquities unto a land not inhabited; and he shall let go the goat in the wilderness. And Aaron shall come into the tabernacle of the congregation, and shall put off the linen garments, which he put on when he went into the holy place, and shall leave them there. And he shall wash his flesh with water in the holy place, and put on his garments, and come forth, and offer his burnt offering, and the burnt offering of the people, and make an atonement for himself, and for the people. And the fat of the sin offering shall he burn upon the altar. And he that let go the goat for the scapegoat shall wash his clothes, and bathe his flesh in water, and afterward come into the camp. And the bullock for the sin offering, and the goat for the sin offering, whose blood was brought in to make atonement in the holy place, shall one carry forth without the camp; and they shall burn in the fire their skins, and their flesh, and their dung. And he that burneth them shall wash his clothes, and bathe his flesh in water, and afterward he shall come into the camp. And this shall be a statute for ever unto you...*[147]

CHAPTER 13

The Offering of Incense

IN ADDITION TO THE sacrifices I have mentioned, there was also a daily offering on the incense altar. In order to explain the nature of this offering I will record first what is said about it in the law, and then any references which may be found outside the law. In Exodus 11:[148] *...and thou shalt bring in the candlestick, and light the lamps thereof. And thou shalt set the altar of gold for the incense before the ark of the testimony... And he put the golden altar in the tent of the congregation before the veil; and he burnt sweet incense thereon...* And in chapter 30, which discusses the construction of the incense altar: *And Aaron shall burn thereon sweet incense every morning; when he dresseth the lamps, he shall burn incense upon it. And when Aaron lighteth the lamps at even, he shall burn incense upon it, a perpetual incense before the Lord throughout your generations.*[149] (I described the procedure for making the incense, and its ingredients, in my discussion of the tabernacle.) So much for the law; now we will see what there is beyond it. In the second chapter of Second Samuel:[150] *And did I choose Aaron out of all the tribes of Israel to be my priest, to offer upon mine altar, to burn incense...* And in the ninth chapter of First Kings: *And three times a year did Solomon offer burnt offerings and peace offerings upon the altar which he built unto the Lord, and he burnt incense upon the altar that was before the Lord...*[151] And chapter 22: *...the people offered and burnt incense yet in the high places.*[152] And in First Chronicles 6: *But Aaron and his sons offered upon the altar of the burnt offering, and on the altar of incense, and were appointed for all the work of the place most holy...*[153] And Second Chronicles 26: *But when Uzziah the king of Judah was strong, his heart was lifted up to his destruction: for he transgressed against the Lord his God, and went into the Temple of the Lord to burn incense upon the altar of incense. And Azariah the priest went in after him, and with him fourscore priests of the Lord... And they withstood Uzziah the king, and said unto him, It appertaineth not unto thee, Uzziah, to burn incense unto the Lord, but to the priests the sons of Aaron, who are consecrated to burn incense; go out of the sanctuary, for thou hast trespassed, neither shall* *it be for thine honor from the Lord God. Then Uzziah was wroth, and had a censer in his hand to burn incense: and while he was wroth with the priests, the leprosy even rose up in his forehead before the priests in the house of the Lord...*[154] And in chapter 29: *Your fathers have forsaken God, and have not burned incense nor offered burnt offerings in the holy place unto the God of Israel.*[155] And in the first chapter of Isaiah: *...of the burnt offerings of rams... I delight not... incense is an abomination unto me...*[156] To these we might also add the famous passage of St. Luke: *And it came to pass, that while Zacharias executed the priest's office before God in the order of his course, according to the custom of the priest's office, his lot was to burn incense when he went into the Temple of the Lord. And the whole multitude of the people were praying without at the time of incense.*[157] Philo in his book on sacrificers offers a straightforward account of the incense offering: *The law commands the building of two altars, which differ in their materials, their location, and their use. One is to be built from selected*[158] *and unpolished stones, and stands in the courtyard near the entrance of the Temple; and it is for slaughtering animal sacrifices. The other altar is, on the other hand, to be made of gold, and to stand behind the first curtain*[159] *in the interior of the Temple, where no one will see it but the priests who are in a state of purity at the time of their service; and it is the burning incense. From this it is clear that a grain of incense offered by a pious man is more welcome to God than a great many animals offered by an unjust one. After all, just as gold is greater than stones, and the sanctuary is greater than the courtyard, so is the burning of incense a more fitting way of giving thanks than the slaughter of animals. This altar, then, draws its majesty not just from the value of its material, the labor of its designers, and the holiness of its location; but from the fact that it is there that the sacred rites begin every day, with the offer of thanks. In fact, it is not allowed to slaughter animals outside the sanctuary before the incense has been offered within, at the very beginning of the day; and this can only mean that God finds pleasure not in the number of sacrifices, but in the good intentions of the sacrificer and his purity of spirit.*[160]

CHAPTER 14

Sacred Gifts

SO MUCH FOR SACRIFICES; now I would like to discuss sacred gifts. These were different in the sense that sacrifices were either completely or partially consumed, while gifts were kept whole and untouched. They were given as required by the law, or to requite a vow, or out of pure generosity. Hence the passage from Numbers 29: *These things ye shall do unto the Lord in your set feasts, beside your vows, and your freewill offerings...* [161] The gifts called for by the law included first fruits, tithes, and the sacred money. [162] We are told about these in general terms in Deuteronomy 12: *Ye shall not do so unto the Lord your God. But unto the place which the Lord your God shall choose out of all your tribes to put his name there, even unto his habitation shall ye seek, and thither thou shalt come. And thither ye shall bring your burnt offerings, and your sacrifices, and your tithes, and heave offerings of your hand, and your vows, and your freewill offerings, and the firstlings of your herds and of your flocks.* [163]

CHAPTER 15

First Fruits and Tithes

"FIRST FRUITS" WERE whatever a person received first, whether from animals, people, or the seeds of the earth. "Tithes" were the tenth part of all the fruits they could coax out of their lands and their flocks in a single year. But the first fruits, whether required by law or offered in payment of a vow, were handed over for the use of the priests.[164] Regarding the obligatory first fruits, God orders as follows in Exodus 22: *Thou shalt not delay to offer the first of thy... first fruits; the firstborn of thy sons shalt thou give unto me. Likewise shalt thou do with thine oxen, and with thy sheep: seven days it shall be with its dam; on the eighth day thou shalt give it me.*[165] And then: *The first of the first fruits of thy land thou shalt bring into the house of the Lord thy God.*[166] And in Numbers 5: *And all the first fruits of the children of Israel, which they bring unto the priest, shall be his. And every man's hallowed things shall be his: whatsoever any man giveth the priest, it shall be his.*[167] As to the voluntary first fruits, God told Aaron and the Levites as follows in chapter 17:[168] *And this is thine: the first fruits of their gift, with all the wave offerings of the children of Israel; I have given them unto thee, and to thy sons and to thy daughters with thee, by a statute for ever; every one who is clean in thy house shall eat of it. All the best of the oil, and all the best of the wine, and of the wheat, the first fruits of them which they shall offer unto the Lord, them have I given thee. And whatsoever is first ripe in the land, which they shall bring unto the Lord, shall be thine; every one that is clean in thine house shall eat of it. Every thing devoted in Israel shall be thine.* Then he taught that the firstborn of people and unclean animals should be redeemed,[169] but not those of cattle, sheep, and goats: *Every thing*, he says, *that openeth the matrix in all flesh, which they bring unto the Lord, whether it be of men or beasts, shall be thine; nevertheless the firstborn of man shalt thou surely redeem, and the firstling of unclean beasts shalt thou redeem. And those that are to be redeemed from a month old shalt thou redeem, according to thine estimation, for the money of five shekels, after the shekel of the sanctuary, which is twenty gerahs. But the firstling of a cow, or the firstling of a sheep, or the firstling of a goat, thou shalt not redeem; they are holy: thou shalt sprinkle their blood upon the altar, and shalt burn their fat for an offering made by fire, for a sweet savor unto the Lord. And the flesh of them shall be thine, as the wave breast and as the right shoulder are thine.*[170] There was also a festival on which the first fruits of the harvest were offered up according to the law (I discussed this above).

As to the tithes, we have learned the following from the law: first, that they were offered to God; and second, that they were handed over for the priests to enjoy. Exodus 22: *Thou shalt not delay to offer the first of thy tithes...*[171] Leviticus 27: *And all the tithe of the land, whether of the seed of the land, or of the fruit of the tree, is the Lord's; it is holy unto the Lord... And concerning the tithe of the herd, or of the flock, even of whatsoever passeth under the rod, the tenth shall be holy unto the Lord.*[172]

In his comments on Ezekiel, however, St. Jerome concludes from the words of the law that there are four types of tithes: the first the people gave to the Levites, and the second the Levites gave to the priests from their own tithe.[173] He also says that both of these types are described in Numbers 18: *Thus speak unto the Levites, and say unto them, When ye take of the children of Israel the tithes which I have given you from them for your inheritance, then ye shall offer up the first fruits of it for the Lord, even a tenth part of the tithe. And these your first fruits shall be reckoned unto you, as though it were the corn of the threshingfloor, and as the fullness of the winepress.*[174] *Thus ye also shall offer first fruits unto the Lord of all your tithes, which ye receive of the children of Israel; and ye shall give thereof the Lord's first fruits to Aaron the priest. Out of all your gifts ye shall offer all the first fruits of the Lord, of all the best thereof, even the hallowed part thereof out of it.*[175]

The third type of tithe was, he says, the part that every member of the people of Israel separated from his crops, so that he could go to the Temple and eat it there in the courtyard, and invite the priests and the Levites to feast with him. This is discussed in Deuteronomy 14: *Thou shalt truly tithe all the increase of thy seed, that the field bringeth forth year by year. And thou shalt eat before the Lord thy God, in the place which he shall choose to place his name there, the tithe of thy corn, of thy wine, and of thine oil, and the firstlings of thy herds and of thy flocks; that thou mayest learn to fear the Lord thy God always. And if the way be too long for thee, so that thou art not able to carry it; or if the place be too far from thee, which the Lord thy God shall choose to set his name there, when the Lord thy God hath blessed thee. Then shalt thou turn it into money, and bind up the money in thine hand, and shalt go unto the place which the Lord thy God shall choose. And thou shalt bestow that money for whatsoever thy soul lusteth after, for oxen, or for sheep, or for wine, or for strong drink, or for whatsoever thy soul desireth; and thou shalt eat there before the Lord thy God, and thou shalt rejoice, thou, and thine household, and the Levite that is within thy gates; thou shalt not forsake him, for he hath no part nor inheritance with thee.*[176] In fact, the above passage from chapter 12 gives the same instruction. It says: *Then there shall be a place which the Lord your God shall choose... thither shall ye bring all that I command you; your burnt offerings, and your sacrifices, your tithes, and the first fruits of your hand, and all your choice vows which ye vow unto the Lord. And ye shall rejoice before the Lord your God, ye, and your sons, and your daughters, and your menservants, and your maidservants, and the Levite who is within your gates; forasmuch as he hath no part nor inheritance with you.*[177] And in Deuteronomy 17:[178] *Thou mayest not eat within thy gates the tithe of thy corn, or of thy wine, or of thy oil... But thou must eat them before the Lord thy God in the place which the Lord thy God shall choose...* And in the first chapter of Tobit: *And went to Jerusalem to the Temple of the Lord, and there adored him, offering faithfully all his first fruits, and his tithes, so that in the third year he gave all his tithes to the proselytes, and strangers.*[179] There are, however, those who disagree with St. Jerome and claim that this third tithe is in fact the same as the first one; and that they may have eaten some of the first tithe and dined along with the Levites in the Temple.

The fourth tithe was not put aside every year but only every third year, for the benefit of the poor. On this we have Deuteronomy 14: *At the end of three years thou shalt bring forth all the tithe of thine increase the same year, and shalt lay it up within thy gates. And the Levite (because he hath no part nor inheritance with thee), and the stranger, and the fatherless, and the widow, who are within thy gates, shall come, and shall eat and be satisfied; that the Lord thy God may bless thee in all the work of thine hand which thou doest.*[180] Likewise chapter 26: *When thou hast made an end of tithing all the tithes of thine increase the third year, which is the year of tithing, and hast given it unto the Levite, the stranger, the fatherless, and the widow, that they may eat within thy gates, and be filled.*[181]

All this is in the law, but all practices were observed thoughout the rest of the Bible; as in Second Chronicles 31: *Moreover* King Hezekiah *commanded the people who dwelt in Jerusalem to give the portion of the priests and the Levites, that they might be encouraged in the law of the Lord. And as soon as the commandment came abroad, the children of Israel brought in abundance the first fruits of corn, wine, and oil, and honey, and of all the increase of the field; and the tithe of all things brought they in abundantly. And concerning the children of Israel and Judah, who dwelt in the cities of Judah, they also*

brought in the tithe of oxen and sheep, and the tithe of holy things which were
consecrated unto the Lord their God, and laid them by heaps.[182]

After the Jews returned from Babylonia, they began to store up the first fruits and the tithes in the treasury. Nehemiah 10: *And we cast the lots... to bring the first fruits of our ground, and the first fruits of all fruit of all trees, year by year, unto the house of the Lord. Also the firstborn of our sons, and of our cattle, as it is written in the law, and the firstlings of our herds and of our flocks, to bring to the house of our God, unto the priests who minister in the house of our God. And that we should bring the first fruits of our dough, and our offerings, and the fruit of all manner of trees, of wine and of oil, unto the priests, to the chambers of the house of our God; and the tithes of our ground unto the Levites, that the same Levites might have the tithes in all the cities of our tillage. And the priest the son of Aaron shall be with the Levites, when the Levites take tithes; and the Levites shall bring up the tithe of the tithes unto the house of our God, to the chambers, into the treasure house. For the children of Israel and the children of Levi shall bring the offering of the corn, of the new wine, and the oil, unto the chambers, where are the vessels of the sanctuary...*[183]

Later on, the Pharisees believed that the law had to be kept so strictly that they even gave tithes on tiny herbs. Christ criticized them for this in chapter 11 of St. Luke: *But woe unto you, Pharisees! for ye tithe mint and rue and all manner of herbs, and pass over judgment and the love of God; these ought ye to have done, and not to leave the other undone.*[184]

CHAPTER 16

Sacred Money and the Treasury

THE NEXT TOPIC on my agenda is the sacred money, which was called the shekel. This was the price they paid to the Lord in exchange for their souls, and it was used for the tabernacle. So God commands in Exodus 30: *When thou takest the sum of the children of Israel after their number, then shall they give every man a ransom for his soul unto the Lord, when thou numberest them; that there be no plague among them, when thou numberest them. This they shall give, every one who passeth among them who are numbered, half a shekel after the shekel of the sanctuary (a shekel is twenty gerahs); a half-shekel shall be the offering of the Lord. Every one who passeth among them that are numbered, from twenty years old and above, shall give an offering unto the Lord. The rich shall not give more, and the poor shall not give less than half a shekel, when they give an offering unto the Lord, to make an atonement for your souls. And thou shalt take the atonement money of the children of Israel, and shalt appoint it for the service of the tabernacle of the congregation; that it may be a memorial unto the children of Israel before the Lord, to make an atonement for your souls.*[185] The priests collected this payment for many years after the Temple was built, and then they stopped; but later on money was needed to repair the Temple, and the priests did not have it, because they had stopped collecting the tax. So King Joash,[186] who wanted it to be paid once again, set up a chest in which everyone could deposit the tax as he entered the Temple. They called this chest *gazophylacium* (which was a combination of Persian and Greek), because it protected the *gaza*;[187] and in Aramaic it was called *corbona*.[188] We are told about this in Second Kings 12: *And Joash said to the priests, All the money of the dedicated things that is brought into the house of the Lord, even the money of every one that passeth the account,*[189] *the money that every man is set at,*[190] *and all the money that cometh into any man's heart to bring into the house of the Lord, let the priests take it to them, every man of his acquaintance; and let them repair the breaches of the house, wheresoever any breach shall be found. But it was so, that in the three and twentieth year of King Joash the priests had not repaired the breaches of the house. Then King*

Joash called for Jehoiada the priest, and the other priests, and said unto them, Why repair ye not the breaches of the house? Now therefore receive no more money of your acquaintance, but deliver it for the breaches of the house. And the priests consented to receive no more money of the people, neither to repair the breaches of the house. But Jehoiada the priest took a chest, and bored a hole in the lid of it, and set it beside the altar, on the right side as one cometh into the house of the Lord; and the priests who kept the door put therein all the money that was brought into the house of the Lord. And it was so, when they saw that there was much money in the chest, that the king's scribe and the high priest came up, and they put up in bags, and told the money that was found in the house of the Lord. And they gave the money, being told, into the hands of them who did the work, who had the oversight of the house of the Lord...[191] We are told the same thing in Second Chronicles 23,[192] but in this case I will quote from the Greek version because it is somewhat clearer,[193] and yet it conveys the same sense as the Latin: *Joash summoned the priests and the Levites, and said to them, Go out into the cities of Judah, and collect money from all of Israel, so that the house of the Lord may be repaired in a few years; and announce this news as quickly as possible. But the Levites did not hurry to do it; so Joash summoned Jehoiada the high priest and said to him, Why did you not see to it that the Levites would collect from Judah and Jerusalem the money which Moses ordered them to pay, when he assembled all of Israel at the tent of meeting? Gotholia*[194] *was an outlaw, and her sons destroyed the house of God! Set up a chest, and put it outside the gate of the house of the Lord; and tell them to announce in Judah and Jerusalem: make your contributions to the Lord, as Moses told Israel in the desert. And all the princes gave, and all the people, and they collected the money and put it in the chest, until it was full; and they had the Levites bring the chest to the king's officials, who saw that it contained a great deal of money. And the king's scribe came, and the viceroy of the great priest, and they emptied the chest and put it back. They did this every day, and so amassed a great deal of money, which the king and Jehoiada the priest gave to the workers who were repairing the house of God.* Josephus also says the same thing, and with somewhat greater clarity. *King Joash*, he says, *was seized with a passion to repair the Temple; so he summoned Jehoiada the high priest, and ordered him to send Levites and priests to every region to collect a half-shekel of silver from everyone for the restoration of the Temple, which had apparently been ruined by Joram, Gotholia, and their sons. But the high priest did not do this, because he knew that no one was going to collect any money. So in the twenty-third year of his reign, Joash berated the high priest and the Levites for their negligence, and ordered them to see to the Temple's restoration in the coming year. Jehoiada then conceived a plan that won the people's favor: he made a wooden chest which he fortified all around, and put a hole in it. And after setting it up in the Temple next to the sanctuary, he instructed each person to put as much money as he wanted into the hole, for the repair of the Temple. Everyone contributed generously to this effort, and they put in a great deal of silver and gold. Afterward they emptied out the chest in the king's presence, while the scribe and the priests counted out all the silver that had been collected; then they put the chest back in the same place. They repeated this process every day.*[195] After the treasury had been set up, King Josiah again drew money from it in order to repair the Temple. It is written in Second Kings: *...King Josiah sent... the scribe to the house of the Lord... to Hilkiah the high priest, that he may sum the silver which is brought into the house of the Lord, which the keepers of the door have gathered of the people; and let them deliver it into the hand of the doers of the work, who have the oversight of the house of the Lord: and let them give it to the doers of the work which is in the house of the Lord, to repair the breaches of the house...*[196] This treasury was destroyed at the same time as the Temple, and it was also restored at the same time; but it was not merely a chest into which money was thrown, but rather a large storehouse which also held the first fruits and tithes of the Levites. As in Nehemiah 10: *And that we should bring the first fruits of... wine and of oil, unto the priests, to the chambers of the house of our God...*[197] And later on: *For the children of Israel and the children of Levi shall bring the offering of the corn, of the new wine, and the oil, unto the chambers...*[198] And then: *And before this, Eliashib the priest, having the oversight of the chamber of the house of our God... And he had prepared for him a great chamber, where aforetime they laid the meat offerings...*[199] And in Second Maccabees: Apollonius *told* Seleucus the king of Syria *that the treasury in Jerusalem was full of infinite sums of money, so that the multitude of their riches, which did not pertain to the account of the sacrifices, was innumerable...*[200] Hence we also read in St. Mark: *And Jesus sat over against the treasury, and beheld how the people cast money into the treasury...*[201] And in St. Luke: *And* Jesus *looked up, and saw the rich men casting their gifts into the treasury.*[202]

A guard was placed in charge of this treasury, whom Isaiah in chapter 22[203] calls *tamias tou hierou*,[204] i.e. the quaestor[205] of the Temple, although the Latin translator calls him "the overseer of the Temple." Josephus, meanwhile, calls him the "Temple treasurer"[206] in Book 18. The high priest's robe, he says, was kept under the seal of the Temple treasurer, who also kept the other ornaments of the Temple.[207] Likewise in Book 7 of the *War*: *They also burned the chests called the Temple treasuries, which contained a great deal of money and clothing... and practically all the wealth of the Jews was gathered there.*[208]

Likewise: *But even the Temple treasurer, i.e. the guardian of the sacred money, was seized, whose name was Phinehas; and he revealed the clothing and belts of the priests.*[209] This concludes my survey of the obligatory offerings.

CHAPTER 17

Votive and Voluntary Offerings

I SHOULD NOW DISCUSS the offerings, or sacrifices, or gifts that were either made to fulfill a vow or given voluntarily. About these we have Leviticus 7: *But if the sacrifice of his offering be a vow, or a voluntary offering...*[210] And chapter 23: *These are the feasts of the Lord, which ye shall proclaim to be holy convocations, to offer an offering made by fire unto the Lord, a burnt offering, and a meat offering, a sacrifice, and drink offerings, every thing upon his day. Beside the Sabbaths of the Lord, and beside your gifts, and beside all your vows, and beside all your freewill offerings, which ye give unto the* Lord.[211]

A "vow" is a thing someone has sworn to render to God in order to win his favor; and not to fulfill it was, God declared, a great crime. Deuteronomy 23: *When thou shalt vow a vow unto the Lord thy God, thou shalt not slack to pay it: for the Lord thy God will surely require it of thee; and it would be sin in thee.*[212] Philo explains this as follows in his work *The Sacrifice of Abel: A vow is a request from God for some sort of good; and he commands us that one whose request has been granted should without delay offer a crown to God... Among the people who fail to do this... there are those who have forgotten the benefits they have received and so absolve themselves of the need to give thanks; and others whose exceptional arrogance convinces them that they, and not God, are the authors of their good fortune... Still others do attribute their blessings to God, but think that they deserved to receive them.*[213]

The formula for taking a vow was as follows. Judges 11: *And he vowed a vow unto the Lord, and said, If thou shalt without fail deliver the children of Ammon into mine hands, then it shall be, that whatsoever cometh forth of the doors of my house to meet me... shall surely be the Lord's, and I will offer it up for a burnt offering.*[214] And in First Samuel: *And she vowed a vow, and said, O Lord... if thou wilt... give unto thine handmaid a man child, then I will give him unto the Lord all the days of his life, and there shall no razor come upon his head.*[215] And Second Samuel 8:[216] *For thy servant vowed a vow... saying, If the Lord shall bring me again indeed to Jerusalem, then I will serve the Lord.*

Someone who fulfilled his promise to God was said to have paid or repaid his vow; as in Leviticus 22: ...*that offereth his oblation, either paying his*
vows, or offering of his own accord.[217] And Second Samuel 8:[218] ...*let me go and*
repay my vow, which I have vowed unto the Lord, in Hebron. And Proverbs 7:
I have peace offerings with me; this day have I repaid my vows.[219]

There was also a law about making and discharging vows, which obligated
men as follows. In Numbers 30: *If a man vow a vow unto the Lord, or swear*
an oath to bind his soul with a bond; he shall not break his word; he shall do
according to all that proceedeth out of his mouth.[220] Whereas if a young woman
under her father's authority or a woman under that of her husband should
make an oath, and her father or husband said nothing, she was obliged to
fulfill it; whereas if he did object she was not. On the other hand, the law
meant for widows and divorced women to be bound by their oaths.

A person could, moreover, vow to God any souls or property that were
in his possession. In the case of a soul, he could buy back the vow;[221] but
in that of an animal, he could not substitute anything for his vow, and the
animal remained sacred to God.[222] If, on the other hand, he vowed his house,
he could redeem it by paying an increased price. Every such valuation was
made in shekels of the sanctuary,[223] and the shekel contained twenty obols.[224]
These and other such matters having to do with vows are discussed at great
length in the last chapter of Leviticus. There was one more type of vow—a
person could consecrate his very self to the Lord. (I will describe this when
I come to discuss the Nazirites.)

We know that vows, like other gifts, were brought to the Temple, from
what Jeremiah says in chapter 33: *The voice... of them who shall bring the*
vows into the house of the Lord...[225]

Voluntary offerings were different both from those that were made
to fulfill a vow and from those that were commanded by law, since they
came entirely from the free will of the giver. Hence Judges 12:[226] ...*All the*
money... that every man is set at, and all the money that cometh into any
man's heart to bring into the house of the Lord. And in the first chapter of
Ezra: ...*let the men of his place help him with silver, and with gold, and with*
goods, and with beasts, beside the freewill offering for the house of God that
is in Jerusalem.[227]

CHAPTER 18

Fasting and Other Punishments of the Body

JUST AS THEY would perform sacrifices or give offerings in order to placate God, they would also fast, cry, put on sackcloth, daub themselves with ashes, throw themselves to the ground, and seek out every possible means of debasing their bodies, all as a way of begging God's favor. Fasts could be either public or private: public fasts were imposed upon the entire nation, and private ones were taken on by individuals as their own consciences dictated. The public fasts were either regular—once a year according to the law—or were added ad hoc, as good judgment or circumstances dictated. Such fasts lasted for seven days, or for three, or until evening.[228] Private fasts were conducted for as long as each person saw fit.

The required and regular fast took place on the tenth day of September, on the Day of Atonement, and was the only fast required by God. This is why that day was called "the Fast" or "the Day of Fasting" (I have already spoken about this).

There is a reference to the special public fast in Second Chronicles 20: *And Jehoshaphat feared, and set himself to seek the Lord, and proclaimed a fast throughout all Judah.*[229] And in Jeremiah 36: *And it came to pass in the fifth year of Jehoiakim... king of Judah, in the ninth month, that they proclaimed a fast before the Lord to all the people in Jerusalem, and to all the people that came from the cities of Judah...*[230] And in the eighth chapter of Ezra: *Then I proclaimed a fast there, at the river of Ahava, that we might afflict ourselves before our God, to seek of him a right way for us...*[231] There is also a very noteworthy mention of a public fast in the fourth chapter of Judith: *And all the people cried to the Lord with great earnestness, and they humbled their souls in fastings, and prayers, both they and their wives. And the priests put on haircloths, and they caused the little children to lie prostrate before the Temple of the Lord... Then Eliakim the high priest of the Lord went about all Israel and spoke to them, saying, Know ye that the Lord will hear your prayers, if you continue with perseverance in fastings and prayers in the sight of the Lord... So they, being moved by this exhortation of his, prayed to the Lord, and continued in the sight of the Lord. So that even they who offered the holocausts to the Lord, offered the sacrifices to the Lord girded with haircloths, and with ashes upon their head. And they all begged of God with all their heart, that he would visit his people Israel.*[232] Likewise in Judges 20: *Then all the children of Israel, and all the people, went up, and came unto the house of God, and wept, and sat there before the Lord, and fasted that day until even, and offered burnt offerings and peace offerings...*[233] And in First Samuel 7: *Gather all Israel to Mizpeh, and I will pray for you unto the Lord. And they gathered together to Mizpeh, and drew water, and poured it out before the Lord, and fasted on that day, and said there, We have sinned against the Lord...*[234] And in the third chapter of First Maccabees: *Wherefore the Israelites assembled themselves together, and came to Mizpeh, over against Jerusalem; for in Mizpeh was the place where they prayed aforetime in Israel. Then they fasted that day, and put on sackcloth, and cast ashes upon their heads, and rent their clothes.*[235] And in Second Maccabees 13: *So when they had... besought the merciful Lord with weeping and fasting, and lying flat upon the ground three days long, Judas, having exhorted them, commanded they should be in a readiness.*[236]

We can deduce the procedure for a private fast from the following passages. The Book of Numbers chapter 30: *Every vow* of a wife, *and every binding oath to afflict the soul through fasting or abstinence from other things, her husband may establish it, or her husband may make it void.*[237] And Second Samuel 12: *David therefore besought God for the child; and David fasted, and went in, and lay all night upon the earth.*[238] Hence David himself said in chapter 12: *...While the child was yet alive, I fasted and wept: for I said, Who can tell whether God will be gracious to me, that the child may live?*[239] And in First Kings 26:[240] *And it came to pass, when Ahab heard those words, that he rent his clothes, and put sackcloth upon his flesh, and fasted, and lay in sackcloth, and went softly.* And in the first chapter of Second Esdras:[241] *And it came to pass, when I heard these words, that I sat down and wept, and mourned certain days, and fasted, and prayed before the God of heaven.*[242] And in the fifth chapter of the Fourth Book of Esdras: *If you have prayed and cried out once again, and fasted seven days, then you will hear things even greater than these.*[243] And in the Book of Judith chapter 8: *And* Judith *made herself a private chamber in the upper part of her house, in which she abode shut up with her maids. And she wore haircloth upon her loins, and fasted all the days of her life, except the Sabbaths, and new moons, and the feasts of the house of Israel.*[244]

Since, then, this was the way the Jews practiced their fasts, it should be obvious why the Pharisees—who wanted to seem more devout than anyone else—embraced fasting so zealously that they practiced it twice a week (as we know from St. Luke)[245] and were astonished that the disciples of Christ did not do the same. But Christ himself approved of fasting, which is clear from the fact that he fasted in the same way as Moses and Elijah;[246] and he explained how people ought to fast: *Moreover when ye fast, be not, as the hypocrites, of a sad countenance; for they disfigure their faces, that they may appear unto men to fast.*[247]

Just as God took more pleasure in offerings of justice and praise than he did in animal sacrifice and blood, he also had more regard for justice and charity than for fasting; and in general, he cared more for trials of the heart than for those of the body. The Book of Isaiah chapter 63[248] makes this point: *Is it such a fast that I have chosen, a day for a man to afflict his soul? Is it to bow down his head as a bulrush, and to spread sackcloth and ashes under him? Wilt thou call this a fast, and a day acceptable to the Lord? Is not this the fast that I have chosen: to loose the bands of wickedness, to undo the heavy burdens, and to let the oppressed go free, and that ye break every yoke? Is it not to deal thy bread to the hungry, and that thou bring the poor that are cast out to thy house? When thou seest the naked, that thou cover him; and that thou hide not thyself from thine own flesh?* Joel says the same thing: *Therefore also now, saith the Lord, turn ye even to me with all your heart, and with fasting, and with weeping, and with mourning. And rend your heart, and not your garments...*[249] These statements were of course directed at Jews who embraced fasting more eagerly than charity, and did without food more readily than they turned away from sin. This is what I have to say about the sacred rites.

BOOK V

Sacred People

CHAPTER 1

Types of Sacred People

LEAD ME IN THY *truth, Lord, and teach me. I will declare thy name unto my brethren.*[1] For what is your name, if not that which is called upon by the people you have summoned to perform your service? It is these people whom I will now discuss. After all, now that I have considered the sacred places, days, and rites, it remains only to consider the people who performed and looked after these places, days, and rites, and the ceremonies in general. Moreover, I use the term "sacred persons" here to refer to those who spent their lives in divine service, or in some way explained the will of God and his laws. These were the high priests, the priests, the Levites, the singers, the porters, and the *nethinim*, as well as the Nazareans, the prophets, and the scribes (together with their sects).[2] Along with explaining the duties of these officials I will set out the responsibilities of the tribe of Levi, which differed from those of the other tribes: the Levites administered the faith, and the others the republic itself. For as it is written in the third chapter of Numbers, God took the Levites to himself instead of the firstborn of the Hebrews, whom he had already set apart at the moment when he struck down the firstborn of Egypt.[3] Though God made it the Levites' fate to be deprived of land, he bestowed on them every other possible reward and honor: he gave them a share in everything that was offered to him by a grateful humanity and made it their special privilege to look after God's worship. As God said when he spoke to Aaron, in Numbers 18: …*Thou shalt have no inheritance in their land, neither shalt thou have any part among them: I am thy part and thine inheritance among the children of Israel. And, behold, I have given the children of Levi all the tenth in Israel for an inheritance, for their service which they serve, even the service of the tabernacle of the congregation.*[4] Let us begin, then, with the high priests.

CHAPTER 2

High Priests

JUST AS THE PEOPLE called priests were in charge of all the sacred rites, so among all these priests one was superior, the one called "high priest." In the holy books this man is therefore called not only "priest," but "first priest," "great priest," and "chief of priests," or (in the Latin manner) "pontiff."[5] Once this office had been established, the others were called simply "priests" and "second priests," or "of the second rank." As in Second Kings 24:[6] *And the king commanded Hilkiah the high priest, and the priests of the second order, and the keepers of the door...* And Judith chapter 4: *Eliakim the great priest of the Lord.*[7] And Nehemiah 3: *Eliashib the great priest...*[8] And Second Kings 25: *And the captain of the guard took Seraiah the chief priest, and Zephaniah the second priest...*[9] This is correct—Seraiah served as high priest, and Zephaniah as a regular priest. If, then, the functions of the high priest carried so much weight in sacred matters that he was ranked above all the others, it stands to reason that by giving a clear description of his office we can also lay the essential foundations for a proper understanding of the priesthood as a whole. I would therefore like to discuss the high priest; but first I would like to point out to the reader that God appointed as high priest Aaron the brother of Moses from the tribe of Levi, and yet made his sons regular priests. From this we are to understand that what the Bible tells us about Aaron refers specifically to the high priest, and about his sons to the other priests. Moreover, I am going to follow the same order in which God (after explaining the tabernacle in Exodus 28) gives his instructions for the high priest—his clothing, his consecration, the conditions imposed upon him, and finally his duties.

The high priest had eight garments: the ephod,[10] the breastplate,[11] the blue robe,[12] the tight linen coat,[13] the linen breeches,[14] the girdle,[15] the mitre,[16] and the gold plate.[17] God ordered Moses to dress Aaron in these garments after he was made high priest. In this case too I have no hesitations about first repeating the words of the law, and then illustrating them with quotes from outside authors.[18] God's instructions for the ephod are as follows: *And they shall make the ephod of gold, of blue, and of purple, of scarlet, and fine twined linen, with cunning work. It shall have the two shoulderpieces thereof joined at the two edges thereof; and so it shall be joined together...* And thou shalt take two onyx stones, and grave on them the names of the children of Israel: Six of their names on one stone, and the other six names of the rest on the other stone, according to their birth.[19] Then he describes the breastplate in this way: *And thou shalt make the breastplate of judgment with cunning work; after the work of the ephod thou shalt make it; of gold, of blue, and of purple, and of scarlet, and of fine twined linen, shalt thou make it. Foursquare it shall be doubled; a span shall be the length thereof, and a span shall be the breadth thereof. And thou shalt set in it settings of stones, even four rows of stones: the first row shall be a sardius, a topaz, and a carbuncle: this shall be the first row. And the second row shall be an emerald, a sapphire, and a diamond. And the third row a ligure, an agate, and an amethyst. And the fourth row a beryl, an onyx, and a jasper: they shall be set in gold in their inclosings. And the stones shall be with the names of the children of Israel, twelve, according to their names, like the engravings of a signet; every one with his name shall they be, according to the twelve tribes... And Aaron shall bear the names of the children of Israel in the breastplate of judgment upon his heart, when he goeth in unto the holy place, for a memorial before the Lord... and Aaron shall bear the judgment of the children of Israel upon his heart before the Lord continually.*[20] Then the blue robe is described as follows: *And thou shalt make the robe of the ephod all of blue. And there shall be a hole in the top of it, in the midst thereof: it shall have a binding of woven work round about the hole of it, as it were the hole of a habergeon, that it be not rent. And beneath upon the hem of it thou shalt make pomegranates of blue, and of purple, and of scarlet, round about the hem thereof; and bells of gold between them round about. A golden bell and a pomegranate... upon the hem of the robe round about. And it shall be upon Aaron to minister; and his sound shall be heard when he goeth in unto the holy place before the Lord, and when he cometh out, that he die not.*[21] Then God adds a bit about the tight linen coat and the other garments: *And thou shalt embroider the coat of fine linen, and thou shalt make the mitre of fine linen, and thou shalt make the girdle of needlework.*[22] *And thou shalt make a plate of pure gold, and grave upon it, like the engravings of a signet, HOLINESS TO THE LORD. And thou shalt put it on a blue lace, that it may be upon the mitre; upon the forefront of the mitre it shall be. And it shall be upon Aaron's forehead, that Aaron may bear the iniquity of the holy things, which the children of Israel shall hallow in all their holy gifts; and it shall be always upon his forehead, that they may be accepted before the Lord.*[23] Finally the breeches are mentioned, in these words:

And thou shalt make them linen breeches to cover their nakedness; from the loins even unto the thighs they shall reach. And they shall be upon Aaron, and upon his sons, when they come in unto the tabernacle of the congregation, or when they come near unto the altar to minister in the holy place; that they bear not iniquity, and die...[24] These are the instructions given in Exodus, but the same information is given in Leviticus 8 as follows: *And Moses put upon* Aaron *the coat, and girded him with the girdle, and clothed him with the robe, and put the ephod upon him, and he girded him with the curious girdle of the ephod, and bound it unto him therewith. And he put the breastplate upon him; also he put in the breastplate the Urim and the Thummin. And he put the mitre upon his head; also upon the mitre, even upon his forefront, did he put the golden plate, the holy crown; as the Lord commanded Moses.*[25] This is what is contained in the law.

Josephus, who lived in the time of the Temple, gives a very clear explanation of just what these garments looked like,[26] and St. Jerome borrowed this description in Letter 128,[27] which I would like to include here for the sake of clarifying matters: *The linen breeches, which reach to the knee, cover the privates; while the upper part is tightly cinched under the navel, so that when they are about to slaughter the animals, and are dragging the bulls and rams and carrying their loads, what is hidden will not be exposed, even if they should slip in the course of carrying out their duties and uncover their thighs,... Josephus tells us... that these breeches used to be woven of twisted linen which was then cut and sewn together, since a garment of this sort could not be made on a loom.*[28]

The second linen robe reaches to the ankles, and is made of a double muslin; Josephus also calls it 'byssus'...[29] because in Hebrew it is given as "linen."[30] *This clings to the body so tightly, and has such narrow sleeves, that it has no creases at all; and it reaches to the legs.*[31] One might call it a common undergarment.

The third kind of garment... is a belt or girdle or zona...[32] *This looks like the skin of a snake that has shed its scales;*[33] *and its shape is so rounded that you might take it for an unusually long sort of pouch. It also has attached to it an underlayer of scarlet, purple, and blue, and into it is woven* byssus *for beauty and strength. And it has been embellished with all sorts of colors in such a way that you might imagine its various flowers and gems to have been attached to it, rather than woven in by the hand of a craftsman. They use this girdle to tie up the linen robe, about which I have spoken, between the navel and the chest; it is four inches wide and at one end it hangs down to the legs. If the priests need to perform the sacrifices in a hurry, they can toss it back over their left shoulders.*

The fourth type of garment is a round cap... as though a sphere were divided in two and one half placed on the head. Both we and the Greeks call this a 'tiara'...[34] *It does not come to a point, nor does it cover the head all the way to the hairline; it leaves a third of the front uncovered. But the band is tied around the back of the head in such a way that it will slip off only with difficulty. It is, moreover, made of* byssus, *and covered with a piece of linen so cleverly that from the outside there is no sign of stitching. These four garments—that is, the breeches, the linen robe, the girdle... and the cap—are worn by both the high priests and the other priests. The other four are particular to the high priest.*

One of these four is *the ankle-length robe entirely of blue, to which sleeves of the same color are attached at the sides. To the upper opening which went over the neck (and which is commonly called the 'capitium')*[35] *is woven a very strong border, so that it will not fray. On the bottom part, i.e. at the feet, are seventy bells and pomegranates, woven with the same colors as the aforementioned girdle. Between every two bells is a pomegranate, and between every two pomegranates a bell, in such a way that they alternate one with the other...*

The sixth garment, which is called in Hebrew 'ephod'... that is, above the shoulders... belongs to the high priests alone; *it is woven from blue, byssus, scarlet, purple, and gold... On it are strung remarkably fine plates of gold... from which are twisted cut threads with an underlayer of three colors—blue, scarlet, and purple—and with linen stitching, and the result is a cloak of astonishing beauty whose brilliance transfixes the eye like a* caracalla,[36] *but without a hood. The area of the chest is left open, to provide a space for the* choshen. *On both shoulders it has a stone which has been enclosed and bound with gold.* The translators have rendered them as onyxes or emeralds...[37] *while Josephus calls them sardonyxes... On each of the stones are six of the patriarchs' names according to which the people of Israel was divided up; on the right shoulder appear Jacob's older sons, and on the left his younger. So when the high priest enters the holy of holies, he carries on his shoulders the names of the people for whom he is asking the Lord's favor.*

The seventh... is called Rational...[38] *It is a short shirt made from gold*[39] *and woven with the same four colors as the 'ephod,' and it measures a handbreadth on all sides. It is woven double to give it strength; for worked into it are twelve stones of enormous size and value, arranged in four rows, so that each column contains three stones. In the first row are a sard, a topaz, and an emerald... in the second, a carbuncle, a sapphire, and a jasper; in the third, a ligure,*[40] *an agate, and an amethyst; and in the fourth, a chrysolite, an onyx, and a beryl. I do wonder why it is that the jacinth (which is the most precious of gemstones) is not included among the others, unless perhaps it is the stone called here ligure...*[41] *On each of the stones is carved one of the names of the twelve tribes, arranged according to age... At the four corners of the Rational are four gold rings, which match up with the four on the* ephod, *so that when the Rational has been fitted to the space which we said was left open in the* ephod *the rings fit together, and are tied to each other with blue threads. And to keep the size and weight of the stones from overwhelming the stitching, they are tied and enclosed by gold. But even this would not be enough to support them if there were not also gold chains—which for the sake of appearance are placed within gold tubes—as well as two larger rings on the top part of the Rational, which were tied to the gold hooks of the* ephod, *and another two at the bottom. For on the back side of the* ephod, *opposite the chest and the stomach, there were gold rings on each side, which were joined to the lower rings of the Rational by means of chains. This was done so as to draw the Rational tightly to the* ephod *and the* ephod *to the Rational, so that they should appear to the eye to be of one piece.*

The eighth is a gold plate... on which is written in four Hebrew letters... the name of God, *which among the Hebrews is not to be pronounced. Though the high priest wears the same linen cap as all the priests, this plate is placed above it and tied in the front by a blue cord, and the name of God crowns and protects all the beauty of the high priest.* This is St. Jerome's account of Josephus.

On the other hand, Jerome neglects to mention some of Josephus' other comments, for example, about the stones of the *ephod* and the breastplate, and about the blue cap. He writes about the stones as follows: *The stones that the high priest wore upon his shoulders were sardonyxes; and whenever God was present at the sacrifices, the stone on his right shoulder would sparkle and give off such a shine that it could be seen even at a great distance, though this stone did not otherwise give off any light... It was, moreover, through the twelve stones of the breastplate that God declared whether a coming battle would be won; for even before the army had set out, they would shine with such splendor that everyone could see that God was on their side... But the breastplate and the sardonyxes ceased to function two hundred years before I wrote this book, because God was angered by the violations of his laws.*[42] (If we reconstruct the chronology of ancient times, this would have happened in the time of King John Hyrcanus.)[43] About the cap he says as follows: *Besides the cap worn by all the priests, the high priest had another cap sewn with various shades of blue. This was surrounded by a gold crown which was divided into three rows, which was surmounted in the middle by a gold cup in the shape of a herb... which the Greeks... call* hyoscyamus.[44] The talmudists likewise report that the stones of the breastplate had ceased to shine, but they say this had already happened when the Second Temple was built. So much for the garments.

The high priest's consecration took place over seven days, and was accomplished as follows. The priest who was to be consecrated was first brought to the altar, then washed with water, and then dressed in the garments I have described. Then the holy oil was poured on his head, and finally he was consecrated by a special sacrifice, and the blood of the offering was sprinkled on the altar and on his clothing. God gives these instructions in Exodus 29: *And this is the thing that thou shalt do unto them to hallow them, to minister unto me in the priest's office... when thou hast washed* Aaron *and his sons with water, thou shalt take the garments, and put upon* him *the coat, and the robe of the ephod, and the ephod, and the breastplate, and gird him with the curious girdle of the ephod; and thou shalt put the mitre upon his head, and put the holy crown upon the mitre... and thou shalt consecrate Aaron and his sons... And thou shalt cause a bullock to be brought before the tabernacle of the congregation,* etc.[45] The instructions given in Exodus are repeated in full in Leviticus chapter 8, namely, that Aaron was brought to the altar, washed, clothed, and anointed: *...and the assembly was gathered together* by Moses *unto the door of the tabernacle of the congregation...* he *brought Aaron... and washed* him *with water. And he put upon him the coat, and girded him with the girdle, and clothed him with the robe, and put the ephod upon him, and he girded him with the curious girdle of the ephod, and bound it unto him therewith. And he put the breastplate upon him; also he put in the breastplate the Urim and the Thummim. And he put the mitre upon his head; also upon the mitre, even upon his forefront, did he put the golden plate, the holy crown... And Moses took the anointing oil, and anointed the tabernacle and all that was therein, and sanctified them. And he sprinkled thereof upon the altar seven times, and anointed the altar and all his vessels, both the laver and his foot, to sanctify them. And he poured of the anointing oil upon Aaron's head, and anointed him, to sanctify him.*[46] Finally he brings the sacred offering of consecration. This is how God ordered the offering to be performed: *And he brought the bullock for the sin offering; and Aaron and his sons laid their hands upon the head of the bullock for the sin offering. And he slew it; and Moses took the blood, and put it upon the horns of the altar round about with his finger, and purified the altar, and poured the blood at the bottom of the altar, and sanctified it, to make reconciliation upon it. And he took all the fat that was upon the inwards, and the caul above the liver, and the two kidneys, and their fat, and Moses burned it upon the altar. But the bullock, and his hide, his flesh, and his dung, he burnt with fire without the camp... And he brought the ram for the burnt offering; and Aaron... laid* his *hands upon the* *head of the ram. And he killed it; and Moses sprinkled the blood upon the altar round about. And he cut the ram into pieces; and Moses burnt the head, and the pieces, and the fat. And he washed the inwards and the legs in water; and Moses burnt the whole ram upon the altar: it was a burnt sacrifice for a sweet savor, and an offering made by fire unto the Lord; as the Lord commanded Moses. And he brought the other ram, the ram of consecration; and Aaron... laid his hands upon the head of the ram. And he slew it; and Moses took of the blood of it, and put it upon the tip of Aaron's right ear, and upon the thumb of his right hand, and upon the great toe of his right foot... and Moses sprinkled the blood upon the altar round about. And he took the fat, and the rump, and all the fat that was upon the inwards, and the caul above the liver, and the two kidneys, and their fat, and the right shoulder. And out of the basket of unleavened bread, which was before the Lord, he took one unleavened cake, and a cake of oiled bread, and one wafer, and put them on the fat, and upon the right shoulder. And he put all upon Aaron's hands... and waved them for a wave offering before the Lord. And Moses took them from off their hands, and burnt them on the altar upon the burnt offering; they were consecrations for a sweet savor: it is an offering made by fire unto the Lord. And Moses took the breast, and waved it for a wave offering before the Lord; for of the ram of consecration it was Moses' part... And Moses took of the anointing oil, and of the blood which was upon the altar, and sprinkled it upon Aaron, and upon his garments... And Moses said unto Aaron... Boil the flesh at the door of the tabernacle of the congregation; and there eat it with the bread that is in the basket of consecrations, as I commanded, saying, Aaron and his sons shall eat it. And that which remaineth of the flesh and of the bread shall ye burn with fire. And ye shall not go out of the door of the tabernacle of the congregation for seven days, until the days of your consecration be at an end: for seven days shall he consecrate you. As he hath done this day...*[47] Philo has described this as follows in the third book of his *Life of Moses: After Moses dressed the priests in their sacred garments, he took very fragrant sweet ointment made by the perfumer's art, and with this he sprinkled first the outdoor apparatus—the altar and the basin—seven times, and then the tabernacle and each of the sacred vessels: the ark, the candelabrum, the incense altar, the table, the goblets, the bowls, and the other sacrificial implements. Finally he brought in the high priest and anointed him, pouring a great deal of the sacred ointment over his head. When he had done all this according to the law, he ordered a calf and two rams to be brought. The calf he would offer as an atonement for sins, to indicate that however good a person may be when he is born, the very fact of his birth makes him sinful; meaning that we must placate God with prayer and sacrifice, so that he will not be provoked to anger. There was also one ram which was offered whole to the maker of all things, because of whose kindness every person enjoys as much of the various elements as is appropriate to him... The other ram was to bring about the complete purification of those who were being sanctified; and it was quite rightly called the ram of consecration, because it was through this offering that the priests of God were initiated. Moses poured some of the blood around the altar, and the rest he caught up in a saucer, and with it he daubed three of the initiates' limbs—the tip of the earlobe, the tip of the hand, and the tip of the foot... This symbolizes the idea that the perfect man should be pure in his speech, his actions, and his entire life; for the ear refers to speech, the hand to action, and the foot to the course of one's entire life... Then he took from the material that had been poured around the altar—from the ointment and all the offerings—mixed it together, and sprinkled the priests with it; this was because he wanted them to have a share not only in that purity which was external and of the open air but also of that which was internal, since they were going to be making offerings within the sanctuary, where everything had been anointed with the sacred ointment. After some other animals had been slaughtered as well, both for the priests and for the elders and the entire people, Moses led his brother into the tabernacle. For this was the eighth day of the consecration and the last of this festival; the previous seven days had been devoted to the initiation of his brother and his nephews.*[48]

Some of the conditions imposed on the high priesthood could keep a man from the position, and others would bind him tightly, so to speak, once he had assumed the office. The first set is spelled out in Leviticus 21: *And he who is the high priest among his brethren, upon whose head the anointing oil was poured, and who is consecrated to put on the garments...* shall not be lame, or feeble, or blind, or limping, or have a blemish, or a white spot in the eye, or any other bodily flaw.[49] Hence Philo wrote about the sacrifices: *No priest is allowed to sacrifice unless he is whole—he may not have even the slightest blemish.*[50] And as Josephus tells us, when King Aristobulus took away the priesthood of his brother Hyrcanus, he cut off his nose—by mutilating his brother's body, he took away his hopes of recovering his office, and even his ability to do so. The second set of conditions is as follows: *...he shall not uncover his head, nor rend his clothes;*[51] *neither shall he go in to any dead body, nor defile himself for his father, or for his mother; neither shall he go out of the sanctuary, nor profane the sanctuary of his God; for the crown of the anointing oil of his God is upon him: I am the Lord. And he shall take a wife in her virginity. A widow, or a divorced woman, or profane, or a harlot, these shall he not take; but he shall take a virgin of his own people to wife. Neither* *shall he profane his seed among his people.*[52] In his book *On Monarchy*,[53] Philo says as follows about these conditions: *Since it is ultimately a mortal man who is chosen to become priest, he will not lose the desire to couple; so for a wife they find him a chaste virgin born to holy parents... He is not allowed even to look at a harlot—whose soul is as impure as her body—even if she has left her profession and turned over a new leaf, because of the corrupt way of life she once practiced.*

Finally, the duties which the law assigns to the high priest were as follows: he was to go into the tabernacle every day to light the lamps; enter the sanctuary to light the incense on the altar; set up the showbread every week and keep the old loaves for himself; and perform the people's offerings on festival days together with the priests. And once a year, on the Day of Atonement, he was to put on the sacred garments, go into the sanctuary where the incense altar was, cleanse the people of its stains and sins, and offer prayers for himself, his house, and the entire people.

On the candelabrum there is Leviticus 24: *Command the children of Israel, that they bring unto thee pure olive oil beaten for the light, to cause the lamps to burn continually. Without the veil of the testimony, in the tabernacle of the congregation, shall Aaron order it from the evening unto the morning before the Lord continually: it shall be a statute for ever in your generations. He shall order the lamps upon the pure candlestick before the Lord continually.*[54] Hence it is written in Second Chronicles 12:[55] *...and the candlestick of gold with the lamps thereof, to burn every evening.* And in the first chapter of Second Maccabees: *...we offered also sacrifices and fine flour, and lighted the lamps, and set forth the loaves.*[56]

On the subject of burning the incense, I would add the following passages to what I said before. In the second chapter of First Samuel: *And did I choose Aaron out of all the tribes of Israel to be my priest, to offer upon mine altar, to burn incense, to wear an ephod before me?*[57] In the sixth chapter of First Chronicles: *But Aaron and his sons offered incense upon the altar of the burnt offering, and on the altar of incense, and were appointed for all the work of the place most holy, and to make an atonement for Israel, according to all that Moses... commanded.*[58] And in chapter 26:[59] *...and Aaron was separated, that he should sanctify the most holy things, he and his sons for ever, to burn incense before the Lord, to minister unto him, and to bless in his name for ever.*

On the showbread, Leviticus 24: *And thou shalt take fine flour, and bake twelve cakes thereof: two tenth deals shall be in one cake. And thou shalt set them in two rows, six in a row, upon the pure table before the Lord. And thou shalt put pure frankincense upon each row, that it may be on the bread for a memorial, even an offering made by fire unto the Lord. Every Sabbath he shall set it in order before the Lord continually, being taken from the children of Israel by an everlasting covenant. And it shall be Aaron's and his sons'; and they shall eat it in the holy place: for it is most holy unto him of the offerings of the Lord made by fire by a perpetual statute.*[60] On the same subject First Samuel 21 has: *And* Ahimelech *the priest answered* David, who was asking him for bread, *and said, There is no common bread under mine hand, but there is hallowed bread... So the priest gave him hallowed bread; for there was no bread there but the showbread, which was taken from before the Lord, to put hot bread on the day when it was taken away.*[61] Hence St. Matthew wrote in chapter 12: *But he said unto* the Pharisees, *Have ye not read what David did, when he was a hungered, and they who were with him; how he entered into the house of God, and did eat the showbread, which was not lawful for him to eat, neither for them who were with him, but only for the priests?*[62] And in the first chapter of Second Maccabees: *...and lighted the lamps, and set forth the loaves.*[63] And in First Chronicles 9: *...of the sons of the Kohathites, were over the showbread, to prepare it every Sabbath.*[64]

In Book 6 of his *War*,[65] Josephus includes an account of the sacrifices that were to be offered on festival days, which adds to the passages I have already quoted from the law about the various offerings and festivals: *The high priest, together with the other priests, would also go up to the Temple on the seventh day, and on the new moon, and on the annual festivals of the people; and he would sacrifice girded in a garment that reached to his privates. Beneath it was a linen garment that reached to the feet, and above it a round blue garment from which hung fringes, at the ends of which were, on alternating knots, golden bells and pomegranates.*

Since I already discussed the offering of expiation when I discussed the Day of Atonement, I would like to repeat from that chapter the passage from Leviticus 16: *...Speak unto Aaron... that he come not at all times into the holy place within the veil before the mercy seat, which is upon the ark; that he die not... Thus shall Aaron come into the holy place: with a young bullock for a sin offering, and a ram for a burnt offering. He shall put on the holy linen coat, and he shall have the linen breeches upon his flesh, and shall be girded with a linen girdle, and with the linen mitre shall he be attired... And he shall take of the congregation of the children of Israel two kids of the goats for a sin offering, and one ram for a burnt offering. And Aaron shall offer his bullock of the sin offering, which is for himself, and make an atonement for himself, and for his house. And he shall take the two goats, and present them before the Lord at the door of the tabernacle of the congregation. And Aaron shall cast lots upon the two goats; one lot for the Lord, and the other lot for the scapegoat. And Aaron shall bring the goat upon which the Lord's lot fell,* *and offer him for a sin offering.*[66] The rest of the passage is a long description of the bullock and the goats which were to be sacrificed in order to atone for sins. (Whoever wishes to learn about this may, as I said, return to the previous passage.) The high priest performed this sacrifice once a year, and he went into the holy of holies alone. He is instructed in Exodus 30: *And Aaron shall make an atonement upon the horns of* the incense altar *once a year with the blood of the sin offering of atonements; once a year shall he make atonement upon it throughout your generations...*[67] St. Paul refers to the same thing in Hebrews chapter 9: *the priests went always into the first tabernacle, accomplishing the service of God. But into the second went the high priest alone once every year, not without blood...*[68] Philo, moreover, states in his *Embassy to Gaius: The high priest entered the sanctuary once a year at the time of the fast, and only in order to light the incense and offer the customary prayer that everyone should have a happy and peaceful year. Anyone else who entered it would pay with his life, with no chance of reprieve. I am not referring solely to Jewish commoners—this law applied even to the priest next in rank to the high priest, or to the high priest himself should he go in twice in the year, or three or four times on the same day. The lawgiver wanted the sanctuary to be so feared that it alone was kept unentered and untouched.*[69] And in the second chapter of his *On Monarchy:*[70] *No one is allowed to see the interior of the Temple except the high priest, and even he is allowed in only once, on the same day of the year, when he sees everything. He carries in the incense, and a censer of burning coals; and there he blows a great deal upon the coals, and the room is filled with smoke, so that his vision is hampered and he cannot see very far.* Likewise Josephus in the sixth book of the *War:*[71] *The high priest used the ephod and the breastplate only when he entered the holy of holies, which he did alone once a year on the day when it was customary to fast.* And in the second chapter of *Against Apion: The Temple was surrounded by four porches, on each of which the law placed its own particular restrictions.*[72] *Everyone was permitted to enter the outer one, including foreigners; only menstruating women were kept out. Into the second porch could come men*[73] *with their wives, if they were pure. Into the third came men who were pure or had been made pure.*[74] *Into the fourth came the priests wearing their priestly garments, while the sanctuary was entered only by the high priests, wearing their own special garments.*[75] St. Augustine interprets Josephus' statement that the high priest alone entered the sanctuary once a year to mean that though he did in fact go in every day for the sake of the incense, only once a year did he go in to perform the expiation with the blood of the sacrifice. But we might also say that while he entered the sanctuary every day, it was in the company of a group of priests, while once a year (on the Day of Atonement) he went in alone, that is, without the priests.[76] For Leviticus 16 says: *And there shall be no man in the tabernacle of the congregation when he goeth in to make an atonement in the holy place, until he come out, and have made an atonement for himself, and for his household, and for all the congregation of Israel.*[77] So much for the topics I set out to discuss: the high priests' garments, their consecration, the conditions placed upon them, and their duties. Now let us look at the method of their selection.

This honor was first given to Aaron at God's command, so that it would remain among his descendants forever. God gave this order in Exodus 28: *...it shall be a statute for ever unto Aaron and his seed after him.*[78] And then: *And the holy garments of Aaron shall be his sons' after him, to be anointed therein, and to be consecrated in them. And that son who is priest in his stead shall put them on seven days, when he cometh into the tabernacle of the congregation to minister in the holy place.*[79] And in First Chronicles 26:[80] *...and Aaron was separated, that he should sanctify the most holy things, he and his sons for ever, to burn incense before the Lord, to minister unto him, and to bless in his name for ever.* So when Aaron died, the high priesthood passed to his son Eleazar. From then on the descendants of Eleazar received this office, the sons succeeding their fathers. This is why God said to Phinehas the son of Eleazar: *And he shall have it, and his seed after him, even the covenant of an everlasting priesthood...*[81] The third in line to receive it were the descendants of Ithamar, who was the brother of Eleazar.[82] Then after several years it returned to the line of Eleazar,[83] where it remained until the time of the Syrian kings, after the return from Babylonia. By that time the system had collapsed, and the high priesthood was being awarded by kings as a favor to families which, though they were Levitical, were not directly descended from Aaron. The first of these kings were the Syrians, the second were the proselyte kings of the Jews,[84] and the third were the Roman governors who ruled the province of Syria and Judea. Moreover, the high priesthood had been so continuously uninterrupted that every occupant held his office until the end of his life; but then the Greek kings started to give it out as they saw fit, for several years at a time. I would add that in the period before the exile, the high priests had taken such good care of the sacred rites at the same time as the kings were in charge of governing the state that (according to Josephus) when the Jews were restored to their homeland, they entrusted to high priests both the sacred rites and the administration of the state. When, therefore, the family of the Hasmoneans, from the tribe of Levi, gained complete control of the nation a short while later, they took over not just the princeship[85] but the high priesthood as well, and then they converted this princeship into a monarchy, which made them both high priests and kings. After they were removed, the divine plan finally brought forth the birth of Jesus Christ, who would forever be both king and high priest of the Jews. For "Christ" means *anointed*, the term used to describe both kings and high priests. Hence St. Paul said in Hebrews 6: *...Jesus, made a high priest for ever after the order of Melchizedek.*[86] Here, then, are the names and the order of the high priests:

AARON, son of Amram, grandson of Kehat, and great-grandson of Levi. The first high priest, invested by his brother, Moses, and consecrated in the Sinai Desert. (Exodus 28, Leviticus 8.)

ELEAZAR, son of Aaron. At God's command, succeeded his father upon his death. (Numbers 20, Joshua 14.) Died after Joshua. (Joshua 24.)

PHINEHAS, son of Eleazar. About him it is written in Numbers 25: *And the Lord spake... Behold, I give unto Phinehas my covenant of peace. And he shall have it, and his seed after him, even the covenant of an everlasting priesthood; because he was zealous for his God...*[87] Joshua 22; Judges 20, where it is written: *...for the ark of the covenant of God was there in those days, and Phinehas, the son of Eleazar, the son of Aaron, stood before it in those days.*[88] It is clear from this that he lived until the time of Samson the Judge. Likewise in the second chapter of First Maccabees: *Phinehas our father in being zealous and fervent obtained the covenant of an everlasting priesthood.*[89]

ABISHUA, son of Phinehas.

BUKKI, son of Abishua.

UZZI, son of Bukki.

Josephus is the only one to mention these high priests, in the last chapter of Book 5 of his *Antiquities*; the scripture passes over them and jumps from the age of Phinehas to the time of Eli.[90]

ELI, descended from the line of Ithamar son of Aaron.[91] (First Samuel; Josephus, Book 8.)[92]

AHITUB, son of Phinehas, grandson of Eli. (First Samuel 14; Josephus, Book 8.)[93]

AHIMELECH, son of Ahitub. Killed by King Saul for taking in David. (First Samuel 21–22; Josephus, Book 8.)[94]

ABIATHAR, after the murder of his father Ahimelech. (First Samuel 23 and 30; Josephus, Book 8;[95] St. Mark, chapter 2.)

ZADOK, son of Ahitub, grandson of Amariah, great-grandson of Meraioth, great-great-grandson of Seraiah, great-great-great-grandson of Uzzi the high priest. After the death of Ahimelech he was high priest together with Abiathar, and both were present when the ark was brought back under King David. He was in charge of the tabernacle at Shiloh. (Second Samuel 15, 17, 19; First Kings 1.) Then later on he served alone, after King Solomon killed Abiathar for joining with his brother Adonijah, who was trying to seize the throne. Hence it is written in First Kings 2: *So Solomon thrust out Abiathar from being priest unto the Lord...*[96] Moreover, Zadok anointed King Solomon, and was the first to serve as priest in his Temple. (First Chronicles 6; Josephus, Book 10.)

AHIMAAZ, son of Zadok. (Josephus, Book 10.)[97]

AZARIAH, son of Ahimaaz. (Josephus, Book 10; but in First Kings 4, he is called "the son of Zadok," as well as in First Chronicles 6.[98] Likewise in chapter 31, "Azariah the first priest of the line of Zadok.")[99]

JORAM, son of Azariah. (Josephus, Book 10.)

IUS,[100] son of Joram. (Josephus, Book 10.)

AXIORAM,[101] son of Ius. (Josephus, Book 10.)

PHIDEAS,[102] son of Axioram. (Josephus, Book 10.)

ZADOK, son of Phideas. (Josephus, Book 10.) There is some question as to whether he is the same as the priest Jehoiada, who anointed Joash king of Judah and is called high priest. (Second Kings 12, and Josephus, Book 10.) Also according to Josephus, he lived 130 years. Zechariah the prophet, who was the son of the high priest Jehoiada, was stoned by King Joram.[103] (Josephus, Book 9.)

JOEL, son of Zadok. (Josephus, Book 10.)

JOTHAM, son of Joel. (Josephus, Book 10.) He is called Azariah, and is the priest who resisted King Uzziah when he was going to light the incense. (Second Chronicles 26; Josephus, Book 9.)[104]

URIAH, son of Jotham. (Josephus, Book 10.)

AMARIAH, son of Uriah. (Josephus, Book 10.)

ZADOK, son of Amariah. (Josephus, Book 10.)

SHALLUM, son of Zadok. (Josephus, Book 10.)

HILKIAH, son of Shallum. (Second Kings 22–23; Second Chronicles 34; Josephus, Book 10.) He found the lost book of Deuteronomy when Josiah was king.

SERAIAH, son of Hilkiah. Killed in Riblah by King Nebuchadnezzar. (Second Kings, last chapter; Josephus, Book 10.)

JEHOZADAK, son of Seraiah. Succeeded his father during the captivity in Babylon; brother of Ezra, who later restored the law. (Josephus, Book 10; Eusebius, Book 3 of the *Proofs of the Gospels*.)[105]

JOSHUA, son of Jehozadak. Returned from Babylon to his ancestral city and began to rebuild the Temple. (Ezra 2; Josephus, Book 10;[106] the prophet Haggai; Eusebius, ibid.)

JOIAKIM, son of Joshua. (Nehemiah, chapter 12; Josephus, Book 11.) Possibly the same one who in the fourth chapter of Judith is called Eliakim the great priest of the Lord. (Eusebius, ibid.)

ELIASHIB, son of Joiakim. (Nehemiah 3, 13; Josephus, Book 11; Eusebius, ibid.)

JOIADA, son of Eliashib. (Nehemiah 12; Josephus, Book 11; Eusebius, ibid.)

JONATHAN, son of Judah. (Nehemiah 12; Josephus in Book 11 calls him John;[107] Eusebius, ibid.)

JADDUA, or JADDUS, son of Jonathan. (Nehemiah 12; Josephus, Book 11; Eusebius, ibid.) He welcomed the victorious Alexander the Great.

ONIAS, son of Jaddus. (Josephus, Book 11; Eusebius, ibid.)

SIMON the Just, son of Onias. (Josephus, Book 12. Eusebius omits him.)

ELEAZAR, son of Onias. (Josephus, Book 12; Eusebius, ibid.) It was to him that Ptolemy Philadelphus, the king of Egypt, wrote for a copy of the Bible, as well as seventy-two interpreters.

MANASSEH, son of the high priest Jaddus. (Josephus, Book 12. Eusebius omits him.)

ONIAS II, son of Simon the Just. (Josephus, Book 12; Eusebius, ibid.) He refused to pay tribute to Ptolemy Euergetes.

SIMON II, son of Onias, grandson of Simon. (Josephus, Book 12; Eusebius, ibid.) This was the time of Jesus Sirach, who wrote the *Wisdom*.[108]

ONIAS III, son of Simon II. (Josephus, Book 12; Eusebius, ibid.) It was to him that Arius king of Lacedaemonia sent an embassy. He was accused before Seleucus the king of Syria by a certain Simon from Benjamin, and this was the cause of an uproar.[109] With his death, Antiochus Epiphanes king of Syria appointed his brother high priest.

JOSHUA, also Jason, son of Simon II. (Josephus, Book 12.) Appointed by Antiochus Epiphanes. Eusebius omits him. Although there had been no disturbances, he was the first to be removed by the above-mentioned Antiochus, and the high priesthood began to be a temporary office.

ONIAS IV, also Menelaus, son of Simon II. Appointed, and later executed, by Antiochus Epiphanes. Jerusalem was plundered. According to the Book of the Maccabees, Menelaus was the brother of the traitorous Simon the Benjaminite. Eusebius omits him.[110]

LYSIMACHUS, brother of Menelaus. (First Maccabees; omitted by Josephus and Eusebius.)

ALCIMUS, also called Joachim; from the line of Levi but not of Eleazar or Ithamar. Appointed by the same king. (First Maccabees.)

ONIAS, son of Onias III, the high priest. Fled to King Ptolemy and founded a temple in Heliopolis in Egypt. Eusebius omits him.[111]

JUDAH Maccabee, son of Mattathias the Hasmonean. Chosen by the people from the line of Levi but not that of Eleazar. (Josephus, Book 12; Eusebius; omitted by the Book of Maccabees.)

JONATHAN, son of Mattathias the Hasmonean. Prince of the Jews, subject of Demetrius king of Syria. (First Maccabees; Josephus, Book 13; Eusebius.)

SIMON the Prince, brother of Jonathan, whom he succeeded. As a result, the high priesthood became hereditary among the Hasmoneans, together with the princeship. (First Maccabees; Josephus, Book 13; Eusebius.)

JOHN Hyrcanus, son of Simon. (Josephus, Book 13; Eusebius.)

ARISTOBULUS, son of John. Took the title of king. (Josephus, Book 13; Eusebius.)

JANNAEUS Alexander, son of John. King. (Josephus, Book 13; Eusebius.)

HYRCANUS, son of Alexander Jannaeus. king. Driven out by his younger brother Aristobulus (Josephus, Book 14; Eusebius.)

ARISTOBULUS, son of Alexander Jannaeus. After expelling his brother Hyrcanus, the king and high priest, he became king and high priest. Then he was expelled by the Roman commander Cn. Pompeius. (Josephus, Book 14; Eusebius.)

HYRCANUS, son of Alexander Jannaeus. Restored by Pompeius and again served as high priest. He was then captured by the Parthians and Antigonus, the son of Aristobulus the king and high priest, and mutilated so that he could never again be high priest.

ANTIGONUS, son of Aristobulus the king and high priest. When his uncle Hyrcanus was captured and mutilated, he became king and high priest. He was killed by King Herod, the son of Antipater from Ashkelon, whom the Romans had set up to challenge him. (Josephus, Book 15.)

HANANEL, a Levite from Babylonia. Set up and removed by King Herod. (Josephus, Book 15.)

ARISTOBULUS, son of Alexandra, the daughter of Hyrcanus the king and high priest. Appointed and removed by King Herod. (Josephus, Book 15.) The brother of Mariamne the wife of Herod.

HANANEL, again installed and removed by King Herod. (Josephus, Book 15.)

JOSHUA, son of Phabi. A foreigner installed and removed by King Herod. (Josephus, Book 15.)

SIMON Boethus of Alexandria,[112] a foreigner and father-in-law of King Herod, who installed and removed him. (Josephus, Book 15.)

MATTATHIAS, son of Theophilus. Installed by King Herod. When once he dreamed that he was having intercourse with his wife, on the following day—which was the Day of Atonement—

JOSEPH, son of Ellemus, his relation, served in his place as high priest. (Josephus, Book 17.) Mattathias was later removed.

JOAZAR, son of Simon Boethus.[113] Brother-in-law of King Herod, who installed him. (Josephus, Book 17.) It was during his term that Jesus CHRIST was born. (Nicephorus in his *Chronology*.)[114] He was later removed by Archelaus, Herod's son and successor. (Josephus, Book 17.)

ELEAZAR, son of Simon Boethus. Installed and removed by King Archelaus. (Josephus, Book 17.)

JOSHUA, son of Zvi. Installed and removed by King Archelaus. (Josephus, Book 17.)

JOAZAR, again appointed by King Archelaus. After Archelaus was banished, he was removed by Quirinius the proconsul of Syria,[115] when Augustus reigned over Judea. (Josephus, Book 18.)

ANNAS,[116] or Ananus, son of Seth. Appointed by Quirinius the proconsul of Syria during the reign of Augustus, and removed by Valerius Gratus the procurator of Judea[117] during the reign of Tiberius. (Josephus, Book 18.)

ISHMAEL, son of Phabi. Installed and removed by Valerius Gratus the procurator. (Josephus, Book 18.)

SIMON, son of Camith. Installed and removed by Valerius Gratus the procurator during the reign of Tiberius. (Josephus, Book 18.)

JOSEPH Caiaphas, son-in-law of Annas the high priest. Installed by Valerius Gratus the procurator during the reign of Tiberius. (Josephus, Book 18; all the Gospels; Acts of the Apostles 4.) It was under him that CHRIST was crucified.

JONATHAN, son of the high priest Annas. Appointed by Vitellius the proconsul of Syria during the reign of Gaius, and removed by Herod Agrippa the king of Judea. (Josephus, *Antiquities* Book 18; *War*, Book 2.)

THEOPHILUS, son of the high priest Annas. Installed and removed by King Herod Agrippa during the reign of Claudius. (Josephus, Book 18.)

SIMON Cantheras, son of Boethus the high priest.[118] Installed and removed by King Herod Agrippa. (Josephus, Book 19.)

MATTATHIAS, son of Annas the high priest. Installed and removed by King Herod Agrippa. (Josephus, Book 19.)

AELIONEUS, son of Simon Cantheras the high priest. Installed by King Herod Agrippa and removed by Herod Agrippa II, king of Chalcidice; who, when his brother Agrippa king of Judea had died, asked Claudius for the right to appoint high priests. (Josephus, Book 20.)

JOSEPH, son of Camytus. Installed and removed by King Agrippa of Chalcidice during the reign of Nero. (Josephus, Book 20.)

ANANIAS, son of Nebedius. Installed and removed by King Agrippa of Chalcidice. (Josephus, Book 20.) It was he whom St. Paul called a "white-washed wall."[119] (Acts 23.)

ISHMAEL, son of Phabi.[120] Installed by King Agrippa of Chalcidice. Held hostage in Rome. (Josephus, Book 20.)

JOSEPH Cabus, son of Simon Cantheras the high priest. Installed and removed by King Agrippa of Chalcidice. (Josephus, Book 20.)

ANNAS or Ananus, son of Annas the high priest. Installed and removed by King Agrippa of Chalcidice. He killed St. James, the younger brother of the Lord. (Josephus, Book 20; Acts 12.)

JOSHUA, son of Damnaeus or Mnaseas.[121] Installed and removed by King Agrippa of Chalcidice. (Josephus, Book 20.)

JOSHUA, son of Gamaliel. Installed and removed by King Agrippa of Chalcidice. (Josephus, Book 20.)

MATTATHIAS, son of Theophilus. Installed and removed by King Agrippa of Chalcidice. (Josephus, Book 20.)

PHANNIAS or Phanassus, son of Samuel. Made high priest by the people when it was in revolt. It was under him that Titus captured and burned Jerusalem. (Josephus, Book 20.)

It is clear from this series of high priests that one succeeded the other in such a way that no two ever held the office at the same time. This is why many scholars have asked, and continue to ask, what St. Luke had in mind when he said at the beginning of his gospel: *Annas and Caiaphas being the high priests, the word of God came unto John...*[122] After all, Josephus tells us that Caiaphas was the only high priest at that time;[123] and it is he whom the scripture calls "chief of the priests" and "great priest," titles I have already mentioned. And when Luke describes the events of three years later—a year in which, according to St. John,[124] Caiaphas was high priest—he writes (4:6): *And Annas the high priest, and Caiaphas...*[125]

In his explanation of St. John,[126] St. Augustine responds that perhaps in those days it was the practice for several high priests to serve together, and to officiate in turn for one year at a time; for the fact is, he says, that either Annas and Caiaphas served as high priest in alternate years, or more than one priest served together in the same year. But since his statement lacks authority, and he himself is not certain he believes it; and since Josephus (who lived very near to those times) reports a clear succession of high priests which flatly contradicts the existence of such a practice, I rather think we ought to look for a different explanation. I would therefore suggest that in part they retained the old custom that there should never be more than one high priest at a time, while simultaneously introducing a new one: that all men of high priestly rank—that is, those who had served in the high priesthood—should be called high priests, just like those men who (in accordance with the ancient custom) had been awarded the title once and kept it until their deaths.[127] This is how they now refer to bishops, even those who have left the Church. But Annas in particular bore this title not because he was then high priest, but because of all the former high priests he was the father-in-law of Caiaphas, who was then high priest, i.e. he was actually serving in the high priesthood. For the same reason, Josephus in the second book of his *War* names Jonathan and Annas as the high priests who served under Claudius,[128] even though at the time it was really only Jonathan who performed the office, while Annas, a former high priest, was his father. Likewise, Josephus later on calls Ananus (the son of this Annas) and Joshua high priests at the same time,[129] even though Ananus had been removed and Joshua appointed in his place. And in Book 4 he calls Ananus the oldest of the high priests, and then Joshua the next closest in age to Ananus[130]—among, that is, the men who had served as high priest. Likewise, after he writes that Phannias had been made high priest, he singles out as the most upright of the high priests Joshua the son of Gamaliel and Ananus the son of Annas, both of whom were former high priests.[131] And he writes that even after Phannias had replaced him, Ananus continued to wear the high priestly garments.[132] And in Book 20 of the *Antiquities*, he says that the high priests competed with the priests.[133] Josephus, then, always uses this turn of phrase—instead of "former high priests" he writes "high priests." In fact, he writes about Annas: *Annas was the most fortunate, because he saw all his sons become high priests of God, and before that he himself held this honor for many years; none of our other high priests have managed this feat.*[134]

CHAPTER 3

Priests

WHILE THERE WAS one and only one high priest, there were also many other priests, although they enjoyed less dignity and authority. This will become clear if we examine priests in the same way as we did high priests, namely by considering their garments, their consecration, the conditions placed upon them, and their duties.

The garments worn by the priests were the ones we said they had in common with the high priest—the linen coat, the girdle, the mitre, and the breeches. The instructions for these are given in Exodus 28:[135] *And thou shalt bring* Aaron's *sons, and put coats upon them. And thou shalt gird them with girdles... and put the mitres upon them; and the priest's office shall be theirs for a perpetual statute...* And then: *And thou shalt make them linen breeches to cover their nakedness; from the loins even unto the thighs they shall reach; and they shall be upon Aaron, and upon his sons, when they come in unto the tabernacle of the congregation, or when they come near unto the altar to minister in the holy place; that they bear not iniquity, and die...*[136] Moreover, we are told that these instructions were carried out, in Leviticus chapter 8: *And Moses brought Aaron's sons, and put coats upon them, and girded them with girdles, and put mitres upon them; as the Lord commanded Moses.*[137]

On special occasions the priests also wore an ephod, i.e. a superhumeral,[138] but one made out of linen. First Samuel 23:[139] *...he fell upon the priests, and slew... fourscore and five persons who did wear a linen ephod.*[140] St. Jerome comments on this passage that this ephod was made of linen, and not (as was the high priest's) of blue, *byssus,* scarlet, purple, and gold. For as St. Eucherius[141] says, *there were two kinds of ephod—one made of linen and unadorned, which the priests wore; the other of many colors and woven from gold, purple, byssus, blue, and gems, which only the high priests used.* The priestly one is called *ephod bad,* that is, a linen superhumeral.

The ceremony of consecration for a priest was the same as that for the high priest—he was brought to the altar, washed, clothed, anointed, and consecrated. Exodus 29: *And* the sons of *Aaron thou shalt bring unto the door of the tabernacle of the congregation, and shalt wash them with water. And thou shalt take the garments... and put linen coats upon them. And thou shalt gird them with girdles... and put the mitres upon them... And thou shalt cause a bullock to be brought before the tabernacle of the congregation...*[142] And Leviticus 8: *And Moses brought Aaron's sons, and put coats upon them, and girded them with girdles, and put mitres upon them; as the Lord commanded Moses.*[143] Then we are told about the offering of a bullock and a ram, which was part of the consecration (I discussed this in connection with the consecration of the high priest). Both the high priest and the other priests were consecrated in the same way, for seven days.

The following conditions were imposed on the priests. Leviticus 10: *And the Lord spake unto Aaron, saying, Do not drink wine nor strong drink, thou, nor thy sons with thee, when ye go into the tabernacle of the congregation, lest ye die...*[144] And chapter 21: *...no priest shall be defiled for the dead among his people; but for his kin, that is near unto him, that is, for his mother, and for his father, and for his son, and for his daughter, and for his brother. And for his sister a virgin, who is nigh unto him... But he shall not defile himself, being a chief man among his people... They shall not make baldness upon their head, neither shall they shave off the corner of their beard, nor make any cuttings in their flesh. They shall be holy unto their God, and not profane the name of their God; for the offerings of the Lord made by fire, and the bread of their God, they do offer: therefore they shall be holy. They shall not take a wife who is a whore, or profane; neither shall they take a woman put away from her husband... And the daughter of any priest, if she profane herself by playing the whore, she profaneth her father: she shall be burnt with fire.*[145] Hence Josephus in Book 6 of the *War*: *Only priests without any sort of blemish would approach the altar and the Temple dressed in garments of* byssus; *most important was that they abstain from pure wine, and this temperance stemmed from a ritualistic fear that they might err in performing any of the divine service.*[146]

Their duties were as follows: to safeguard the oils, to look after the vessels of the tabernacle, to offer the incense every day, and to make the daily sacrifices. And if on occasion it was necessary to make a special offering on behalf of the people or for private individuals, they would see to it; and on festival days they would make the people's sacrifice, and flay the hides of the burnt offerings.

The fourth chapter of Numbers describes as follows the incense, the daily offering, the oils, and the vessels: *And to the office of Eleazar the son of Aaron the priest pertaineth the oil for the light, and the sweet incense, and the daily meat offering, and the anointing oil, and the oversight of all the tabernacle, and of all that therein is, in the sanctuary, and in the vessels thereof.*[147] And (as I said) in the sixth chapter of First Chronicles: *But Aaron and his sons offered upon the altar of the burnt offering, and on the altar of incense, and were appointed for all the work of the place most holy, and to make an atonement for Israel, according to all that Moses... had commanded.*[148] And chapter 26:[149] King Uzziah *went into the Temple of the Lord to burn incense upon the altar of incense. And Azariah the priest went in after him, and with him fourscore priests of the Lord, who were valiant men; and they withstood Uzziah the king, and said unto him, It appertaineth not unto thee, Uzziah, to burn incense unto the Lord, but to the priests the sons of Aaron, who are consecrated to burn incense: go out of the sanctuary; for thou hast trespassed, neither shall it be for thine honor from the Lord God. Then Uzziah was wroth, and had a censer in his hand to burn incense; and he was wroth with the priests... in the house of the Lord, from beside the incense altar. And Azariah the chief priest, and all the priests, looked upon him, and, behold, he was leprous in his forehead, and they thrust him out from thence...* Both of these duties were later confirmed during the reign of Joash by the high priest Jehoiada, about whom it is written: *...he handed the care of the Temple to the priests and the Levites according to the instruction of David, ordering that they bring in every day the prescribed sacrifices of the burnt offerings, and light the incense according to the law.*[150] Hence the first chapter of St. Luke: *...while* Zacharias *executed the priest's office before God in the order of his course, according to the custom of the priest's office, his lot was to burn incense when he went into the Temple of the Lord.*[151] And St. Paul in chapter 8 of the Letter to the Hebrews:[152] Christ the high priest *needeth not daily, as those* other[153] *priests, to offer up sacrifice, first for his own sins, and then for the people's...*

On the subject of the special offerings made on behalf of the people and of private individuals, I will add the following passages to the ones I quoted above where I wrote about the burnt offerings and the other sacrifices. On sacrifices for the people, there is chapter 29 of Second Chronicles—after King Hezekiah has told the sons of Aaron to make an offering on the altar of the Lord, the text continues as follows: *So they killed the bullocks, and the priests received the blood, and sprinkled it on the altar; likewise, when they had killed the rams, they sprinkled the blood upon the altar; they killed also the lambs, and they sprinkled the blood upon the altar. And they brought forth the he-goats for the sin offering before the king and the congregation; and they laid their hands upon them; and the priests killed them, and they made reconciliation with their blood upon the altar, to make an atonement for all Israel: for the king commanded that the burnt offering and the sin offering should be made for all Israel.*[154] And for the private individual, the law is recorded in Leviticus 17: *What man soever there be of the house of Israel, who killeth an ox, or lamb, or goat, in the camp, or who killeth it out of the camp, and bringeth it not unto the door of the tabernacle of the congregation, to offer an offering unto the Lord before the tabernacle of the Lord... To the end that the children of Israel may bring their sacrifices, which they offer in the open field, even that they may bring them unto the Lord, unto the door of the tabernacle of the congregation, unto the priest, and offer them for peace offerings unto the Lord... And they shall no more offer their sacrifices unto devils, after whom they have gone a whoring...*[155]

I have already discussed the offerings for festivals in the section on high priests.

The task of flaying the hides of the burnt offerings is described in the first chapter of Leviticus, which deals with the burnt offering made by the high priest: *And the high priest*[156] *shall kill the bullock before the Lord; and the priests, Aaron's sons, shall bring the blood, and sprinkle the blood round about upon the altar... And they shall flay the burnt offering, and cut it into its pieces. And they shall put fire upon the altar, and lay the wood in order upon the fire; and they shall lay the parts... in order upon the wood that is on the fire which is upon the altar.*[157] And in chapter 29 of Second Chronicles: *But the priests were too few, so that they could not flay all the burnt offerings...*[158]

God restored all of these practices after the Jews returned from the Babylonian exile, as it is written in chapter 44 of Ezekiel: *But the priests...,*[159] *the sons of Zadok, who kept the charge of my sanctuary when the children of Israel went astray from me, they shall come near to me to minister unto me, and they shall stand before me to offer unto me the fat and the blood... They shall enter into my sanctuary, and they shall come near to my table, to minister unto me, and they shall keep my charge. And it shall come to pass, that when they enter in at the gates of the inner court, they shall be clothed with linen garments; and no wool shall come upon them, while they minister in the gates of the inner court... They shall have linen bonnets upon their heads, and shall have linen breeches upon their loins; they shall not gird themselves with anything that causeth sweat. And when they go forth into the outer court, even into the outer court to the people, they shall put off their garments wherein they ministered, and lay them in the holy chambers, and they shall put on other garments; and they shall not sanctify the people with their garments. Neither shall they shave their heads, nor suffer their locks to grow long; they shall only poll their heads. Neither shall any priest drink wine, when they enter into the inner court. Neither shall they take for their wives a widow, nor her who is put away; but they shall take maidens of the seed of the house of Israel, or a widow who had a priest before... And they shall come at no dead person to defile themselves; but for father, or for mother, or for son, or for daughter, for*

brother, or for sister who hath had no husband, they may defile themselves.
And after he is cleansed, they shall reckon unto him seven days. And in the
day that he goeth into the sanctuary, unto the inner court, to minister in the
sanctuary, he shall offer his sin offering... And it shall be unto them for an
inheritance: I am their inheritance; and ye shall give them no possession in
Israel: I am their possession. They shall eat the meat offering, and the sin of-
fering, and the trespass offering; and every dedicated thing in Israel shall be
theirs. And the first of all the first fruits of all things, and every oblation of
all, of every sort of your oblations, shall be the priest's; ye shall also give unto
the priest the first of your dough, that he may cause the blessing to rest in
thine house. The priests shall not eat of anything that is dead of itself, or torn,
whether it be fowl or beast.[160]

Now that I have explained all this, I will show how the priests were selected and arranged into twenty-four divisions. The first priests, then, were
Nadab, Abihu, Eleazar, and Ithamar the sons of Aaron; they were clothed
and consecrated at God's command. But after Nadab and Abihu died because
they had put foreign rather than sacred fire to the sacrifices, only Eleazar and
Ithamar remained to father the lines of high priests and priests.

Since, moreover, there were in David's time sixteen families descended
from Eleazar and eight from Ithamar, he assigned all the priests to twenty-
four divisions, and named each division after the person who was at that time
the head of his family. The order of the divisions was, however, determined
purely by chance—one was called "first," another "second," and so on. Hence
St. Eucherius called them the twenty-four lots.

These were the names of the men who were heads of their families and
gave their names to the divisions; they were in the following order, as we see
in First Chronicles 24: *Now the first lot came forth to Jehoiarib, the second to*
Jedaiah, the third to Harim...,[161] and so forth, as follows:

1. Jehoiarib
2. Jedaiah
3. Harib[162]
4. Seorim
5. Malchijah
6. Benjamin[163]
7. Hakkoz
8. Abijah
9. Jeshuah
10. Shecaniah
11. Eliashib

12. Jakim
13. Huppah
14. Jeshebaal[164]
15. Bilgah
16. Immer
17. Jethi[165]
18. Aphses
19. Pethahiah
20. Jehezekel
21. Jachin
22. Samuel[166]
23. Delaiah
24. Jebeli[167]

Josephus also mentions the first division, Jehoiarib, in his *Antiquities*—he writes that Mattathias the priest was the grandson of Hasmoneus of the division of Jehoiarib, and a Jerusalemite.[168] And in his *Life*, he says: *My family comes not only from the priests but from* Jehoiarib, *the first of the twenty-four divisions.*[169] The eighth, which was called Abijah, is mentioned by St. Luke: *...a certain priest named Zacharias, of the course of Abijah.*[170] For although I have called them "divisions" in the Roman style,[171] the Latin translation renders them sometimes as "courses" and sometimes as "companies," and the Greek as *ephemeriae*[172] and *ephemerides*, as we will see later on. Moreover, according to Theophylact[173] the *ephemeriae* were the same thing as weeks. This is clear from Second Chronicles 24:[174] *...for Jehoiada the priest dismissed not the companies which were accustomed to succeed one another every week* (here instead of "companies" the Greek has *ephemeriae*). As in Second Chronicles 25: *according to our ephemeriae, established by David.*[175] The courses or divisions that David initiated were later laid out by Solomon along the lines set out by his father, as we are told in chapter 5 of Second Chronicles: *In the time of Solomon, when the ark was brought into the Temple, there were not yet courses, and the order of service among the priests had not been given out.*[176] And in the eighth chapter: *And* Solomon *appointed, according to the order of David his father, the courses of the priests to their service...*[177] The reasoning behind this arrangement seems to have been as follows: David wanted not that all the priests be occupied with their sacred duties every day, but rather that a single division be on duty each and every week. So first he chose by lot the order of the divisions, and then he ordered the priests of each division to cast lots to see which function each one would perform in his given week—who, for example, would burn the incense, and who would offer the sacrifices. For so it is described in St. Luke: ...*while Zacharias executed the priest's office before God in the order of his course, according to the custom of the priest's office, his lot was to burn incense when he went into the Temple.*[178] And Josephus writes in the second book of his *Against Apion*: *Granted that there are twenty-four divisions of priests, each of which contains more than five thousand men; and yet on any given day only one division is in service. When they have completed their turn others come to replace them at the offerings, and gathering in the Temple at midday they accept from their predecessors the keys to the Temple and the tally of the vessels (though nothing used for eating or drinking is brought into the Temple).* Though I supported the suggestion of St. Ambrose[179] and St. Augustine that Zacharias was the high priest because he lit the incense, which no one but the high priest was permitted to do, the idea that this was his particular privilege can be called into question. Zacharias, after all, could not have been the high priest that year, since according to Josephus Joazar was in charge of the office. Nor had St. Luke been talking about a high priest: *a certain priest.*[180] Besides, the high priests (unlike the others) did not belong to courses and lots; and as I have already shown, the priests were just as likely to offer incense as the high priest. We must therefore conclude that he was simply a priest. There is, besides, another reference to these courses in Ezra chapter 6: *And they set the priests in their divisions, and the Levites in their courses...*[181]

Now, there were in fact certain priests in charge of each of the priestly divisions; and they, like the high priest, were called as a group *archiereis*, and in the Latin version "chiefs of the priests" and "high priests."[182] This fact has plunged the whole subject into an unfathomable darkness. This is how Ezra puts it in the eighth chapter: *...keep them, until ye weigh them before the chiefs of the priests and the Levites, and chiefs of the families... in Jerusalem.*[183] And in St. Mark 14: *And they led Jesus away to the chief priest Caiaphas... And the chief priests... sought for witness against Jesus...*[184] All in all, throughout the entire trial of Christ there is on the one hand a high priest and on the other the chiefs of the priests, who are described as attending the high priest.[185] Ezra himself was one of these men—he is called "chief of the priests," and yet he did not serve as high priest.[186] So too were John and Alexander, about whom it is written in Acts chapter 4: *And Annas the chief of the priests,*[187] *and Caiaphas, and John, and Alexander, and as many as were of priestly descent...*[188] For it was really Caiaphas who was high priest, while Annas (as I explained above) was a former high priest; and the others were chiefs of the priestly divisions, which is explicit in the Greek: *ek genos archieratikou;*[189] that is, from the class of the chiefs of the priests.[190] For the council to which this verse refers was composed of not only the high priest, but also the chiefs of the priestly divisions (as I will show later on). Finally, we are told in Acts 19 of another chief priest named Scaeva: *And there were seven sons of one Scaeva, a Jew, and chief of the priests...*[191] Now there was never a Scaeva who served as high priest, or who could have done so in Ephesus, where this verse takes place.[192]

Since, therefore, all the priests were descendants of Eleazar and Ithamar, it is generally agreed that they were from the tribe of Levi, which God had set aside for the priesthood. Hence St. Paul wrote in Hebrews chapter 7: *For he of whom these things are spoken pertaineth to another tribe, of which no man gave attendance at the altar. For it is evident that our Lord sprang out of Judah; of which tribe Moses spake nothing concerning priesthood.*[193] Josephus wrote the following about the whole class of priests, in the first book of his *Against Apion*: *From the very start, not only did they appoint to perform these functions men of the highest character who had been taught how to propitiate God, but they also saw to it that the line of the priests would continue uncorrupted. For it is only right that any man who was going to serve as a priest should be born*[194] *of a woman from that family... and that the family should be validated by an ancient pedigree and many witnesses. This, of course, we do not only in Judea itself,*[195] *but wherever our lineage is found the purity of priestly marriages is maintained—in Egypt, and Babylonia, and anywhere at all that members of the priestly line have settled. For they send letters to Jerusalem with the family name of the bride on her father's side and the names of her distant ancestors, who provided the proof of her lineage. And if a war should break out... then those of the priests that survive investigate whatever women remain; for they are not willing to marry any women who have been taken prisoner, fearing that they may have had relations with foreigners... And in the case of every high priest we have appointed for the last two thousand years, the sons have been listed right after their fathers. But if anyone should lie, he is forbidden either to approach the altar or to perform any other sacred function.*[196]

CHAPTER 4

Levites

AFTER THE PRIESTS came the Levites, which included two types of people: everyone who came from the tribe of Levi and was therefore called a Levite (including the high priests and the priests), as well as all the other members of this tribe, who were authorized to play particular roles in the sacred rites. It is the latter whom I will now discuss. All the Levites of this type, then, were descendants of Levi but did not trace their ancestry to the families of Eleazar or Ithamar. Levi left three sons—Gershon, Kohath, and Merari; and Kohath left Amram, Izhar, Hebron, and Uzziel. To Amram were born Moses and Aaron, and from Aaron came Eleazar and Ithamar. And just as the lines of high priests and priests descended from Aaron through the offspring of Eleazar and Ithamar, so all the other types of sacred functionaries, whom we call Levites, came from the other sons and grandsons of Levi.

These were organized into two groups, the first established by Moses and the second by David. I will begin with the first group: God entrusted to these Levites the care of the tabernacle and its vessels and utensils, and the ark of the covenant; these they were to carry around and protect, while at the same time seeing to the needs of the priests. In the first chapter of Numbers: *Only thou shalt not number the tribe of Levi, neither take the sum of them among the children of Israel; but thou shalt appoint the Levites over the tabernacle of testimony, and over all the vessels thereof... and they shall minister unto it, and shall encamp round about the tabernacle. And when the tabernacle setteth forward, the Levites shall take it down; and when the tabernacle is to be pitched, the Levites shall set it up; and the stranger that cometh nigh shall be put to death.*[197] And in the third chapter: *Bring the tribe of Levi near, and present them before Aaron the priest, that they may minister unto him. And they shall keep his charge, and the charge of the whole congregation before the tabernacle of the congregation, to do the service of the tabernacle. And they shall keep all the instruments of the tabernacle of the congregation, and the charge of the children of Israel, to do the service of the tabernacle. And thou shalt give the Levites unto Aaron and to his sons; they are wholly given unto him out of the children of Israel. And thou shalt appoint Aaron and his sons, and they shall wait on their priest's office; and the stranger who cometh nigh shall be put to death... And I, behold, I have taken the Levites from among the children of Israel instead of all the firstborn who openeth the matrix among the children of Israel: therefore the Levites shall be mine, because all the firstborn are mine; for on the day that I smote all the firstborn in the land of Egypt I hallowed unto me all the firstborn in Israel, both man and beast: mine shall they be...*[198] Then God distributed duties to each of the families of the Levites, as follows: *Number the children of Levi after the house of their fathers, by their families: every male from a month old and upward shalt thou number them. And Moses numbered them... And these were the sons of Levi by their names: Gershon, and Kohath, and Merari. And these are the names of the sons of Gershon by their families: Libni, and Shimei. And the sons of Kohath by their families: Amram, and Izhar, Hebron, and Uzziel. And the sons of Merari by their families: Mahli, and Mushi. These are the families of the Levites according to the house of their fathers...* The Libnites and the Shimeites *shall pitch behind the tabernacle westward. And the chief of the house of the father of the Gershonites shall be Eliasaph the son of Lael. And the charge of the sons of Gershon in the tabernacle of the congregation shall be the tabernacle, and the tent, the covering thereof, and the hanging for the door of the tabernacle of the congregation, and the hangings of the court, and the curtain for the door of the court, which is by the tabernacle, and by the altar round about, and the cords of it for all the service thereof...* The Amramites, the Izharites, the Hebronites, and the Uzzielites, *keeping the charge of the sanctuary, shall pitch on the side of the tabernacle southward. And the chief of the house of the father of the families of the Kohathites shall be Elizaphan the son of Uzziel. And their charge shall be the ark, and the table, and the candle-stick, and the altars, and the vessels of the sanctuary wherewith they minister, and the hanging, and all the service thereof...* The Mahlites and the Mushites under *Zuriel the son of Abihail: these shall pitch on the side of the tabernacle northward. And under the custody and charge of the sons of Merari shall be the boards of the tabernacle, and the bars thereof, and the pillars thereof, and the sockets thereof, and all the vessels thereof, and all that serveth thereto, and the pillars of the court round about, and their sockets, and their pins, and their cords. And Eleazar the son of Aaron the priest shall be chief over the chief of the Levites, and have the oversight of them who keep the charge of the sanctuary.*[199] But those who encamp before the tabernacle toward the east, *even before the tabernacle of the congregation eastward, shall be Moses, and Aaron and his sons, keeping the charge of the sanctuary for the charge of the children of Israel; and the stranger who cometh nigh shall be put to death.*[200]

Then chapter 4 explains what each of them was supposed to do and to carry: the ark, the veil, the table, the curtains, the covering of the tabernacle, the hanging, the cords, the vessels, the boards, the bars, the pillars, the sockets, and all the furniture. Finally, in chapter 8 a law is brought: *This is it that belongeth unto the Levites: from twenty and five years old and upward they shall go in to wait upon the service of the tabernacle of the congregation... to keep the charge, and they shall do no service.*[201] They continued to serve these functions until the time of David, which is why in Joshua's time they were the ones who carried the ark across the Jordan River. In that passage they are called "priests of Levitical stock," since the term "priest" was used in a broader sense then.[202]

Then David established a second order of Levites, since the first one had fallen somewhat into abeyance. He took away from them the duty of transporting the ark, and appointed some of the Levites as assistants of the priests and the Temple (these were called simply "Levites"), others as singers, others as porters, and still others as scribes and judges.

Of the assistants there were 24,000, of the scribes and judges 6,000, and 4,000 each of the singers and the porters. This information may be found in chapter 23 of First Chronicles: *And* David *gathered together all the princes of Israel, with the priests and the Levites. Now the Levites were numbered from the age of* twenty[203] *years and upward; and their number by their polls, man by man, was thirty and eight thousand. Of which, twenty and four thousand were to set forward the work of the house of the Lord; and six thousand were scribes and judges. Moreover four thousand were porters; and four thousand praised the Lord with the instruments which I made, said David, to praise therewith. And David divided them into courses among the sons of Levi, namely, Gershon, Kohath, and Merari.*[204] And later on: *For David said, The Lord God of Israel hath given rest unto his people, that they may dwell in Jerusalem for ever. And also unto the Levites; they shall no more carry the tabernacle, nor any vessels of it for the service thereof. For by the last words of David the Levites were numbered from twenty years old and above; because their office was to wait on the sons of Aaron for the service of the house of the Lord, in the courts, and in the chambers, and in the purifying of all holy things, and the work of the service of the house of God; both for the showbread, and for the fine flour for the meat offering, and for the unleavened cakes, and for that which is baked in the pan, and for that which is fried, and for all manner of measure and size; and to stand every morning to thank and praise the Lord, and likewise at even; and to offer all burnt sacrifices unto the Lord in the Sabbaths, in the new moons, and on the set feasts, by number, according to the order commanded unto them, continually before the Lord; and that they should keep the charge of the tabernacle of the congregation, and the charge of the holy place, and the charge of the sons of Aaron their brethren, in the service of the house of the Lord.*[205] Likewise in the ninth chapter: *And certain of the Levites had the charge of the ministering vessels, that they should bring them in and out by tale. Some of them also were appointed to oversee the vessels, and all the instruments of the sanctuary, and the fine flour, and the wine, and the oil, and the frankincense, and the spices. And some of the sons of the priests made the ointment of the spices. And Mattithiah, one of the Levites, who was the firstborn of Shallum the Korahite, had the set office over the things that were made in the pans. And other of their brethren, of the sons of the Kohathites, were over the showbread, to prepare it every Sabbath.*[206] And David organized these assistants into twenty-four divisions, and named them after the Gershonites, the Kohathites, and the Merarites.[207] Hence the leaders mentioned in the eighth chapter of Ezra were no less Levites than they were priests.[208]

The innovations begun by David were later completed by Solomon, in chapter 8 of Second Chronicles: *And he appointed, according to the order of David his father, the courses of the priests to their service, and the Levites to their charges, to praise and minister before the priests, as the duty of every day required; the porters also by their courses at every gate...*[209] When, therefore, King Hezekiah had determined to restore the worship of God, which had fallen into disuse, he summoned the priests and the Levites and said to them (Second Chronicles 29): *...Hear me, ye Levites, sanctify now yourselves, and sanctify the house of the Lord... and carry forth the filthiness out of the holy place... My sons, be not now negligent: for the Lord hath chosen you to stand before him, to serve him, and that ye should minister unto him, and burn incense.*[210] Then it continues: *Then the Levites arose... And they gathered their brethren, and sanctified themselves, and came... to cleanse the house of the Lord. And the priests went into the inner part of the house of the Lord, to cleanse it, and brought out all the uncleanness... And the consecrated things were six hundred oxen and three thousand sheep. But the priests were too few, so that they could not flay all the burnt offerings; wherefore their brethren the Levites did help them, till the work was ended, and until the other priests had sanctified themselves; for the Levites were more upright in heart to sanctify themselves than the priests.*[211] Then it is written in chapter 31: *And Hezekiah appointed the companies (i.e. ephemeriae, or courses) of the priests and the Levites after their divisions, every man according to his service, the priests and Levites for burnt offerings and for peace offerings, to minister, and to give thanks, and to praise in the gates of the tents of the Lord.*[212] Later on Josiah restored the Temple, and he also revived the duties of the Levites; as it is written in chapter 35: *And said unto the Levites that taught all Israel, which were holy unto the Lord, put the holy ark in the house which Solomon... did build; it shall not be a burden upon your shoulders; serve now the Lord your God, and his people Israel, and prepare yourselves by the houses of your fathers, after your courses, according to the writing of David... and according to the writing of Solomon... And stand in the holy place according to the divisions of the families of the fathers of your brethren the people, and after the division of the families of the Levites. So kill the passover, and sanctify yourselves...*[213] But it seems that the chief responsibility of the Levites was to flay the hides of the burnt offerings instead of the priests; for a little farther on it adds: *...and the Levites* stood *in their courses, according to the king's commandment... and the Levites flayed the hides of the burnt offerings.*[214] I would either say that this was Josiah's innovation, or put it back in the time of Hezekiah, when the Levites took this duty upon themselves because there were so few priests available. And in fact, to this day no one has discovered why St. Jerome wrote about this passage that though it was the custom for the Levites to flay the hides of the burnt offerings, the priests did so in the case of sin offerings. For Ezekiel seems to be saying in chapter 44 that in later times this was entirely the responsibility of the Levites: *Yet the Levites shall be ministers in my sanctuary, having charge at the gates of the house, and ministering to the house: they shall slay the burnt offering and the sacrifice for the people, and they shall stand before them to minister unto them... And they shall not come near unto me, to do the office of a priest unto me, nor to come near to any of my holy things, in the most holy place...*[215]

CHAPTER 5

Singers

WE SAID THAT THE singers were established by David to offer thanks and to sing to the Lord with instruments. These instruments were of several kinds—horns, cymbals, psalteries, citharas, and the instrument specifically called an organ.[216] They would also sing the hymns composed by David, Asaph, Jeduthun, Heman, and Ethan; and in giving thanks they often used the words: *O give thanks unto the Lord; for he is good; for his mercy endureth for ever.*[217] Moreover, they wore coats of *byssus* so they could be told from the priests, who wore linen ones. David assigned this duty to the three sons of Joel, who were descended from Gershon; namely, Asaph, Heman, and Jeduthun.[218] Between them they had twenty-four sons—Asaph four, Jeduthun six, and Heman fourteen; each of these gave his name to one of the twenty-four divisions which were assigned at random on the basis of lots. And it is written about them in the same passage: *These were the sons of the Levites after the house of their fathers. These likewise cast lots over against their brethren the sons of Aaron in the presence of David the king, and Zadok, and Ahimelech, and the chief of the fathers of the priests and Levites, even the principal fathers over against their younger brethren. Moreover David and the captains of the host separated to the service of the sons of Asaph, and of Heman, and of Jeduthun, who should prophesy with harps, with psalteries, and with cymbals; and the number of the workmen according to their service was:... the sons of Asaph... four, under the hands of Asaph, who prophesied according to the order of the king... the sons of Jeduthun... six, under the hands of their father Jeduthun, who prophesied with a harp, to give thanks and to praise the Lord... the sons of Heman, fourteen... the king's seer in the words of God, to lift up the horn... All these were under the hands of their father for song in the house of the Lord, with cymbals, psalteries, and harps, for the service of the house of God, according to the king's order... So the number of them, with their brethren who were instructed in the songs of the Lord... was two hundred fourscore and eight. And they cast lots, as well the small as the great, the teacher as the student.*[219] They were arranged into twenty-four courses, which are then set out in order as follows:

1. Joseph
2. Gedaliah
3. Zaccur
4. Izri
5. Nethaniah
6. Bukkiah
7. Jesharelah
8. Jeshaiah
9. Mattaniah
10. Shimei
11. Azareel
12. Nashabiah[220]
13. Shubael
14. Mattithiah
15. Jeremoth
16. Hananiah
17. Joshbekashah
18. Hanani
19. Mallothi
20. Eliathah
21. Hothir
22. Giddalti
23. Mahazioth
24. Romamtiezer

Descriptions of their duties are to be found in many passages, but above all in the seventh chapter of Second Chronicles, under the reign of Solomon: *And the priests waited on their offices; the Levites also with instruments of music of the Lord, which David the king had made... and the priests sounded trumpets before them...*[221] And in chapter five: *And it came to pass, when the priests were come out of the holy place (for all the priests who were present were sanctified, and did not then wait by course; also the Levites who were the singers, all of them of Asaph, of Heman, of Jeduthun, with their sons and their brethren, being arrayed in white linen, having cymbals and psalteries and harps, stood at the east end of the altar, and with them a hundred and twenty priests sounding with trumpets); it came even to pass, as the trumpeters and singers were as one, to make one sound to be heard in praising and thanking the Lord; and when they lifted up their voice with the trumpets and cymbals and instruments of music, and praised the Lord, saying, For he is good; for his mercy endureth for ever: that then the house was filled with a cloud, even the house of the Lord; so that the priests could not stand to minister by reason of the cloud.*[222] And in chapter 20: ...King Jehoshaphat *appointed singers unto the Lord, and who should praise the beauty of holiness, as they went out before the army, and to say, Praise the Lord; for his mercy endureth for ever.*[223] Likewise in the third chapter of Ezra: *And they sang together by course in praising and giving thanks unto the Lord; because he is good, for his mercy endureth for ever...*[224] And chapter 13:[225] *For in the days of David and Asaph of old there were chiefs of the singers, and songs of praise and thanksgiving unto God.*

Josephus also adds in Book 8[226] that this same Solomon made 200,000 robes of *byssus* for the Levites who sang hymns; and in Book 20 that in the time of Agrippa king of Judea, they were given priestly linen in place of the *byssus. All the members of the tribe,* he says, *who were singers of hymns persuaded the king to convene a session of the council, and to give them the right to wear a linen robe just as the priests did... And the king, in accordance with the judgment of the members of the council, allowed them to put aside their former garments and dress in linen. And since part of the tribe served in the Temple, they were permitted to learn the hymns which they had requested to sing. And both these things were contrary to the laws.*[227]

CHAPTER 6

Porters

THE PORTERS WERE attendants who kept watch at the doors to the Temple and guarded the sacred chests[228] about which we are told in First Chronicles: *And the porters were Shallum, and Akkub, and Talmon, and Ahiman, and their brethren; Shallum was the chief, who hitherto waited in the king's gate eastward; they were porters in the companies of the children of Levi. And Shallum the son of Kore... and his brethren... were over the work of the service, keepers of the gates of the tabernacle; and their fathers, being over the host of the Lord, were keepers of the entry. And Phinehas the son of Eleazar was the ruler over them in time past, and the Lord was with him. And Zechariah the son of Meshelemiah was porter of the door of the tabernacle of the congregation. All these who were chosen to be porters in the gates were two hundred and twelve. These were reckoned by their genealogy in their villages, whom David and Samuel the seer did ordain in their set office. So they and their children had the oversight of the gates of the house of the Lord, namely, the house of the tabernacle, by wards. In four quarters were the porters, toward the east, west, north, and south... For these Levites, the four chief porters, were in their set office, and were over the chambers and treasuries of the house of God. And they lodged round about the house of God, because the charge was upon them, and the opening thereof every morning pertained to them.*[229]

These men too were organized into twenty-four divisions or courses, as it is written in chapter 26. The first seven of these were named after the sons of Shelemiah[230]—Zechariah, Jediael, Zebadiah, Jathniel, Elam, Jehohanan, and Elioenai; the next eight after the sons of Obededom—Shemaiah, Jehozabad, Sacar, Nethaneel, Ammiel, Issachar, and Peulthai;[231] and the last six after the sons of Shemaiah the firstborn—Othni, Rephael, Obed, Elzabad, Elihu, and Semachiah. The rest were named after the sons of Hosah—Simri, Hilkiah, Tebaliah, and Zechariah.[232] After setting this out it adds: *Among these were the divisions of the porters, even among the chief men, having wards one against another, to minister in the house of the Lord. And they cast lots, as well the small as the great, according to the house of their fathers, for every gate. And the lot eastward fell to Shelemiah. Then for Zechariah his son... northward. To Obededom southward; and to his sons the house of Asuppim. To Shuppim and Hosah the lot came forth westward, with the gate Shallecheth, by the causeway of the going up, ward against ward. Eastward were six Levites, northward four a day, southward four a day, and toward Asuppim two and two. At Parbar westward, four at the causeway, and two at Parbat. These are the divisions of the porters among the sons of Kore, and among the sons of Merari.*[233] After this is finished, we are told about the custody of the sacred funds: And the Levites their brethren... *were over the treasures of the house of God, and over the treasures of the dedicated things... And Shebuel... was ruler of the treasures. Eliezer* and his brothers...[234] *were over all the treasures of the dedicated things, which David the king, and the chief fathers, the captains over thousands and hundreds, and the captains of the host, had dedicated. Out of the spoils won in battles did they dedicate to maintain the house of the Lord.*[235]

Then, during the reign of Joash, the high priest Jehoiada appointed certain Levite porters to guard the Temple, whose task was to bar anyone impure from entering. This is found in Second Chronicles 23.[236] And chapter 24 of Second Kings tells us that these same porters collected the sacred money: *Go up to Hilkiah the high priest, that he may sum the silver which is brought into the house of the Lord, which the keepers of the door have gathered of the people.*[237] Philo describes the subject as follows, in his work on the rewards of priests:[238] *Some of the guardians worked as porters... others watched the courtyard... still others were chosen to guard the Temple in shifts, by day and by night... some were in charge of sweeping the colonnades and the atrium, and carrying out the scraps and refuse, and seeing that the place was pure.*[239]

Now the duties of the priests, the Levites, the singers, and the porters are even more clearly laid out in Second Chronicles 35, which describes the famous Passover celebrated by King Josiah: *So the service*, it says, *was prepared, and the priests stood in their place, and the Levites in their courses* (Greek: *in their divisions*), *according to the king's commandment. And they killed the passover, and the priests sprinkled the blood from their hands, and the Levites flayed them. And they removed the burnt offerings, that they might give according to the divisions of the families of the people, to offer unto the Lord, as it is written in the book of Moses... And they roasted the passover with fire according to the ordinance; but the other holy offerings sod they in pots, and in caldrons, and in pans, and divided them speedily among all the people. And afterward they made ready for themselves, and for the priests; because the priests the sons of Aaron were busied in offering of burnt offerings and the fat until night; therefore the Levites prepared for themselves, and for the priests the sons of Aaron. And the singers the sons of Asaph were in their place, according to the commandment of David... and Heman, and Jeduthun the king's seer; and the porters waited at every gate; they might not depart from their service; for their brethren the Levites prepared for them. So all the service of the Lord was prepared the same day, to keep the Passover, and to offer burnt offerings upon the altar of the Lord, according to the commandment of King Josiah.*[240]

CHAPTER 7

Nethinim

THE NETHINIM WERE closely associated with the porters, as we learn from the first chapter of Ezra, where he reviews in order the priests, the Levites, the singers, the porters, and the *nethinim* who returned from Babylonia. Just as the Levites were in charge of ministering to the priests, the *nethinim* ministered to the Levites; so if we may call the Levites deacons, then the *nethinim* were subdeacons. In chapter 9 of First Chronicles: *Now the first inhabitants who dwelt in their possessions in their cities were the Israelites, the priests, Levites, and the nethinim.*[241] And in Ezra chapter 2: *All the nethinim, and the children of Solomon's servants, were three hundred and ninety and two.*[242] At one time they were called Gibeonites; the latter are discussed in Joshua chapters 5, 9, and 20: ...Joshua *delivered the* Gibeonites *out of the hand of the children of Israel, that they slew them not. And Joshua made them that day hewers of wood and drawers of water for the congregation, and for the altar of the Lord, even unto this day, in the place which he should choose.*[243] Then David gave them a new name (though not a new function) and instead of Gibeonites he called them *nethinim.*[244] This is clear from Ezra chapter 8: *Also of the nethinim, whom David and the princes had appointed for the service of the Levites...*[245] Hence it is written in chapter 2: *So the priests, and the Levites, and some of the people, and the singers, and the porters, and the nethinim, dwelt in their cities.*[246]

CHAPTER 8

Nazirites

TILL NOW I HAVE been describing the people who saw to the sacred rites. There was as well a certain class of men who, though they did not touch anything sacred, nevertheless dedicated their efforts to God. These people either consecrated their own bodies to him, or poured forth his prophecies, or explained his laws. The first group were called Nazirites, the second, prophets, and the third, scribes. The latter went on to spawn various sects—Sadducees, scribes, Pharisees, Herodians, and others.[247]

The Nazirites, then, were men who had dedicated themselves to God with a vow. The procedure is explained in Numbers chapter 6: *When either man or woman shall separate themselves to vow a vow of a Nazirite, to separate themselves unto the Lord, he shall separate himself from wine and strong drink, and shall drink no vinegar of wine, or vinegar of strong drink, neither shall he drink any liquor of grapes, nor eat moist grapes, or dried. All the days of his separation shall he eat nothing that is made of the vine tree, from the kernels even to the husk. All the days of the vow of his separation there shall no razor come upon his head; until the days be fulfilled, in which he separateth himself unto the Lord, he shall be holy, and shall let the locks of the hair of his head grow. All the days that he separateth himself unto the Lord he shall come at no dead body. He shall not make himself unclean for his father, or for his mother, for his brother, or for his sister, when they die; because the consecration of his God is upon his head. All the days of his separation he is holy unto the Lord. And if any man die very suddenly by him, and he hath defiled the head of his consecration; then he shall shave his head in the day of his cleansing, on the seventh day shall he shave it. And on the eighth day he shall bring two turtledoves, or two young pigeons, to the priest, to the door of the tabernacle of the congregation; and the priest shall offer the one for a sin offering, and the other for a burnt offering, and make an atonement for him, for that he sinned by the dead, and shall hallow his head that same day. And he shall consecrate unto the Lord... but the days that were before shall be lost, because his separation was defiled.*[248] I find three particular examples of Nazirites among the Hebrews—Samson, Samuel, and James the Just, the brother of the Lord. On Samson, there is Judges chapter 22:[249] *Now therefore beware, I pray thee, and drink not wine nor strong drink, and eat not any unclean thing; for, lo, thou shalt conceive, and bear a son; and no razor shall come on his head: for the child shall be a Nazirite unto God from the womb...* As for Samuel, Hannah vows her son to God in First Samuel, with these words: *...I will give him unto the Lord all the days of his life, and there shall no razor come upon his head.*[250] About James, Hegesippus[251] says as follows, according to Clement of Alexandria: *He was sacred from his mother's womb, he did not drink wine or strong drink, nor did he eat any animals, and iron never touched his head.*[252] On the other hand, Philo describes this vow of sanctification explicitly in his book on sacrificers: *When someone has offered up first fruits and tithes from all his produce... and does not have anything more with which to demonstrate his piety, he dedicates his own self; and this is therefore called the great vow... For no one possesses anything more valuable than himself which he may then give up. The person who makes such a vow takes on the following obligations: first, that he should not drink wine or any other beverage made from grapes... then, that on the appointed day he should make, in the required fashion, three votive offerings—a sheep, a ewe, and a ram; the sheep as a burnt offering, the ewe as a sin offering, and the ram as a peace offering. All these offerings are fitting for the person who has made a vow: the burnt offering because he is dedicating to God not only his property, but himself; the sin offering because however blameless he may be, as a man he is not without sin; and the peace offering because he attributes to God, his true savior, the contentment he has received.*[253]

CHAPTER 9

Prophets

NEXT WERE THE MEN who were filled with the spirit of God, and at his command warned the Hebrews of both the good and bad things that were going to happen. At first they were called seers, and then prophets. As it is written in chapter 9 of First Samuel: *Beforetime in Israel, when a man went to inquire of God, thus he spake, Come, and let us go to the seer: for he who is now called a prophet was beforetime called a seer.*[254] And just as God declared to the Hebrews that he was going to give them more guardians,[255] he made them a particular promise that he would raise up prophets from among them. But even before he sent them the prophets promised in the law, he blessed many of the patriarchs with the prophetic spirit, as in the cases of Abraham, Isaac, Jacob, and Joseph. (Their prophecies still exist, sealed in the narrative of the sacred text.)[256] Soon afterward he endowed several foreigners with this distinction, including Balaam, Job,[257] and a number of others.

But the first prophet God sent, and the greatest of them all, was Moses, about whom we are told in Numbers 12: *If there be a prophet among you, I the Lord will make myself known unto him in a vision, and will speak unto him in a dream. My servant Moses is not so... With him will I speak mouth to mouth, even apparently, and not in dark speeches; and the similitude of the Lord shall he behold...*[258] Then he said that he would send others after him, which he did (as Moses himself bears witness in Deuteronomy 18): *I will raise them up a prophet from among their brethren, like unto thee, and will put my words in his mouth; and he shall speak unto them all that I shall command him. And it shall come to pass, that whosoever will not hearken unto my words which he shall speak in my name, I will require it of him. But the prophet, who shall presume to speak a word in my name, which I have not commanded him to speak, or who shall speak in the name of other gods, even that prophet shall die. And if thou say in thine heart, How shall we know the word which the Lord hath not spoken? When a prophet speaketh in the name of the Lord, if the thing follow not, nor come to pass, that is the thing which the Lord hath not spoken, but the prophet hath spoken it presumptuously: thou shalt not be afraid of him.*[259] And in chapter 18: Moses said, If *the Lord thy God will raise up unto thee a prophet from the midst of thee, of thy brethren, like unto me, unto him ye shall hearken...*[260] And chapter 34: *And there arose not a prophet since in Israel like unto Moses...*[261]

This was the prophetic spirit, with which God filled Moses more than anyone else; and from him it passed to the seventy elders, who themselves began to give prophecy. This is described in Numbers 11: *And Moses went out, and told the people the words of the Lord, and gathered the seventy men of the elders of the people, and set them round about the tabernacle. And the Lord came down in a cloud, and spake unto him, and took of the spirit that was upon him, and gave it unto the seventy elders; and it came to pass, that, when the spirit rested upon them, they prophesied, and did not cease. But there remained two of the men in the camp, the name of the one was Eldad, and the name of the other Medad; and the spirit rested upon them; and they were of them who were written, but went not out... and they prophesied in the camp. And there ran a young man, and told Moses, and said, Eldad and Medad do prophesy in the camp. And Joshua the son of Nun, the servant of Moses, one of his young men, answered and said, My lord Moses, forbid them. And Moses said unto him, Enviest thou for my sake? Would God that all the Lord's people were prophets, and that the Lord would put his spirit upon them!*[262]

Then in the time of the judges we are told about Deborah (Judges chapter 4), who is said to have been a prophet and to have judged the people by herself. And in chapter 6 we are told of another prophet[263] in these words: *And it came to pass, when the children of Israel cried unto the Lord because of the Midianites, that the Lord sent a prophet unto the children of Israel, who said unto them, Thus saith the Lord...*[264]

Finally God produced Samuel, who outstripped all the others in his glory at a time when... *the word of the Lord was precious... there was no open vision.*[265] In the second chapter of First Samuel:[266] *...So Samuel went and lay down in his place. And the Lord... called three times... and... said to Samuel, Behold, I will do a thing in Israel, at which both the ears of every one who heareth it shall tingle... And Samuel grew, and the Lord was with him, and... all Israel... knew that Samuel was established to be a prophet of the Lord.* After Samuel there appeared, so to speak, an established organization of prophets, and groups of them could be found in every age and in every state. Hence First Samuel 28: *And when Saul inquired of the Lord, the Lord answered him not, neither by dreams, nor by priests, nor by prophets.*[267] Samuel, moreover, stood at the head of a large retinue of men who devoted themselves energetically to explaining the scripture, and from among whom God chose a number to serve as prophets. Following Samuel, then, there was a steady succession of prophets until Malachi in the time of Darius, when the Temple was restored. We are told about Samuel's retinue, and how God inspired them, in First Samuel 10, where Samuel says to Saul: *...thou shalt come to the hill of God, where is the garrison of the Philistines: and it shall come to pass, when thou art come thither to the city, that thou shalt meet a company of prophets coming down from the high place with a psaltery, and a tabret, and a pipe, and a harp, before them; and they shall prophesy; and the Spirit of the Lord will come upon thee, and thou shalt prophesy with them, and shalt be turned into another man.*[268] And a little after: *And when they came thither to the hill, behold, a company of prophets met him; and the Spirit of God came upon him, and he prophesied among them. And it came to pass, when all who knew him beforetime saw that, behold, he prophesied among the prophets, then the people said one to another, What is this that is come unto the son of Kish? Is Saul also among the prophets?*[269] And chapter 19: *And Saul sent messengers* to Ramah *to take David; and when they saw the company of the prophets prophesying, and Samuel standing as appointed over them, the Spirit of God was upon the messengers of Saul, and they also prophesied. And when it was told Saul, he sent other messengers, and they prophesied likewise. And Saul sent messengers again the third time, and they prophesied also. Then went he also to Ramah... and the Spirit of God was upon him also, and he went on, and prophesied, until he came to Naioth... And he stripped off his clothes also, and prophesied before Samuel in like manner, and lay down naked all that day and all that night. Wherefore they say, Is Saul also among the prophets?*[270] So after Samuel there was a great crop of prophets, though not all their names have been recorded in the text. We know this from Second Kings 2, where it is written: *And Elijah said unto Elisha, Tarry here, I pray thee; for the Lord hath sent me to Bethel... So they went down to Bethel. And the sons of the prophets who were at Bethel came forth...*[271] And: *...tarry here, I pray thee; for the Lord hath sent me to Jericho... And the sons of the prophets who were at Jericho.*[272] And afterward: *Tarry, I pray thee, here; for the Lord hath sent me to Jordan... And they two went on. And fifty men of the sons of the prophets went...*[273] And after Elijah was snatched up:[274] *And when the sons of the prophets who were to view at Jericho saw him, they said, the spirit of Elijah doth rest on Elisha.*[275] The names of the prophets who lived under the kings and during the Babylonian exile were more or less as follows: The ones whose prophecies were not recorded are Gad, Nathan, Asaph, Jeduthun, Ahijah, Shemaiah, Iddo, Azariah, Hanani, Jehu, Jahaziel, Eliezer, Zechariah,[276] Elijah, and Elisha.[277] The ones who did record their prophecies were Hosea, Joel, Amos, Obadiah, Jonah, Micah, Nahum, Habakkuk, Zephaniah, Haggai, Zechariah, and Malachi (these are called the lesser prophets, because the

books of prophecy they left us are rather short); and Isaiah, Jeremiah, Ezekiel, and Daniel (who are called greater because they wrote larger collections
of prophecies).[278] They predicted the disasters that were going to befall the
kingdoms of Israel and Judah, and they added a great deal about the coming
of Christ. The last of them was Malachi, who announced the forerunner of
Christ as follows: *Behold, I will send my messenger, and he shall prepare the
way before me...*[279] And until John the Baptist, whom he had predicted, there
were no more prophets of any note among the Jewish people.

Since I have been discussing the prophets, to whom (more than anyone else) people turned when they wished to consult with God himself,
I have decided for the sake of clarity to add some general remarks about
the procedure for consulting with God. The Hebrews, then, consulted him
principally through oracles; and they were said to have consulted such an
oracle whenever they approached the mercy seat of the ark of the covenant,
where they made their requests of God and he answered them. God himself instructs Moses about this in the twenty-seventh chapter of Exodus,[280]
when he tells him: *...I will commune with thee from above the mercy seat,
from between the two cherubim which are upon the ark of the testimony, of
all things which I will give thee in commandment unto the children of Israel.*
Moses, in fact, then carried out God's instructions in this passage, in the
eighth chapter of Numbers:[281] *And when Moses was gone into the tabernacle
of the congregation to speak with the oracle,*[282] *then he heard the voice of one
speaking unto him from off the mercy seat that was upon the ark of the testimony, from between the two cherubim: and he spake unto him.* Likewise in
the first chapter of Judges: *Now after the death of Joshua it came to pass, that
the children of Israel asked the Lord, saying, who shall go up for us against the
Canaanites first, to fight against them? And the Lord said, Judah...*[283] And in
the twentieth chapter: *they went up to the house of God, and asked counsel of
God, and said, which of us shall go up first to the battle against the children
of Benjamin? And the Lord said, Judah...*[284] And afterward: *...they went up
and wept before the Lord... and asked counsel of the Lord, saying, shall I go
up again to battle against the children of Benjamin my brother? And the Lord
said, go up against him.*[285] And in the tenth chapter of First Samuel: *Therefore they inquired of the Lord further, if* Saul *should yet come thither. And
the Lord answered, behold he hath hid himself among the stuff.*[286] And in the
twenty-first chapter of Second Samuel: *and David inquired of the oracle of
the Lord. And the Lord answered...*[287] This method of consulting the oracle
was practiced only as long as the First Temple stood; during the Second (the
talmudists say) there was no longer an ark, but only, as I have said, a stone
that stood three inches high.[288]

In addition to the oracle, God answered sometimes through prophets, sometimes through priests, and sometimes through dreams. Hence (as I said) it is written: *And when Saul inquired of the Lord, the Lord answered him not, neither by dreams, nor by priests, nor by prophets.*[289] *By priests* means "by high priests," which I believe is proven by the reference to Abiathar the high priest in the thirtieth chapter of First Samuel: *And David said to Abiathar the priest... I pray thee, bring me hither the ephod. And Abiathar brought thither the ephod to David. And David inquired of the Lord, saying, Shall I pursue after this troop? Shall I overtake them? And he answered him, Pursue: for thou shalt surely overtake them, and without fail recover all.*[290] The same point is made in the eighteenth chapter of Judges: *And they said unto him, Ask counsel, we pray thee, of God, that we may know whether our way which we go shall be prosperous. And the priest said unto them, Go in peace...*[291] In fact, we are told later that this priest had an ephod.[292] And because it is written in the twenty-fifth chapter of Exodus that onyx stones and gems were to adorn the ephod and the breastplate, the talmudists added that the Urim and Thummim stones, i.e. those of Teaching and Truth, were located on the high priest's pectoral,[293] and that by looking at these stones—which would sometimes shine more brightly than normal—the priests could understand hidden truths and relay them to the people. If, on the other hand, the stones kept their natural color, this meant that nothing out of the ordinary was going to happen. And as I said above, even these stones stopped shining when the Second Temple was built.[294]

I have already spoken about the prophets. *Beforetime*, it says in First Samuel, *when a man went to inquire of God, thus he spake, Come, and let us go to the seer,*[295] i.e. to the prophet. And in the eighth chapter of Second Kings: *...go, meet the man of God, and inquire of the Lord by him, saying, Shall I recover of this disease?*[296] I will also include here a striking passage about the prophets consulted by Kings Jehoshaphat and Ahab, in the eighteenth chapter of Second Chronicles: *Therefore* Ahab *the king of Israel gathered together of prophets four hundred men, and said unto them, Shall we go to Ramothgilead to battle, or shall I forbear? And they said, Go up; for God will deliver it into the king's hand...* Then Micaiah was summoned; and at first he said the same thing; but after he was sworn to tell the truth he added, *The Lord hath put a lying spirit in the mouth of these thy prophets, and the Lord hath spoken evil against thee.* Then Zedekiah... one of the prophets, who had predicted a success, *came near, and smote Micaiah upon the cheek, and said, Which way went the Spirit of the Lord from me to speak unto thee? And Micaiah said, Behold, thou shalt see...* And to the king: *If thou certainly return in peace,* *then hath not the Lord spoken by me.*[297] But as I said earlier, the prophets too ceased after the building of the Second Temple.

The procedure for dreams was as follows. God forbade the observation of dreams—he did not want the divine message contained within them to be taken lightly.[298] He also included a prohibition in the eighteenth chapter of Deuteronomy: *There shall not be found among you any one... who useth divination, or an observer of dreams, or an enchanter, or a witch. Or a charmer, or a consulter with familiar spirits, or a wizard, or a necromancer. For all that do these things are an abomination unto the Lord...*[299] Accordingly, in the thirty-third chapter of Second Chronicles King Manasseh is rebuked for observing dreams and devoting himself to the evil arts. And it is written in chapter 23 of Jeremiah: *The prophet who hath a dream, let him tell a dream; and he who hath my word, let him speak my word faithfully. What is the chaff to the wheat? saith the Lord.*[300] There are, however, many cases in which God chose to use a dream to deliver a message. In the twelfth chapter of Numbers: *If there be a prophet among you, I the Lord will make myself known unto him in a vision, and will speak unto him in a dream. My servant Moses is not so... With him will I speak mouth to mouth, even apparently, and not in dark speeches; and the similitude of the Lord shall he behold...*[301] When, therefore, in the seventh chapter of Judges one person tells another that he had a dream, Gideon accepts as true the interpretation given to it.[302] And in the third chapter of First Kings: *In Gibeon the Lord appeared to Solomon in a dream... and God said, Ask what I shall give thee. And he said... Give me... an understanding heart... And Solomon awoke; and, behold, it was a dream. And he came to Jerusalem, and stood before the ark of the covenant of the Lord...*[303] God continued to use this method of informing people until the very end.[304] As St. Matthew writes: *But while he thought on these things, behold, the angel of the Lord appeared unto him in a dream, saying, Joseph, thou son of David, fear not to take unto thee Mary thy wife...*[305] And in Joel chapter 2: *And it shall come to pass afterward, that I will pour out my spirit upon all flesh; and your sons and your daughters shall prophesy, your old men shall dream dreams, your young men shall see visions.*[306] Because naturally occurring dreams are so often unclear and spring from such uncertain sources, God warned us not to take any notice of them, as opposed to those which he himself had sent. He also made it possible for a man to see that such dreams ought not to be rejected and that they contain a degree of truth, like the dreams that Joseph and Daniel pieced together, and which won them such praise for their ingenuity.

There were four ways in which God either was consulted by people and responded to them, or was not consulted but sent them a message: he himself spoke directly, or used a vision or a dream; or an angel spoke directly for him, or through a vision or dream. A case of the first would be: *God said to Abraham/Jacob/Joshua.* Of the second: *The word of the Lord came unto Abraham in a vision, saying...*[307] Of the third: *And the angel of the Lord called unto him out of heaven, and said...*[308] And of the fourth: *The angel of the Lord appeareth to Joseph in a dream, saying...*[309]

The interpreters of the sacred text explain that though God did use words, they were not the sort of words that could be perceived with the ears. Rather, he shaped the thoughts of those to whom he spoke in such a way that they could see things with their eyes as though they had actually occurred, and could feel themselves being addressed by God through his divine power. The effect was just as though they had heard God speaking and were no less aware of what they themselves had said. Things said in this way were prophecies, and the people to whom they were said were called prophets. Hence in the thirteenth chapter of First Kings, a certain prophet says: *For it was said to me by the word of the Lord, thou shalt eat no bread nor drink water there...* Then King Jeroboam *said unto him, I am a prophet also as thou art; and an angel spake unto me by the word of the Lord, saying, Bring him back with thee into thine house, that he may eat bread and drink water...*[310] Moreover, what I have said about the word of God was written by St. Basil in his commentary on Psalm 28: *The voice of God is different* from the voices that are registered by our ears; *for it happens that the minds of men to whom he wishes to communicate are shaped by a kind of vision, just as happens in dreams. In dreams our minds seem to be impressed with the forms of various words, even though no sound has fallen on our ears, and instead the mind itself has been shaped by various symbolic representations; and so should we understand the voice of God, which the prophets are said to have heard.*[311] And in any case, not everyone about whom it is written *God said to him* was given this information directly by God himself; rather he got it from a prophet whose mind God had filled. And when we are told that God came to someone, this is considered not prophecy but a simple admonition, as in the cases of Laban and Abimelech.[312]

The prophets, then, were informed about the future either while they were awake (in a vision) or while they slept (in a dream); and either with or without a messenger (in what is called an imagined vision).[313] Only Moses himself is thought to have been instructed without dreams or messengers, but with (as they call it) an intellectual vision, and to have predicted what was going to happen. But sacred speech, as Philo tells us in his book on dreams, is like a king ordering what he wants done; or a teacher giving useful instruction; or a counselor giving timely advice to people who cannot decide upon their own plan; or a friend passing on secret information which is not meant to be heard by the uninitiated. God could also ask a question of someone, as he did of Adam.[314] Even though the scriptures usually speak of God with great reverence,[315] they do sometimes liken him to a man for the sake of penetrating our brute ignorance; and with an eye toward educational utility rather than the truth, they give God limbs, motions, and words. Most people, after all, are incapable of imagining God without a physical body, and they cannot devote themselves to him unless they hear that he comes, and goes, and gets angry, and takes revenge, and has his bolts at the ready to punish evildoers, and sometimes even calls people by name.[316]

CHAPTER 10

Scribes

JUST AS THE PROPHETS declared God's wishes, so the scribes interpreted his law. The beginnings of this institution date back to Moses himself—he used one kind of language to describe handing things down to the people, and another for committing things to writing. The first was called tradition and the second, law. But the things that Moses taught orally he first communicated to Joshua, and then Joshua to the elders, the elders to the prophets, and the prophets to the scribes. In the later scholarship of the Hebrews these traditions are called "historical kabbala."[317] St. Luke makes a reference to the traditions of Moses in the sixth chapter of Acts: *For we have heard him say, that this Jesus of Nazareth... shall change the customs which Moses delivered us.*[318] The elders[319] are mentioned in the second chapter of Judges: *And the people served the Lord all the days of Joshua, and all the days of the elders who outlived Joshua, who had seen all the great works of the Lord, which he did for Israel.*[320] We are also told about their traditions in SS. Matthew and Mark: *Why do thy disciples transgress the tradition of the elders? For they wash not their hands when they eat bread. But Jesus answered and said unto them, Why do ye also transgress the commandment of God by your tradition?*[321] And: *For the Pharisees, and all the Jews, except they wash their hands oft, eat not, holding the tradition of the elders.*[322]

Just as Moses was the first to give the law, he was also the first to explain it. We know this from what is written in the Gospels about the "seat of Moses."[323] The leaders who came after him continued to keep the same practice; hence it is written in Leviticus 10: *And the Lord spake unto Aaron, saying, Do not drink wine nor strong drink, thou, nor thy sons with thee, when ye go into the tabernacle of the congregation, lest ye die... And that ye may put difference between holy and unholy, and between unclean and clean; and that ye may teach the children of Israel all the statutes which the Lord hath spoken unto them by the hand of Moses.*[324] Josephus accordingly wrote in the second book of his *Against Apion*: *The lawgiver did not want his people to hear the law only once, but that once a week they should put aside their labors and gather to listen to it and learn it perfectly.*[325] Philo writes the same thing in the third book of his *Life of Moses:*[326] *It was the custom... on Sabbaths... to devote time to philosophy; the leader stood before the people and taught what they ought to say and do, and everyone else listened. This is why even today they philosophize on the Sabbath according to their ancestral custom... for our places of prayer, in whatever city they are found, are teachers of all the virtues*[327] *with which we may understand and correct our dealings in both divine and human matters.* It was also required by law that every seventh year, the Levites had to pass on to the people the words of the law.[328]

This was the state of affairs when David became king and put his stamp on this institution, as he had all the others of the state. Once he had calculated the number of Levites, he made six thousand of them into scribes and judges; and then, when he was assigning the sacred duties of the Levites to their families, he also set some of them over Israel *to teach and to judge*, as we find in First Chronicles 23 and 26.[329] To this day, as far as I know, no one has demonstrated who exactly these scribes and judges who taught and judged were. The Greek translation has, in the first passage I mentioned,[330] *grammateis* and *kritai*;[331] and in the second[332] *to grammateuein* and *diakrinein*.[333] These were the terms used to describe the two duties of those who interpreted the law: first, to read the words of the law; and second, to explain it whenever the necessity arose. *Grammateis* is, therefore, better translated as "lectors"[334] (a word also used by the Christian Church)[335] than as "scribes." We can prove this from Ezra chapter 3, where Ezra is called *ho anagnōstēs tou nomou*, i.e. the reader of the law, whereas in other passages he is called *grammateus* or scribe. And in the tenth chapter of St. Luke, where Christ is speaking to a certain *legis peritus*[336] (or scribe) who had said *what shall I do to inherit eternal life? He said unto him, What is written in the law? How readest thou?*[337] That is, "How can you claim to be an interpreter if you don't know what questions to ask?" On the other hand, chapters 5, 6, 10, and 11 call men of this type *grammateis, nomikoi*, and *nomodidaskaloi*;[338] that is, experts in the law and doctors of the law. And yet the fact that the same people are called *kritai*, i.e. judges, and are said *diakrinein*, i.e. to judge or distinguish, refers entirely to their method of interpretation, which required them to make judgments and draw distinctions.[339] This is especially important for the Hebrew language, which is generally thought to have very few words, which have different meanings depending on their particular markings and punctuation.[340] Philo proves this in his book called *That Every Good Man Is Free*, where he discusses the Jews called Essenes as follows: *Their most established observance is the seventh day, when they rest from all other work and gather at their sacred places (which are called synagogues); they sit*

ranked by age from youngest to oldest and listen with the appropriate comport-
ment. Then one of them starts to read from the Bible, while another—one of
their most learned men—explains what is least familiar; for most of their
traditions are passed on through ancient symbols and allegory.[341] St. Paul, who
lived at the same time as the Essenes, proves the same thing, since what he
writes to the Corinthians agrees with this practice: *Let the prophets speak*
two or three, and let the others judge.[342] In Greek it has *diakrinetōsan,* i.e. *let*
two read, and the others explain.[343] And after the time of David, when King
Jehoshaphat saw that this practice had fallen into disuse and that most people were ignorant of the law, *he sent the priests and the Levites through all*
the cities of Judah, to teach it.[344] In Second Chronicles 17: *Also in the third*
year of his reign he sent to his princes... to teach in the cities of Judah. And
with them he sent Levites... and with them... priests. And they taught in Ju-
dah, and had the book of the law of the Lord with them, and went about
throughout all the cities of Judah, and taught the people.[345] Afterward King
Josiah did the same thing as well, when the book of Deuteronomy (which
was thought to have vanished) was found in the Temple. In Second Kings
23: *And the king went up into the house of the Lord, and all the men of Judah*
and all the inhabitants of Jerusalem with him, and the priests, and the proph-
ets, and all the people... and he read in their ears all the words of the book of
the covenant which was found in the house of the Lord.[346] Then followed a
few years later the Babylonian exile; this lasted seventy years, after which the
Jews were restored to their homeland. From then on the law seems to have
been placed under the complete control of the chief priests and the scribes,
as will become clear from the following remarks: there is no question that
in the chaos of that time the law was either lost, neglected, or corrupted,
and desperately needed to be studied and corrected. So Ezra (who is called
a priest, a scribe, and the chief of the priests and scribes) returned to his
homeland after the Temple had been restored, and searched out the copies
of the law that had been lost in the recent exile and destruction. He corrected texts that had been distorted, and marked them with the punctuation
that they have today in the traditions of the Hebrews.[347] He also taught the
law to the people, who were ignorant of it. This is how it is described in his
book: *For Ezra had prepared his heart to seek the law of the Lord, and to do*
it, and to teach... statutes and judgments.[348] Likewise: *And... were gathered*
together the chief of the fathers of all the people, the priests, and the Levites,
unto Ezra the scribe, even to understand the words of the law.[349] And in the
ninth chapter of the Third Book of Esdras: *Ezra, the priest and the reader of*
the law, stood upon a wooden platform which had been built for him... and
took up the book before the entire crowd.[350] All those others who have

interpreted the law, resolved its difficulties, and kept its books from becoming corrupted are thought to have begun with Ezra, for the same passage goes on to say: *He told Ezra, the chief of the priests and the reader, and the Levites who teach the masses.*[351] Notice that Ezra, who was called a priest and a scribe, is now being called the chief of the priests and the reader of the law—the author obviously understood *Levites who teach the masses* to mean "chiefs of the priests and scribes." These men were summoned by Ezra, and they consulted together with him about fixing certain distorted passages of the holy books, and (as the talmudists claim) they created a canon of those books which they had most rigorously examined.[352] From that time on, therefore, it was the chiefs of the priests and the scribes who were primarily responsible for interpreting the law, and they not only were called "doctors of the law" but were regarded as such. Hence the passage in Matthew 13: *...Therefore every scribe who is instructed unto the kingdom of heaven is like unto a man who is a householder, who bringeth forth out of his treasure things new and old.*[353] And chapter 16:[354] *And his disciples asked him, saying, Why then say the scribes that Elijah must first come?* And Mark 16:[355] *...How say the scribes that Christ is the son of David?* It is therefore understandable that when King Herod, who was a proselyte or adoptive Jew, heard about the birth of Christ but had no idea where he was going to appear, he consulted with the chiefs of the priests and the scribes. For as St. Matthew writes, he summoned the chiefs of the priests and the scribes and asked them where Christ would be born.[356] And later on, when Christ—who was neither chief of the priests, nor scribe, nor Levite—had begun to teach in the Temple, he drew particular attention from the chiefs of the priests and the scribes. This is why they were particularly interested to know by whose authority he was doing this. For St. Luke reports as follows in chapter 20: *...as* Jesus *taught the people in the Temple, and preached the gospel, the chief priests and the scribes came upon him... saying, Tell us, by what authority doest thou these things? Or who is he who gave thee this authority?*[357] Thus SS. Matthew and Mark, as though in response to this question, write that Christ taught not like the scribes but as though on his own authority, that is, not like an interpreter of the law but like a lawgiver. For while the interpreters were always resorting to the phrase *the Lord says*, Christ said: *Ye have heard that it was said of them of old time... But I say unto you...*[358] It was a scribe of this sort whom St. Paul writes about in the First Letter to the Corinthians: *Where is the wise? Where is the scribe?*[359] That is, the expert in the law. Such a scholar was Nicodemus, whom Christ called a master of the law and whom he refuted;[360] and such scholars were the men with whom Christ, at the age of twelve, debated the law in the Temple.[361] Such a man was that Pharisee about whom St. Matthew says in chapter 22: *Then one of them... asked him a question, a Pharisee, named Gamaliel, a doctor of the law, and in reputation among all the people...*[362] Finally, such a man was Josiah the Pharisee scribe, about whom it is written in the life of St. James the elder:[363] *Josiah was one of the scribes of the Pharisees; he laced a rope around the neck of the apostle, but then he was converted and suffered martyrdom alongside him.*[364]

The scribes taught the law in two places, the Temple and the synagogues. St. Luke informs us about the Temple when he says that Christ was found there among the teachers, asking and answering questions. All the Gospels likewise report that he often taught and lectured in the Temple. Hence in chapter 18 of the gospel of St. John, he says about himself: *I spake openly to the world; I ever taught in the synagogue, and in the Temple, whither the Jews always resort...*[365] And St. Paul writes in Acts 24: *And they neither found me in the Temple disputing... neither in the synagogues...*[366] This is the reason some scribes were called "scribes of the Temple." The proof of this is the decree of Antiochus the Great[367] found in Book 12 of Josephus: *Let the Senate, the priests, the scribes of the Temple, and the sacred singers be exempt from the tribute levied on every person.*[368] In fact, Hilkiah the high priest *gave the law which he found to Shaphan, the scribe of the Temple, so that he would read it to King Josiah.*[369] And King Josiah sent the scribe of the Temple to Hilkiah the high priest, to ask for the funds for the restoration of the Temple (Second Kings).[370]

The synagogues were, as I said, sanctuaries where the Jews were accustomed to gather on Sabbath days to listen to the law. Hence the passage in Acts 11:[371] *For Moses of old time hath in every city them who preach him, being read in the synagogues every Sabbath day.* To add to my previous comments on the sort of teaching that went on in the synagogues, I would also like to draw on what Philo says about the Essenes, and from the Gospels' description of how Christ roamed about the synagogues of the Galilee preaching the truth. In St. Matthew chapter 4: *And Jesus went about all Galilee, teaching in their synagogues, and preaching the gospel of the kingdom... And Jesus came to Nazareth... and, as his custom was, he went into the synagogue on the Sabbath day... And there was delivered unto him the book of the prophet Isaiah... And he came down to Capernaum, a city of Galilee, and taught them on the Sabbath days. And they were astonished at his doctrine; for his word was with power.*[372] Likewise chapter 13: *And Jesus was teaching in one of the synagogues of the Jews on the Sabbath... and he healed a woman... And the ruler of the synagogue answered with indignation, because that Jesus had healed on the Sabbath day...*[373] All this took place when Christ was alive; but it is recorded that after his death his teachings spread to synagogues beyond Judea and the

Galilee. Acts 9: *And Saul... desired of* the high priest *letters to Damascus to the synagogues, that if he found any of this way, whether they were men or women, he might bring them bound unto Jerusalem...* then he was converted, and he *preached Christ in the synagogues, that he is the son of God.*[374] And in chapter 13: *And when they were at Salamis,* Paul and Barnabas *preached the word of God in the synagogues of the Jews... And: ...they came to Antioch in Pisidia, and went into the synagogue on the Sabbath day, and sat down. And after the reading of the law and the prophets the rulers of the synagogue sent unto them... Now when the congregation was broken up, many of the Jews... followed... And the next Sabbath day came almost the whole city together to hear the word of God.*[375] And chapter 14: *And it came to pass in Iconium, that they went both together into the synagogue of the Jews, and so spake, that a great multitude both of the Jews and also of the Greeks believed.*[376] And in 17: *...they came to Thessalonica, where was a synagogue of the Jews; and Paul, as his manner was, went in unto them, and three Sabbath days reasoned with them out of the scriptures...* And when he had come to *Beroea, coming thither* he *went into the synagogue of the Jews... But when the Jews of Thessalonica had knowledge that the word of God was preached of Paul at Beroea, they came thither also...* Paul *then reasoned in the synagogue* in Corinth *every Sabbath... And he departed thence, and entered into a certain man's house, named Justus, one who worshipped God, whose house joined hard to the synagogue. And Crispus, the chief ruler of the synagogue, believed in the Lord with all his house... And he came to Ephesus... entered into the synagogue, and reasoned with the Jews.*[377] Then in 19: *And he went into the synagogue* of Ephesus, *and spake boldly for the space of three months, disputing and persuading the things concerning the kingdom of God.*[378] But the Jews had synagogues not only in Asia but even in Rome, and especially the synagogue of the freedmen, who (it is clear from Acts) also had a synagogue in Jerusalem.[379] Philo attests to this in his *Embassy to Gaius:* Tiberius *did not hide the fact that he admired the Jews... because they detested flattery.* Otherwise he would not have permitted them to settle *across the Tiber,* which was a choice part of the city. *These Jews were Romans, and for the most part freedmen; they had been brought to Italy as captives and then granted freedom by their masters.*[380] *They were forced to change very few of their ancestral practices; Tiberius, after all, knew that they gathered together to pray,*[381] *and especially on the seventh day when they taught their traditional philosophy in public. He also knew that they stored up the sacred money from their first fruits and sent it to Jerusalem; and yet he did not expel them from Rome, or strip them of their Roman citizenship, or replace their prayers with new ones, or forbid them to gather to hear their laws interpreted.*[382] So much for the scribes, that is, the teachers of the law.

CHAPTER 11

The Seven Jewish Sects

SINCE I HAVE BEEN discussing the interpreters of the law, this would be an obvious place to consider the Jewish philosophies that were popular in those final days;[383] these were of seven different kinds, which they called the seven sects. According to the testimony of St. Epiphanius, they were: Sadducees, scribes, Pharisees, hemerobaptists, Nazareans, Ossenes,[384] and Herodians. I would like to discuss these groups, first one at a time and then all together.

The Sadducees took their name from Zadok the disciple of Antigonus, who had defected to the temple of Mount Gerizim built by Manasseh in the territory of Samaria, and introduced the sect of the Sadducees during the reign of Alexander the Great. This is according to Rabbi Abraham in his *Historical Kabbala*.[385] These men, Josephus tells us, denied the power of fate and attributed everything to human judgment. They said that our souls were mortal and therefore would not be resurrected; they did not believe that God sees all our transgressions; and they were misanthropes who shunned all social interactions.[386] And as St. Epiphanius writes, they knew nothing of the angels and the Holy Spirit, and kept exactly the same customs as the Samaritans even though they were Jews and sacrificed in Jerusalem.[387]

On the other hand, the scribes were (according to St. Epiphanius)[388] *interpreters of the law, one might say the practitioners of a kind of grammatical discipline; and though in other respects they behaved just like Jews, they introduced a rather overwrought kind of interpretation that was given to sophistry. They not only lived according to the letter of the law, but went beyond it. That is, they practiced the immersion and purification of pitchers, cups, dishes,[389] and the other vessels they used in their service; and they frequently washed their hands and purified themselves in the bath,[390] as though to demonstrate that they were clearly devoted to upright and holy lives. Moreover, they wore certain fringes to show off their elegance,[391] so that they might advertise their rank and win the praise of passersby, and they added phylacteries to their own cloak (that is, broad purple stripes)...[392] They had, moreover, four types of* explanations:[393] *first in the name of Moses their prophet, second in that of their teacher called Akiba or Bar Akiba,*[394] *third in that of Andan or Annan, who was also called Judah,*[395] *and fourth in the name of the sons of Hasmoneus.*[396] There is no doubt that these were among the men whom I called teachers of the law.

The Pharisees, according to Josephus, *claimed to have more reliable knowledge of the required rites; they lived lives of poverty and owned nothing that was soft or delicate... Though they attributed everything to fate, they did not do away with man's free will; they believed that God would one day pass judgment and men would receive rewards and punishments as they deserved them. They also believed that the soul is immortal, and that after we die some souls are consigned to an eternal prison, and others are restored to life; but that while the souls of good men are reborn into the bodies of human beings, those of bad men are put into cattle.*[397] St. Epiphanius has this to say about them: *The Pharisees held the same beliefs as the scribes, for they were close to one another... They were very serious about chastity and temperance, they prayed frequently, and they took care not to pollute themselves with any bodily stain... They slept only on the hardest beds... They fasted twice a week, on the second and fifth days. They took tithes, and they gave first fruits and thirtieths and fiftieths... They rendered up their sacrifices and vows with great exactness. They wore the clothing of the scribes, which I have already described: cloaks and other embellishments, and effeminate mantles; and on their feet they wore sandals with straps. They were called Pharisees because they kept apart from others, on account of the excessive religiosity which they had willingly taken upon themselves; for in the Hebrew language* phares *means separation.*[398]

The hemerobaptists[399] *had the same beliefs as the scribes and Pharisees, though like the Sadducees they denied the resurrection of the dead... Their most characteristic feature was that they baptized themselves every day, which is the source of their name.*[400]

Now the Nazareans, *although they originally came from the areas of Gilead and Bashan and from beyond the Jordan... kept all the practices of the Jews... circumcision, the Sabbath, and all the festivals... But they did not offer sacrifices or eat animals... Though they acknowledged the patriarchs who are mentioned in the five books of Moses... they did not accept the books themselves... They said that it was Moses who got the law, but that it was a different law from the one that has been handed down in his name.*[401]

The Ossenes *originated in the Nabatean region, Iturea, Moab, and Areilitis,*[402] *which is beyond the Dead Sea... Although Jews by ancestry they were inconsistent in their practices, and they used their intellectual powers with great cunning.*[403] Josephus calls these people Essenes, and in the second book of his *War* he describes them as follows: *The Essenes have rejected marriage and adopted other people's children... They spurn wealth... they do not live in any particular towns... and they share their possessions with their fellow members... They never buy new clothes or shoes unless the old ones have worn out. Among themselves they have no business dealings; they provide whatever a person lacks, and they will get back in return whatever they themselves may need... They are incredibly pious... they immerse themselves every day in cold water... They maintain complete silence while they eat... They take no one into their company... unless he has demonstrated to them his self-control... And when they do admit such a person they make him swear a great oath that he will cherish God, faith, and justice... If any of them have been found to sin they are driven out of the fellowship... and forbidden to take any food that might be brought to them... They carry out the severest sort of justice... and they have no fear of death... or crucifixion. They believe that... the souls of good men... go off to the blessed isles... and those of evil men to the underworld.[404] In Book 18 of the Antiquities he says as follows: The Essenes attribute everything to God, they believe that the soul is immortal... they prohibit offerings to the Temple.[405] They don't participate in sacrifices with the people because they believe that they possess a superior purity and sanctity...[406] Their way of life is ideal, all their energies are devoted to agriculture... they share everything with one another... and they have neither wives nor slaves... They choose their best men to be priests... They eat simple food, and their clothing is spare and pure.[407]* And in Pliny Book 5: *On the western shore the Essenes have fled beyond the range of the dangerous waters;[408] they are a solitary people, and more remarkable than any other in the world; they live without women, as they have given up all sexual contact; they have no money, and only the palm trees for company. Every day brings an equal number of new arrivals; they come in such huge numbers because they are tired of life, and the storms of fortune have driven them to adopt the ways of the Essenes. Thus (amazing as it seems) for countless generations this people in which no one is born goes on without fail; they reap a great harvest from the fact that others repent of their lives. Below them was the town of Engedi; though it was second only to Jerusalem in its fertility and its palm groves, now it is just another ruin.[409] Next is the cliffside fortress of Masada, which is itself not far from the Dead Sea.[410]* But Philo does a much more impressive job of describing them in his book *That Every Good Man Is Free: In Syria,* he says, *and Palestine (which contain the greatest numbers of Jews) are a certain group called Essenes, who number more than four thousand; in Greek they are called "Essene" after* hosioi, *that is, holy,[411] since they are especially devoted to God. They do not sacrifice any animals, because they consider it their task to sanctify their minds. They live here and there, avoiding the cities because of the corruption of the officials who govern them... Some of them work in agriculture, the others practice the trades of peacetime... They do not amass gold or silver, or buy up large tracts of land in hopes of the large returns they will get from them, but acquire only what they need to survive... None of them manufactures weapons; even in peacetime... they do not engage in any sort of trade... They have no slaves; they are all free, and they supply each other with whatever help is needed... They reject the logical... and physical parts of philosophy...*[412] *but they accept that part which has to do with God. Their greatest interest is moral philosophy, which they study with the help of their ancestral laws... These they teach primarily on the seventh day... They are, moreover, filled with holiness, justice, and the other virtues,*[413] *and they hold to three principles: God, virtue, and the love of their fellow men.*[414] *The proof... that they love God is that they practice perpetual chastity, and do not make oaths or tell lies; and that they consider God to be the source of everything delightful but of nothing evil. We can see how much they love virtue from the fact that they despise money and reputation, they reject physical pleasure... and they never waver. We can see their burning love for humanity from the affection and companionship with which they treat one another... for they all share the same home... the same clothing... the same treasury, and the same expenses... They live their lives in common... They even pool together their profits... they care jointly for the sick... and they treat their elders like their own parents.*[415]

The Herodians, as Epiphanius says,[416] *were certainly Jews, but for them it was a hypocritical sham—they thought that Herod was the Lord Christ who was predicted by all the scriptures, the law, and the prophets; and misled by this idea they claimed that he was Herod, based on the verse: A prince shall not be missing from Judah, and a leader from its loins, until he should come for whom it is kept waiting.*[417] *The one, they say, for whom it is kept waiting means a foreigner.* Likewise Tertullian in his *On Rules: The Pharisees distinguished themselves from other Jews by making certain additions to the law... The Herodians said that Herod was Christ.*[418]

But of all these groups, it was the Pharisees and Sadducees who flourished before the arrival of Christ. Thus, as Josephus tells us, the commoners of Jerusalem were in league with the Pharisees, and its aristocrats with the Sadducees.[419] When John the Prince[420] grew unhappy with the exceptional authority that the Pharisees were enjoying in the state, he suspended the laws they had passed (these were new traditions, not found in the ancient Mosaic law).[421] And yet the Pharisees amassed so much power that later on, they waged war on Alexander the king of the Jews[422] with the assistance of Demetrius Eucerus the king of Syria, and forced him to give up the territories of Moab and Gilead.[423] Then, after Alexander died and was succeeded by Queen Alexandra, they won her over and got back their laws; and they devoted themselves with even greater zeal to their harsh way of life, both in the city and throughout the kingdom.[424] This conflict eventually came down to the royal brothers Hyrcanus and Aristobulus—one was a Pharisee, the other a Sadducee.[425] When Christ was beginning to spread his gospel among the people, it was the scribes, the Pharisees, the Sadducees, and the Herodians who were particularly popular. They are therefore mentioned by name in the gospel as the only ones who could have offered any sort of opposition to Christ's new teaching. And just as they kept harassing him with all sorts of questions in an effort to expose him, and tried to trap him with their words, so he too went after them and did all he could to lay bare their hypocrisy and the fact that their teachings conformed so little to the way they lived their lives. I will quote in order the relevant passages of the Gospels, so that this issue will be perfectly clear. St. Mark chapter 3: *And the Pharisees went forth, and straightway took counsel with the Herodians against him, how they might destroy him.*[426] And chapter 7: *...the Pharisees, and certain of the scribes... when they saw some of the Lord's disciples eat bread with defiled, that is to say, with unwashen, hands, they found fault. For the Pharisees, and all the Jews, except they wash their hands oft, eat not, holding the tradition of the elders. And when they come from the market, except they wash, they eat not. And many other things there be, which they have received to hold, as the washing of cups, and pots, brazen vessels, and tables.*[427] St. Luke chapter 11: *...ye Pharisees make clean the outside of the cup and the platter.*[428] St. Matthew 15: *Then came to Jesus scribes and Pharisees, which were of Jerusalem, saying, why do thy disciples transgress the tradition of the elders? For they wash not their hands when they eat bread. But he answered and said unto them, why do ye also transgress the commandment of God by your tradition? For God commanded, saying, honor thy father and mother; and he that curseth father or mother, let him die the death. But ye say, whosoever shall say to his father or his mother, it is a gift, by whatsoever thou mightest be profited by me; and honor not his father... he shall be free. Thus have ye made the commandment of God of none effect by your tradition.*[429] St. Jerome, in Letter 151, explains these traditions as follows: *I cannot possibly express just how many traditions (which they now call* deuterōseis*)*[430] *the Pharisees have, or how ridiculous their stories are. My book is not nearly long enough for the task, and they are frequently so filthy that I would blush to discuss them. Yet I will give one example of how disgraceful this hateful people is: They have in charge of their synagogues certain very wise men who are given a disgusting duty—if they cannot tell by sight whether the blood of an unmarried woman is pure (because she is menstruating) or impure,*[431] *they examine it by taste.*[432] *Not only that,* *because they have been commanded to sit in their own houses on the Sabbath and not to go out or leave the place where they live, when we try to hold them to the letter of their law—meaning that if they want to keep their commandments they cannot lie down, or walk, or stand, but only sit—they usually respond with "Rabbi Akiba, and Simon, and Hillel our teachers handed down to us that we are allowed to walk two thousand feet on the Sabbath," and other things of this sort. They prefer the teachings of man to those of God.* Hence St. Eucherius says[433] about the phrase in the first chapter of Acts— *which is a Sabbath day's journey*[434]—that "a Sabbath day's journey" means a thousand paces, since Jews had been allowed on the Sabbath to walk to the Mount of Olives,[435] and clearly they gave themselves permission to walk this same distance no matter where they where. In fact, we also have St. Mark chapter 8: *...beware of the leaven of the Pharisees, and of the Sadducees, and of the Herodians.*[436] St. Matthew 16: *The Pharisees also with the Sadducees came, and tempting desired him that he would show them a sign from heaven... So Jesus said unto them, Take heed and beware of the leaven of the Pharisees and of the Sadducees... Then understood they how that he bade them not beware of the leaven of bread, but of the teaching of the Pharisees and of the Sadducees.*[437] And chapter 12: *But when the Pharisees saw* his disciples picking grain on the Sabbath, *they said unto him, Behold, thy disciples do that which is not lawful to do upon the Sabbath day.*[438] Likewise: *Then certain of the scribes and of the Pharisees answered, saying, Master, we would see a sign from thee.*[439] And in chapter 22: *...came to him the Sadducees, which say that there is no resurrection, and asked him... in the resurrection whose wife shall she be of the seven? For they all had her.*[440] And afterward: *But when the Pharisees had heard that he had put the Sadducees to silence, they were gathered together. Then one of them, which was a lawyer, asked him a question, tempting him...*[441] And in St. Mark chapter 12: *...they send unto him certain of the Pharisees and of the Herodians... saying, Is it lawful to give tribute to Caesar, or not?*[442] So, angered by these attempts, Christ laid bare their behavior and their way of life, as in St. Matthew 22[443] and St. Luke 20:[444] *...The scribes and the Pharisees sit in Moses' seat: All therefore whatsoever they bid you observe, that observe and do; but do not ye after their works: for they say, and do not. For they bind heavy burdens and grievous to be borne, and lay them on men's shoulders; but they themselves will not move them with one of their fingers. But all their works they do for to be seen of men: they make broad their phylacteries, and enlarge the fringes of their garments, and love the uppermost rooms at feasts,*[445] *and the chief seats in the synagogues, and greetings in the markets, and to be called of men, Rabbi, rabbi... Woe unto you, scribes and Pharisees, hypocrites! for ye devour widows' houses, and for* *a pretense make long prayer... for ye compass sea and land to make one proselyte, and when he is made, ye make him twofold more the child of hell than yourselves... for ye pay tithe of mint and anise and cummin, and have omitted the weightier matters of the law, judgment, mercy, and faith; these ought ye to have done, and not to leave the other undone... for ye make clean the outside of the cup and of the platter, but within they are full of extortion and excess... for ye are like unto whited sepulchers, which indeed appear beautiful outward, but are within full of dead men's bones, and of all uncleanness... because ye build the tombs of the prophets, and garnish the sepulchers of the righteous.* These fringes and phylacteries of the Pharisees are, by the way, commanded by God as follows in Numbers 15: *Speak unto the children of Israel, and bid them that they make them fringes on the borders of their garments throughout their generations, and that they put upon the fringe of the borders a ribbon of blue; and it shall be unto you for a fringe, that ye may look upon it, and remember all the commandments of the Lord, and do them; and that ye seek not after your own heart...*[446] On the other hand, St. Epiphanius explains all the customs of the Pharisees as follows:[447] *They had a sort of fringes that symbolized their elegance, which they wore to show off their rank and win the admiration of the crowds; and to their cloaks they added phylacteries, which were broad purple stripes... The fringes were... at the edges and borders... while the phylacteries were figures woven of that famous color purple which the Lord said had been spread out.*[448] *For everyone wore the fringes on the four corners of their cloaks along with certain ornaments, and the corners were tied with that same thread;*[449] *so as long as they wore them, they behaved modestly and their actions were pure.*[450] Then the Book of Acts contains frequent references to these people, such as in chapter 4: *And as the apostles in Jerusalem spake unto the people, the priests, and the captain of the Temple, and the Sadducees, came upon them, being grieved that they taught the people, and preached through Jesus the resurrection from the dead.*[451] And in chapter 5: *Then the high priest rose up, and all they who were with him (which is the sect of the Sadducees), and were filled with indignation.*[452] And in 24:[453] *But when Paul perceived that the one part were Sadducees, and the other Pharisees, he cried out in the council, Men and brethren, I am a Pharisee, the son of a Pharisee: of the hope and resurrection of the dead I am called in question. And when he had so said, there arose a dissension between the Pharisees and the Sadducees... For the Sadducees say that there is no resurrection, neither angel, nor spirit; but the Pharisees confess both.* So much for the seven sects.

There was an offshoot of the Pharisees called the Golanites. They came into being during the reign of Herod the Great. In fact, their movement sprang from the following circumstances: Augustus Caesar did away with taxes and imposed a regular tribute on every person and on property; and to that end he ordered the entire Roman population to be counted. This was done in such a way that he ordered even Judea—which he had placed under Herod after declaring him king—to be counted up, and a tribute levied on all its inhabitants.[454] When this was done a certain Judah appeared, and together with Zadok the Pharisee he declared that the people of God should not recognize any master but God, nor should Augustus be allowed to carry out his census, because it would prove that they were in fact his slaves. Judah's followers pushed the people not to give Caesar any tribute, and they were contemptuous of death and punishment. In their clothing and in other respects they were identical to the Pharisees; hence the latter also sometimes asked Christ, in order to test him, whether tribute ought to be given to Caesar, because at the time this question had provoked a number of different responses. Christ, however, answered that what was Caesar's should be given to Caesar, and what was God's to God, and he himself paid two drachmas during the census (for himself and for St. Peter).[455] Above all, Judah managed to stir up the *sicarii* and the Zealots, who backed up their ideology with swords and daggers[456] and killed anyone who disagreed with them; no sort of punishment could dislodge them from their beliefs, to the point that even the young boys who were drafted to this cause astonished onlookers with how stubbornly they resisted the tortures inflicted on them. The sources for this are: Luke chapter 2; Matthew 17; Josephus, *Antiquities* 18 and *War* 7; and Isidore, *Etymologies*, Book 5 chapter 36.[457]

Such was the character of the worship which, in any sacred community, men are required to give to God. The point of this worship is ultimately that we live life according to the proper principles, and shape it according to his commands and his will. We can easily accomplish this if we give his law a permanent place in our mouths, our hearts, and our hands; if, that is, we can harmonize with it our words, our intentions and our actions. And ultimately we will show such diligence that we will love God, and try to be loved by him. That this was his will, he demonstrated through the covenant he forged with the Hebrews—he would be their God, and they would be his people.

BOOK VI

Councils and Courts

CHAPTER 1

The State

NOW THAT I HAVE finished the longest and most difficult part of this analysis—i.e. the section on religion—and made it as polished as I think it should be, it is time to move on to what remains. After all, we have yet to discuss the state: that is, how a republic is administered by its citizens. I do not, in fact, agree with Marcus Varro, the most learned man of ancient times,[1] who at the beginning of his book about human and divine matters states that he is going to begin with human affairs because states first had to arise before they could establish religion.[2] In fact, this sequence was the complete reverse of what he imagined. True religion, as St. Augustine tells us, was not founded by some earthly city—it was in fact, and without question, the very foundation of the celestial city itself.[3] That city was inspired and taught by the God who grants eternal life, and whom Varro and his contemporaries knew nothing about. So I decided that I would discuss the state *after* I finished with religion, and divide the entire subject into three parts—councils, courts, and magistracies. (This is the same scheme I used in my book about the Athenian republic.)[4] My approach to these issues has been guided by the following principle: *Every civil society* (says Aristotle in his *Politics*) *is bound together by the union of what is useful and what is just.*[5] Human beings are the only creatures to have acquired some understanding of these two concepts because they alone have been made capable of speech, through which they can share them with one another as circumstances require. Now, councils try to find utility and courts look for fairness; and since these bodies are made up, respectively, of councilors and judges, they need some sort of leader or chief to call them together and bring before them the matters of utility and law that require their attention. After all, a mass of people cannot be governed without some sort of head.[6] The people in charge of councils and courts are called magistrates; so in the next two books I will examine the civil administration of the Hebrew republic, with a particular emphasis upon (once again) councils, courts, and magistracies.

CHAPTER 2

Councils

I USE THE TERM "councils" for those bodies that were particularly responsible for whatever concerned the welfare of the entire state, such as war, peace, the grain supply, borders, the passage of legislation, the appointment of magistrates, and things of that sort. All this amounts to nothing more than making decisions about everything of practical concern which could not be included within the law. Just as in other republics, so in the Jewish state there were two councils—one was drawn from the entire people regardless of qualification, and the other from a select few who were older than the rest. The general council was called an assembly,[7] and the restricted one a senate. Even David seems to have been aware of this in the Psalms: when he addresses the praises of God that were to be sung in all—and by all—gatherings of men, he refers in poetic terms to both the assembly and the senate. As when he says: *I will praise the Lord with my whole heart, in the council of the upright, and in the congregation.*[8] And elsewhere: *Let them exalt him also in the ecclesia*[9] *of the people, and praise him in the seat of the elders.*[10] Likewise: *I have hated the ecclesia of evildoers; and will not sit with the wicked.*[11] Instead of "assembly" he used the words "congregation" (in Greek *synagōgē*) and *ecclesia*; and instead of "senate" he used "council" (or *boulē*); while the "seat of the elders" shows that he was prepared to add yet a third body if it should serve the needs of the state under his guidance.[12]

CHAPTER 3

The Assembly

IT IS CLEAR FROM the passages I have just cited that the popular assembly is generally referred to in the holy books by either of two Greek terms, *synagoga* or *ecclesia*, since the split between the Synagogue and the Church which arose after Christ gave us his gospel had not as yet occurred.[13] And as I remarked at the beginning of this book,[14] there were three popular assemblies which paralleled the three estates of the Hebrews—those of the entire people, the individual tribes, and the individual cities within each tribe. The first assembly included all the tribes of Israel gathered together; the second, all the families within each tribe; and the third, all the men of every city. I will now describe what I have learned about each of these in turn.

The assembly of the entire people was established by God. The proof of this is that he often says to Moses in Exodus: *Speak to the children of Israel. Speak to the whole body of Israel.*[15] To which the people respond: *...All that the Lord hath said will we do, and be obedient.*[16] And since God ordered that all his commands, precepts, statutes, judgments, and testimonies be taught to all the children of Israel, he was clearly responsible for the popular assembly, which is now my concern. Hence the wording of Exodus 35: *And Moses gathered all the congregation of the children of Israel together...*[17] And Numbers 27: Joshua *will stand before Eleazar the priest, and before all the congregation; and give him a charge in their sight. And he shall put some of* his *honor upon him, that all the congregation*[18] *of the children of Israel may be obedient.*[19] And Deuteronomy 9: *And the Lord delivered unto me two tables of stone... in the day of the assembly.*[20]

No one could convene this assembly of the entire people except men with supreme authority,[21] such as generals, judges, kings, and princes. We learn about generals from Joshua 23: *And Joshua called for all Israel, and for their elders, and for their heads, and for their judges, and for their officers...*[22] And in the next chapter: *And Joshua gathered all the tribes of Israel to Shechem, and called for the elders of Israel, and for their heads, and for their judges, and for their officers...*[23] About judges, from chapter 7 of First Samuel: *And*

Samuel the judge *said, Gather all Israel to Mizpeh...*[24] About kings, from Second Samuel 13:[25] *And* King *David gathered all the people together...* And in Second Chronicles 15:[26] *...he assembled... all Israel, unto Jerusalem.* Then in chapter 11 of First Kings,[27] after the ten tribes have split off: *And when* King *Rehoboam was come to Jerusalem, he assembled all the house of Judah, with the tribe of Benjamin...* Finally, princes are explicitly mentioned in the decree by which Simon was made prince[28] in First Maccabees, where it says: *...that it should be lawful for* no one... *to gather an assembly... without him.*[29]

As for the procedure for convening the people, it is written in the law that whenever they were to be gathered they would be summoned by various trumpet blasts. *Make thee* (says God in Numbers 10) *two trumpets of silver; of a whole piece shalt thou make them: that thou mayest use them for the calling of the assembly, and for the journeying of the camps. And when they shall blow with them, all the assembly shall assemble themselves to thee at the door of the tabernacle of the congregation. And if they blow but with one trumpet, then the princes, which are heads of the thousands of Israel, shall gather themselves unto thee. When ye blow an alarm, then the camps that lie on the east parts shall go forward. When ye blow an alarm the second time, then the camps that lie on the south side shall take their journey... But when the congregation is to be gathered together, ye shall blow, but ye shall not sound an alarm. And the sons of Aaron... shall blow with the trumpets...*[30]

It was customary for the people to gather for three reasons: to listen, to pray, and to act. "To listen," as they did at the very beginning when they gathered to hear God's commands,[31] as in Deuteronomy 4: *Gather me the people together, and I will make them hear my words...*[32] This is why it is written in First Chronicles 29: *Furthermore David the king said unto all the congregation...*[33]

When, on the other hand, the people gathered to pray, their most usual meeting place was in a town of Judah called Mizpeh. As in Judges 11: *...and Jephthah uttered all his words before the Lord in Mizpeh.*[34] And in the third chapter of First Maccabees: *Wherefore the Israelites assembled themselves together, and came to Mizpeh, over against Jerusalem; for in Mizpeh was the place where they prayed aforetime in Israel. Then they fasted that day, and put on sackcloth, and cast ashes upon their heads, and rent their clothes.*[35] This is exactly right, for as Samuel had said in First Samuel 7: *...Gather all Israel to Mizpeh, and I will pray for you unto the Lord.*[36] And since in Mizpeh there was no tabernacle or ark at that time, it follows that there was some sort of altar there, just as there had been at the "high places." (The tabernacle and the ark were in Shiloh, as it is written in Judges 20:[37] leaving Mizpeh... *the*

people came to the house of God in Shiloh, and abode there... before God...
and wept...) This is why, when they went to Mizpeh in order to pray, they
were said to have gone up to the Lord. For as it says in the next chapter:[38]
And all the people went to Gilgal... and there they sacrificed sacrifices of peace
offerings before the Lord... And yet the tabernacle was not in Gilgal at that
time. And in chapter 15: *...And Samuel hewed Agag in pieces before the Lord*
in Gilgal.[39] In fact, Samuel also built an altar in Ramah (First Samuel 7).[40]

When they gathered to act, it was for two purposes—to appoint judges,
kings, and princes; and to declare or conduct wars. On appointing judges, it
is written in Judges chapter 8: *The people said to Gideon: rule over us.*[41] And
on kings, First Samuel 10: *And Samuel called the people together unto the Lord*
to Mizpeh; and said unto the children of Israel, Thus saith the Lord God of
Israel, I brought up Israel out of Egypt... And ye have... rejected your God...
and ye have said unto him... set a king over us. Now therefore present your-
selves before the Lord by your tribes, and by your thousands.[42] And afterward:
And the people immediately sent men to fetch Saul, because he had hidden
at home, and when they brought him to Mizpeh the people shouted... God
save the king.[43] On princes, we have as follows in First Maccabees 2:[44] *Now*
therefore we have chosen thee this day to be our prince... instead of Judah...

They also convened in Mizpeh in order to declare war—first against the
Ammonites, then against the Benjaminites, and then against the Philistines.
On the Ammonites, Judges 10: *...And the children of Israel assembled them-*
selves together against the Ammonites, and encamped in Mizpeh.[45] On the
Benjaminites of Gibeah, chapter 20: *Then all the children of Israel... were*
gathered together as one man, from Dan even to Beersheba, with the land of
Gilead, unto the Lord in Mizpeh. And the chiefs of all the people, even of all
the tribes of Israel, presented themselves in the assembly of the people of God,
four hundred thousand footmen who drew sword... To whom the Levite said,
Behold, ye are all children of Israel; give here your advice and counsel. And
all the people arose as one man, saying, We will not any of us go to his tent,
neither will we any of us turn into his house. But now this shall be the thing
which we will do to Gibeah...[46] And on the same subject in the following
chapter: *Now the men of Israel had sworn in Mizpeh... There shall not any of*
us give his daughter unto Benjamin to wife.[47] And afterward: *...What one is*
there of the tribes of Israel who came not up to Mizpeh to the Lord?[48] On the
other hand, Samuel says about the Philistines in the seventh chapter of First
Samuel: *And Samuel said, Gather all Israel to Mizpeh, and I will pray for you*
unto the Lord. And they gathered together to Mizpeh, and drew water, and
poured it out before the Lord, and fasted on that day, and said there, We have

*sinned against the Lord. And Samuel judged the children of Israel in Mizpeh...
And the men of Israel went out of Mizpeh, and pursued the Philistines...* So
much for the assembly of the entire people.[49]

As for the individual tribes, it seems very likely that each tribe had its own
leaders, on whose authority it assembled, deliberated, administered justice,
and declared war. (We will look into some of their other activities when we
discuss the leaders of these tribes.) We have the following two references to
fighting wars. First, Joshua 19: *...the children of Dan went up to fight their
own war against Leshem, and took it.*[50] Then, the Ephraimites did as follows
to Jephthah the judge (Judges 12): *Behold a rebellion arose in Ephraim. And
the men of Ephraim gathered themselves together, and went northward, and
said unto Jephthah, Wherefore passedst thou over to fight against the children
of Ammon, and didst not call us to go with thee?... And Jephthah said unto
them, I and my people were at great strife with the children of Ammon; and
when I called you, ye delivered me not out of their hands... wherefore then
are ye come up unto me this day, to fight against me? Then* Jephthah *called
all the men of Gilead, and fought with Ephraim...*[51]

We may also conclude that every city contained a particular group that
made up the citizen body of that city, from the fact that within each city were
magistrates—called "chiefs of the city"—who were in charge of such a group.
We are at any rate well informed about the people of Jerusalem, as in First
Chronicles 30:[52] *For the king had taken counsel, and his princes, and all the
congregation in Jerusalem...* And then: *the king, and the princes, and the entire
congregation in Jerusalem, decreed that they should make the passover.*[53] But in
First Kings 8: *And Solomon stood before the altar of the Lord in the presence
of all the congregation of Israel...*[54] It appears from these passages that there
was both a Jerusalemite people and an Israelite or Judean people. But given
that the republic of the Hebrews was far from being a democracy[55]—it was,
as I have already said, either an aristocracy or a monarchy—the people had
very little influence over its affairs. When it was an aristocracy the senate
was in charge, and when a monarchy, the king. But if the people ever did
have any kind of strength or grandeur,[56] it was above all after the kingdom
was destroyed in the Babylonian exile, when the people took the Hasmoneans as their princes and set up a republic in the Greek style.[57] For it is
written in the first chapter of Second Maccabees that proclamations were
published with the following heading: *...the people that were at Jerusalem...
and the council, and Judah, sent greeting... unto Aristobulus, King Ptolemy's
master.*[58] And in chapter 14:[59] *...unto Simon the high priest, and the elders...
and* the entire *people.*[60] And in Book 20 of Josephus: *Claudius Caesar... to
the magistrates, senate, people, and nation of the Jews...,*[61] as though the

people actually played a part in the state. Likewise: *The Pharisees stood with the people against the king.*[62] And in Cicero's speech on behalf of Flaccus: *It was an act of the greatest import to pay no mind, for the sake of the state, to the passionate mob of Jews who often attend assemblies.*[63] But then it is well known how great an uproar the people of Jerusalem, who were up in arms, instigated at the trial of Christ.

From all this it seems that the popular assembly enjoyed some sort of power not only when Judea was subject to its kings, but even when it was ruled by the people and the emperor of Rome.[64] It was like the other cities of Asia[65] where the Roman proconsul held assizes, administered justice, and tried capital cases, and left any other cases to be tried by the people whenever they would convene a legitimate assembly.[66] By "legitimate assembly" I mean one that convened on fixed days according to the law, just as we call "disordered" one that meets at random and on the spur of the moment. The proof of this lies not only in the Greek and Roman testimony which I have collected in my books about provincial law and the Athenian republic (in which I discuss the system of assizes and the procedure for summoning assemblies). We also find it in the book of St. Luke, who was familiar with Greek and Roman customs and wrote as follows about the Roman assizes and the legitimate assemblies of the Ephesians, which the latter called an *ecclesia* (Acts 19): *And when they heard these sayings, they were full of wrath, and cried out, saying, Great is Diana of the Ephesians. And the whole city was filled with confusion... And when Paul would have entered in unto the people, the disciples suffered him not... for the congregation was disordered...*[67] And then: *And when the town clerk had appeased the people, he said... if Demetrius, and the craftsmen who are with him, have a matter against any man, the courts are open, and there are proconsuls; let them implead one another. But if ye inquire any thing concerning other matters, it shall be determined in a lawful ecclesia... And when he had thus spoken, he dismissed the congregation.*[68] There is no doubt that if the translator of this passage had rendered *ecclesia* as "assembly," he would have expressed the idea much more clearly. Aeschines[69] also refers to both disordered and legitimate assemblies in his speech about the false embassy: *You have caused more assemblies to convene through fear and chaos than you have according to the dictates of the law.*[70] Ulpian, moreover, cites Demosthenes to the effect that assemblies were legally convened three times a month,[71] which St. John Chrysostom confirms in his comments on Acts.[72] The clerk was therefore quite right to tell the Ephesians, after quieting the crowd, that they had convened a disordered assembly, and therefore, "If you have a charge to make against anyone which you would like to lodge, go to the proconsul of Asia when he holds the courts and assizes," i.e. when he holds court in Ephesus. "But if you have some other kind of case, wait for the legitimate assembly of the Ephesian people, and take it up there." After that he dismissed the assembly, which was disordered (i.e. it was convened ad hoc rather than according to the law). Strabo,[73] in Book 13, says about the courts and assizes of Asia: *the borders of Phrygia, Lydia, Caria, and Mysia are practically indistinguishable, because they blend into one another. The Romans added more than a little to this confusion—rather than dividing these regions according to their peoples, they used another scheme to draw up the dioceses in which they held assizes and administered justice.*[74] These dioceses, or assizes, or forums of Asia,[75] were (according to Pliny):[76] the Laodicean, the Synnadian, the Apamean, the Alabandan, the Sardian, the Smyrnean, the Ephesian, the Adramyttian, and the Pergamene. On the tumultuous assemblies of Asia and Greece, Cicero says as follows in his speech for Flaccus: *All the states of Greece are governed by the recklessness of a sitting assembly. The Greece of the old days failed in only one respect, the unbounded freedom and license of its assemblies: it was men of no experience, with no political education or training at all, who sat in the theater. And if this was what used to happen at Athens, can you imagine how little restraint there was in the assemblies of Phrygia or Mysia? It is usually people from those very nations who disturb our own assemblies;*[77] *so what do you suppose must happen when they are all by themselves?*

CHAPTER 4

The Senate

NOW THAT I HAVE explained the assembly, I should discuss the senate. This too was a Hebrew institution, and like the people it took three forms: the first consisted of the elders of the entire people; the second, of those who belonged to each tribe; and the third, of those who lived in each of the cities.

The senate of the entire people was formed by God from those seventy men who were the oldest of all the Israelites; as God says in Numbers 15:[78] *...Gather unto me seventy men of the elders of Israel, whom thou knowest to be the elders of the people, and officers over them; and bring them unto the tabernacle of the congregation, that they may stand there with thee... the burden of the people with thee, that thou bear it not thyself alone.*[79] Thus the Greeks called the men who belonged to this order "senate," "elders," "older men," and "senators";[80] while they called the council *boule*, its meeting place *bouleterion*, and the men themselves *bouletai* (which mean, so to speak, "the council," "the council room," and "the councilmen").

These men assembled in the capital city before the highest head of state, and at his behest they (along with the heads of the people) gave counsel on the highest matters of state. Hence Josephus reports this provision of the law: *Let the king do nothing without the advice of the high priest and the senators.*[81] Now follows the evidence for these senates. In Deuteronomy chapter 5, Moses says: *...ye came near unto me, even all the chiefs of your tribes, and your elders.*[82] And in chapter 27: *And Moses with the elders of Israel commanded the people, saying, Keep all the commandments which I command you...*[83] Likewise in Joshua 23: *And Joshua called for all Israel, and for their elders, and for their chiefs, and for their judges, and for their officers...*[84] Then in the time of the judges, in Judges 21: The elders decided that the Benjaminites should capture the young women of Shiloh as wives.[85] Then during the reign of Solomon, in the seventh chapter of First Kings:[86] *Then Solomon assembled the elders of Israel... unto King Solomon in Jerusalem...* And in the first chapter of Second Chronicles:[87] King Hezekiah *took counsel with his elders...*[88] *to stop the waters* *of the fountains...* Even though after the division of the kingdom the senate of the Judeans was drawn only from the tribes of Judah and Benjamin, they continued to keep the figure of seventy elders. So Ezekiel says in chapter 7:[89] *And there stood before them seventy men of the ancients of the house of Israel...*, even though in his time the ten tribes of Israel were in Assyria.[90] And in Jeremiah 19 the prophet mentions the elders of the people: *...get a potter's earthen bottle, and take of the elders of the people, and of the elders of the priests.*[91] The senate was active not only during the monarchy—even though the monarchy itself had been done away with, the senate was restored again when the Jews came back from Babylonia. As it is written in the first chapter of Isaiah: *And I will restore thy judges... and thy counselors as at the beginning...*[92] And in the tenth chapter of Ezra: *And that whosoever would not come within three days, according to the counsel of the princes and the elders, all his substance should be forfeited...*[93] And in First Maccabees 12: *Jonathan the high priest, and the elders of the nation, and the priests, and the other of the Jews...*[94] And in the first chapter of Second Maccabees: *...the people that were at Jerusalem... and the council, and Judah, sent greeting... unto Aristobulus, King Ptolemy's master.*[95] And in chapter 11: *...King Antiochus sendeth greeting unto the council, and the rest of the Jews.*[96] And in 14:[97] *...unto Simon the priest* and the elders, *and to all the people.* And in St. Luke 12:[98] *And as soon as it was day, the elders of the people... came together...* In Greek this is *the* presbyterium *of the people.*[99] Josephus also tells us that in the last days of the city, Florus the procurator of Judea summoned the chief senators and announced in the senate that he wanted to leave the city;[100] and he says that the senate house, which he calls *bouleuterium*, was burned along with the Temple.[101] And whereas it was always the role of the senate to offer advice,[102] it is clear even so that when the kings had control of the state they showed no obedience to the laws, and they issued decrees even without the approval of the senate as though they had supreme authority. Their decrees were not what God would have commanded, but what they themselves wanted.[103]

The idea that each of the tribes had its own senators, who were different from the senators of the entire people, is based more on conjecture than on any solid authority. It is true that it is written in Second Kings 20:[104] *...they gathered unto* King Josiah *all the elders of Judah and of Jerusalem*; and in First Samuel 30: David *sent of the spoil unto the elders of Judah, even to his friends...*;[105] and that God said in Jeremiah 19: *And I will make void the counsel of Judah...*[106] But it could be that the men called "elders of Judah" here are in fact the same as the "elders of the people."

On the other hand, each of the cities most certainly had its own senators, who were different from the ones we have already discussed. Hence the passage: *they gathered unto* King Josiah *all the elders of Judah and of Jerusalem.* And in Josephus Book 12:[107] *The elders of Jerusalem were upset that the brother of Jaddua the high priest had married a foreign-born woman.* And in Judges 11: *And it was so, that when the children of Ammon made war against Israel, the elders of Gilead went to fetch Jephthah... And they said unto Jephthah, Come, and be our captain...*[108] And in chapter 8: *He caught a young man of the men of Succoth, and inquired of him; and he described unto him the princes of Succoth, and the elders thereof...*[109] And in Ruth chapter 4: *And Boaz took ten men of the elders of the city* of Bethlehem, *and said...*[110]

CHAPTER 5

The Courts

I HAVE DISCUSSED the councils, which were primarily concerned with the well-being of the state. Next I should discuss the courts, which determined what was fair to each individual—something that could not be provided for or spelled out in the law.[111] The Greek translators of the Bible sometimes call these courts *krisis*,[112] and sometimes *dikē*,[113] obviously because they had in mind the dual function of the courts, which could either condemn or absolve. As I explained above, they described these two functions with two different terms: judgment and justice (or statute).

There were two courts of justice among the Hebrews—one in every city, called *krisis*; and one found only in Jerusalem, called *sunedrion*. (The Latin translation renders them as "court" and "council.") Hence Christ said in the gospel of St. Matthew: ...*whosoever is angry with his brother without a cause shall be in danger of the court; and whosoever shall say to his brother, Raca,*[114] *shall be in danger of the council.*[115] We know that the court was not the same as the council from what David says in the first Psalm: *Therefore the ungodly shall not stand in the court, nor sinners in the council of the righteous.*[116]

CHAPTER 6

The Courts of Cities

LET US DEAL FIRST with the courts of the cities, and then with the council of Jerusalem: when they were established and confirmed, who their members were, who was in charge, where they met, and the procedures by which they tried cases.

I am of the opinion that the judges of the cities, along with their superiors (who in Greek were called *grammatoeisagogeis*),[117] were appointed by Moses in the desert—first at the behest of his father-in-law, Jethro, and then at the command of God. For when Moses took it upon himself that first year in the desert to hear court cases, his father-in-law, Jethro, advised him to save himself the effort and to appoint men of wisdom, knowledge, and discernment to give judgments in his place, leaving for himself only the most difficult cases. He therefore appointed chiefs (whom I will discuss later on), tribunes, centurions, heads of fifty, and heads of ten; or (as the Greek has it) *chiliarchoi*, *hekatontarchoi*, *pentekontarchoi*, and *dekadarchoi*,[118] who were the introducers of cases for the judges (or grammatoisagogues).[119] In Exodus chapter 18: *And Moses chose able men out of all Israel, and made them heads over the people, rulers of thousands, rulers of hundreds, rulers of fifties, and rulers of tens. And they judged the people at all seasons...*[120] This is why forty years later, when Moses was recounting to the people the things he had done, he mentioned in the first chapter of Deuteronomy: *And I spake unto you... How can I myself alone bear your cumbrance, and your burden, and your strife? Take you wise men, and understanding, and known among your tribes, and I will make them rulers over you. And ye answered me, and said, The thing which thou hast spoken is good for us to do. So I took the chief of your tribes, wise men, and known, and made them heads over you, tribunes, and centurions, and captains over fifties, and captains over tens, and officers among your tribes, who will teach you everything. And I charged your judges at that time, saying, Hear the causes between your brethren, and judge righteously between every man and his brother, and the stranger that is with him. Ye shall not respect persons in judgment; but ye shall hear the small as well as the great; ye shall not be afraid of the face of man, for the judgment is God's; and the cause that is too hard for you, bring it unto me, and I will hear it.*[121] The Greek, however, is more explicit and better able to explain this system of judges: *And he appointed them to be over you as heads of thousands, heads of hundreds, heads of fifties, heads of tens, and grammatoisagogues for your judges.* (Instead of the Latin translation—*who will teach you everything*—the Greek has *grammatoisagogues for your judges.*)[122] Then follows a law of God which defines the provisions for these judges as follows (chapter 16): *Judges and officers shalt thou make thee in all thy gates, which the Lord thy God giveth thee, throughout thy tribes; and they shall judge the people with just judgment. They shalt not wrest judgment; they shalt not respect persons, neither take a gift...*[123] (In this passage the Greek has "grammatoisagogues" instead of "officers.") Josephus describes this law in a way that makes clear that these judges were also chosen by lot: *The men who were chosen by lot to go out and judge in the cities should be held in the highest respect, and insults should not be spoken in their presence... The judges should, moreover, have the right to pronounce sentence as they see fit, unless it has been proven that they accepted gifts in exchange for a verdict, or there was some other way they judged wrongly.*[124]

Just as Moses established these judges, afterward King Jehoshaphat confirmed their authority in the kingdom of Judea, as we are told in chapter 29 of Second Chronicles:[125] *And he set judges in the land throughout all the fenced cities of Judah, city by city, and said to the judges, take heed what ye do: for ye judge not for man, but for the Lord, who is with you in the judgment. Wherefore now let the fear of the Lord be upon you; take heed and do it: for there is no iniquity with the Lord our God, nor respect of persons, nor taking of gifts.*

Though the courts were suspended while the Jews were in Babylonia, on returning to their homeland they restored them along with their other institutions. Isaiah foresaw that this was going to happen in the first chapter of his book, where he proclaimed these words of God: *And I will restore thy judges as at the first...*[126] And then King Artaxerxes commanded that this be done, as it is written in Ezra chapter 6:[127] *And thou, Ezra, after the wisdom of thy God, which is in thine hand, set judges and scribes who may judge all the people...* (He refers to as "scribes"[128] the ones we called grammatoisagogues.) According to St. Athanasius,[129] it was in the restoration of these judges that the Psalmist was rejoicing when he sang in Psalm 121 of his great joy that, just as the Lord had predicted, the city of Jerusalem had been rebuilt, and the judges restored: *I was glad when they said unto me, Let us go into the house of the Lord. Our feet shall stand within thy gates, O Jerusalem. Jerusalem is built as a city that is compact together; whither the tribes go up, the tribes of the Lord, unto the testimony of Israel, to give thanks unto the name of the Lord. For there are set thrones in judgment* (or *for judgment* in the Greek),[130] *the thrones of the house of David.*[131] And this was the situation until the last days of the Judeans.

These judges seem to have been chosen from among the body of senators within each city, just as among the Romans it was from earliest times the senators who managed the courts.[132] The law itself shows this in many places. Deuteronomy 18: *If the striker shall flee to one of these cities, the senate of that city will send and receive him...*[133] And in chapter 19: *...and he fleeth into one of these cities; then the elders of his city shall send and fetch him thence.*[134] And in 21: *If one be found slain... and it be not known who hath slain him; then the senate of that city*[135] *shall come forth, and they shall measure unto... him who is slain...*[136] Hence Ruth chapter 4: *And Boaz took ten men of the elders of the city* of Bethlehem, *and said, Sit ye down here and be witnesses... And... the people who were in the gate, and the elders, said, We are witnesses...* and in their presence he accepted the property of Elimelech.[137]

In his book *On the Judge*,[138] Philo concludes from the law that there were four conditions placed upon upstanding judges.[139] The first was that they should not listen to frivolous suits—the translator renders the passage in Exodus 23 as: *Thou shalt not accept the voice of a lie...*[140] Philo gives the reason for this injunction: *The eyes*, he says, *interact directly with the objects they see, and they somehow carry out their duties... with the help of light, by means of which everything is illuminated and perceived. The ears, however, as one of the ancients correctly pointed out,*[141] *are less reliable than the eyes because they engage not with the objects themselves, but with the words that describe them; and these are not always accurate.*[142] The second condition was that they should not accept gifts, which blind even wise men to the truth and subvert the words of the just.[143] For it is a man of criminal character who would let gifts lead him to an unjust decision, and a less-than-upright one who would not deliver the proper verdict without receiving some reward for his efforts. After all, there are men of a character somewhere between just and unjust who have been given the task of protecting the oppressed from their oppressors, and yet do not want to rule on behalf of the better cause without being paid for it. And it is right that a judge's verdicts should be not merely within the law but beyond reproach. The third condition was that before reaching a decision they should consider the claims of the litigants with no regard at all for the parties themselves—that is, whether or not they are citizens, friends, or family members. Neither goodwill nor hatred should have any influence on the proceedings. And the fourth condition was that in rendering their verdicts they should not be swayed by any pity for the poor; for the law says: *Neither shalt thou countenance a poor man in his cause.*[144] Philo gives an explanation for this dictum as well: Only in court are we not allowed to pity the poor—we owe our pity to the unfortunate, and anyone who does wrong of his own free will is not unfortunate but unjust. Besides, the unjust are promised punishments, and the just rewards; so the punishment of an unfortunate should not be rescinded because of his miserable circumstances—he deserves not pity but anger. And when a man comes to deliver a judgment, he should approach it like a good moneychanger, who recognizes the differences between one transaction and another, and doesn't mix up the die marks of his coins and confuse good money with bad.[145] This is what I have to say about the judges.

Trials were held at the gates of cities, which were called "gates of judgment." This is clear from a law in Deuteronomy 21:[146] *And if the man like not to take his brother's wife, then let his brother's wife go up to the gate unto the senate...* Likewise: *If a man have a stubborn... son, who will not obey the voice of his father, or the voice of his mother... Then shall his father and his mother lay hold on him, and bring him out unto the elders of his city, and unto the gate of his place; and they shall say unto them, This your*[147] *son is stubborn and rebellious...*[148] And in the next chapter: If someone shall out of hatred accuse his wife of not being a virgin, *Then shall the father of the damsel, and her mother, take and bring forth the tokens of the damsel's virginity unto the elders of the city in the gate.*[149] And in chapter 25: *...let his brother's wife go up to the gate unto the elders of that city.*[150] Moreover, in Joshua 8[151] it is written: *...he shall stand at the entering of the gate of the city, and shall declare his cause in the ears of the elders of that city.* And in Ruth chapter 4: *And Boaz took ten men of the elders of the city* of Bethlehem, *and said, Sit ye down here and be witnesses... And... the people who were in the gate, and the elders, said, We are witnesses...* and in their presence he accepted the property of Elimelech.[152] Hence Proverbs 22: *...neither oppress the afflicted in the gate; for the Lord will plead their cause.*[153] And in 31: *Her husband is known in the gates, when he sitteth among the elders of the land.*[154] And Psalm 126: *...they shall not be ashamed, but they shall speak with the enemies in the gate.*[155]

The procedure was as follows: when a person wanted to bring suit against someone, he approached one of the chiefs of the judges—who were called grammatoisagogues—and explained his case to him, and asked him to bring it before the judges. And if the grammatoisagogue accepted the dispute (for he could in fact reject it), he would bring it before the judges on the day set aside for this; this is why he was called "the introducer." I will give proof of all this in the section where I present my thesis about the chiefs of the judges (I would prefer not to repeat myself, and to put everything in its own place and in the setting most appropriate to it). The talmudists report that trials were conducted as follows: whenever someone had a grievance, he went first to the judges of his own city, and if they would not listen,[156] he went to the judges of the city closest to it. If they too would not give him a hearing, he approached the judges of Jerusalem, who sat at two of the gates. If from these judges too he was unable to get satisfaction, he had recourse to the council called Sanhedrin. According to an account written by a former Hebrew named Pietro Galatino,[157] the talmudists said as follows:[158] *At first there were no disputes in Israel; rather, the courts of seventy-one judges sat in different places: one court met in the gate of the mountain of the House, i.e. the Temple, and another in the gate of the courtyard; while the other courts, of twenty-three judges, sat in each of the cities of Israel.*[159] *When there was a question to be asked, it was handled by the court of that city. If they heard, they told them;*[160] *and if not, the parties went to the court in the closest city. If they heard, they told them; but if not the parties went to the court at the gate of the Lord's mountain, and they said, "So I have explained it, and so my colleagues have explained it; so I have taught, and so my colleagues have taught." If they heard, they told them; but if not the two sides went to the court at the gate of the courtyard of the House of the Lord; and they said, "So I have explained it, and so my colleagues have explained it; so I have taught, and so my colleagues have taught." If they heard, they told them; but if not, the two sides went to the chamber called* gazith,[161] *where the Sanhedrin met from morning until evening, though on Sabbaths and festivals they sat in the wall.*[162] This is what the talmudists have to say.

The law, moreover, has this to say about hearing witnesses. In Deuteronomy 17: *At the mouth of two witnesses, or three witnesses, shall he who is worthy of death be put to death; but at the mouth of one witness he shall not be put to death.*[163] And in chapter 19: *One witness shall not rise up against a man for any iniquity, or for any sin, in any sin that he sinneth; at the mouth of two witnesses, or at the mouth of three witnesses, shall the matter be established.*[164] And then it says that false witnesses are to be given the harshest sentences.[165] Hence Josephus says in his discussion of this issue: *We are to rely not on one witness but on three or two whose character has been investigated. Women cannot be trusted because they can be flighty or impulsive; and neither can slaves, who are an inferior breed—their testimony will very likely be influenced by bribery or fear. Anyone who has given false witness will be arrested, and punished with the same penalty as would have been the man about whom he gave his testimony.*[166] The same law also prohibited anyone from being condemned until he was given a hearing; for as Nicodemus says in the seventh chapter of St. John: *Doth our law judge any man, before it hear him, and know what he doth?*[167] Finally, there is a law about passing sentence in Deuteronomy chapter 25, as follows: *If there be a controversy between men, and they come unto judgment, that the judges may judge them; then they shall justify the righteous, and condemn the wicked. And it shall be, if the wicked man be worthy to be beaten, that the judge shall cause him to lie down, and to be beaten before his face, according to his fault, by a certain number. Forty stripes he may give him, and not exceed; lest, if he should exceed, and beat him above these with many stripes, then thy brother should seem vile unto thee.*[168]

CHAPTER 7

The Jerusalem Council

THE CHAMBER CALLED *gazith*—which the Greek sources called *sunedrion* and *cathedra*, the Latin ones *concilium*, and the talmudists *sanhedrin*—was, in the rank and number of its judges, the greatest of all the tribunals in this city which God had chosen and placed in charge of both the sacred rites and the government. It was established first in Shiloh and then in Jerusalem—or first in the tribe of Ephraim and then in Judah—with the idea that whenever the judges of the various cities were unable to reach a decision because they disagreed on a matter of law, of fact, or of opinion, the matter could be referred to the capital. I will deal with this tribunal as follows: first I will explain everything the talmudists have to say about it, and then I will add whatever I myself have learned from reading the sacred authors. The talmudists say in various places:[169] *In the time of Moses, God ordered seventy elders to be chosen, advanced in age and known for their wisdom, who would help Moses to govern the people. Their task was to clarify and delimit all the difficult provisions of the law, and to give judgment in serious matters and hard cases. It is written about them in Deuteronomy*: If there arise a matter too hard for thee in judgment... then shalt thou arise, and get thee up into the place which the Lord thy God shall choose *to call on his name...*[170] *These men were called the Sanhedrin,* and they met in the chamber called *gazith* to render the judgments of souls.[171] *They were also called 'mehokekim,' that is, scribes or legislators, because whatever they handed down or wrote was treated by the others as though it were law. It was their body that was symbolized by the scepter that the Holy Spirit gave to the house of Jacob, and it was upon them that this scepter depended.*[172] *This is why their power to pass judgment was in force not only when the Jews were subject to kings and commanders*[173]—*even when they no longer had such kings or commanders the authority of the Sanhedrin remained in force... They had received from the tradition four methods of execution—stoning, burning, killing,*[174] *and strangulation.* It was therefore their custom *that when they killed someone, that is, when they sentenced someone to death, they would eat nothing that entire day...* Moreover, *judgments about*

*money and movable goods were handled by three judges, and capital cases by
twenty-three... But only the court of seventy-one judged a tribe, a scepter,[175] a
false prophet, or a high priest; and without the approval of the court of seventy
they did not declare war or add to the city,[176] or to the payments of the Temple.[177] And the tribes did not convene any Sanhedrins, i.e. assemblies of judges,
without their approval... The great house... contained seventy-one judges, and
the lesser house twenty-three. There were, moreover, seventy elders, about whom
we are told in Numbers 11: Gather unto me seventy men of the elders,[178] and
Moses was one more... None of the lesser Sanhedrins could be ordained except
by the superior assembly of the seventy... for those seventy judges ordained the
assemblies of the other judges who were in charge in all the other cities and
regions, on the condition that the courts of each region would be subordinate
to the great court of their superiors that met in Jerusalem, in the place called
gazith.[179] The judges were appointed by the laying on of hands, in such a way
that five were needed in order to grant that privilege.[180] King Herod took away
these Sanhedrins; others were put in their place, but they lacked the power to
give death sentences. Hence they answered Pilate, It is not lawful for us to
put any man to death.[181] Then, when the Temple was burned by the Romans
because of the false conviction of Christ forty years before, the Sanhedrin was
driven from the chamber called gazith and settled in Hamith;[182] but they were
permitted to try capital cases only in the chamber called gazith, as in Deuteronomy 17: And you shall do according to the word which they will tell you
from that place...[183] Likewise: then shalt thou arise, and get thee up into the
place...[184] In the end all these judges were again killed by the Romans.[185]* And
this, according to Pietro Galatino, is the account of the talmudists, who claim
to have absolute knowledge of these matters.

To the knowledge which those men acquired with their own eyes (so
to speak) and then wrote down, I will add what I have learned from the
sacred treasuries of the Old and New Testaments, and in particular from the
historical narratives of Josephus, and with these I will explain the origins,
confirmation, rights, and powers of the council. So to begin with, it seems
that God established this tribunal so that it would develop from a court of
judges to a council of elders and priests.[186] So it is written in Deuteronomy
chapter 17, where Moses is commanded by God to say to the people: *If
there arise a matter too hard for thee in judgment, between blood and blood,
between plea and plea, and between leprous and not leprous,[187] being matters
of controversy within thy gates: then shalt thou arise, and get thee up into
the place which the Lord thy God shall choose, so that you may call his name
there;[188] and thou shalt come unto the priests the Levites, and unto the judge
that shall be in those days, and inquire; and they shall show thee the sentence*

of judgment; and thou shalt do according to the sentence, which they of that place which the Lord shall choose shall show thee; and thou shalt observe to do according to all that they inform thee. According to the sentence of the law which they shall teach thee, and according to the judgment which they shall tell thee, thou shalt do; thou shalt not decline from the sentence which they shall show thee, to the right hand, nor to the left. And the man who will do presumptuously, and will not hearken unto the priest who standeth to minister there before the Lord thy God, or unto the judge, even that man shall die... [189] This passage implies that judgment was in the hands of the king, the priests, and the elders of the people; for they more than anyone were in charge of the place that the Lord had chosen. Josephus' account of this law therefore makes particular mention of the senate. He writes as follows: *But if the judges are unable to reach a decision about the matter before them... they will hand the entire case on to the holy city; and the high priest, the prophet, and the senate convene and give whatever judgment they think best.* [190] Afterward, Moses explicitly mentions as judges those whom I have described as priests. He says in chapter 19: *If a false witness rise up against any man to testify against him that which is wrong; then both the men... shall stand before the Lord, before the priests and the judges, which shall be in those days.* [191] And Josephus also mentions these same priests in the second book of his *Against Apion*: Moses *gave the priests the tasks of examining everyone, judging disputes, and punishing the guilty.* [192]

But Moses himself tried in the council the case of the man who collected wood on the Sabbath (in Leviticus 15).[193] As Philo says in Book 3 of his *Life of Moses*:[194] *They arrested the man and brought him to the prince, who was joined in the council by the priests; and the entire people was also there to listen... on the Sabbath day... While Moses, who did not know what punishment the man deserved... consulted with* God... *who answered that he should be stoned to death...*

Just as Moses set up this tribunal, so later on Jehoshaphat king of Judah ratified it, just as he also confirmed the courts of the cities. It is written as follows in Second Chronicles: *Moreover in Jerusalem did* he *set of the Levites, and of the priests, and of the chiefs of the fathers of Israel, for the judgment of the Lord, and for controversies, when they returned to Jerusalem. And he charged them, saying, Thus shall ye do in the fear of the Lord, faithfully, and with a perfect heart. And what cause soever shall come to you of your brethren who dwell in your cities, between blood and blood, between law and commandment, ceremonies and statutes* (the Greek has *precept, command, statutes, and judgments*),[195] *ye shall even warn them, that they trespass not against the Lord, and so wrath come upon you, and upon your brethren: this do, and ye shall not trespass. And, behold, Amariah the chief priest is over you in all matters of the Lord; and Zebadiah the son of Israel,*[196] *the ruler of the house of Judah, for all the king's matters; also the Levites shall be officers* (in Greek *scribes*) *before you...*[197]

We can see from these passages that the council was composed of the king, along with the leaders of the people and the seventy elders of the people; the high priest, along with the leaders of the priests; and the scribes, that is, the teachers (this is perfectly clear from the Gospels, which describe the trial of Christ).[198] By "leaders of the people" I mean the chiefs of the twelve tribes, who attended the king; while the elders were the seventy senators of the people whom I have described. Joseph of Arimathea, then, was a senator or a noble decurion as well as a member of the council,[199] for it is written that he did not agree with the others to condemn Christ.[200] By "leaders of the priests" I mean the men who were in charge of each of the twenty-four divisions or courses of priests, while the scribes were the teachers of the law whom Josephus calls prophets.[201]

Though the council was discontinued during the Babylonian exile, when the Jews returned to their homeland they restored all their remaining institutions,[202] and even the power to judge on the council was given to the priests. Ezekiel predicted this in chapter 44, where God commands him to say: *And the priests shall teach my people the difference between the holy and profane, and cause them to discern between the unclean and the clean. And they shall be present at the judgment of blood,*[203] *so that they may make the decision; and they shall justify my statutes, and judge my judgments; and they shall keep my laws and my statutes in all mine festivals...*[204] That is, they will try religious and capital cases, and they will *justify men*, i.e. absolve them; and *judge* them, i.e. condemn them, as this is what must be done with laws (a point I made before when I showed which people deserved punishment and which reward).[205] Some claim that later on this council was chosen from the members of David's family and that they were afterward removed by King Herod. But if this is true, it remains to be seen whether it is the point of the phrase in the Psalm which (according to St. Athanasius)[206] was sung upon the restoration of Jerusalem: *For there*, i.e. in Jerusalem, *are set thrones of judgment, the thrones upon the house of David,*[207] i.e. thrones from the house of David.

The council was convened by either the king or the high priest, depending on whether the accusation at hand was a matter of state or of religion,[208] and the procedure for a trial before the judges was more or less as follows. When a person wanted to accuse someone else, he generally approached the king, or the high priest, or the leaders, and brought his charge. Once this was done, they sent officers to seize the man, and if the situation called for it, they even sent a company of men given to them by the overseer of the Temple. They had the man brought to them, and they generally kept him in prison and under military guard until they could pass judgment on him. Then the entire council was convened, and it devoted itself to the trial. The prosecutor tendered the charge and the penalty in these words: *This man is worthy of death, because he did this or that.* The defender then rebutted the charge with: *This man is not worthy of death, because he did not do it, or he did it with good reason.*[209] When both sides had stated their cases, the judges took a vote, and the defendant was either absolved or condemned according to the number of votes in favor or against. But after the Romans took charge, the council had the power to condemn but not to punish: this only the Roman governor could do. This is what happened at the trial of Christ—the council condemned Christ and sentenced him to death, while the people (at the instigation of the council) demanded that Pilate the governor have him crucified, which Pilate decided to do.[210]

The formula for introducing or rebutting a charge is found in chapter 26 of Jeremiah: *Then spake the priests and the prophets unto the princes and to all the people, saying, This man is worthy of death; for he hath prophesied against this city... Then said the princes... unto the priests... This man is not worthy to die: for he hath spoken to us in the name of the Lord our God.*[211] On the other hand, the formula of condemnation is found in St. Matthew chapter 26: *...Behold, now ye have heard his blasphemy. What think ye? They answered and said, He is guilty of death.*[212] Mark puts this as: *...And they all condemned him to be guilty of death.*[213] But everything I have said will be more easily understood if I review every one of the trials held by this court for which we have a literary account.

There is a reference to the court and the council in the first Psalm: *Therefore the ungodly shall not stand in the court, nor sinners in the council of the righteous.* But the first trial about which we are told explicitly that it was conducted by the council took place under the Hasmoneans, and specifically under Hyrcanus. Josephus tells us in Book 14 that Herod, who later became king, was the defendant. Now, at that time there was a law—which Josephus himself mentions here—that no criminal could be executed unless he had first been condemned by a vote of the council or (to use the Greek name) *synedrion. Herod the son of Antipater,* writes Josephus, *had killed* some robbers... *without the approval of the council,* and his power was throwing everyone into a state of panic. *So many* people *urged King Hyrcanus and the people to force Herod to defend his actions in the council; and Hyrcanus... ordered him to appear there to plead his case... But he so frightened the entire*

*council by coming in with his troops that no one dared step forth to accuse
him. But even though they all held their tongues, a man named Sameas, who
was a man of principle,... did speak up: "Members of the council, and Your
Majesty... I believe that none of you has ever seen such a man as this one
standing here in our council. As a rule, the people who have come here to
plead their cases have made it their practice to stand here humbly and beg for
your mercy... their hair disheveled, and dressed in black. But this man, who
is here to defend himself on a charge of murder,... stands there in purple, and
carefully groomed, and surrounded by armed men. This means that if he is
convicted according to the law, it is he who will punish us with death, and
use force to evade the truth. But it is not Herod I accuse! He has never paid
any attention to the law but only to his own interests; while you, and the king,
have given him the unbridled freedom to do it! Be aware that there is only
one God, who is the greatest; and that is why this man, whom you want to
set free for the sake of Hyrcanus, will someday torment you and even the king
himself." ...When Hyrcanus saw that the judges were leaning toward executing
Herod, he postponed the verdict till the next day, and tipped him off so that
he could leave the city.*[214]

After Aristobulus was defeated and Judea subjected to Roman rule and
made into a province,[215] Herod's father Antipater was appointed governor,
and given such authority that the high priest could not assemble the council
without his knowledge and permission; nor could the council punish those
they had convicted until he approved the decision. Josephus tells us this in
Book 20, where he speaks about St. James the brother of the Lord.[216]

Then, as Josephus tells us, P. Gabinius the proconsul of Syria[217] was called
into action by Alexander the son of Aristobulus,[218] and after winning a new
victory he again remade Judea's government: he added four more councils
and divided the nation into five districts. According to Josephus, the first
was based in Jerusalem, the second in Gadara, the third in Amathus, the
fourth in Jericho, and the fifth in Sepphoris in the Galilee.[219] Since there
were in fact five councils, Christ was right to tell the apostles in chapter 10
of Matthew: *But beware of men: for they will deliver you up to the councils*
(in Greek *eis synedria*, i.e. *to the councils*), *and they will scourge you in their
synagogues.*[220]

When (as Josephus also tells us)[221] the Romans named Herod king and
he took possession of Jerusalem, he informed the council about certain
suspicious letters written by Hyrcanus.[222] And as the latter had already lost
his kingdom, Herod now had him killed (just as Sameas had predicted) and
along with him the seventy elders. In their place he put men of less exalted
origins, as both the talmudists and Philo tell us. Philo writes in his book

On Times: In the thirtieth year of his reign, Herod took the Sanhedrin away from the house of David.[223]

After Herod died and his son King Archelaus was banished to Vienne[224] by the emperor Augustus, Judea was again made a Roman province and placed under the authority of a procurator, and Herod's son Herod Antipas was given the Galilee in his capacity as tetrarch.[225] At that time the Pharisees and Sadducees (who were, as I have explained, two sects that had arisen in the days of the Hasmoneans and were especially powerful at the time) had great influence in the council—some of the elders, priests, scribes, and leaders belonged to the one sect, and the rest to the other. This is why Christ, who was preaching his gospel in those days, often mentions this council and the men who belonged to it. For example, he mentions the court and the council when he teaches for the first time a long lesson on the mountain in which he proposes a change in the old law and prescribes a new category of murder (as an expert in Jewish customs, he derived new spiritual crimes from the temporal ones prescribed at that time by the law). For just as it says in the Psalm: *Therefore the ungodly shall not stand in the court, nor sinners in the council of the righteous*, so he himself said: *Ye have heard that it was said of them of old time, Thou shalt not kill; and whosoever shall kill shall be in danger of the judgment; but I say unto you, that whosoever is angry with his brother without a cause shall be in danger of the court; and whosoever shall say to his brother, Raca, shall be in danger of the council; but whosoever shall say, Thou fool, shall be in danger of hell fire.*[226] By this he meant that a man called before the council faced more serious consequences than one called before the court (Matthew calls the first of these *sunedrion*, and the second *krisis*). For since the court dealt with less serious crimes than did the council, its penalties were correspondingly lighter where the council's were harsher; and according to tradition, hell was the place where the bodies of the damned were cast into the flames.[227] St. Augustine, however, interpreted this verse very differently: *There are three types of verdicts here: of the court, of the council, and of the fires of hell. For although in the court people still have the opportunity to defend themselves, the council—even though it is also a kind of court—differs in a way that is implied by this passage: it seems that it is the role of the council to pronounce the sentence of a condemned man, since at this point it is no longer a question of whether the defendant is guilty; it is instead the task of the judges to decide just how the condemned man ought to be punished.*[228] It seems to me, though, that Augustine did not have a clear notion of Hebrew legal reasoning.[229] Then, in another passage, Christ predicts before his disciples the death penalty which the Jerusalem council is going to inflict on him. He says in Matthew 16: *...that he must go unto*

Jerusalem, and suffer many things of the elders and chief priests and scribes, and be killed, and be raised again the third day.[230]

Once word of Christ's prediction spread, and he came to be seen as a threat to the old law, it was the council above all that made every effort to stand in his way. St. Luke writes as follows in chapter 20: *...the chief priests and the scribes with the elders, asked Christ... Tell us, by what authority doest thou these things? Or who is he who gave thee this authority...?* And when they failed to catch him this way, *they watched him, and sent forth spies, which should feign themselves just men, that they might take hold of his words, so they might deliver him unto the power and authority of the governor. And they asked him, saying... Is it lawful for us to give tribute unto Caesar, or no?*[231] And in John chapter 11: *But some of them went their ways to the Pharisees, and told them what things Jesus had done. Then gathered the chief priests and the Pharisees a council, and said, What do we? For this man doeth many miracles. If we let him thus alone, all men will believe in him; and the Romans shall come and take away both our place and our nation. And one of them, named Caiaphas, being the high priest that same year, said unto them, Ye know nothing at all, nor consider that it is expedient for us, that one man should die for the people, and that the whole nation perish not... Then from that day forth they took counsel together for to put him to death.*[232] And later on: *Now both the chief priests and the Pharisees had given a commandment, that, if any man knew where he were, he should show it, that they might take him.*[233]

Then followed the most famous trial the council would ever hold, in which Christ was condemned to death and executed. I would like to narrate the course of this trial by combining into one the many gospel passages that describe it, because this is the best way to put its character into sharp focus. I will, moreover, follow the general sequence of events without quoting any particular passages (all of which should be familiar enough to the reader). As we know, the chiefs of the priests, the scribes, and the elders of the people met in the court of the high priest—who was called Caiaphas—and considered how they might entrap Christ and kill him.[234] It was then that Judas, one of the twelve disciples of Christ, approached the priests and promised that he would hand Christ over to them in exchange for thirty denarii, and having been paid he watched for an opportunity to hand him over without any fuss. In the meantime, Jesus celebrated Passover with his disciples and made the Last Supper, where he said that one of them was going to betray him. Then, when all the rites had been completed, he went out with Peter and the sons of Zebedee[235] to a garden outside the city and gave himself over to prayer. Then Judas came by night with the servants and troops he had gotten from the chiefs of the priests, the elders of the people, and the magistrates of the

Temple, and handed him over. And Jesus said to this crowd that had surrounded him:[236] "Have you come out to arrest me with swords and clubs, as
though I were a thief? When I sat with you every day in the Temple, you
did not lay a hand on me." But the troops, and the tribune,[237] and the servants of the Jews seized him and brought him in chains to Caiaphas, who
was high priest that year. And the high priest asked him about his followers
and his teachings. While the men who were holding him mocked and beat
him, others were pestering his disciple Peter in various ways as he stood by
the hearth.[238] At dawn the elders of the people, the chiefs of the priests and
the scribes, together with the entire council, gathered together in order to
hand him over for execution. They brought him into their council, where
they tried to produce false testimony against him but were unsuccessful.[239]
Then they said, "If you are the messiah, tell us." He replied: "Were I to tell
you, you would not believe me or let me go. But from now on the son of
man will be sitting at the right hand of the power of God." Then they all
said, "So are you the son of God?" To which he replied, "You say that I am."
Then they said, "What more proof do we need? We have heard it from his
own mouth." And they condemned him to death.[240] And the whole crowd
rose up and took him from Caiaphas to the governor's house, to Pilate the
governor, to hand him over for execution. And Pilate came out to see them
and said, "Of what crime do you accuse this man?" They answered: "If this
man were not wicked, we would not have handed him over to you." Pilate said
to them, "Take him yourselves and judge him according to your laws." The
Jews said, "We are not allowed to kill anybody.[241] We found him subverting
our nation and keeping people from paying their tribute to Caesar, and saying
that he was the King Messiah." So Pilate asked him if he were the Messiah,
king of the Jews; to which he replied, "It is you who says it." So Pilate said
to the chiefs of the priests and the crowd: "I find no fault in this man." But
they grew more insistent and said, "Throughout all Judea, from the Galilee
down to here, he stirs up the people with his teachings." When Pilate heard
"Galilee," he asked whether Christ was a Galilean, and as he was aware that
this meant he was under Herod's jurisdiction,[242] he sent him to Herod (who
was in Jerusalem). But when Herod failed to get any answers out of him he
threw him out, and sent him back to Pilate dressed in white. Pilate assembled
the chiefs of the priests, the leaders, and the people, and said to them: "You
have brought this man to me on the charge that he is subverting the people;
but I find no fault in him, and neither does Herod."[243] And since it was the
custom that on festivals the governor would release to the people any prisoner
they wished, and he had in chains a notorious robber named Barrabas, he
asked the people whether he should release Barrabas or Jesus. And stirred

up by the chiefs of the priests and the elders, they said, "Barrabas." Then he said, "What shall I do with Jesus?" And they said, "Crucify him." So Pilate said, "I find no fault in him."[244] They answered, "We have a law, and according to this law he deserves to die because he made himself the son of God." And when Pilate asked them if he could release Jesus, the Jews shouted, "If you release him, you are no friend of Caesar's. For whoever makes himself a king is disloyal to Caesar."[245] So when Pilate saw that there was nothing he could do, he sat at the tribunal and washed his hands before the people, and he said: "I am innocent of this man's blood; you will see to that." And the entire people answered, "His blood will be on us and on our children." Then Pilate, who wanted to placate the people, ruled that their request for Christ's crucifixion should be granted. So the soldiers took Jesus away and led him out of the city carrying his own cross, to the place of Calvary; and they crucified him in the sixth hour.[246] It is clear from this account that (as I have suggested) the council assembled early in the morning;[247] they brought Christ into their council; they met in the Chamber of Hewn Stone; and Christ was brought there from the home of the high priest and there condemned to death. Then the people declared the manner of his execution, which was approved with the consent of Pilate the governor.

Proceeding in chronological order, the third trial of this council is mentioned in the Book of Acts, in the story of St. Peter and St. John in chapters 3 and 4: When Peter and John entered the Temple and healed *a certain man lame from his mother's womb*, and the people were amazed and spoke about it for a long time, *the priests, and the captain of the Temple, and the Sadducees, came upon them, being grieved that they taught the people, and preached through Jesus the resurrection from the dead. And they laid hands on them, and put them in hold... And it came to pass on the morrow, that their rulers, and elders, and scribes, and Annas the high priest, and Caiaphas, and John, and Alexander, and as many as were of the kindred of the high priest, were gathered together at Jerusalem. And when they had set them in the midst, they asked, By what power... have ye done this?*[248] And then: *But when they had commanded them to go aside out of the council...*[249] For even though in this passage Caiaphas is the high priest and Annas the former high priest, the latter wields the power of his son-in-law Caiaphas, while John and Alexander were (as I explained above) the chiefs of the priests.

The fourth trial is in chapter 5, which deals with the signs and wonders wrought by the apostles:[250] *Then the high priest rose up, and all they that were with him (which is the sect of the Sadducees), and were filled with indignation, and laid their hands on the apostles, and put them in the common prison... But the high priest came, and they that were with him, and called the council together, and all the elders* (in Greek *pasa gerousia*) *of the children of Israel, and sent to the prison to have them brought... Now when the high priest and the captain of the Temple and the chief priests heard* that no one was found in the prison, *they doubted of them whereunto this would grow... Then went the captain with the officers, and brought them without violence... And when they had brought them, they set before the council the men* whom the high priest had warned not to speak in the name of Jesus... *Then Peter... answered and said, We ought to obey God rather than men... Then stood there up one in the council, a Pharisee, named Gamaliel, a doctor of the law...,* and commanded to put the apostles forth a little space.[251] And finally: *And to him they agreed; and when they had called the apostles, and beaten them, they commanded that they should not speak in the name of Jesus, and let them go.*[252]

The fifth trial was that of St. Stephen in chapter 6: *Then they suborned men, which said, We have heard him speak blasphemous words against Moses, and against God. And they stirred up the people, and the elders, and the scribes, and came upon him, and caught him, and brought him to the council, and set up false witnesses, which said, This man ceaseth not to speak blasphemous words against this holy place, and the law.*[253] And much farther on: *Then they cried out with a loud voice, and stopped their ears, and ran upon him with one accord.*[254]

There is a sixth trial, that of St. Paul, in chapter 23:[255] *...and the chief captain also was afraid, after he knew that he was a Roman, and because he had bound him. On the morrow, because he would have known the certainty wherefore he was accused of the Jews, he loosed him from his bands, and commanded the chief priests and all their council to appear... And Paul, earnestly beholding the council, said, Men and brethren, I have lived in all good conscience before God until this day. And the high priest Ananias commanded them that stood by him to smite him on the mouth. Then said Paul unto him, God shall smite thee, thou whited wall; for sittest thou to judge me after the law, and commandest me to be smitten contrary to the law? And they that stood by said, Revilest thou God's high priest? Then said Paul, I wist not, brethren, that he was the high priest; for it is written, Thou shalt not speak evil of the ruler of thy people. But when Paul perceived that the one part were Sadducees, and the other Pharisees, he cried out in the council, Men and brethren, I am a Pharisee, the son of a Pharisee; of the hope and resurrection of the dead I am called in question. And when he had so said, there arose a dissension between the Pharisees and the Sadducees; and the multitude was divided.*

The seventh trial was that of St. James the Younger,[256] about whom Josephus writes in Book 20: Ananus, who was appointed high priest by King Agrippa, *was a man of exceptional arrogance; and as a Sadducee he was severe in his conduct of trials... And thinking that he had the perfect opportunity, since Festus the procurator had died and Albinus was still on his way, he convened the council of judges and called before it James the brother of Jesus, who was called Messiah, along with several others who were brought up on charges for violating the law... But there were people of a kindlier nature who were upset about this, and they secretly contacted the king, asking him to restrain Ananus from carrying out such a plan... Some of them even intercepted Albinus on the road... and informed him that it was against the law for Ananus to convene the council without his consent. So Albinus... ordered Ananus not to attempt any such thing unless he was willing to pay the price, and this was the reason that he removed him from the high priesthood...*[257]

The eighth trial was that of St. Matthew, as it is described in his biography: *...when the Jews found Matthew giving a rather vehement sermon about Jesus they were filled with zeal; so they took him away in chains, and told the high priest and the elders: "We have seized a disciple of Jesus whom we caught corrupting the people in the synagogue." They ordered him brought before them, so the Jews went out with their servants and brought him to the council. The high priest harangued Matthew for a long time, but he responded, "I am a servant of Christ." Then the high priest covered his ears and gritted his teeth, and said, "Matthew has committed blasphemy! Let him hear the law: whoever has blasphemed the Lord's name must die by death;*[258] *the entire people will stone him with stones."*[259] *And once he had been condemned, they brought him to the place of stoning.*

The ninth trial is to be found in Josephus, in Book 4 of his *War*, where he writes: *In accordance with the law they assemble seventy of the most well-respected commoners to play the part of judges, even though these men lack any real power; and before these they accuse Zacharias of betraying them to the Romans.*[260]

The tenth trial, which is mentioned by Josephus son of Gorion,[261] took place in the same year that Titus destroyed the city of Jerusalem. He says that Jochanan[262] *assembled* the judges of the people and the seventy *elders* (who were also called the Sanhedrin), *and said to* all the priests, and the elders, and the judges: *Unless you judge whomever we send to you according to our wishes, you will all die.*[263]

And this is what I have to say about the Jerusalem council. I have paid particular attention in this discussion to how the Hebrews tried capital crimes.

CHAPTER 8

Punishments

NOW THAT I HAVE explained all this, the next logical step is to describe the various kinds of penalties or punishments. The law categorizes these under more or less the following headings: restitution, fines, retribution, lashes, exile, sale, and death.

Restitution, as in Exodus 22: *If a man shall steal an ox, or a sheep, and kill it, or sell it; he shall restore five oxen for an ox, and four sheep for a sheep.*[264]

Fines, as in Exodus 21: *If... one hurts a woman with child, so that her fruit depart from her, and yet no mischief follow; he shall be surely punished, according as the woman's husband will lay upon him; and he shall pay as the judges determine.*[265]

Retribution, as in the following: *And if any mischief follow, then thou shalt give life for life, eye for eye, tooth for tooth, hand for hand, foot for foot, burning for burning, wound for wound, stripe for stripe.*[266]

Lashes, as in Deuteronomy 25: *And it shall be, if the wicked man be worthy of being beaten, that the judge shall cause him to lie down, and to be beaten before his face, according to his fault, by a certain number. Forty stripes he may give him, and not exceed; lest, if he should exceed, and beat him above these with many stripes, then thy brother should seem vile unto thee.*[267]

Sale, as in chapter 22: *...if he have nothing with which to make restitution, then he shall be sold for his theft.*[268]

Exile, as in chapter 21: *And if a man lie not in wait, but God deliver him into his hand; then I will appoint* him *a place whither he shall flee.*[269]

There are three types of execution explicitly spelled out in the law: burning, crucifixion, and stoning; all the rest fall into the general category of killing.[270]

Burning is mentioned in Leviticus 20: *And if a man take a wife and her mother, it is wickedness; they shall be burnt with fire, both he and they, that there be no wickedness among you.*[271]

The law of crucifixion is handed down by God in Deuteronomy 21: *And if a man have committed a sin worthy of death, and he be put to death, and thou hang him on a tree; his body shall not remain all night upon the tree, but thou shalt in any wise bury him that day (for he who is hanged is accursed of God); that thy land be not defiled, which the Lord thy God giveth thee for an inheritance.*[272] Then it is written in the eighth chapter of Joshua: *And the king of Ai he hanged on a gibbet until eventide; and as soon as the sun was down, Joshua commanded that they should take his carcass down from the cross, and cast it at the entering of the gate of the city...*[273] The Greek translator calls it neither a gibbet nor a cross but rather a doubled wood,[274] because crosses were constructed of two pieces of wood. And in chapter 10: Joshua *hanged the five kings on five trees, and they were hanging upon the trees until the evening; and it came to pass at the time of the going down of the sun, that Joshua commanded, and they took them down off the gibbets...*[275] Then in Second Samuel 21: *...and the Gibeonites crucified the sons of Saul with King David's consent, in the hill before the Lord;*[276] that is, before the tabernacle, which at that time was in Gibeon. And in Esther chapter 7: *Behold also, the gallows fifty cubits high, which Haman had made for Mordecai... standeth in the house of Haman. Then the king said, Hang him thereon. So they hanged Haman on the gallows that he had prepared for Mordecai...*[277] And in Ezra chapter 6: *Also I have made a decree,*[278] *that whosoever shall alter this word, let timber be pulled down from his house, and being set up, let him be nailed thereon...*[279] And in Acts chapter 5, it says about Christ: *...whom ye slew and hanged on a tree.*[280] David says about this cross in Psalm 21: *...they pierced my hands and my feet. They numbered all my bones...*[281]

There were, however, no cases in which a court assigned the penalty of crucifixion, except for one occasion when the judge was God and another when it was the council. In the first instance we have a passage in Numbers 25: *...and the anger of the Lord was kindled against those who had sinned with the daughters of Moab, and the Lord said unto Moses, Take all the heads of the people, and hang them up before the Lord against the sun, that the fierce anger of the Lord may be turned away from Israel.*[282] In the second case, when Christ was condemned, we have a description in the Gospels: after the members of the council sentenced him to death, they brought him to Pilate the governor, so that he would carry out the execution, and told him that Christ had been calling himself the king of the Jews. *And Pilate answered and said again unto them, What will ye then that I shall do unto him whom ye call the king of the Jews? And they cried out again, Crucify him... And so Pilate, willing to content the people... delivered Jesus, when he had scourged him, to be crucified. And the superscription of his accusation was written over,* *the king of the Jews. And with him they crucify two thieves; the one on his* *right hand, and the other on his left.*[283] *The Jews therefore, because it was the* *preparation,*[284] *that the bodies should not remain upon the cross on the Sabbath* *day... besought Pilate that their legs might be broken, and that they might be* *taken away. Then came the soldiers, and brake the legs of the first, and of the* *other which was crucified with him. But when they came to Jesus, and saw* *that he was dead already, they brake not his legs; but one of the soldiers with a* *spear pierced his side, and forthwith came there out blood and water.*[285] I also believe that they demanded Christ's crucifixion in accord not with their own laws but with those of the Romans, who (as I have shown in my book on Roman legal procedures)[286] would put on the cross men convicted of treason. Christ was also accused of *maiestas*[287] for claiming that he was the king of the Jews when Caesar alone was king. It was, moreover, accepted practice[288] to allow the relatives of the crucified man to bury him, and this practice was observed both in the case of Christ and in other cases (as Philo tells us in his *Flaccus*):[289] *I know of several cases of crucified men being taken down* *from the cross on the eve of* the festival of the Augusti,[290] *and (in accord with* *the custom) handed over to their families for burial.*[291]

On the subject of stoning, I have learned the following. It was applied above all to those people who had deserted God by worshiping other gods, cursing God, neglecting the Sabbath, or committing adultery. The person who discovered such a crime gave his testimony and threw the first stones; then the people took hold of the man, and pursued him with stones beyond the borders of the city, until he died. It is commanded as follows in Leviticus 24: *Bring forth him who hath cursed without the camp; and let all who* *heard him lay their hands upon his head, and let all the congregation stone* *him... Whosoever curseth his God shall bear his sin. And he that blasphemeth* *the name of the Lord, he shall surely be put to death, and all the congrega-* *tion shall certainly stone him: as well the stranger, as he that is born in the* *land...*[292] Then Deuteronomy 13: When a person has persuaded others to worship foreign gods... *neither shall thine eye pity him, neither shalt thou* *spare, neither shalt thou conceal him; but thou shalt surely kill him; thine* *hand shall be first upon him to put him to death, and afterward the hand of* *all the people. And thou shalt stone him with stones, that he die.*[293] Likewise chapter 17: ...*man or woman, who hath wrought wickedness in the sight of* *the Lord thy God, in transgressing his covenant, and hath gone and served* *other gods, and worshiped them... And it be told thee, and thou hast heard of* *it, and inquired diligently, and, behold, it be true, and the thing certain, that* *such abomination is wrought in Israel; then shalt thou bring forth that man* *or that woman, who have committed that wicked thing, unto thy gates, even that man or that woman, and shalt stone them with stones, till they die. At the mouth of two witnesses, or three witnesses, shall he that is worthy of death be put to death; but at the mouth of one witness he shall not be put to death. The hands of the witnesses shall be first upon him to put him to death, and afterward the hands of all the people. So thou shalt put the evil away from among you.*[294] And in Numbers 15: *And while the children of Israel were in the wilderness, they found a man who gathered sticks upon the Sabbath day. And they who found him gathering sticks brought him unto Moses and Aaron, and unto all the congregation. And they put him in ward, because it was not declared what should be done to him. And the Lord said unto Moses, The man shall be surely put to death: all the congregation shall stone him with stones without the camp. And all the congregation brought him without the camp, and stoned him with stones, and he died...*[295] As for adultery, Deuteronomy 22 says as follows: *If a damsel who is a virgin be betrothed unto a husband, and a man find her in the city, and lie with her; then ye shall bring them both out unto the gate of that city, and ye shall stone them with stones that they die; the damsel, because she cried not, being in the city; and the man, because he hath humbled his neighbor's wife...*[296]

This is more or less what the law has to say about stoning. It is also described by several of the sources outside the law. For example, First Kings 21 refers to blasphemy: *...and the men of Belial witnessed against him, even against Naboth, in the presence of the people, saying, Naboth did bless God and the king. Then they carried him forth out of the city, and stoned him with stones, that he died.*[297] (They used to say "bless" instead of "curse," for good luck.) Likewise in John 10: *The Jews answered him, saying, For a good work we stone thee not; but for blasphemy...*[298] And in Acts 6, about St. Stephen: *Then they suborned men, which said, We have heard him speak blasphemous words against Moses, and against God. And they stirred up the people, and the elders, and the scribes, and came upon him, and caught him, and brought him to the council, and set up false witnesses, which said, This man ceaseth not to speak blasphemous words against this holy place, and the law.*[299] And then after Stephen has spoken it adds: *Then they cried out with a loud voice, and stopped their ears, and ran upon him with one accord, and cast him out of the city, and stoned him; and the witnesses laid down their clothes at a young man's feet, whose name was Saul.*[300] The same thing happened to St. Matthew the apostle, who was convicted of blasphemy: *When they had brought him to the place of stoning, the two witnesses—in accordance with the dictates of the law—laid their hands on him and threw the first stones.* On adultery, John chapter 8 says as follows: *And the scribes and Pharisees brought unto him a woman taken in adultery; and when they had set her in the midst, they say* *unto him, Master, this woman was taken in adultery, in the very act. Now Moses in the law commanded us, that such should be stoned; but what sayest thou?...* He answered them, *He that is without sin among you, let him first cast a stone at her.*[301] This proves that, as I have said, the verdict belonged to the council and the punishment to the people.

The other types of execution are less well known, for example, beheading. On this we have Matthew 14: *And...* King Herod *beheaded John in the prison.*[302] As for strangulation or hanging, it is not mentioned except for the case of Judas the betrayer, who *burst down the middle because of his hanging.*[303] And this is what I have to say about the courts.

BOOK VII

Magistrates

CHAPTER 1

Types of Magistrates

AFTER THE COUNCILS and courts came the magistrates; they were of course in charge of these councils and courts, or (to be more specific) their authority gave them control over some public decisions and judgments. The Greek translator calls them *archontes*, and the Latin, *principes*. And since *archein* means not only "to be in charge" and "to be a leader" but also "to rule" and "to command," it follows that the magistrates had two kinds of power: first, to be in charge of the people and tell it what to do; and second, to issue laws and make judgments[1] (or as the scripture says, *he should do judgment and justice*).[2] This is why the sacred text calls the magistrates sometimes "rulers of the people" and sometimes "judges." We can see this clearly in the Books of Kings, where (we are told) the kings both ruled the people and judged them. We can prove that they were rulers from the ninth chapter of First Samuel, where God says about Saul: *...thou shalt anoint him to be ruler over my people Israel.*[3] And in the fifth chapter of Second Samuel, he says to David: *...Thou shalt feed my people Israel, and thou shalt be a ruler over Israel.*[4] And after David, we are told about Solomon in the first chapter of First Kings: *...for* Solomon *shall be king in my stead; and I have appointed him to be ruler over Israel and over Judah.*[5] As for judgments, there is a passage in First Samuel in which the people say to Samuel: *...now make us a king to judge us.*[6] And in the eighth chapter of Second Samuel: *...and* King *David executed judgment and justice unto all his people.*[7] And in the first chapter of Second Chronicles,[8] Solomon is told:[9] *...therefore* God *made thee king over* Israel, *to do judgment and justice.* Hence in Psalm 9: *For thou hast maintained my judgment and my justice; thou satest in the throne judging right*; that is, you fulfilled the tasks which I entrusted you to do with respect to my law.[10] In all these passages the Greek has *krisis*, *dikē*, and *dikaiosunē*, which correspond to the terms God uses in the law, *krimata* and *dikaiōmata* (or *judgments* and *statutes*). These are the means by which the law condemns the guilty and absolves the innocent.[11] After all, a magistrate is the living and speaking embodiment of the law, or rather its executor and guarantor.

And that the magistrate combines both kinds of powers—that of a ruler and that of a judge—we know from the Egyptian in the second chapter of Exodus, who turned to Moses after he had killed an Egyptian man and said: *Who made thee a prince and a judge over us?*[12] They exercised their authority as rulers by waging wars and debating issues of state, and as judges by administering justice.

This power of ruling or judging was first granted to Moses, who was made the leader of the Hebrew people even before the law itself was written. This happened when God commanded him to lead the people, which had been made slaves to the king, out of Egypt. So at first the people and the senate came willingly to consult with Moses and to accept the laws he gave them, without the need for judges or magistrates. But later on, when his father-in-law, Jethro, came to him during his first year in the desert and saw that he was expending all his energy on judging cases, he came up with the idea that Moses should hand the judgment of easier cases over to a group of officials, men of exceptional wisdom and fairness, and keep for himself the more serious ones (and in particular those that had to do with God).[13] As he was dying, Moses passed this authority on to Joshua the son of Nun, who led the people into the land of Canaan. And when he too died, the people began to make use of the government God had handed down to them, as Moses had told them to do in the fortieth year in the land of Moab, when he discussed the things that had to be done once the people had gained possession of the land of Canaan: *Ye shall not do after all the things that we do here this day, every man whatsoever is right in his own eyes. For ye are not as yet come to the rest and to the inheritance, which the Lord your God giveth you.*[14]

Since, moreover, the republic had three levels of government—for the entire people, for each of the tribes, and for each of the cities—magistrates were to be found at all these levels. The magistrates of the entire people were first judges, then kings, then princes, and finally kings again,[15] and their seat was the capital city. Each of the tribes had phylarchs[16] and patriarchs, and each of the cities had either "chiefs of cities" or judges—that is, tribunes, centurions, heads of fifty, and heads of ten.[17] Circumstances require that I deal with each of these separately.

CHAPTER 2

The Judges of Israel

THOUGH THE MEN who administered the first government of the Hebrews in the land of Canaan—that is to say, the aristocracy—had the authority both to rule and to judge, they were called not "rulers" because they ruled but "judges" because they judged, and they considered this the more important of their functions. As "judges," they were given by law the power and authority either to condemn or to absolve. The Greeks used two terms to express this idea—*kritēs* and *dikastēs*, *krinein* and *dikadzein*, *krisis* and *dikaiōsis*[18]—and with these they indicated the two categories of law particular to this magistracy, i.e. judgment and statute; these categories (which I have already singled out many times as being particularly worthy of our attention) are called in the law *krima* and *dikaiōma*. After all, it was said of Othniel, Ehud, and Deborah that *ekrinon* they judged Israel, and about Samuel that *edikadze*;[19] while his sons, who were trained by their father to give judgment, were called not *kritai* like the others but *dikastai*.[20] And in the second chapter of Baruch, such men are called *hoi dikastai hoi dikasantes Israel*.[21]

The particular province of these judges, then, was to control the courts, make deliberations of state, and conduct wars; and they wielded their judicial power, both to absolve and to condemn, without consulting any of the lesser judges. As I have already shown, Moses first created this power on the authority of his father-in-law, and God confirmed it through his law; and not only did the judges wield it in the cities in which they lived (for in their time Jerusalem had not yet been appointed the seat of power),[22] but they also traveled throughout the tribes and held assizes in certain cities where they performed the duties I have described. Hence it is written in the fourth chapter of Judges: *And Deborah... judged Israel at that time. And she dwelt under the palm tree... between Ramah and Bethel in Mount Ephraim; and the children of Israel came up to her for judgment.*[23] And in the seventh chapter of First Samuel: *And Samuel judged Israel all the days of his life. And he went from year to year in circuit to Bethel, and Gilgal, and Mizpeh, and judged Israel in all those places. And his return was to Ramah; for there was his house, and there he judged Israel, and there he built an altar unto the Lord.*[24] Of course, they did not enjoy the right to execute anyone they wished, since in all cases they were bound by the law (though the kings were later freed from this limitation).[25]

It is harder to say for certain whether the judges had the power to summon the people, to assemble the senate, or to set before either body whatever proposals they considered to be in the interest of the state. But since Moses and Joshua did have this right in the days before the judges and the kings had it after them, it is reasonable to assume that they themselves enjoyed it as well. The fact is, though, that these powers are not spelled out in the book that contains the history of the judges, which is written so sparingly that it hardly mentions the order in which they succeeded one another or the wars they fought.[26]

Now, there is in fact proof that the judges had the authority to declare war, in the account of Jephthah in Judges 11: *And it was so, that when the children of Ammon made war against Israel, the elders of Gilead went to fetch Jephthah... And they said unto Jephthah, Come, and be our captain, that we may fight with the children of Ammon.*[27] Certainly every war that was fought in the time of the judges was under their command as though they had been commanders in chief,[28] and yet the decision to declare war was not their own.[29] If not for that, their power would have equaled even that of the kings who came after them.

Moreover, their office was not hereditary—it was bestowed by the acclaim of the people whenever God chose a hero from among them. This situation is described by the expression *the Lord raised them up a deliverer.*[30] Thus the office did not always remain in the same family, or even in the same tribe. And when the Bible says that God raised up for the people this or that deliverer, it means that he planted within the people the idea that they should choose this or that judge to command their war. For as the angel of the Lord says to Gideon: *...Go in this thy might, and thou shalt save Israel from the hand of the Midianites... as one man.*[31] And the elders say to Jephthah: *...Come, and be our captain, that we may fight with the children of Ammon.*[32]

These were the judges: Othniel from the tribe of Judah, Ehud from the tribe of Ephraim, Deborah from the tribe of Ephraim (along with Barak from the tribe of Naphtali), and Gideon from the tribe of Manasseh.[33] Then Abimelech the son of Gideon, who took power by force—even though he killed his brothers, he was chosen by people of his city.[34] After him was Tola from the tribe of Issachar; then Jair who was from the tribe of Manasseh across the Jordan, as was Jephthah;[35] then Ibzan from the tribe of Judah; then

Elon from the tribe of Zebulon, Labdon[36] from the tribe of Ephraim, and Samson from the tribe of Dan; then Eli and finally Samuel, both of whom were Levites.[37]

CHAPTER 3

The Kings

THE JUDGES WERE then succeeded by the kings, who were very unlike them—the manner of their investiture was different and they enjoyed much greater power and authority, which came not so much from the laws as from the king's own preferences and desires. The Hebrew concept of a king was like that of Aristotle—he was freed from the laws and ruled with unlimited powers.[38] The king's coronation was as follows: first he was given his crown with the support of the entire people, and then he was anointed with the holy oil, and finally he was placed on the royal throne amid a great deal of pomp. As for his authority, he was first of all given control over the twelve tribes; for we are told about Saul: ... *When thou wast little in thine own sight, wast thou not made the head of the tribes of Israel, and the Lord anointed thee king over Israel?*[39] Second, he judged the tribes, and he had—both in conjunction with the council and by himself—absolute power to grant life or death as he saw fit; he was, in a sense, above the law. Third, he declared and waged wars as he liked. Now, I would like to discuss these matters in their proper order; so I will review from beginning to end the Bible's account of the kings, quoting from the holy books their description first of Saul, and then of David, and finally of Solomon. Once I have set out all this material, it will be easy for the reader to see the truth of my claims.

Since, then, God had known from the beginning that the Hebrews would not settle for judges, i.e. an aristocracy, and would long to be dominated by a king, he included among his laws one which they were meant to employ should the lust for a king ever overwhelm them. This law prescribed both the method of installing a king and his rights once he had been enthroned, in the following words in Deuteronomy 17: *When thou art come unto the land which the Lord thy God giveth thee, and shalt possess it, and shalt dwell therein, and shalt say, I will set a king over me, like all the nations that are about me; thou shalt in any wise set him king over thee, whom the Lord thy God shall choose: one from among thy brethren shalt thou set king over thee; thou mayest not set a stranger over thee, who is not thy brother. But he shall*

not multiply horses to himself, nor cause the people to return to Egypt, to the
end that he should multiply horses; forasmuch as the Lord hath said unto you,
Ye shall henceforth return no more that way. Neither shall he multiply wives
to himself, that his heart turn not away; neither shall he greatly multiply to
himself silver and gold. And it shall be, when he sitteth upon the throne of
his kingdom, that he shall write himself a copy of this law in a book out of
that which is before the priests the Levites; and it shall be with him, and he
shall read therein all the days of his life: that he may learn to fear the Lord
his God, to keep all the words of this law and these statutes, to do them; that
his heart be not lifted up above his brethren, and that he turn not aside from
the commandment, to the right hand, or to the left: to the end that he may
prolong his days in his kingdom, he, and his children, in the midst of Israel.[40]
Josephus describes the law as follows in Book 4 of his *Antiquities: But if*
you have been overwhelmed by the desire for a king, make him one of your
own nation; and see that he always pays close attention to justice, along with
all the other virtues. He should also take care not to consider himself smarter
than the laws or than God; nor should he do anything without the advice of
the high priest and the senators, or take many wives, or chase after large sums
of money or horses. It is through such practices that a king's arrogance[41] *is*
swept beyond the limits of the laws. And he should also take care that even if
he has indulged any of these appetites, he should not become more powerful
than your own interests would permit.[42] So much for Josephus. What God had
foreseen—i.e. that the Hebrews would someday be seized by the desire for a
king—actually happened in the time of Samuel, the prophet and judge. As it
is written in First Samuel, the people were distressed by the unfair judgments
of Samuel's sons Joel and Abijah, whom he—now fettered by age—had appointed to administer justice in his place. So the elders approached Samuel
and demanded of him a king to make their laws for them, just like the other
nations had. In effect, they were asking for a king who was above the law,
or was exempt from the body of legal codes.[43] The matter has been passed
down to us as follows: The elders *said unto him, Behold, thou art old, and*
thy sons walk not in thy ways; now make us a king to judge us like all the
nations. But the thing displeased Samuel... And Samuel prayed unto the Lord.
And the Lord said unto Samuel, Hearken unto the voice of the people... for they
have not rejected thee, but they have rejected me, that I should not reign over
them... howbeit yet protest solemnly unto them, and show them the manner
of the king who shall reign over them. And Samuel told all the words of the
Lord unto the people who had asked of him a king. And he said, This will be
the manner of the king who shall reign over you: He will take your sons, and
appoint them for himself, for his chariots, and to be his horsemen; and some

shall run before his chariots. And he will appoint him captains over thousands, and captains over fifties; and will set them to ear his ground, and to reap his harvest, and to make his instruments of war, and instruments of his chariots. And he will take your daughters to be confectionaries, and to be cooks, and to be bakers. And he will take your fields, and your vineyards, and your olive-yards, even the best of them, and give them to his servants. And he will take the tenth of your seed, and of your vineyards, and give to his officers, and to his servants. And he will take your menservants, and your maidservants, and your goodliest young men, and your asses, and put them to his work. He will take the tenth of your sheep; and ye shall be his servants. And ye shall cry out on that day because of your king whom ye shall have chosen you; and the Lord will not hear you on that day. Nevertheless the people refused to obey the voice of Samuel; and they said, Nay; but we will have a king over us; that we also may be like all the nations; and that our king may judge us, and go out before us, and fight our battles. And Samuel reported all the words of the people... And the Lord said to Samuel, Hearken unto their voice, and make them a king. And Samuel said unto the men of Israel, Go ye every man unto his city.[44] The passage reveals that among his duties the king had two above all, which were required by the law: he was in charge of trials and of wars. As the people say: *...and that our king may judge us, and go out before us, and fight our battles.* All this serves to demonstrate well enough that the kings did indeed have powers that outstripped those of the judges (I have already discussed what Aristotle has to say about their powers).[45]

Now I will move on to some other issues having to do with the king's selection and anointment. The next thing to happen was that God ordered Samuel to anoint with oil Saul the son of Kish from the tribe of Benjamin, who had come to him looking for his father's lost asses. Samuel kissed Saul and said:[46] *...Is it not because the Lord hath anointed thee to be captain over his inheritance? And thou shalt deliver his people out of the hands of their enemies, that are round about them.* And he ordered Saul to wait for him in Gilgal... Then he assembled the people in Mizpeh so that they could choose a king. There all the tribes cast lots, and the lot fell on Benjamin; and the tribe itself cast lots, and the lot fell on the family of Matri. And then the draws proceeded all the way to Saul the son of Kish. So the people immediately sent for Saul, who was found hiding at home; and when he was brought to Mizpeh, they shouted: *...God save the king. Then Samuel told the people the manner of the kingdom, and wrote it in a book, and laid it up before the Lord. And Samuel sent all the people away, every man to his house.* Then the Bible describes Saul's consecration, which was done by means of anoint-ment.[47] This is why the king is often called "the anointed of the Lord," as in

Psalm 17: *...and showeth mercy to his anointed, to David.*[48] And in First Samuel 24: *...that I should not do this thing unto my master, the Lord's anointed...*[49] When, moreover, several men had said that they were not going to obey Saul, Samuel told the people: *Come, and let us go to Gilgal, and renew the kingdom there. And all the people went to Gilgal; and Samuel anointed King Saul; and there they sacrificed sacrifices of peace offerings...*[50] Where the Latin has *renew the kingdom there*, the Greek has *enkainidzōmen*;[51] and *enkainidzein* means not only "to renew," but also "to consecrate" and "to dedicate." This is why the consecration of the Temple is called *encaenia*,[52] as in First Maccabees chapter 4, where it is written: *...the altar of holocausts... according to the day wherein the heathens had defiled it, in the same was it renewed.*[53] In Greek it is *enekainisthē*, that is, "it was dedicated." Hence a little farther on, *enkainismos* is rendered as "dedication."[54]

Then God rejected Saul because he had violated custom by making a burnt offering without waiting for the priest,[55] and as king he chose David the son of Jesse from the tribe of Judah, who was still a boy and a shepherd. Samuel was sent to the house of Jesse so that he could look over his seven sons and finally anoint David.[56] So after David, who was the youngest of the brothers, had been anointed king, he was summoned to the court of King Saul to serve as a harp player. Saul kept him there, and David went on to perform many brave and difficult deeds for him; but in particular he struck down the Philistine giant Goliath, who had challenged him to single combat. This victory provoked Saul to jealousy against him and led him to persecute David in various ways. Then when Saul was killed, David was again anointed king by the men of Judah, in Hebron in the tribe of Judah, while the other tribes anointed Saul's son Ishbosheth.[57] After Ishbosheth was killed by his own men, David was anointed a third time, over all of Israel and by the entire people; as it is written later on in the fifth chapter of Second Samuel: *Then came all the tribes of Israel to David unto Hebron, and spake, saying, Behold, we are thy bone and thy flesh... So all the elders of Israel came to the king to Hebron; and King David made a league with them in Hebron before the Lord; and they anointed David king over Israel. David was thirty years old when he began to reign, and he reigned forty years. In Hebron he reigned over Judah seven years and six months; and in Jerusalem he reigned thirty and three years over all Israel and Judah.*[58] During his reign he expelled the Jebusites who were holding Jerusalem and built a fortress on Mount Zion, where he came to live, and which was therefore called the city of David. It was there that he moved the ark of the covenant and readied the materials for building the Temple; and finally he chose his son Solomon to rule after him and ordered him anointed. So we are told in the first chapter of First

Kings: *The king also said unto* Zadok the priest, and Nathan the prophet, and Benaiah, *Take with you the servants of your lord, and cause Solomon my son to ride upon mine own mule, and bring him down to Gihon; and let Zadok the priest and Nathan the prophet anoint him there king over Israel: and blow ye with the trumpet, and say, God save King Solomon. Then ye shall come up after him, that he may come and sit upon my throne; for he shall be king in my stead; and I have appointed him to be ruler over Israel and over Judah.*[59] And all this was carried out according to his orders.

Then, after David's death, Solomon became king. He built the Temple and placed the ark in the holy of holies, and in his wealth and glory he far outrivaled all the other kings, as it is written in Second Chronicles.[60]

When Solomon left this mortal coil, all of Israel assembled in Shechem to appoint his son Rehoboam as king. But when he answered rather acerbically the people's request that he relieve them of the tribute that his father had placed upon them,[61] ten of the tribes deserted him and took as their king Jeroboam the son of Nebat, from the tribe of Ephraim. This is how the kingdom was split into two parts: one was the tribe of Judah, which was joined by the tribe of Benjamin, and the other was the remaining ten tribes, which were known altogether as the kingdom of Israel.

Judah was ruled at all times by the same tribe and by the family of David, so that a father usually left the kingdom to his son, while the kingdom of Israel was passed among a number of tribes and families, because instead of keeping to the law of God it turned to the worship of idols. Yet even though the kingship of Judah was hereditary, it was confirmed by the acclaim of the people. Hence in the twelfth chapter of First Kings: *...all Israel were come to Shechem to make Rehoboam king.*[62] And in the twenty-third chapter:[63] *And the inhabitants of Jerusalem made Ahaziah his... son king in* his father's stead... So it was in all the other cases. Moreover, there was a king of Judah named Joash, whose coronation is described with such precision that I would like to quote the account from the twenty-third chapter of Second Chronicles: *Then they brought out* Joash *the king's son, and put upon him the crown, and gave him the testimony, and made him king. And Jehoiada and his sons anointed him, and said, God save the king.*[64] And in chapter 26:[65] *Then the people of the land took Jehoahaz the son of Josiah, and anointed him,*[66] *and made him king in his father's stead...* The Israelite kingdom fell much more quickly than the Judean: while the former lasted until Hosea, whom Shalmaneser the king of Assyria defeated and carried off to Assyria along with the population of Israel,[67] the latter fell only many years later under Zedekiah, who was transported to Babylonia by its king, Nebuchadnezzar, along with all the Judeans.

It is easy to understand from these passages the procedure with which the kings of the Jews were installed, and the powers they enjoyed, and the fact that they reached this lofty rank not only because of their birth but with the support of the people. In order to see this even more clearly, one need only look closely at the stories of each of the remaining kings.

The king judged the people in three different ways, but in only one was he the sole judge. As in Second Samuel, chapter 15: *And Absalom rose up early, and stood beside the way of the gate; and it was so, that when any man who had a controversy came to the king for judgment, then Absalom called unto him... And in this manner did Absalom to all Israel that came to the king for judgment...*[68] This is why I said before that David performed justice and judgment for the entire people. In fact, David himself asked God to bless as follows his son Solomon, whom he had chosen to succeed him: *Give the king thy judgments, O God, and thy justice unto the king's son. He shall judge thy people with justice, and thy poor with judgment:*[69] Nor was he wrong to do so; for it is written in Psalm 96: *...justice and judgment are the habitation of God's throne.*[70] And in Psalm 98: *...thou dost establish equity, thou executest judgment and justice in Jacob.*[71]

The king executed a second type of judgment when he formed a judicial council, of the sort I have already described, together with the elders and the priests. In the third type, the king summoned the elders and the magistrates so that he could hold trials and issue verdicts. I will prove this in a little while, when I discuss the leaders of the tribes.

As I explained above, the kings convened the senate and summoned the people to public meetings.

That wars were declared at the king's behest, and fought under his leadership, is clear from the Books of Kings[72] and Chronicles, which are full of descriptions of royal wars. To these we may add the statement of the Hebrews when they requested a king: *and that our king may judge us, and go out before us, and fight our battles.*

CHAPTER 4

The Princes of the Jews, and the Last Kings

ALTHOUGH THE EPHRAIMITES never returned to their ancestral territories or recovered the sovereignty of their kingdom, after seventy years of captivity the Judeans were allowed by Cyrus the king of Persia to return from Babylonia. According to Josephus, they handed the leadership over to their high priests, while the kings of Persia, then of Egypt, and then of Syria[73] held military control over Judea and exacted tribute from the Jews. Then, after an internal conflict over the high priesthood,[74] Antiochus Epiphanes the king of Syria deprived the priests of their freedom and their religious rites, and they began to serve for only a few months at a time. Stung by this indignity, the Hasmoneans (who were Levites) took back control of the Jewish state by means of arms and political strategy. At first they called themselves princes, and then kings; in fact, they used the term "prince" to mean "commander in battle" and "trial judge"—it is written in the second chapter of First Maccabees that when they made Mattathias their prince *then many who sought after justice and judgment went down...*[75] This was as it should be—whoever is given the power to carry out justice and judgment is called "prince" or "archon."[76] Mattathias' son Judah Maccabee succeeded him as prince, and to this office he added the high priesthood.[77] He was followed by his brother Jonathan,[78] about whom it is written: *Now therefore we have chosen thee this day to be our prince and captain in* Judah's *stead, that thou mayest fight our battles. Upon this Jonathan took the governance upon himself at that time...*[79] Then his brother Simon was chosen:[80] *...Thou shalt be our leader instead of Judah and Jonathan thy brother. Fight thou our battles, and whatsoever thou commandest us, that will we do.*[81] Likewise, a bit farther on: *Also that the Jews and priests were well pleased that* Simon *should be their governor and high priest for ever, until there should arise a faithful prophet; moreover that he should be their captain, and should take charge of the sanctuary, to set them over their works, and over the country, and over the armor, and over the fortresses... Beside this, that he should be obeyed of every man, and that all the writings in the country should be made in his name, and that he should* *be clothed in purple, and wear gold; also that it should be lawful for none of the people or priests to break any of these things, or to gainsay his words, or to gather an assembly in the country without him, or to be clothed in purple, or wear a buckle of gold; and whosoever should do otherwise, or break any of these things, he should be punished. Thus it liked all the people to deal with Simon, and to do as hath been said. Then Simon accepted hereof, and was well pleased to be high priest, and captain and governor of the Jews and priests, and to defend them all. So they commanded that this writing should be put in tables of brass, and that they should be set up within the compass of the sanctuary in a conspicuous place; also that the copies thereof should be laid up in the treasury, to the end that Simon and his sons might have them.*[82] Then Demetrius the king of Syria freed them from all forms of tribute; thus the Jews, in a word, got back their former sovereignty under their own kings. About this First Maccabees says: *As for any oversight or fault committed unto this day, we forgive it, and the crown tax also, which ye owe us, and if there were any other tribute... and let there be peace betwixt us.*[83] Then there follows: *Thus the yoke of the heathen was taken away from Israel in the hundred and seventieth year. Then the people of Israel began to write in their instruments and contracts, In the first year of Simon the high priest, the governor and leader of the Jews.*[84] Then Antiochus the son of Demetrius added some other privileges, writing as follows: *...I confirm unto thee all the oblations which the kings before me granted thee, and whatsoever gifts besides they granted. I give thee leave also to coin money for thy country with thine own stamp. And as concerning Jerusalem and the sanctuary, let them be free; and all the armor that thou hast made, and fortresses that thou hast built, and keepest in thine hands, let them remain unto thee. And if anything be, or shall be, owing to the king, let it be forgiven thee from this time forth for evermore.*[85]

Then Simon was succeeded by his son John,[86] and John by his son Aristobulus,[87] who (as Josephus tells us) raised the princeship to the status of a monarchy and was the first to place a crown on his head. This happened 471 years and three months after the people was freed from its captivity in Babylonia and returned home.[88] Aristobulus was followed by his brother Alexander Jannaeus, to whom Aristobulus' widow Salome (or Alexandra) gave the throne after she married him. After he died Alexandra herself took power,[89] and afterward her son Hyrcanus, who was driven out by his brother Aristobulus.[90] And when the Roman commander Pompey was fighting the war against Mithridates, he took control of Syria, made King Aristobulus a prisoner, and occupied Judea;[91] reorganizing it into a province and appointing as its procurator Antipater of Ashkelon.[92] And when soon after Antigonus the son of Aristobulus seized the city and took back the kingdom, the

Romans responded by appointing Herod the son of Antipater as king;[93] he died after accomplishing some great things[94] and left part of his kingdom to his son Archelaus.[95] This Herod was king when Jesus Christ, whom God had foretold so long before, was born. Then Archelaus was banished to Vienne by the emperor Augustus for abusing his authority,[96] and Judea was once again reformed as a province and placed under a procurator. This explains why Pontius Pilate was procurator when Christ was crucified. Then Herod Agrippa, the son of Aristobulus and the grandson of Herod, was named king of Judea by the emperor Claudius,[97] and when he died Judea was for a third time governed by Roman procurators in the manner of a province. When Vespasian was emperor and Gessius Florus was his procurator, the city was destroyed together with the nation and its Temple. These were the names of the kings and princes:

KINGS OF JUDAH AND ISRAEL

SAUL	The first king, son of Kish from the tribe of Benjamin. Twenty years.
DAVID	Son of Jesse from the tribe of Judah. Forty years.
SOLOMON	Son of David. Forty years.

KINGS OF JUDAH FROM THE HOUSE OF DAVID

REHOBOAM	Son of Solomon. Seventeen years.
ABIJAH	Son of Rehoboam. Three years.
ASA	Son of Abijah. Four years.
JEHOSHAPHAT	Son of Asa. Twenty-five years.
JORAM	Son of Jehoshaphat. Eight years.
AHAZIAH	Son of Joram. One year.
ATHALIAH	Wife of Joram. Seven years.
JOASH	Son of Ahaziah. Forty years.
AMAZIAH	Son of Joash. Twenty-nine years.
AZARIAH	Or Uzziah, son of Amaziah. Five years.
JOTHAM	Son of Azariah. Sixteen years.
AHAZ	Son of Jotham. Sixteen years.

HEZEKIAH	Son of Ahaz. Twenty-nine years.
MANASSEH	Son of Hezekiah. Fifteen years.
AMON	Son of Manasseh. Two years.
JOSIAH	Son of Amon. Thirty-one years.
JEHOAHAZ	Son of Josiah. Three months.
ELIAKIM	Or Jehoiakim, son of Josiah. Eleven years.
JEHOIACHIN	Or Jeconiah, son of Jehoiakim. Three months.
ZEDEKIAH	Son of Josiah. Eleven years.

The Jews were deported to Babylon, and when they returned seventy years later, they were governed by their high priests. Then the princeship of the Hasmoneans was established during the reign of Antiochus Epiphanes, the king of Syria.

PRINCES

MATTATHIAS	The Hasmonean. One year.
JUDAH	Maccabee, son of Mattathias. Four years.
JONATHAN	Son of Mattathias. Eighteen years.
SIMON	Son of Mattathias. Eight years.
JOHN	Hyrcanus, son of Simon. Thirty-six years.

KINGS AGAIN

ARISTOBULUS	Son of John Hyrcanus. Called himself king. One year.
ALEXANDER	Jannaeus, son of John Hyrcanus. Twenty-seven years.
SALOME	Or Alexandra. Wife of Alexander. Nine years.
HYRCANUS	Son of Alexander. Three months.
ARISTOBULUS	Son of Alexander. Expelled by his brother Hyrcanus. Six years.

JUDEA UNDER THE ROMANS

ANTIPATER   Of Ashkelon, procurator of Judea. Three years.

KINGS FOR A THIRD TIME

ANTIGONUS   Son of Aristobulus. The city taken by the
                         Romans, he is the last of the Hasmoneans.
                         Three years.

HEROD   The Great, son of Antipater of Ashkelon.
                         Made king by the Romans in opposition to
                         Antigonus. Thirty-seven years.

JESUS CHRIST IS BORN

ARCHELAUS   Son of Herod the Great. King of Judea.
                         Nine years. His brother, Herod Antipas, was
                         tetrarch of the Galilee. Thirty-four years.

JUDEA AGAIN UNDER THE ROMANS

C. COPONIUS   Made procurator of Judea by Augustus.
                         Two years.

M. AMBIVIUS   The same. One year.

ANNIUS RUFUS   The same. One year.

VALERIUS GRATUS   Made procurator by Emperor Tiberius.
                         Eleven years.

PONTIUS PILATE   The same. Ten years.

THE PASSION OF CHRIST

MARCELLUS   The same. Three years.

KINGS FOR THE FOURTH TIME

HEROD AGRIPPA   Son of Aristobulus, grandson of Herod the
                             Great. Made king of Judea by the emperor
                             Gaius.[98] Ten years.

JUDEA UNDER THE ROMANS FOR THE THIRD TIME

CUSPIUS FADUS   Made procurator by Emperor Claudius.
                             Three years.
TIBERIUS ALEXANDER   The same. Two years.
CUMANUS   The same. Three years.
ANTONIUS FELIX   The same. Three years.
PORCIUS FESTIUS   Made procurator by Nero. Three years.
ALBINUS   The same. Three years.
GESSIUS FLORUS   The same. Three years.

The city of Jerusalem, along with the Temple, was destroyed by Titus Caesar while his father, Vespasian, was emperor.

CHAPTER 5

The Chiefs of the Tribes, or Phylarchs

THE SECOND LEVEL of government consisted of the chiefs of the tribes and the families, whom I will discuss next. It was these chiefs who led each tribe and looked after its registers.[99] So just as there were twelve tribes, there were twelve chiefs. After naming them in the fifth chapter of Numbers,[100] the text adds: *These are those who were numbered, whom Moses and Aaron numbered, and the princes of Israel, being twelve men: each one was for the house of his fathers.* And in the fourth chapter: *And Moses and Aaron and the chiefs of the congregation numbered the sons of the Kohathites...*[101] And in the thirteenth chapter:[102] *And Moses, and Eleazar the priest, and all the chiefs of the congregation, went forth...* (The "congregation" is the assembly of the entire people.) And in Joshua 22: *...they sent unto* the children of Reuben, and to the children of Gad... *ten chiefs, of each house a chief.*[103] And since the tribes are called *phylai*, the Septuagint calls their chiefs *phylarchoi, archiphyloi, archontes*, and *archēgoi tōn phylōn*; and it also calls them "chiefs of Israel." For at Numbers 6,[104] where the Latin has *chiefs of Israel*, the Greek has *the twelve chiefs of Israel, the chiefs of the tribes*. Hence Philo said in his book on fugitives: *There are twelve chiefs of this sort, who are called phylarchs.*[105] True, First Chronicles 27 mentions two chiefs of the tribe of Manasseh and one of the tribe of Levi, and if we added these the total would be fourteen;[106] but the round number, namely twelve, is used more frequently.

These men had the following privileges: they stood at the king's side, and they accompanied him both to give their advice and to render judgments for the various tribes; and they bound themselves along with the king whenever they believed it was necessary to validate something by means of a public oath. The proof that they convened to give advice is as follows.[107] Numbers 30: *And Moses spake unto the heads of the tribes of the children of Israel...*[108] And in the fifth chapter of Deuteronomy: *...ye came near unto me, even all the heads of your tribes, and your elders.*[109] And in 31: *Call to me your phylarchs and your elders.*[110] (The Latin is less exact: *Gather unto me all the elders throughout your tribes...*) And in 29: *Ye stand this day all* *of you before the Lord your God; your chiefs, your tribes, and your elders...*[111] (in Greek *archiphyloi*).[112] And in First Chronicles 28: *And David assembled all the princes of Israel, the princes of the tribes...*[113] And in the fifth chapter of Second Chronicles: *Then* King Solomon *assembled the elders of Israel, and all the heads of the tribes...*[114] And in the eighth chapter of First Kings: *Then Solomon assembled the elders of Israel, and all the heads of the tribes...*[115] David also referred to this when he said about his own coronation as king: *Who is like unto the Lord our God, who dwelleth on high, who humbleth himself to behold the things that are in heaven, and in the earth! He raiseth up the poor out of the dust, and lifteth the needy out of the dunghill; that he may set him with chiefs, even with the chiefs of his people.*[116] That is, that he may enthrone the king among the twelve chiefs of the tribes who sit by his side; for this is the sense of the Greek.[117]

We know from the following passages that the chiefs administered justice. Psalm 121, which has to do with the restoration of Jerusalem after the Babylonian exile: *Whither the tribes go up, the tribes of the Lord, unto the testimony of Israel, to give thanks unto the name of the Lord. For there are set thrones of judgment, the thrones of the house of David.*[118] Isaiah alludes to the same thing in chapter three: *The Lord standeth up to plead, and standeth to judge the people. The Lord will enter into judgment with the ancients of his people, and the chiefs thereof...*[119] And in 32: *Behold, a king shall reign in righteousness, and chiefs shall rule in judgment.*[120] Each of them, moreover, had his own seat from which he rendered justice for his own tribe. Christ shows this very clearly when he says about this practice that he was going to sit like a king on the celestial throne of majesty, and that the twelve apostles—just like the twelve phylarchs—would sit on twelve thrones to judge the twelve tribes. For there is no question that Christ has in mind the ancient republic of the Hebrews, which flourished in the time of David. This is what he says in Matthew 19: *...Verily I say unto you, that ye which have followed me, in the regeneration when the son of man shall sit in the throne of his glory, ye also shall sit upon twelve thrones, judging the twelve tribes of Israel.*[121]

It is clear from the seventh chapter of First Kings that Solomon gave these judges a place in the Temple—there it is written: *Then he made a porch... wherein is the tribunal, even the porch of judgment... And his house where he dwelt had another court within the porch...*[122] For the Greek translator has "*thronos*" instead of "tribunal," i.e. a throne; and he calls this place *kritērion*, that is, *judicatorium*.[123]

As for the fact that they took oaths, this is clear from the ninth chapter of Joshua: *And Joshua... made a league with* the Gibeonites... *and the princes of the congregation*—that is, of the people—*sware unto them.*[124] But even after the ten tribes were torn from the body of the state and deported to the region of Assyria, the Judeans continued to refer to twelve chiefs of tribes, just as they referred to the seventy elders.[125] We know this from the sixth chapter of Ezra: the Jews who returned from Babylonia sacrificed *for a sin offering for all Israel, twelve he goats, according to the number of the tribes of Israel.*[126] While in the seventh chapter of the Third Book of Esdras it says: *the number of the phylarchs*, that is, of the chiefs of the tribes *of Israel.*[127] And then: *Then I separated twelve of the phylarchs, and of the chief of the priests...*[128] This is why Christ was also quite right to say that *the apostles, just like the twelve phylarchs, will judge the twelve tribes.*[129] As for the idea that these chiefs also took part in the council, I have already proven this point.[130]

CHAPTER 6

The Heads of Families, or Patriarchs

AFTER THE CHIEFS of the tribes come the heads of families. In order to understand just who they were, we must first understand what was meant by "family": just as the people of Israel was divided into twelve tribes, each tribe was divided into many families; and just as the people as a whole was named after Israel, and each of the tribes after his sons, so the families took their names from his grandchildren. The Latin translator uses a number of different terms to describe these families, calling them generations, nations, kin, houses, and families. (For these the Greek has *Geneseis, syngeneai, dēmoi, oikoi,* and *patriai*.) As in the first chapter of Numbers: *Take ye the sum of all the congregation of the children of Israel, after their kin, by the houses of their families... And the children of Reuben... by their generations, after their families... by their houses... forty... thousand and five hundred.*[131] The names of the families that sprang from each of the sons of Israel are recorded in Numbers 26. From Reuben, the Hanochites, the Palluites, the Hezronites, and the Carmites. From Simon, the Nemuelites, the Jaminites, the Jachinites, the Zarhites, and the Shaulites. From Gad, the Zephonites, the Haggites, the Shunites, the Oznites, the Erites, the Arodites, and the Arelites. From Judah, the Shelanites, the Pharzites, the Zarhites, the Hezronites, and the Hamulites. From Issachar, the Tolaites, the Punites, the Jashubites, and the Shimronites. From Zebulon, the Sardites, the Elonites, and the Jahleelites. From Manasseh, the Machirites, the Gileadites, the Jeezerites, the Helekites, the Asrielites, the Shechemites, the Shemidaites, and the Hepherites. From Ephraim, the Shuthalhites, the Bachrites, the Tahanites, and the Eranites. From Benjamin, the Belaites, the Ashbelites, the Ahiramites, the Shuphamites, the Huphamites, the Ardites, and the Naamites. From Dan, the Shuhamites. From Asher, the Jimnites, the Jesuites, the Beriites, the Heberites, and the Malchielites. From Naphtali, the Jahzeelites, the Gunites, the Jezerites, and the Shillemites. From Levi, the Gershonites, the Kohathites, and the Merarites. Hence it is written in Joshua chapter 7: *In the morning, therefore, ye shall be brought according to your nations: and it shall be, that the tribe which the Lord taketh shall come according to the men thereof... So Joshua rose up early in the morning, and brought Israel by their tribes; and the tribe of Judah was taken; and he brought all the kindred of Judah; and he took the kin of the Zarhites; and he brought the kin of the Zarhites man by man, and the family of Zabdi was taken.*[132] And in chapter 19: *And the lot of the tribe of the children of Benjamin came up according to their families... And the second lot came forth to Simeon, even for the tribe of the children of Simeon according to their kindred...*[133] And in Judges 17: *And there was a young man out of Bethlehemjudah of the kindred of Judah.*[134] And in First Samuel 10: *Now therefore present yourselves before the Lord by your tribes, and by your families. And when Samuel had caused all the tribes of Israel to come near, the tribe of Benjamin was taken. When he had caused the tribe of Benjamin to come near by their kindred, the kin of Matri*[135] *was taken, and Saul the son of Kish was taken...*[136]

These, then, were the families of the Israelites while they were in the desert. Some of these families disappeared later on, while others flourished; for example, among the families of the tribe of Judah was that of David, which appeared later on.[137] Hence he himself says in First Chronicles 28: *...God... hath chosen Judah to be the ruler; and of the house of Judah, the house of my father...*[138] And while the ten tribes more or less disappeared in their exile in Assyria, the others survived in Babylonia. When they returned, they reconstituted the Jewish people.

Since the system was set up in such a way that the families (or whatever else one might call them) were part of the tribes, it follows that just as the tribes had chiefs, so did the families; and these too were called by a number of different names: *Dēmarchoi, archontes tōn geneseōn* (or *syngeneōn*), *patriarchai, archipatriōtai,* and *archontes tōn patriōn* and *tōn oikōn.* That is, chiefs "of the people," "of generations," "of families," and "of houses." The general term for all of these is "patriarchs."[139] These terms appear very often, as for example in the first chapter of Numbers: *And with you there shall be the chiefs of the tribes, and of the houses in their kindreds.*[140] And in chapter 6:[141] *That the chiefs of Israel, heads of the families, who were in the tribes, and were over them who were numbered, offered.* And in 36: *And the chiefs of the families of the children of Gilead... came near, and spake before Moses, and before the chiefs of the children of Israel...*[142] And in Joshua 14: *...and the chiefs of the families throughout the tribes of Israel.*[143] And in chapter 19: *These are the inheritances, which... the chiefs of the families and of the tribes of the families of Israel, divided for an inheritance by lot in Shiloh...*[144] And in 21: *Then came near the chiefs of the families of the Levites unto Eleazar the priest, and unto*

Joshua the son of Nun, and unto the heads of the kindred of the tribes...[145] (in Greek, *archipatriōtai* and *archiphyloi patriōn*). And in First Chronicles 24: *Among the sons of Eleazar there were sixteen chief men of the families, and eight among the sons of Ithamar according to their families and houses.*[146] And in chapter 8, which has to do with the Benjaminites: *These were the patriarchs, and the chiefs of their kindred. These dwelt in Jerusalem.*[147] This is all there is to say about the identity of these families and their chiefs.

It remains to explain what their duties were: they were to call together the families in their charge and bring to them any matters of public concern, and to serve as their leaders in wartime. They were also retained by the kings to give advice and conduct trials. We know they reported to their families from the fact that during the Babylonian exile they were the only magistrates who were allowed to keep even a portion of their authority, so that they could administer their families in the public interest. When, therefore, the people are about to be brought back from Babylonia, it is only the chiefs of the families who are mentioned, and (we are told) called forth from among the three remaining tribes—Judah, Benjamin, and Levi.[148] This is how it is recorded in the third chapter of Ezra, whereas the Greek narrative mentions these officials in various other places.[149] For example, it is written in chapter 2: *...the archiphylites*[150] *of the families of Judah and Benjamin, and the priests and Levites were assembled.*[151] And in chapter 5: *There were chosen to go up, the leaders of the houses of the families according to their tribes.*[152] And likewise: *These are the names of those who went up according to their families, to the leadership of the faction,* i.e. the *meridarchia.*[153] And: *Who were in charge of the families.* And: *Who led their families.*[154] The Latin translator does not make this clear because he uses "districts" rather than "families," but in Nehemiah chapter 8, it is written: *...were gathered together the chiefs of the families of all the people, the priests, and the Levites, unto Ezra the scribe, even to understand the words of the law.*[155] We may also conclude that they were military leaders as well, from the fact (which I will discuss later) that in the army the military tribunes were patriarchs.[156] We know that the chiefs of the families were retained by the kings to give advice from the fifth chapter of Second Chronicles, where it is written: *Then King Solomon assembled the elders of Israel, and all the chiefs of the tribes, the heads of the families of the children of Israel...*[157] And we know about trials from chapter 19: *King Jehoshaphat set of the Levites, and of the patriarchs of Israel, for the judgment of the Lord...*[158]

CHAPTER 7

Rulers of the Cities, Tribunes, Centurions, Heads of Hundreds, and Heads of Fifties

THE THIRD LEVEL of government, which was the network of individual cities, consisted of the magistrates or chiefs who belonged to each of these cities. For just as the families followed the tribes of which they were a part, so they in turn were followed by the cities into which the parts of these families were organized.[159] As we said above, each tribe founded many cities, among which the families of that tribe were distributed. The men who were in charge of those communities were called "rulers of the cities," as in the ninth chapter of Judges, which deals with the Ephraimite city of Shechem: *And when Zebul the ruler of the city heard the words of Gilead,*[160] *his anger was kindled.*[161] And then: *But there was a strong tower within the city, and thither fled all the men and women, and all the rulers of the city...*[162] And in the twenty-fourth chapter:[163] *...Joshua the ruler of the city...*, i.e. one of the rulers of the city.[164]

Many such rulers—chiliarchs, hecatonarchs, pentecontarchs, and decadarchs—were appointed to be in charge of both deliberations and judgments, which is why they are sometimes called "rulers of the cities" and sometimes called "chiefs of the judges." Josephus adds that there were seven of them in every city.[165] The chiliarchs were in charge of a thousand men, the hecatonarchs of a hundred, the pentecontarchs of fifty, and the decadarchs of ten. The Latin translator calls them—in the Roman fashion—tribunes, centurions, *quinquagenarii,* and *decani.*[166]

Moses first established these officials in the desert, and placed them in charge of the people and the judges—at first at the suggestion of his father-in-law, Jethro, and then at the command of God. Jethro makes this suggestion in the eighteenth chapter of Exodus, and Moses repeats it in the first chapter of Deuteronomy, in the passage I quoted before:[167] *How can I myself alone bear your cumbrance, and your burden, and your strife? Take you wise men, and understanding, and prudent, and I will place them over you. And ye answered me, and said, The thing which thou hast spoken is good for us to do. So I took from among you wise men, and understanding, and prudent, and I made them heads over you, chiliarchs, and hecatonarchs, and pentecontarchs, and decadarchs, and grammatoisagogues for your judges.*[168] (This is the text of the Greek version, which is somewhat clearer than the Latin.)[169] When, moreover, Moses says that *I made them heads over you, chiliarchs, and hecatonarchs, and pentecontarchs, and decadarchs,* he is clearly implying that one of their functions is to govern the people; and when he adds *and grammatoisagogues for your judges* he is pointing to their other function, that of governing the judges. From this we see that they had two different duties—to be in charge of the councils of the cities, on one hand, and of the judges, on the other. In their first capacity, they convened the senate of their city and discussed with it matters of public concern, and as long as they did so, they were called "rulers of the city." In their second capacity, they would bring before some of the senators—as one would before authorized judges[170]—the cases that required judgment. On such occasions they were called "heads of the judges" and "grammatoisagogues," or "introducers of the disputes." (If we compare the two translations of this passage, it becomes clear that the Greek conveys this information with much greater precision than does the Latin.) On the heads of the judges there is Exodus 18: *And Moses chose able men out of all Israel, and made them heads over the people, rulers of thousands, rulers of hundreds, rulers of fifties, and rulers of tens. And they judged the people at all seasons...*[171] And in First Chronicles 28: *And David assembled all the chiefs of Israel, the commanders of the tribes, and the captains of the companies...*[172] The Greek, however, is more complete: *He assembled all the chiefs of Israel, the heads of the judges and the tribes, and all the heads of the daily divisions.*[173] On the grammatoisagogues, the first chapter of Deuteronomy says as follows: *and made them heads over you, tribunes, and centurions, and captains over fifties, and captains over tens, who will teach you everything.* And in 16: *Judges and officers shalt thou make thee in all thy cities...*[174] And in Deuteronomy 29: *Ye stand this day all of you before the Lord your God; your chiefs, and your tribes, your elders, and your teachers...*[175] And in 31: *Gather unto me all the elders of your tribes, and your teachers...*[176] And in Joshua 23: *And Joshua called for all Israel, and for their elders, and for their heads, and for their judges, and for their officers...*[177] And in 24: *And Joshua... called for the elders of Israel, and for their heads, and for their judges, and for their officers...*[178] The same passages appear in Greek as: *I placed grammatoisagogues over your judges.* And: *You will establish for yourselves judges and grammatoisagogues in all your cities.* And: *You stand today before the Lord your God, your heads of tribes, and your senate, and your judges, and your grammatoisagogues.* And: *Summon to me all your heads of tribes, and your elders, and your judges, and your grammatoisagogues.* And: *he summoned all of Israel, the elders, the chiefs, and the judges, and the scribes.* And: *he called for the elders, and the chiefs, and the judges, and the scribes.* It is absolutely clear from these passages that there was a single magistrate placed over the judges, who was called the grammatoisagogue. As I see it, we still know less than we should about who these *grammatoeisagogeis* were. But St. Augustine, in the second book of his *Questions on Exodus,* has written as follows:[179] *It is not clear just who were the people whom the text mentions as* grammatoe-isagogeis *just after the heads of ten,*[180] *since this title is never used for any of the offices or magistracies. In fact, they have been understood as teachers of a sort, i.e. as those "instructors of writing" who teach the rudiments of the alphabet, just as the Greek term suggests. This surely means that the Hebrews had writing before the giving of the law,*[181] *though it may never be possible to figure out when this took place. It is a common belief that writing began with the first men and from them was handed down to Noah, and from him to the ancestors of Abraham, and then to the people of Israel; but I don't see how one could prove this.* And in Book 18, chapter 39 of the *City of God: Finally, Moses appointed men whose task was to teach the people to read before they might learn any of the words of the divine law. The scripture calls these men* grammatoisagogues, *which could be translated into Latin as "those who bring in or introduce the letters," because in a sense they bring in or introduce these letters to the minds of the students, or rather they bring to them those whom they teach.* From this it seems that St. Augustine understood "grammatois-agogues" to mean "instructors"[182] who taught the people to read. The ancient translation[183] seems to refer to the same thing—it has *scholars, teachers, and those who teach everything.*

But since these men were not, as St. Augustine seems to think, appointed as teachers for the entire people but rather (as we can see from the passages I have cited) were for the judges only, the grammatoisagogues were more properly the teachers and instructors of the judges. Now, should someone find this explanation less persuasive than the other one, he can distance himself from it a bit by saying that the task of the grammatoisagogues was not to teach the judges how to read but to bring their cases to them, and (as I said) to govern their actions.[184] The law of God which I quoted above seems to point in this direction: *You will establish for yourselves judges and grammatoisagogues in all your cities, and they shall judge the people with just judgment.* Josephus explains this as follows: *Each city would be governed by seven men who stood out in their love of virtue and justice. Each of these chiefs would be given two officers from the tribe of Levi.*[185] Likewise in the third chapter of Ezra:[186] ...*set judges and magistrates, which may judge all the people.* "Magistrates" means "governors of the judges."

These men were endowed with the authority to either accept or reject the cases brought to their attention, and to bring those they did accept before the judges. Hence Isaiah says in his first chapter: *Every one of thy princes... loveth gifts, and followeth after rewards; they judge not the fatherless, neither doth the cause of the widow come unto them.*[187] The Greek here is clearer and more appropriate: *And they do not accept the cause of the widow.*[188] The translators of the Septuagint got this term[189] from the Athenians—they had the same kind of magistrates, whom they called *Eisagōgeis tōn graphōn.*[190] As I have written at some length in my book on the Athenian state, what the latter call *graphai* is called by the Septuagint *grammata*;[191] and there were magistrates who brought cases or accusations to the judges assigned to a particular trial.[192] Caesar also uses this manner of speaking in the first book of his *Civil War*: *Whatever disputes the soldiers had among themselves they brought to Caesar of their own free will.*[193]

Given all this, the procedure for bringing suit certainly seems (as I said before) to have gone as follows: when a person wanted to bring charges against someone else, he brought his opponent to one of these officials and somehow dragged him into court.[194] If the official took notice of the charge or accusation, he brought the matter to trial. The judges then heard the case and either absolved the man or convicted him. If convicted, he was handed over to the collector, who threw him in jail. There he would remain imprisoned until he had paid off his fine. Hence Christ says in chapter 12 of St. Luke: *When thou goest with thine adversary to the magistrate, as thou art in the way, give diligence that thou mayest be delivered from him; lest he hale thee to the judge, and the judge deliver thee to the collector, and the collector cast thee into prison... thou shalt not depart thence, till thou hast paid the very last mite.*[195] The tribunes, centurions, heads of fifty, and heads of ten were, therefore, magistrates whose duties included being in charge of the judges and bringing them their cases, and perhaps teaching them as well; this is what is done today in Venice by the officials called "advocates of the commune."[196] Hence it is written in the first chapter of Second Chronicles: *Then Solomon spake unto all Israel, to the captains of thousands and of hundreds, and to the judges...*[197]

The third duty of these officials was to appear before the king to offer him (and the other officials) advice on matters of state, and to judge certain cases alongside the king. The evidence for their advisory role is the same set of passages I quoted above in the previous discussion.[198] In Deuteronomy 29: *You stand today before the Lord your God, your heads of tribes, and your senate, and your judges, and your grammatoisagogues.*[199] And in 31: *Summon to me all your heads of tribes... and your grammatoisagogues.*[200] And in First Chronicles, chapter 13: *And David consulted with the captains of thousands and hundreds, and with every leader* about bringing back the ark.[201] And in chapter 38:[202] *David assembled all the magistrates of Israel, the chiefs of the judges and of the tribes.*[203] And in the first chapter of Second Chronicles: *Solomon summoned* among others *the officials, the tribunes, and the centurions*, on his way to offer sacrifice.[204] There is a reference to trials in Second Chronicles 29: *Then Hezekiah the king... gathered the rulers of* Jerusalem, *and went up to the house of the Lord.*[205] Likewise in Jeremiah 36:[206] When Micaiah reported to the officials sitting in the house of the king, in the storehouse, that he had heard Baruch reciting Jeremiah's prophecy about the coming destruction of the city, they quickly summoned Baruch and ordered him to recite his book. What they heard astonished them, so they went to King Jehoiakim and told him everything that had happened. Though the king wanted to burn the book, some of them objected, but it did them no good. Likewise in chapter 37: *...so Irijah took Jeremiah*, on the pretense that he was fleeing to the Chaldeans, *and brought him to the princes. Wherefore the princes... smote Jeremiah, and put him in prison... Then they said unto the king, We beseech thee, let this man be put to death... Then Zedekiah the king said, Behold, he is in your hand: for the king is not he who can do anything against you.*[207] And in Second Chronicles 18:[208] King Ahab sent Micaiah to Amon, the ruler of the city, so that he would put him in prison. And in chapter 20 of St. Luke: *...and they sent forth spies, which should feign themselves just men, that they might take hold of his words, so they might deliver him unto the leadership, and unto the authority of the governor.*[209] When the verse uses the term "leadership"[210] it means "the magistrates of the Jews," and when it uses "governor"[211] it means "the Roman procurator."[212]

If, therefore, one of the "rulers of the city" was a chiliarch, that is, the head of a thousand men, then we may clearly understand the famous passage of the prophet Micah on the subject of Bethlehem, where Christ was to be born. In chapter 5: *But thou, Bethlehem Ephratah, though thou be little among the thousands of Judah, yet out of thee shall he come forth unto me who is to be ruler in Israel...*[213] The Greek is more explicit: *And you, Bethlehem, home of Ephratah, are too small to be among the thousands of Judah. From you he shall come forth to me, to be a prince of Israel...* This is what it means: though you, Bethlehem, are so small a city that you do not have a thousand men, and cannot appoint a ruler of a thousand, or chiliarch; nevertheless from you will come Christ the archon,[214] that is, the ruler not just of one city but of all Israel.

CHAPTER 8

The Scribes, or Recorders

NOW, IT IS TRUE that I have already written in my discussion of religion[215] that the scribes were jurists who interpreted the law for the people, what in Greek are called *grammateis*.[216] But now I must add that they also wrote things down, and that it was with this writing that they performed their duty to the magistrates, the people, and the senate. We know that they wrote from Psalm 44: *...my tongue is the pen of a scribe writing swiftly.*[217] And from Jeremiah 36, where it says that Jeremiah had given his vision to Baruch the scribe to write down and recite, but that when King Jehoiakim heard it he cut it up with the scribe's[218] own razor.[219] And from chapter 8, where it says: *...Lo, certainly in vain made he it; the pen of the scribes is in vain.*[220] Now, we are not well-informed as to whether these men were also among the interpreters of the law, or whether the latter made up another group entirely. It does seem that this second type of scribe interpreted the law in public, while the first type was a kind of recorder.[221] But the reader may apply his own judgment to the relevant passages of scripture. The first mention of the scribes, then, is in the fifteenth chapter of Numbers.[222] God says to Moses: *Gather unto me seventy men of the elders of Israel...* and the scribes, *and bring them unto the tabernacle of the congregation.*[223] The other mention is in the twentieth chapter of Deuteronomy: *The scribes shall speak to the people...*[224] In the Greek, "scribes" is always rendered as *grammateis*. It is in fact unclear whether they performed exactly the same tasks for the people, the senate, and the magistrates, and whether they contributed to the code of laws or merely recorded the acts passed by those other officials. But they do seem to have seen to the latter's needs, and to have devoted their efforts to them.

That the kings had scribes we know first of all from Seraiah, who was the scribe of King David; and Elioseph and Abiah,[225] who were Solomon's; and Shebna, who was Hezekiah's.[226] And in Second Kings 12: *And it was so, when they saw that there was much money in the chest, that the king's scribe and the high priest came up, and they put up in bags, and told the money that was found in the house of the Lord.*[227] There are many passages like these. Josephus, moreover, shows us that the chiefs of the tribes also had scribes—he says in the seventh book of his *Antiquities*: Joab the lieutenant of King David *went to count the number of the Hebrews, and he took with him the heads of tribes and the scribes, and traveled throughout all of Israel.*

Josephus also informs us about the rulers of the state[228] in his description of the law. He says: *Each of these rulers would be given two officers from the tribe of Levi.*[229] Clearly by "officers" he means two scribes, who recorded legal pronouncements. That they were in fact from the tribe of Levi is also clear from First Chronicles,[230] which mentions *...scribes and officers of the Levites...*[231]

The following passages prove that the people also had scribes. In the twentieth chapter of Deuteronomy: The scribes *shall speak to the people...*[232] And in the first chapter of Joshua: Joshua commanded the scribes of the people to order the people to prepare food.[233] And in the third chapter: The scribes passed through the camp, and told them to follow the Levites who were carrying the ark.[234]

The proof that some scribes served the people and others the senate is a passage in the twenty-seventh chapter of First Chronicles: *the tribunes, the centurions, and the scribes who served the people.*[235] And Josephus (in Book 5 of his *War*) mentions Aristeus, a famous man and the scribe of the senate.[236] And Jeremiah, in chapter 52, mentions a man who had been deported from Jerusalem and was *...the principal scribe of the host, who mustered the people of the land.*[237] In Greek this is: *Ton grammatea tōn dynameōn ton grammateuonta tō laō pasēs tēs gēs*; that is, "the scribe of the troops, who recorded documents for the people of all the land."

Be that as it may, though the Greek always uses the one word *grammateis*, the Latin version varies between *duces*, *principes*, and *praecones*.[238] This proves decisively that while the translator himself was not sure just who the *grammateis* were, he did not regard them as teachers of law. But it is possible that a scribe who recorded documents might have had many additional public duties.

CHAPTER 9

Military Matters

UP TO THIS POINT we have discussed the civilian functions of the people, the senate, and the magistrates. Now seems the time to examine the conduct of external, that is to say military, affairs. After all, generals (as Aristotle tells us) are as integral a part of the perfect state as are priests and judges. True, there is not a great deal to say on this subject, because the holy book does not provide us with a great deal of information; but we will look first at the rules God left us about fighting wars, then at the people who led them, and then at the wars that the Hebrews waged. On the conduct of war, God orders in Deuteronomy 20 that: *When thou goest out to battle against thine enemies, and seest horses, and chariots, and a people more than thou, be not afraid of them; for the Lord thy God is with thee, who brought thee up out of the land of Egypt. And it shall be, when ye are come nigh unto the battle, that the priest shall approach and speak unto the people, and shall say unto them, Hear, O Israel, ye approach this day unto battle against your enemies: let not your hearts faint, fear not, and do not tremble, neither be ye terrified because of them; for the Lord your God is he who goeth with you, to fight for you against your enemies, to save you. And the officers shall speak unto the people, saying, What man is there who hath built a new house, and hath not dedicated it? Let him go and return to his house, lest he die in the battle, and another man dedicate it. And what man is there who hath planted a vineyard, and hath not yet eaten of it? Let him also go and return unto his house, lest he die in the battle, and another man eat of it. And what man is there who hath betrothed a wife, and hath not taken her? Let him go and return unto his house, lest he die in the battle, and another man take her. And the officers shall speak further unto the people, and they shall say, What man is there who is fearful and fainthearted? Let him go and return unto his house, lest his brethren's heart faint as well as his heart. And it shall be, when the officers have made an end of speaking unto the people, that they shall make captains of the armies to lead the people. When thou comest nigh unto a city to fight against it, then proclaim peace unto it. And it shall be, if it make thee*

*answer of peace, and open unto thee, then it shall be, that all the people who
are found therein shall be tributaries unto thee, and they shall serve thee.
And if it will make no peace with thee, but will make war against thee, then
thou shalt besiege it; and when the Lord thy God hath delivered it into thine
hands, thou shalt smite every male thereof with the edge of the sword; but the
women, and the little ones, and the cattle, and all that is in the city, even all
the spoil thereof, shalt thou take unto thyself; and thou shalt eat the spoil of
thine enemies, which the Lord thy God hath given thee. Thus shalt thou do
unto all the cities which are very far off from thee, which are not of the cities of these nations. But of the cities of these people, which the Lord thy God
doth give thee for an inheritance, thou shalt save alive nothing that breatheth;
but thou shalt utterly destroy them; namely, the Hittites, and the Amorites,
the Canaanites, and the Perizzites, the Hivites, and the Jebusites; as the Lord
thy God hath commanded thee. That they teach you not to do after all their
abominations, which they have done unto their gods; so should ye sin against
the Lord your God. When thou shalt besiege a city a long time, in making war
against it to take it, thou shalt not destroy the trees thereof by forcing an axe
against them; for thou mayest eat of them, and thou shalt not cut them down
(for the tree of the field is man's life) to employ them in the siege; only the trees
which thou knowest that they be not trees for meat, thou shalt destroy and
cut them down; and thou shalt build bulwarks against the city that maketh
war with thee, until it be subdued.*[239] From this, says Philo, *it is clear that the
nation of the Jews was friendly toward all who loved peace, and should not be
condemned for having had courage enough to repel the violence of those who
decided to attack without provocation. It also drew a distinction in war between
those who threatened it and those who did not; for it is a mark of incredible
savagery to launch a merciless attack on people who do not deserve it or pose
only a minor threat; and to slaughter women… as readily as men. And only a
great love of justice would prohibit even the destruction of the enemy's fields,
or cutting down trees in order to do away with the fruit.*[240]

CHAPTER 10

The Chief of the Army

OF THE MAGISTRATES who dedicated themselves to military affairs, the most important was the general, or chief of battle; after the king he had the greatest authority over the conduct of wars. The Latin translator calls him *princeps militiae*,[241] and the Greek, *archistratēgos tēs dynameos* and *archōn pantōn archontōn tēs dynameos*; that is, the chief commander of the army. Such a commander of all the army's commanders was Abner, while Saul was king. As it says in Second Samuel 2: *Abner the son of Ner, captain of Saul's host...*[242] And in chapter 3: *ho hēgoumenos megas*, i.e. David called him the great commander. While David was king, this task was performed by Joab and Amasa, who are called in the same book *chiefs of the soldiers of Israel, and over all the army*.[243] On Joab, chapter 24 says: David commissioned Joab, the chief of his army, to count the entire Hebrew people and calculate the total number of soldiers.[244] And to Amasa David says as follows, in chapter 19: *God do so to me, and more also, if thou be not captain of the host... continually...*[245] In fact, it is written in Second Kings 24 that Nebuzaradan, the general of Nebuchadnezzar, deported to Babylonia Sopher, the chief of the army, who used to train the recruits from the people of the land,[246] though the Greek has *the scribe of the chief of the army, who was counting the people of the land*.[247] That the chief of the soldiers was very important even to the king, we know from what Elisha says to the widow[248] in the fourth chapter of Second Kings: *what is to be done for thee? Wouldest thou be spoken for to the king, or to the captain of the host?...*[249]

CHAPTER 11

Tribunes and Centurions

THE GENERAL COMMANDED the chiliarchs, the hecatonarchs, the pentecontarchs, and the decadarchs. Moses established these officials to be in
charge of groups of a thousand, a hundred, fifty, and ten men. As I have
said, the Latin translator calls them tribunes, centurions, heads of fifty,²⁵⁰ and
heads of ten.²⁵¹ It was generally from among these officials that the chiefs
of the families were drawn. As it is written in the first chapter of Numbers:
*they are the phylarchs according to their families, the chiliarchs of Israel.*²⁵² This
is as though to say that of all these officials, it was usually those who were
patriarchs within their own tribes who were raised to the rank of chiliarch
(though of course not all the patriarchs were tribunes).²⁵³ The chiliarchs, in
fact, are also called *archontes* and *archēgoi tōn chiliadōn*, that is, chiefs of
thousands, for example, in First Chronicles 12: *And there fell some of Manasseh to David... Adnah, and Jozabad... captains of the chiliads...*²⁵⁴ And in
chapter 24:²⁵⁵ *David summoned... the chiefs of the chiliads, so that he could
bring back the ark.* There is also a reference in the Book of Judges to a chiliad
of soldiers: when Gideon is summoned²⁵⁶ to take command, he refuses it,
saying: *My chiliad is humble in Manasseh, and I am the least in my family.*²⁵⁷
And likewise in Micah: *And you, Bethlehem... are too small to be among the
thousands...;*²⁵⁸ that is, to set up a chiliad and a chiliarch.

The centurions, whom the Greek calls *hekatonarchoi*, are also called
archontes tōn hekatontadōn, i.e. "chiefs of centuries." It says, for example, in
Second Chronicles 28 that David assembled the heads of the chiliads and the
centuries, i.e. the tribunes and the centurions.²⁵⁹ Moreover, the tribunes and
the centurions are often mentioned in connection with war, as when David
is about to send the army against his son Absalom in Second Chronicles
18.²⁶⁰ After reviewing his men he assigns them tribunes and centurions, and
divides them into three groups under three commanders, who between them
would be in charge of the entire army. And in Second Kings 11: Jehoiada
summoned the centurions in order to crush Queen Athaliah.²⁶¹ (In Second
Chronicles 23,²⁶² it is instead the "heads of families" who are said to have been

summoned.)[263] And in Second Chronicles 25: When King Amaziah was about to go out to war, *he gathered together Judah, and assigned all of Judah and Jerusalem to tribunes and centurions according to the houses of their families, and counted them from twenty years and upward; and he found that there were three hundred chiliads capable of going to war.*[264] And in the third chapter of First Maccabees,[265] Judah the prince is said to have appointed on the eve of battle the men who would lead the people, the tribunes, and the centurions. In fact, sometimes the scripture also calls them *archontes tēs dynameos* and *stratēgoi*, i.e. the chiefs of the army, as in Numbers 31: *And Moses was wroth with the officers of the host, with the captains over thousands, and captains over hundreds...*[266] (though the Greek has here not "officers" but *episcopi*, i.e. overseers). And in Second Samuel 24: *...And Joab and the captains of the host went out from the presence of the king, to number the people of Israel.*[267]

CHAPTER 12

The Heads of Fifty, and of Ten

THE PENTECONTARCHS and decadarchs are mentioned not only in Exodus, where they are appointed by Moses, but also in the first chapter of Second Kings, where it says: *Then* Ahaziah king of Judah *sent unto* Elijah *a captain of fifty with his fifty...* then another, then a third.[268] Likewise in First Maccabees: *And after this Judah ordained captains over the people, even captains over thousands, and over hundreds, and over fifties, and over tens.*[269]

The king appointed all these officials as he saw fit. That this was also true of the chief of the army is clear from the passage quoted above about Amasa.[270] The following passages are our evidence for the tribunes and centurions. In First Samuel 8: *And* the king *will appoint him* your sons as *captains over thousands, and captains over hundreds...*[271] And in chapter 28:[272] *Saul made David his captain over a thousand...* And in Second Samuel 18: *And David numbered the people who were with him, and set captains of thousands, and captains of hundreds over them.*[273] And afterward: *...And the king stood by the gate side, and all the people came out by hundreds and by thousands.*[274] And in the second chapter of First Chronicles:[275] *And David said, Whosoever smiteth the Jebusites first shall be chief and captain...* In Greek this is *Eis archonta kai stratēgon,* that is, "I will make him leader of the state and commander of the army." And in Second Chronicles 25: King Amaziah *made the Judeans, by their families, captains over thousands, and captains over hundreds...*[276] In Greek, *he appointed them according to the houses of their families as tribunes and centurions...* From this it seems that the tribunes were chosen not always from the heads of families, but sometimes from the families themselves.[277] In the third chapter of First Maccabees we have: *And after this Judah ordained captains over the people, even captains over thousands, and over hundreds, and over fifties, and over tens.*

CHAPTER 13

Magistrates of the Temple

RIGHT AFTER THE HEADS of the army came the men called in Greek *prostatai* and *stratēgoi tou hierou*, i.e. governors of the Temple and commanders of the Temple forces. They were in charge of both the Temple guard which Judah Maccabee had set up and the fortress of Antonia, which Judah's successors[278] had built alongside the Temple. On the Temple guard, it is written in First Maccabees: Judah built up *Mount Zion with high walls and strong towers round about, lest the gentiles should come and tread it down as they had done before. And they set there a garrison to keep it...*[279] Josephus writes about this fortress: *The Hasmonean princes... built a particularly strong fortress contiguous with the Temple... which they called Baris, and there they ordered the high priest's garments to be stored... Later on, King Herod had this fortress strengthened in order to protect the Temple, and named it Antonia to please his friend, the triumvir Mark Antony.*[280] We also know from St. Matthew 27 that the Jews assigned soldiers to serve in this garrison, for when they petitioned Pilate to order Christ's tomb to be guarded for three days he answered: *...Ye have a watch: go your way, make it as sure as ye can.*[281] As we will soon see, this garrison was in the hands of a single military tribune—or possibly more—and his troops.

Besides the soldiers who guarded the Temple, there were also attendants, i.e. lictors,[282] whose job was to arrest criminals at the behest of the high priest and the people. But when people were convicted of profaning the Temple, or showing contempt for the faith, or any other serious crime, then in addition to the lictors they sent soldiers to serve as guardsmen. They did the same with people who had so much power that the authorities were afraid of them. The lictors would call on these soldiers to lay hands on the criminal and bind him, so that they would be able to meet whatever resistance he might offer. The story of Christ is proof of all this: first Judas the betrayer goes to the chief priests and proposes that he will hand Christ over to them if they pay him; then he goes with several of them to the military tribune, from whom he gets a troop of men; then he gets the attendants. Finally, armed with all of these he sets off to arrest Christ.[283] I will quote here the passages from the Gospels, though I should first warn the reader that the Latin translator has done a poor job by rendering *stratēgos* as "magistrate"—first, because it does not convey the military command contained in the word *stratēgos*; and second, because he has confused this office with the "chiefs of the people"[284] who later served with the elders on the same court,[285] and whom he also calls "magistrates" (whereas the Greek calls them not *stratēgoi* but *archontes*). In Matthew 26 and Mark 14:[286] ...*Judas... went unto the chief priests, and said unto them, What will ye give me, and I will deliver him unto you?* But Luke adds to the chief priests the chiefs of the people, whom the translator calls magistrates: *And* Judas *went his way, and communed with the chief priests and magistrates, how he might betray him unto them.*[287] While John says in chapter 18: *Judas then, having received a band of men and officers from the chief priests and Pharisees, cometh thither...*[288] And then: *Then the band and the tribune and officers of the Jews took Jesus, and bound him.*[289] Luke, chapter 22: *Then Jesus said unto the chief priests, and magistrates of the Temple, and the elders, which were come to him...*[290] (Instead of "magistrates of the Temple" the Greek has *stratēgoi tou hierou*.)[291] We can see the same thing in the narrative of the apostles. In Acts 4: *And as the apostles spake unto the people, the priests, and the magistrate of the Temple* (i.e. the *stratēgos tou hierou*), *and the Sadducees came upon them.*[292] And in chapter 5: *Now when the magistrate of the Temple and the chief priests heard these things, they doubted of them whereunto this would grow... Then went the magistrate with the officers, and brought them without violence...*[293] It is clear from these passages that the "magistrates of the Temple" were military commanders whose job was to arrest criminals; and if my theory about these magistrates is correct, then it follows that an error has been committed by the scholars who used these passages to illustrate their claim that the latter were judges who held trials in the Temple.

CHAPTER 14

The Wars of the Jews

NOW THAT I HAVE explained all this, I should satisfy the curiosity of those readers who would like a brief introduction to the wars fought by the Hebrews. These wars were in fact very different from one another. First, the Hebrews fought with the inhabitants of Arabia while they were passing through it under the leadership of Moses, in the days before they crossed the Jordan; they fought, for example, with the Amalekites, Arad the king of the Canaanites, Sihon the king of the Amorites, Og the king of Bashan, the Moabites,[294] and the Midianites.[295] Then, after they crossed the Jordan, they fought under Joshua with the Amorites, the Canaanites, the Girgashites, the Hittites, the Hivites, the Jebusites, and the Perizzites, who were living in the land of Canaan, which God had promised to them; and after driving those peoples out of the land through no small effort, they distributed it by lot.[296] Then the land was divided up, and settlements were founded throughout, and for a long time the Israelites were plagued by the wars they fought with their neighbors—the king of Mesopotamia, the Canaanites, the Midianites, the Moabites, the Ammonites, and the Philistines.[297] The latter attacked them continuously until the time of David, when they held five cities on the Mediterranean coast toward Egypt—Gaza, Ashkelon, Ekron, Gath, and Azotus. Most of these wars took place in the time of the judges; after that King Saul was the first to conquer Nahash the king of the Ammonites, to harass the Philistines, and (at God's order) to crush Agag the king of the Amalekites, even though his kingdom was quite far away.[298] Then David fought with Ishbosheth the son of King Saul, whom his people had proclaimed king against David; with the Jebusites, whom David expelled from the city of Jerusalem; with the Moabites and the Ammonites; with his son Absalom and with Sheba, both of whom had rebelled against him; and four times with the Philistines.[299] When he had finally crushed them, and added Syria of Damascus[300] and the Idumeans[301] to his kingdom, he was able to leave to his son Solomon an empire entirely at peace. Under Solomon this peace was solidified; then, when the kingdom split in two after his death—one part was called Judah, the other Israel—there was frequent civil war between the two sides. They also suffered from foreign enemies, the most powerful kingdoms of those times—Egypt, Assyria, Babylonia, and Syria.[302] Because of their sins they were unable to resist these enemies: the Israelites (who were composed of the ten tribes) were deported by the Assyrians to Nineveh, and the Judeans were taken by the Babylonians to Babylon. But afterward Cyrus the king of Persia allowed the Jews to recover the ancient soil of their fathers: at first they were tribute-paying subjects of the Persians, and then of the Macedonian kings of Egypt and Syria, the successors of Alexander the Great.[303] In the end Epiphanes stripped them of both their freedom and their faith, so they finally took up arms and were able to harass the very kings of Syria, until they won complete sovereignty. Then, after they had conquered the Idumeans, the Samaritans, the Itureans, the Moabites, and the Gileadites,[304] they began to fight among themselves over the kingship, and succeeded in bringing the Roman army down upon their heads. They endured three wars in particular: the first with Cn. Pompey, who captured the city;[305] the second with C. Sosius, who exiled King Aristobulus from the city and installed Herod;[306] and the third with Titus Caesar, who destroyed the city and wiped out the nation itself.[307]

As we may conclude from these examples, the Jews could have successfully fought a series of wars so exceptional in their size, their variety, and the frequency with which they took place only if they had at their disposal both commanders and a knowledge of the military arts. The Jews did not participate in other people's wars, or hire themselves out to gentile armies, or recruit gentiles for their own: the law banned them from having any kind of interaction with other nations.[308] So when Tiberius Caesar saw that they refused to fight for him in accordance with their ancestral laws, he inflicted on them the most heinous punishments possible, as Josephus tells us in Book 18.[309]

CHAPTER 15

The Final Situation of the Jews

I WILL NOW DISCUSS what Philo has to say in his writings about the final situation of the Jews, and after explaining this point I will bring my work to an end. Philo's *Embassy to Gaius* tells us above all just how many Jews were scattered throughout the nations of the world in the reign of the emperor Gaius: *The nation of the Jews*, he says, *is so populous that it is not restricted like other nations to the limits of one region only—it lives all over, throughout practically the entire world. It has spread among all the provinces and islands of the continent, so much so that the Jews are only slightly fewer in number than the local inhabitants... Leaving aside the numberless masses that live in Judea itself... they have also settled in Babylon and in many other districts... and every year they send sacred money to the Temple—which they call first fruits—despite the difficulty of the journey.*[310] Philo then adds a remark about the colonies founded by the Jews in various places, as follows: *The holy city... is the metropolis*[311] *not only of the region of Judea but of many others, on account of the colonies that in the past were founded nearby on the borders of Egypt, Phoenicia, and Syria (both Syria in general and the part called Hollow), as well as farther away in Pamphylia, Cilicia, most of Asia*[312] *as far as Bithynia, and the innermost recesses of Pontus.*[313] *Likewise in Europe,*[314] *in Thessaly, Boeotia, Macedonia, Aetolia, Attica, Argos, Corinth, and certain parts of the Peloponnese. However, it is not only the provinces of the continent that are full of Jewish colonies, but even the most famous of the islands—Euboea, Cyprus, and Crete. And this is not to mention the cities across the Euphrates; for with the exception of a small part of Babylon and other districts, every city that has arable land has been settled by Jews.*[315] Then he writes as follows about the majesty of the Temple: *From its very beginnings the Temple has never permitted any images made by human hands, because it is the dwelling place of God. For works of painting and sculpture are the representations of gods that can be perceived with the senses; whereas our ancestors believed that it was wrong to paint or sculpt an image of a God that cannot be seen. Agrippa*[316] *visited there and paid his respects... and Augustus in his letters ordered that first fruits should be sent there from all over, and even established a daily sacrifice there... No Greek, no barbarian, no king or satrap or anyone else however hostile, no rebellion, war, enslavement, or devastation, nothing at all caused such complete havoc as when a man-made image was placed in the Temple in violation of ancient custom. For even when its neighbors were hostile, they always left the Temple alone to conduct its rites, since it was sacred to the creator and father of all things. They knew that those who had violated it often paid the price for their actions with unbearable suffering.*[317] Finally he says about the synagogues: *When Augustus... was informed that the sacred first fruits were being neglected, he sent letters ordering the governors of the provinces of Asia to grant the Jews the unique privilege of gathering in their synagogues. For (he said) they were not a Bacchanal...*[318] or a conspiracy of rebels *meeting in order to destroy the peace, but schools of justice and self-control where the study of virtue flourished; and that first fruits were to be brought every year* from which sacrifices would be offered, *and sent by this holy delegation to the Temple in Jerusalem. Then Augustus declared that no one should keep the Jews from gathering together and making their collections, or from sending them to Jerusalem in the fashion of their ancestors.*[319] Philo is also quite correct to say that the Jews observed their ancestral rites: *All nations readily keep the rites of their ancestors, but the Jews do so more than all the others; for since they believe that their laws were given to them by oracles... and they study them even as children, they carry about the impressions of these laws etched firmly in their minds. And as they are always thinking about them, they hold them up as the most upright of all laws; and even the foreigners who keep these principles they embrace as equal to their own citizens. But those who hate or attack the laws they regard as enemies; and they go to such lengths to avoid anything even slightly against their law, that no change of fortune or worldly success could persuade them to transgress it. The proof that there is nothing they revere as steadfastly as the Temple is that they declare certain death for anyone who ventures beyond its inner barrier (for they allow past the outer one the Jews who visit from all the parts of the world).*[320] Hence Rutilius[321] wrote of the Jews who were scattered all over after the victory of Titus:

> *Would that Judea never had been crushed*
> *By Pompey's wars and Titus' command,*
> *Disease once rooted out spreads much more widely,*
> *And victors are oppressed by those they trounce.*

This is what I have learned about the republic of the Hebrews, and I have explained it as clearly and distinctly as I can. Now that these issues have received careful reflection and analysis, anyone who would again attempt to examine the holy books will be able, without a doubt, to understand much more clearly many of the things that had hitherto been wrapped in a dense fog; and with a clear draught of this learning he will slake the thirst for heavenly knowledge that has been growing deep within him. Moreover, I do not believe I should be held at fault if I have used the Greek translation in a few places for the sake of strengthening my claims, by appealing (where appropriate) to the authority of the sacred texts; or if I have produced some evidence from the Third Book of Esdras.[322] For I have done so only in order to dispel the terrible obscurity of the issues with which I am dealing, and which obviously cannot be clarified in any other way. I have also done this in order to promote the authority of the holy fathers who made use of the Septuagint translation—I am, to be sure, dealing not with questions of dogma, but only with the times of the ancients.[323] I also felt that I could shed some light on early institutions and customs by turning to the most ancient of sources, and with this in mind I have always put my trust in Philo and Josephus, the most learned of men, since I knew that the holy fathers themselves had gotten from them a great deal of important corroboration for the events of ancient times. But I freely submit these observations, and any similar ones I may have made, to the painstaking censure and judgment of the Church. After all, I have no doubts at all that people who have been spurred by these questions to bring their own particular talents to investigate others like them will produce even better things; just as a person who was admitted to a very sumptuous banquet but had to leave before eating his fill longs for many more such occasions. If, then, they will carry before them the kind of torch that will banish the darkness from the hidden recesses of these questions, they will be able to track down with much greater success the secret mysteries contained within them. I am in fact aware of the mystery, i.e. that heavenly and eternal life, which according to St. Augustine is prefigured in this republic—he claims that the Hebrew people was assembled into the only state that represented the sacrament of eternal life.[324] For, he says, every prophecy and all the laws that governed their lives, in a word the rites, the priesthoods, the ceremonies and festivals, are signifiers and foreshadowings, which—through the eternal life of those who have faith in Christ—we believe were fulfilled, we see are fulfilled, and we trust will be fulfilled. And would that God himself, in his incredible mercy, might see to it that I will merit after my death to see in heaven that state which in life I have described on earth; so that when I come to the house of the Lord, joyful because of the things we were told were going to be, I will finally and truly be able to say with the prophet: *As we have heard, so have we seen in the city of the Lord of hosts, in the city of our God. Blessed are they who dwell in thy house; they will be still praising thee.*[325]

NOTES

DEDICATION

1. Sigonio seems to have in mind here the interpretation of Old Testament passages within the New Testament.

2. In 1578 Gregory XIII commissioned Sigonio to write a history of the Church. See the discussion in the introduction, pp. xii–xiii.

3. Gabriele Paleotti (1522–1597) was archbishop of Bologna.

4. Here Sigonio seems to be representing his work as a loyal and useful tool in the Catholic reaction to the Reformation.

BOOK I

1. I.e. the Vulgate Bible.

2. A paraphrase of Psalms 118:2.

3. That is, the Old Testament can be interpreted only by reference to the New.

4. Compare the accusation made by St. Stephen against the Temple in Acts chapter 7: *Our fathers who came after... found favor before God, and desired to find a tabernacle for the God of Jacob. But Solomon built him a house. However, the most High dwells not in temples made with hands...*

5. A fifth-century Gallic chronicler who wrote a history of the world from creation until his own time. In 1582, Sigonio published a commentary on his *Historia Sacra*.

6. Since in Latin the term *Judaeus* can mean either "Judean" or "Jew," I have tried to translate it appropriately according to context. Although Sigonio does distinguish between these two terms, it is not always clear which one he has in mind, and in some cases he seems to be blurring the distinction.

7. See below, p. 10.

8. Genesis 14:13.

9. Sigonio may be referring to the fact that Abraham fathered not only Isaac but Ishmael, considered the father of the Arabs, and was the father of still other nations through the children of his concubines (cf. Genesis 25:2–6).

10. Genesis 12:1–3.

11. Genesis 15:5.

12. Perhaps Sigonio has in mind the special inheritance given to Caleb in Joshua 14–15.

13. Joshua 21:41–42.

14. Numbers 1:49.

15. Judges 17:7–9.

16. Sigonio's Latin is much closer to the Hebrew than the Vulgate is here.

17. Numbers 36:8.

18. Judges 19:1.

19. 2 Chronicles 22:11.

20. Jeremiah 7:15.

21. 2 Chronicles 11:13–14.

22. In 711 BCE.

23. 2 Kings 17:33–36, 40–41.

24. In 586 BCE.

25. Hosea 1:6–7.

26. Died 530 BCE.

27. 521–486 BCE.

28. Perhaps Sigonio has in mind Josephus *Jewish Antiquities* 11.3.8: "[Darius] also enjoined the Idumeans and Samaritans, and the inhabitants of Coelesyria, to restore those villages which they had taken from the Jews."

29. I.e. over the Jews.

30. In 167 BCE.

31. For the interpretation of the law and Sigonio's sources, see the discussion in the introduction, pp. xviii–xxii.

32. A combination of Deuteronomy 6:5 and Leviticus 19:18.

33. Exodus 17:35–36.

34. I.e. the Ten Commandments were expanded into the body of laws contained in the Torah, which can then be grouped into four categories.

35. I.e. the many individual laws contained in the text.

36. I.e. where in the text.

37. Exodus 15:25–26.

38. Leviticus 25:18.

39. Leviticus 26:3.

40. Leviticus 26:46.

41. Numbers 36:13.

42. Deuteronomy 4:14.

43. Deuteronomy 4:5.

44. Deuteronomy 4:44–45.

45. Deuteronomy 6:1.

46. Joshua 24:25.

47. 1 Kings 2:3.

48. 2 Kings 17:13.

49. 2 Chronicles 19:8, 10.

50. 2 Chronicles 34:31.

51. Psalms 118:4–5, 14, 16, 24, 27.

52. Psalms 17:22.

53. Psalms 104:45.

54. Psalms 147:19.

55. Nehemiah 10:29.

56. Ezekiel 44:24.

57. Gk. *dikaiōmata*.

58. The Latin term—which, following the King James, I have translated as "statute"—is *justificatio*, which as in English implies the approval of an action.

59. Psalms 7:8.

60. Isaiah 5:22.

61. Leviticus 24:22.

62. Deuteronomy 25:1.

63. Proverbs 17:15.

64. Matthew 12:37.

65. Genesis 15:14.

66. 2 Chronicles 20:11–12.

67. John 12:47.

68. John 7:51.

69. Cf. Exodus 22:2–3.

70. Cf. Deuteronomy 19:4–5.

71. Nehemiah 9:34.

72. 2 Kings 17:15.

73. Exodus 19:5–6.

74. Deuteronomy 11:22–23.

75. Luke 1:6.

76. Deuteronomy 17:18–19.

77. Deuteronomy 31:10–12.

78. 2 Chronicles 17:7, 9.

79. 2 Kings 22:11.

80. 2 Kings 23:3.

81. Ezra 7:10.

82. Ruled 285–247 BCE.

83. 1 Maccabees 1:43, 45–53, 57–60.

84. Since the New Testament is consistently critical of "scribes," Sigonio must draw some distinction between Ezra and his successors in the time of Jesus.

85. Cf. Matthew 5:17.

86. Matthew 5:20.

87. I.e. that the law of the New Testament goes beyond that of the Old.

88. Perhaps Sigonio is referring here to the institution of kingship.

89. "The best," Cicero's preferred term for aristocrats of old family.

90. Deuteronomy 12:8–9.

91. Sigonio, like his contemporaries, uses *pontifex*—the title of the most important Roman priest—to refer to the Jewish high priest, and the more generic *sacerdos* for the other priests.

92. Joshua 1:7.

93. Joshua 1:16–17.

94. Chapter 23.

95. Judges 2:7.

96. I.e. the land of Israel.

97. Josephus *Jewish Antiquities* 4.8.17.

98. 1 Samuel 8:5.

99. 1 Samuel 8:7.

100. 1 Samuel 8:9.

101. As in Roman political thought, it is not the amount of power a king enjoys but its arbitrariness that distinguishes monarchy from aristocracy.

102. Aristotle *Politics* 1287a16. Sigonio has added here "a king" in order to reinforce the anti-monarchic meaning of the passage. See the discussion in the introduction, pp. xxiv–xxv.

103. 1 Samuel 8:11, 13–14, 16–18.

104. Psalms 2:6–9.

105. Aristotle *Politics* 1287a16.

106. The point is presumably that both "king" and "prince" are used in the Bible to describe leaders ("prince" is the usual translation of *nasi*, a generic term for a leader of the people).

107. Though Josephus describes Herod's family as Idumean and therefore among the forced converts of the Hasmonean John Hyrcanus, there was a later belief, preserved in Eusebius' *History of the Church* (1.7.11), that Herod's father Antipater had been born a temple slave in Ashkelon.

108. Judges 17:6.

109. In classical political thought, "the people" are the non-aristocratic segment of the citizen body.

110. Joshua 23:2.

111. Genesis 17:12, 14.

112. Exodus 12:48–49.

113. The Bible itself makes no distinction between the term *ger* ("stranger") as it is used in this passage and any other sort of foreigner living in the land of Israel. It is only in Second Temple and rabbinic Judaism that the *ger* mentioned alongside the native Israelite came to be regarded as a convert with a different legal status from other gentiles.

114. Leviticus 17:8–9.

115. Leviticus 24:22.

116. Genesis 34.

117. Judith 14:6.

118. Matthew 23:15.

119. 2 Chronicles 30:25.

120. Ezekiel 14:7.

121. Acts 2:10.

122. The northwestern coastal region that contained the capital, Antioch.

123. In the southeast.

124. The Roman province of Arabia was divided into two districts.

125. Pliny *Natural History* 5.71.

126. The Kinneret, or Sea of Galilee.

127. Cf. John 4:5.

128. The Mediterranean.

129. Deuteronomy 12:4-6, 17-18.

130. Deuteronomy 17:8.

131. Sigonio is giving both the biblical and post-biblical names.

132. Joshua 18:1.

133. Joshua 22:12.

134. Judges 21:2.

135. Judges 21:19.

136. Jeremiah 7:12.

137. Jeremiah 7:14.

138. Cf. Joshua 15:63.

139. 2 Chronicles 6:5-6.

140. 2 Kings 21:7.

141. Josephus *Jewish Antiquities* 4.8.5-7.

142. Psalms 77:68-69. The Hebrew of this verse could read, depending on the vocalization, either *ramim*, "high up," or *remim*, which appears elsewhere as an alternate spelling of *re'emim*, a kind of horned animal. Some Vulgate texts therefore have here "unicorn."

143. Genesis 48:21-22: *And Israel said unto Joseph... Moreover I have given you one portion more than your brothers, which I took out of the hand of the Amorite with my sword and my bow.*

144. Joshua 24:32: *And the bones of Joseph, which the children of Israel brought up out of Egypt, they buried in Shechem, in a parcel of ground which Jacob bought from the sons of Hamor the father of Shechem for a hundred pieces of silver.*

145. I.e. Mount Gerizim, near Shechem.

146. John 4:20.

147. Joshua 20:7.

148. Psalms 121:3–5.

149. That is, the tribes.

150. Joshua 15:63: *As for the Jebusites, the inhabitants of Jerusalem, the children of Judah could not drive them out; the Jebusites dwell with the children of Judah at Jerusalem to this day.*

151. Deuteronomy 33:12.

152. Sigonio draws this conclusion from Judges 19:11–14: *And when they were by Jebus, the day was nearly over; and the servant said to his master: Please come and let us turn in into this city of the Jebusites, and lodge in it. And his master said to him: We will not turn aside here into the city of a stranger, who is not of the children of Israel... let us draw near to one of these places to lodge all night, in Gibeah or in Ramah... and the sun set on them when they were by Gibeah, which belongs to Benjamin.* The city of Jebus, or Jerusalem, was therefore in the neighborhood of the cities of Benjamin.

153. The texts that come closest to this topic are Josephus *Jewish War* 5.5.1 and *Jewish Antiquities* 8.6.1, though neither is specific on the issue of Solomon's fortifications.

154. For Jehoiakim, cf. 2 Kings 24:1: *In his days Nebuchadnezzar king of Babylon came up, and Jehoiakim became his servant three years: then he turned and rebelled against him.* For Jehoiachin, 24:10: *At that time the servants of Nebuchadnezzar king of Babylon came up to Jerusalem, and the city was besieged.* For Zedekiah, 24:20–25:2: *...Zedekiah rebelled against the king of Babylon... and Nebuchadnezzar king of Babylon came with all his army against Jerusalem and besieged it... so the city was besieged until the eleventh year of King Zedekiah.*

155. Perhaps Sigonio is referring to the rebuilding of the city's walls and gates mentioned in chapter 3 of Nehemiah.

156. In 63 BCE.

157. The nation that controlled the territory east of the Euphrates and was often in conflict with the Roman Empire, whose influence extended to its boundaries.

158. I.e. provincial governor.

159. Herod became king in 41 BCE.

160. After the Bar Kochba rebellion in 131–135 CE. Sigonio is referring to the genesis of Christianity rather than to its adoption by the emperors, which took place only in the fourth century.

BOOK II

1. Heb. *bamot.*

2. Sigonio gives us two names because the Vulgate, in the passage which follows, also calls the "mercy seat" (*propitiatorium*) an "oracle," even where the Hebrew uses only the term *kaporet.*

3. To cover the entrance of the tabernacle.

4. Exodus 25:8–9.

5. Exodus 25:8–10, 12–21.

6. This is the Vulgate version; the Hebrew has: *You shall overlay it with pure gold, and make a molding of gold around it. And you shall make around it a frame a handbreadth wide, and a molding of gold around the frame.*

7. Exodus 25:23–31, 37–38.

8. Exodus 26:31, 33–35.

9. Exodus 26:36; 27:1, 3–4, 9–10.

10. Exodus 27:20–21; 30:1–3, 6–7, 18, 23–27, 34–35.

11. Leviticus 17:3–4, 8–9.

12. Exodus 37:25–26; 38:1–7.

13. Exodus 40:16–33.

14. Deuteronomy 10:5.

15. Leviticus 6:12.

16. The Latin *testimonium* is the Vulgate's regular translation of the Hebrew *edut*, the "testimony" or "witness" placed in the tabernacle. Since *testamentum* does not appear in the Pentateuch at all, Sigonio seems to be using it as a synonym. *Pactum*, on the other hand, is used interchangeably with *foedus* to mean "covenant."

17. Exodus 19:5.

18. Leviticus 26:3, 11–12.

19. Hebrews 9:2–5.

20. That is, he entered it just as the high priest entered the tabernacle in Jerusalem.

21. Jerome, Letter 64, section 9.

22. The church fathers followed the Septuagint's translation of *shittim*, the kind of wood used to build the tabernacle, as *aseptos*, "undecaying."

23. Joshua 18:1.

24. Joshua 19:51.

25. Exodus 34:23-24.

26. Judges 18:31. This refers to the cult of the city of Dan, in the north.

27. Judges 20:18.

28. Judges 20:26.

29. Judges 21:19.

30. 1 Samuel 4:3-4.

31. 1 Samuel 4:11.

32. The Philistines had deliberately chosen nursing cows, supposing that if they were willing to leave their young behind, it was only because God was encouraging them to return the ark.

33. The Hebrew source (1 Samuel 7:1) has here "brought it to the house of Abinadab on the hill," but the Vulgate instead of "hill" has *Gabaa*, on the misunderstanding that the Hebrew *giv'a* is in fact the town of Giveah in Benjamin; and Sigonio makes this explicit.

34. 1 Samuel 21:1-6: *Then David came to Nob to Achimelech the priest... and David said to Achimelech the priest... Give me five loaves of bread, or whatever is here. And the priest answered David, I have no common bread at hand, but there is holy bread... So the priest gave him the holy bread; for there was no bread there but the bread of the Presence, which is removed from before the Lord, to be replaced by hot bread on the day it is taken away.*

35. 2 Chronicles 1:3.

36. 1 Chronicles 16:39-40.

37. 1 Chronicles 21:29.

38. 2 Chronicles 1:3-4.

39. 1 Kings 8:6-9; 1 Chronicles 5:7-10.

40. 2 Maccabees 1:19.

41. 2 Maccabees 2:4-8.

42. 2 Maccabees 1:20-22, 31-32.

43. Perhaps Sigonio is thinking of 1 Maccabees 4:49: *They also made new holy vessels, and into the Temple they brought the candlestick, and the altar of burnt offerings, and of incense, and the table.*

44. Deuteronomy 12:2-4. This source is not relevant, because it refers to actual idolatry rather than to the *bamot*—"high places"—mentioned in Kings and Chronicles. Though the Torah itself does not mention such places, Sigonio has been influenced by the constant criticism leveled at them by Kings, which describes them in language

the Torah reserves for idolatry, and judges each ruler according to whether or not he fought the "high places."

45. Judges 6:19.

46. Though Augustine never wrote a commentary on Judges, this passage does resemble one in the commentary of the eighth-century German abbot Hrabanus.

47. 1 Samuel 9:12.

48. 2 Chronicles 1:3.

49. 1 Kings 3:2–4.

50. Sigonio again conflates the "high places" with the worship of foreign gods and idols.

51. 2 Kings 17:9–11.

52. 1 Kings 14:23, which does not explicitly blame Rehoboam.

53. 1 Kings 22:43.

54. 2 Kings 16:4.

55. 2 Kings 21:3.

56. 2 Chronicles 34:3.

57. 2 Kings 23:5, 8–9, 13, 15, 19.

58. Augustine, Letter 185.5.19.

59. Deuteronomy 12:4–6.

60. Deuteronomy 12:13–14.

61. 1 Chronicles 28:2–4.

62. 1 Chronicles 28:6.

63. 2 Samuel 7:5–6.

64. 2 Samuel 7:12–13.

65. David had brought on the plague by calling for a census of the people, which angered God: 1 Chronicles 21.

66. In Chronicles, which sees David as by far the most important of the Judean kings, it is he rather than Solomon who lays the groundwork for the Temple.

67. 1 Chronicles 22:7–11.

68. This statement appears in 1 Chronicles 22:17–18 but not in 1 Kings.

69. I.e. Kings and Chronicles.

70. 1 Kings 6:19; 7:6, 48–51.

71. 1 Chronicles 3:10, 14; 4:1–2, 6–8, 19–20, 22.

72. 1 Kings 8:3–4, 6–7, 9.

73. Cf. 1 Kings 8; 2 Chronicles 6.

74. 1 Kings 8:63–64; 9:2–7.

75. 1 Kings 9:25.

76. Cf. 1 Kings 12:26–33.

77. I.e. out of fear that the Temple would summon more loyalty than the monarchy.

78. The spelling of the name in the Septuagint.

79. Perhaps Sigonio has in mind 2 Chronicles 24:7: *For the sons of Athaliah, that wicked woman, had broken into the house of God; and had also used all the dedicated things of the house of the Lord for the Baals.*

80. We are told in 2 Chronicles 24 that Joash revived the practice of collecting the half-shekel that Israelites were required to donate to the Temple, which had stopped because the sons of Athaliah had been raiding the treasury. He then used this money to make repairs.

81. 2 Kings 12:4–16; 2 Chronicles 24:4–14.

82. According to 2 Kings 16, Ahaz used the Temple treasury to pay Tiglat-pileser, the king of Assyria, for his help in withstanding an attack by Israel, and he had an altar built on the model of one he saw in Damascus, which he used instead of the bronze altar as the main place of sacrifice.

83. 2 Chronicles 29:6–7.

84. 2 Chronicles 29:18–19.

85. Josiah's father Manasseh was considered one of the worst offenders—he built foreign altars and reintroduced the "high places" (2 Kings 33).

86. 2 Kings 22:5.

87. One of the priestly garments.

88. Cf. Hosea 3:4. The teraphim were religious images that (depending on where in the Bible they are mentioned) may or may not have been considered idolatrous.

89. 528–521 BCE.

90. 1 Maccabees 1:21–22, 29, 54.

91. Sigonio's account comes from Josephus rather than 1 Maccabees, and he has confused the relationship between Onias and the sons of Tobias (a powerful family in the region); according to Josephus (*Jewish Antiquities* 12.5.1) it was Onias whom they supported against the latter's brother Jason. Moreover, the murder of Onias happened some time later, after Antiochus' death.

92. The "abomination of desolation" referred to by 1 Maccabees 1:54, which was apparently the center of the new cult.

93. 1 Maccabees 4:36–38, 41–54, 56, 59–61.

94. Josephus *Jewish Antiquities* 15.11.1.

95. Josephus *Jewish Antiquities* 15.11.2–7.

96. One of "three men" (with Octavian and Lepidus) who formed a government at Rome.

97. I.e. it was on an open, curved slope like the natural depressions that originally served as theaters.

98. The passage is a selection and paraphrase of Josephus *Jewish Antiquities* 15.11.4–6.

99. John 2:19.

100. John 2:20.

101. I.e. who had seen Herod's project for themselves.

102. 31 BCE–14 CE.

103. 14–37 CE.

104. Strictly speaking, Josephus wrote the *Jewish Antiquities* in the 70s CE, about ninety years after the Temple was rebuilt.

105. His opponents were trying to make Jesus' claim seem all the more ridiculous.

106. 37–41 CE.

107. Sigonio seems to be referring to Josephus' statement (*Jewish Antiquities* 18.8.1) that the Jews of Alexandria were accused before Caligula of not honoring him in their rites the way the other Alexandrians did.

108. John 19:15.

109. Josephus mentions only the conflict over worshiping Caligula's image. Either Sigonio is being unclear here, or he is misrepresenting Josephus in order to corroborate the New Testament.

110. Josephus *Jewish War* 6.4.5–7.

111. 117–134 CE.

112. Cf. Matthew 24:2.

113. Sigonio seems to be distinguishing between the destruction of the earthly Temple, which was deserved and affected only the Jews, and Hadrian's attack, which was aimed at the faith and was therefore a crime against Christianity.

114. Cf. *History of the Church* 4.6.4. Eusebius, however, mentions only the bare facts; he has nothing to say about Hadrian's motives.

115. Bishop of Nola, in Italy (354–431 CE). A collection of his letters survives to this day.

116. The chronicler Sulpicius Severus.

117. Paulinus of Nola, Letter 31.3.

118. Sulpicius Severus *Sacred History* 2.31.

119. Daniel 9:27.

120. This is presumably a reference to *Jewish Antiquities* 11.8.7, where Josephus says that the Samaritan temple became a refuge for Jews who had to flee charges that they had violated the law.

121. Cf. Psalms 78:55–69: *He... settled the tribes of Israel in their tents. Yet they tested and rebelled against the most High God, and did not observe his testimonies, but turned away and acted treacherously... For they provoked him to anger with their high places; they moved him to jealousy with their graven images. When God heard, he was full of wrath, and he utterly rejected Israel. He forsook his dwelling at Shiloh, the tent where he dwelt among men... He rejected the tent of Joseph, he did not choose the tribe of Ephraim; but he chose the tribe of Judah, Mount Zion, which he loves. He built his sanctuary like the high heavens, like the earth, which he has founded for ever.*

122. King of Egypt (180–145 BCE).

123. Cf. Josephus *Jewish Antiquities* 13.3.4.

124. Josephus (*Jewish Antiquities* 12.5.5) says it was Zeus Hellenios, i.e. of the Greeks.

125. Josephus *Jewish Antiquities* 13.9.1.

126. This is a nice illustration of the fact that Sigonio lets his narrative follow its sources: the scope of the discussion suddenly shifts from the history of the Samaritan nation (as told by Josephus) to "the Samaritan woman" (as told by the gospel of John).

127. He is called "the Jew" here in accordance with the following verse: *ye* (i.e. the Jews) *say that in Jerusalem...*

128. John 4:20–21.

129. Cf. Josephus *Jewish Antiquities* 13.3.1. Josephus says that the murdered high priest was Onias' uncle, and he does not suggest that anyone else was forced to leave. Sigonio presumably wants to explain where the new temple's devotees had come from.

130. Josephus *Jewish War* 7.10.4.

131. I.e. Hannukah.

132. 2 Maccabees 1:1–18.

133. Asia Minor.

134. Greece and the eastern Mediterranean.

135. Sigonio quotes from Gilbert Génébrard, *Chronographiae libri quatuor* (Paris: Martinum Iuvenem, 1580), p. 94.

136. Acts 6:9.

137. John 18:20.

138. Acts 15:21.

139. Acts 9:1–2.

140. Luke 7:4–5.

141. John 9:22.

142. John 12:42.

143. See, for example, Luke 20:46: *Beware of the scribes, who desire to walk in long robes, and love greetings in the markets, and the highest seats in the synagogues, and the chief rooms at feasts.*

144. A famous medieval allegory.

BOOK III

1. This "civil calendar," which begins with the month of Nisan, is the one used by the Bible. The "natural calendar," beginning with Tishri, is used in Jewish law and practice.

2. This process is now accomplished by inserting an additional thirty-day month into seven of every nineteen years of the calendar cycle.

3. 1 Kings 4:7.

4. Daniel 4:29.

5. Esther 3:7.

6. In other words, Tishri.

7. Exodus 23:16. This is Tabernacles, which falls in the middle of Tishri.

8. Exodus 34:22.

9. I.e. the sabbatical year, during which the land rested, and the fiftieth or jubilee year, when land was restored to its original owners, and slaves were freed.

10. In this case the Targum Jonathan, the traditional translation of the Prophets.

11. I.e. Ethanim, the biblical name of Tishri.

12. 1 Kings 8:2 has simply "the seventh month"; the translator believed that since Tishri was the month in which the world was created, it was originally the first month, but Nisan supplanted it when the Israelites, who were about to leave Egypt, were told (Exodus 12:2): *This month shall be for you the beginning of months; it shall be the first month of the year for you.*

13. Josephus *Jewish Antiquities* 1.3.3. Josephus goes on to say: "...for so did they order their year in Egypt. But Moses appointed that Nisan, which is the same with Xanthicus, should be the first month for their festivals, because he brought them out of Egypt in that month."

14. Exodus 12:2.

15. Exodus 13:4.

16. Exodus 34:18. Though Sigonio translates these phrases differently because the Vulgate does, in the Hebrew both passages use the same term, *aviv*, to describe the first month. But since *aviv* can mean either "spring" or "ear of grain," the Vulgate wants to recognize both options.

17. If, that is, the new month were always to begin with a new moon, the year would always fall short relative to the sun.

18. That is, although the dates on which these festivals fell were lunar, their celebration was to coincide with the seasons of the solar calendar.

19. Of the seven-year cycle.

20. If the intercalation were done every two years, the 11.25-day gap would come to 22.5 days. There is no evidence that such a short month was ever added, in biblical times or later. Sigonio's assumption about biblical practices seems to have been based on theory rather than on any knowledge of, or interest in, actual historical realities.

21. The biblical name.

22. Heb. *maleh* and *haser*.

23. Leviticus 23:5.

24. Numbers 9:11.

25. 1 Chronicles 27:2, 4–5, 7–9.

26. Since the Vulgate referred to the Old Testament books of Ezra and Nehemiah as 1 and 2 Esdras, it called this apocryphal book 3 Esdras. Sigonio, however, also mentions 2 Esdras, by which he means not Nehemiah (which he calls by that name) but the apocryphal 4 Esdras.

27. 3 Esdras 5:6.

28. Baruch 1:8.

29. Zechariah 7:1.

30. Zechariah 1:7.

31. 1 Maccabees 16:14.

32. Esther 3:7 and passim.

33. 1 Maccabees 16:14.

34. 1 Kings 6:37–38.

35. 1 Kings 8:2.

36. 2 Chronicles 23:8.

37. This verse does use "Sabbath" to mean "week," but in the section before the part quoted here.

38. Luke 18:12.

39. Mark 16:2.

40. Mark 16:9.

41. Matthew 28:1.

42. Acts 20:7.

43. John 1:10.

44. Jerome *Against Vigilius* 13.

45. 1 Corinthians 16:2.

46. 3 Esdras 1:1.

47. The time between sunrise and sunset was divided into twelve equal hours, so that the first hour began with sunrise.

48. John 11:9.

49. Cf. Matthew 20:1–6: *For the kingdom of heaven is like a householder, who went out early in the morning to hire laborers for his vineyard... And he went out about the third hour, and saw others standing idle in the marketplace, and said to them, You too may go into the vineyard... Again he went out about the sixth and ninth hours, and did likewise. And about the eleventh hour he went out, and found others standing idle, and said to them, Why do you stand here all day idle?*

50. I.e. they were holidays on which work was not forbidden.

51. The Vulgate does use the term "Kalends" here.

52. This is actually the amount for a bull, but Sigonio has skipped over the intervening text.

53. Numbers 28:11–14.

54. Josephus *Jewish Antiquities* 3.10.1.

55. 2 Chronicles 2:4.

56. 2 Chronicles 8:12–13.

57. Ezra 3:5.

58. Isaiah 1:14.

59. Exodus 29:38–42; Numbers 28:3–8. The translation follows the passage in Numbers.

60. Leviticus 23:37. This verse refers not to the daily offering, but to the various offerings prescribed for different festival days.

61. Josephus *Jewish Antiquities* 10.1.1.

62. 2 Chronicles 2:4. The same verse is quoted above in reference to the new moon, but with different deletions.

63. In the following chapters Sigonio limits himself to festivals commanded and/or described in the Bible, including the Apocrypha; he has no interest in the Jewish festivals as such—he does not call the first of Tishri the New Year, for example. He is also careful to distinguish between the three pilgrimage festivals and other ceremonies, such as the Festival of Unleavened Bread, which occurred at the same time but are mentioned separately in the text. Though in general the post-pentateuchal festivals mentioned by Sigonio are explicitly established in the texts which mention them, there are two exceptions at the very end of Book 3: Nicanor Day, which is mentioned only in Josephus; and the Fast of Gedaliah, which alludes to an event in the Bible but does not itself appear there.

64. Leviticus 19:3. This verse has traditionally been interpreted as a reference to the seventh day rather than the festivals.

65. Leviticus 23:32.

66. Leviticus 23:39.

67. Hannukah.

68. Exodus 20:8–11.

69. Exodus 35:3.

70. Leviticus 23:3.

71. Numbers 28:9–10.

72. Exodus 24:5, 8.

73. Philo *On the Special Laws* 35.169–175.

74. Exodus 12:2–3, 5–9, 11–14.

75. Exodus 12:15–17, 19.

76. Exodus 12:25–27.

77. Leviticus 23:5–8.

78. Deuteronomy 16:8.

79. Because the Roman calendar is entirely solar, its months never agree completely with those of the Jewish calendar.

80. Exodus 13:4.

81. Deuteronomy 16:1.

82. Philo *Life of Moses* 2.41.222–224.

83. Though this presumably refers to the Roman calendar, the latter did originally begin in March and end in December (the tenth month). Since like the Hebrew calendar it was agricultural, it took no notice of the wintertime.

84. Philo *On the Ten Commandments* 30.159–160.

85. Heb. *atzeret.* Cf. Deuteronomy 16:8, though there (and in other passages) *atzeret* is usually understood to mean an "assembly" or "convocation" of the people. Cf. also chapter 13 below.

86. Luke 22:1.

87. Luke 22:7.

88. Mark 14:12.

89. 1 Corinthians 5:7.

90. An early medieval Jewish chronology of biblical and Second Temple times. Sigonio did not quote directly from this work, but from Génébrard's *Chronographiae*. See the discussion in the introduction, pp. xxxii–xxxiv.

91. The rabbinic rule is that Passover may not begin on Monday, Wednesday, or Friday (though this is not discussed in the *Seder Olam*).

92. Sigonio quotes from Génébrard, *Chronographiae*, pp. 28, 114.

93. I.e. the paschal sacrifice would take place on Friday afternoon.

94. Which seems to mean that he was celebrating the festival a day before everyone else.

95. The Roman official in charge of administering justice.

96. According to the Gospels, the crucifixion took place on Friday and the Last Supper—the "Passover"—the night before (cf. John 13:1: *Now before the Feast of the Passover, when Jesus knew that his hour was come that he should depart out of this world...*); but the passage in John (18:28) which mentions the *paraskeue* implies that when Jesus was brought before Pilate early on Friday morning, the priests had not yet celebrated the paschal sacrifice. The problem is further complicated by the fact that John does not explicitly call this meal the "Passover" (cf. 13:1–2).

97. Acts 12:3–4. Sigonio seems to be endorsing another solution to this problem: since all the days of the holiday were called "Passover," it is possible that the Last Supper was in fact the Seder and took place when it was supposed to, while the "Passover" to which John refers in 18:28 was a different sacrifice associated with the holiday.

98. Deuteronomy 16:5-6.

99. Joshua 5:10-11.

100. 2 Chronicles 30:2-3.

101. 2 Chronicles 30:21-23, 26.

102. 2 Kings 23:22-23.

103. 2 Chronicles 35:1.

104. 3 Esdras 1:1.

105. Ezra 6:19, 22.

106. Heb. *bikurim.*

107. From the Greek for fifty, because it took place fifty days after Passover.

108. Heb. *shavuot.*

109. Leviticus 23:10-13.

110. Leviticus 23:15-19.

111. There is no reference in Numbers to the Festival of Weeks.

112. Deuteronomy 16:9-10.

113. Leviticus 2:14-16.

114. Josephus says it is wheat flour.

115. Josephus *Jewish Antiquities* 3.10.5-6.

116. This is somewhat confusing, because the term "first fruits" (*bikurim*) is usually used with reference to Shavuot rather than Passover; cf. Leviticus 23:17 and Numbers 28:26, where Shavuot is called "the day of *bikurim.*" The second day of Passover, on the other hand, does not have a name of its own. Sigonio may have been misled by the Vulgate, where the same term (*primitiae*) is used for both "first fruits" and the first cutting of the grain on Passover.

117. 2 Maccabees 12:31-32.

118. Acts 2:1.

119. Leviticus 23:24-25.

120. In Genesis 22, Abraham is given the ram as a substitute for Isaac, whom he had been ordered to sacrifice. This story was linked to the New Year because the *shofar* used to sound the blasts was made of a ram's horn.

121. Psalms 80:3-4.

122. Philo *On the Ten Commandments* 30.159.

123. Leviticus 23:27-29.

124. Leviticus 16:29-34.

125. Jeremiah 36:6. According to verse 9, this was not the Day of Atonement but a public fast declared by the king "in the ninth month."

126. Josephus *Jewish War* 5.5.7.

127. Heb. *hag ha'asif*. As in his description of Passover, Sigonio has somewhat confused the situation. Whereas the term "gathering" (*asif*) in the passages quoted here refers to the gathering of produce at the time of the holiday, the eighth-day "gathering" (*atzeret*) was an assembly of the people. Sigonio's belief that the eighth day celebrated the harvest seems to have been influenced by three of the passages he quotes here: Leviticus 23:36, which refers to the *coetus et collecta*, "an assembly and a gathering"; Deuteronomy 16:13, which uses the verb *colligare* (collect or gather) to refer to the harvest of the season; and Nehemiah 8:18, where the eighth day assembly is called *collecta*. Sigonio has therefore combined these two ideas (though he does, confusingly, omit the part of the Leviticus passage that says the *collecta* was on the eighth day). He may also have been misled by the fact that the Vulgate routinely translates the term *mikra kodesh*, which describes both the first and eighth days of Passover and Tabernacles, as "called holy" (*mikra* is from the same root as *kara*, "call") rather than as "a holy convocation," as in the King James. Sigonio may have been aware he was offering a controversial interpretation, because in the Leviticus and Nehemiah passages the word *collecta* is printed in capital, boldface letters.

128. I.e. the first fruits.

129. Leviticus 23:34–36, 39–43.

130. This is from the section of the passage that deals with the sacrifice of the New Year; it is not clear whether Sigonio thought it was somehow part of the sacrifices for Tabernacles.

131. Numbers 29:1–2, 12–13, 17, 20, 23, 26, 29, 32, 35–36, 39.

132. Deuteronomy 16:13–14.

133. Exodus 23:16.

134. Exodus 34:22.

135. Nehemiah 8:14–18.

136. This is a literal translation of Josephus, who is himself unclear.

137. Though in Latin this usually means "peach," here Sigonio is translating literally Josephus' term *persea*.

138. Josephus has "the same number plus one more" (i.e. fourteen lambs).

139. Josephus *Jewish Antiquities* 3.10.4.

140. Building of booths.

141. Cf. John 7:2–10: *Now the Jew's Feast of Tabernacles was at hand... Then Jesus said to them, My time is not yet come, but your time is always ready... Go up to this feast; I am not yet going to this feast, for my time has not yet fully come... But*

when his brothers had gone up, then he too went up to the feast, not openly, but as it were in secret.

142. By "many festivals" Sigonio seems to mean occasions like the Feast of Unleavened Bread, which coincided with one of the three pilgrimage holidays.

143. Deuteronomy 16:16.

144. Exodus 23:14–16.

145. 1 Chronicles 8:12–13.

146. Luke 6:1.

147. 2 Chronicles 30:2–3.

148. I.e. the expression should really be "first second," because the Passover of the first month fell in the second.

149. Mark 2:23.

150. The Pharisees criticize Jesus twice in chapter 2, in this story and in the previous one. Cornelius Jansen (1510–1576) was a Flemish cleric and Bible scholar.

151. Exodus 23:10–11.

152. Leviticus 25:2–6.

153. Leviticus 25:20–22.

154. Deuteronomy 15:1, 3–4, 6, 9, 12–14.

155. Leviticus 25:8–11, 14–16.

156. Numbers 36:3–4.

157. Numbers 36:6–7.

158. Heb. *yovel*="Jubilee."

159. Cf. Leviticus 25:9.

160. Joshua 6:4. The Vulgate adds the phrase "which are used in the Jubilee," while the Hebrew has simply *yovelim*, which makes the verse irrelevant to the Jubilee but does prove Sigonio's claim that *yovel* means "ram's horn."

161. ἐγκαινίζειν. This verb has the same root as *encaeniis*, the Latin transliteration of the term for "dedication."

162. Here Sigonio is blurring the distinction between ceremonies that occurred only once, and yearly commemorations.

163. 1 Kings 8:63, 65.

164. 2 Chronicles 7:8–10.

165. Ezra 6:15–16.

166. Josephus *Jewish Antiquities* 11.3.7.

167. 1 Maccabees 4:56, 59.

168. 2 Maccabees 1:18.

169. John 10:22–23.

170. Josephus *Jewish Antiquities* 15.11.4–6.

171. Judges 11:30–31, 34, 39.

172. Judges 11:39–40.

173. 2 Maccabees 1:18.

174. In Book II, chapter 3.

175. Josephus (*Jewish Antiquities* 12.7.7) uses this term to refer to Hannukah, not to the day of Nehemiah's fire.

176. Judith 16:31.

177. Though Judith says nothing about when the festival occurred, by the talmudic period the story had come to be associated with Hanukkah.

178. Esther 9:17–26.

179. 2 Maccabees 15:36.

180. Josephus *Jewish Antiquities* 12.10.4.

181. Though Gedaliah, who had been put in charge of the Judeans who remained after the deportations, was well received by them, he was assassinated by a member of the former royal family.

182. 2 Kings 25:25.

183. This reconstruction, like Sigonio's suggestion that the lunar year was intercalated by the addition of a short month every two years, is an entirely theoretical and synthetic picture of how the calendar worked. In both the Second Temple system (the earliest we know of) and the later standardized calendar, the length of various months (whether 29 or 30 days) varied from one year to the next, as did the days of the week on which specific dates such as festivals fell out. There were also restrictions placed on which days of the week certain holidays could fall. Sigonio assumes that the seventh day of the first month was a Sabbath, and continues on from there.

184. Cf. 1 Maccabees 13:49–52: *They also of the tower in Jerusalem were in such straits that they could neither come forth, nor go into the country, nor buy, nor sell... Then they cried to Simon, beseeching him to be at one with them: which he granted them... he cleansed the tower from pollution, and entered into it the twenty-third day of the second month in the hundred seventy and first year, with thanksgiving, and branches of palm trees... He ordained also that that day should be kept every year with gladness...*

185. This was not a Jewish practice, but an ancient Roman one from before the time of the Julian calendar reform: an additional short month was added every two

years between February 23 and 24 (February being the last month of the lunar year) in order to reconcile the lunar and solar calendars.

BOOK IV

1. Cf. Cicero *On the Nature of the Gods* 1.6.

2. Leviticus 1:3.

3. 1 Samuel 3:14.

4. Hebrews 8:3.

5. Hebrews 5:1.

6. Sigonio may be referring to Numbers 15:20, which mentions the "heave offering" (*tenufah*) of the threshing floor.

7. Although the word "libation" usually applies to an offering of wine, here Sigonio is using it as the Vulgate does in Leviticus 6:14, to refer to the various meal offerings prepared with flour in the three types of vessels mentioned above. For the vessels, cf. Leviticus 7:9.

8. θυσία, "offering."

9. Origen *Homilies on Leviticus* 23. Origen, Greek church father, was an important Christian philosopher and theologian of the second and third centuries.

10. Heb. *ola*.

11. Heb. *nesech*.

12. Heb. *shlamim*.

13. Heb. *hatat*.

14. Heb. *asham*.

15. Heb. *miluim*.

16. Philo wrote about biblical and Jewish topics in Greek, using the allegorizing methods of the neoplatonist philosophers.

17. Moses.

18. Philo *On the Special Laws* 36.194.

19. Philo has here *two*.

20. Philo *On the Special Laws* 36.195–197.

21. I.e. outside the Pentateuch.

22. An expression often used in Leviticus to describe sacrifices.

23. I.e. the meal offerings.

24. Origen *Homilies on Leviticus* 5.2.

25. Leviticus 1:2–9.

26. Leviticus 6:9–13.

27. Philo *On the Special Laws* 37.198–199.

28. Cf. Leviticus 9:24, where the inauguration of Aaron is described: *And a fire came out from before the Lord, and consumed upon the altar the burnt offering and the fat; and when all the people saw this, they shouted and fell on their faces.*

29. Leviticus 10:1–2.

30. Cf. Psalms 66:13–15: *I will go into your house with burnt offerings… I will offer you burnt sacrifices of fatlings, with the incense of rams; I will offer bullocks with he-goats.*

31. Philo *Life of Moses* 22.30.158.

32. As above, Sigonio uses the term "libation" to refer to the Hebrew *minha*, which the King James translates as "meat offering."

33. Leviticus 2:1–16.

34. Leviticus 6:14–18.

35. Cf. Numbers 15:4, 9.

36. Peaceful.

37. Sacrifices for peace.

38. Sacrifices of the peace offerings.

39. Sacrifices for well-being.

40. εἰρηνικὰ, "peaceful."

41. θυσία εἰρηνικὴ, "sacrifice for peace."

42. σωτήριον, "safety offering."

43. Sacrifice for peace. (This is the same as the second Greek term. Perhaps Sigonio could not think of distinctive translations for two of the Latin phrases, but if so he has the Greek in the wrong order, because the corresponding Latin terms are clearly different from one another.)

44. Heb. *neder, nedava.*

45. Heb. *toda.* This is the "thank offering," or "sacrifice of thanksgiving."

46. Leviticus 3:1–5.

47. Leviticus 3:13–17.

48. Following the Vulgate, Sigonio translates the terms "heave offering" (*teruma*) and "wave offering" (*tenufa*) as "first fruits."

49. See note 48 above.

50. See note 48 above.

51. Leviticus 7:11–33.

52. Here Sigonio, following the Vulgate, has *salutaris*, the term translated above as "sacrifice for well-being."

53. Leviticus 10:14–15.

54. Philo *On the Special Laws* 39.212; 40.220, 222–225.

55. Leviticus 22:29–30.

56. Psalms 115:12–13, 17.

57. This should properly be the high priest, but Sigonio is following the text of Leviticus, which (as it often does) has here simply "the priest."

58. Heb. *nasi*, a generic term for a ruler that was not used as an actual title of office until the Hasmonean period.

59. Leviticus 4:3–12.

60. Leviticus 6:25–30.

61. I.e. about the whereabouts of something that he had found, or that had been entrusted to him.

62. I.e. an unintentional sin.

63. I.e. a false oath.

64. Cf. Leviticus 5:14–26.

65. Leviticus 5:21–26.

66. Leviticus 7:1–10.

67. The text of Philo does not mention any additional animals here, while the Bible (Leviticus 4:27–31) mentions a female goat as the offering for unintentional sins.

68. Philo *On the Special Laws* 1.42.226–228.

69. Philo *On the Special Laws* 1.43.235–236.

70. Cf., for example, Augustine *To Simplicianus* 12.1; *Against Faustus* 22.22, 27.

71. There is no reason to think that Augustine was deliberately rejecting the Bible's definition of "trespass" (*delictum*) as "unintentional sin"—the passage from Leviticus 6 ("If a soul sin...") does not explicitly define this kind of sin as a "trespass," and the description of the trespass offering in chapter 7 says nothing about the sin itself. Augustine may have chosen the term *delictum* to describe a deliberate offense, because it was used in Roman law to describe private injuries as opposed to public crimes.

72. Cf. Leviticus 9:24.

73. I.e. after the death of his sons.

74. Leviticus 9:8–24; 10:1–2, 12–20.

75. From the Greek *holokaustos*, "burned whole."

76. I.e. a mature animal.

77. Leviticus 4:23 mentions a goat but not a bull.

78. I.e. an *issaron*, or a tenth of an ephah.

79. The *chous* was a liquid measure equal to about 3.2 liters.

80. Josephus *Jewish Antiquities* 3.9.1–4.

81. Joshua 8:31.

82. Joshua 22:23.

83. Judges 6:19–21.

84. 1 Samuel 7:9.

85. 1 Samuel 10:8.

86. 1 Samuel 13:9.

87. 1 Samuel 13:12.

88. 2 Samuel 6:17.

89. 1 Kings 3:15.

90. 1 Kings 9:25.

91. 2 Kings 16:13.

92. 2 Kings 16:15.

93. 2 Chronicles 29:31.

94. 2 Chronicles 30:22.

95. 2 Chronicles 29:21–24.

96. 2 Chronicles 29:31.

97. 2 Chronicles 29:35.

98. Ezra 6:17.

99. 1 Maccabees 4:56.

100. I.e. Joshua through Chronicles.

101. Psalms 39:6. Christian writers like Sigonio considered the Book of Psalms to be a prophetic work that contained references to the coming of Christ.

102. Ezekiel 45:17.

103. Proverbs 7:14.

104. As in the Pauline Letter to the Hebrews 13:15: *By him, therefore, let us offer the sacrifice of praise to God continually, that is, the fruit of our lips giving thanks to his name.*

105. In the Latin liturgy, the phrase "offering of praise" is used in the sense of "prayer offered in place of sacrifice."

106. Proverbs 21:3.

107. Psalms 39:6.

108. Psalms 4:5.

109. Hosea 6:6.

110. Letter of James 1:27. *Religio* in classical Latin often refers to ritual obligations such as sacrifice.

111. Mark 12:33.

112. Hebrews 13:16.

113. Psalms 49:14.

114. Psalms 115:17.

115. Psalms 106:22.

116. Hebrews 13:15.

117. Hosea 14:2.

118. As at the beginnings of Psalms 104, 105, 106, 117, and 135.

119. A kind of harp.

120. 1 Chronicles 23:30–31.

121. 2 Chronicles 5:12–13.

122. 2 Chronicles 29:27–28.

123. 2 Chronicles 31:2.

124. Ezra 3:10–11.

125. Psalms 110:3.

126. 1 Chronicles 16:27.

127. The apocryphal book also known as Sirach.

128. Ecclesiasticus 39:19–20.

129. Ezra 10:11.

130. ὁμολόγησις and αἴνεσις, "praise."

131. Luke 1:46.

132. τελείωσις, "fulfillment."

133. Leviticus 6:19–23.

134. Leviticus 7:37–38.

135. The Bible does not consider this a separate type of offering; it consisted of various combinations of burnt offerings, sin offerings, trespass offerings, and meal offerings.

136. See the next chapter.

137. I.e. the seven days a woman would normally have to wait after her menstrual period.

138. The comparison here is apparently between the nature of the impurity in the two situations, not the amount of time they lasted.

139. Leviticus 12:2–8.

140. Luke 2:22–24.

141. I.e. the symptoms described in Leviticus 13.

142. Leviticus 14:2–7.

143. Leviticus 15:13–15.

144. This passage has to do with the woman who menstruates outside her cycle. Sigonio has left out the section that describes normal menstruation.

145. Leviticus 15:25–30, 32–33.

146. I.e. the Day of Atonement.

147. Leviticus 16:2–29.

148. Exodus 40:4–5, 26–27.

149. Exodus 30:7–8.

150. 1 Samuel 2:28.

151. 1 Kings 9:25.

152. 1 Kings 22:43.

153. 1 Chronicles 6:49.

154. 2 Chronicles 26:16–19.

155. 2 Chronicles 29:7.

156. Isaiah 1:11, 13.

157. Luke 1:8–10.

158. I.e. selected to fit together rather than hewn into shape.

159. There were two curtains in the Temple, between the courtyard and the outer room of the sanctuary, and between the latter and the inner room or holy of holies.

160. Philo *On the Special Laws* 51.273–277.

161. Numbers 29:39. Although Sigonio seems to want this to illustrate his three-part system of gifts, the "things" mentioned in the verse are actually obligatory sacrifices.

162. The half-shekel tax for the Temple.

163. Deuteronomy 12:4–6.

164. Whereas the tithes were eaten by the Levites, the poor, foreigners, and the owner himself.

165. Exodus 22:29–30.

166. Exodus 23:19.

167. Numbers 5:9–10.

168. Numbers 18:11–14.

169. I.e. their equivalent value given to the Temple.

170. Numbers 18:15–18.

171. Exodus 22:29. This is the same verse quoted earlier in the passage, but since the Vulgate reads, "tithes and first fruits," Sigonio has omitted "tithes" above and "first fruits" here.

172. Leviticus 27:30, 32.

173. Jerome *Commentary on Ezekiel* 14 (on Ezekiel 45:13–14).

174. I.e. as though it were produce the Levites had grown themselves and therefore needed to tithe.

175. Numbers 18:26–29. Jerome does not quote this text.

176. Deuteronomy 14:22–27.

177. Deuteronomy 12:11–12.

178. Deuteronomy 12:17–18.

179. Tobit 1:6.

180. Deuteronomy 14:28–29.

181. Deuteronomy 26:12.

182. 2 Chronicles 31:4–6.

183. Nehemiah 10:34–39.

184. Luke 11:42.

185. Exodus 30:12–16.

186. Also called Jehoash.

187. The Persian term for a treasury, while *phylacium* was from the Greek *phylakein*, "guard."

188. This is the term Josephus uses (*Jewish War* 2.9.4) to describe the Temple treasury. Though in Hebrew it means "sacrifice," it is sometimes used in both rabbinic and Greek sources to refer to property vowed to the Temple. Cf. Mishnah Nedarim 1:4; Josephus *Against Apion* 1.22; Mark 7:11.

189. The Hebrew phrase, *kesef over*, is unclear—it could mean either money given by people who passed by or money that came into the Temple.

190. I.e. his personal valuation (cf. Leviticus 27:1–8).

191. 2 Kings 12:4–11.

192. 2 Chronicles 24:4–14.

193. The Greek version, in Sigonio's translation at least, is not noticeably different from the Vulgate account.

194. I.e. Athaliah.

195. Josephus *Jewish Antiquities* 9.8.2.

196. 2 Kings 22:3–5.

197. Nehemiah 10:37.

198. Nehemiah 10:39.

199. Nehemiah 13:4–5.

200. 2 Maccabees 3:6. This passage actually has a man named Simon speaking to Apollonius about the treasury; but since the latter then goes on to report this conversation to the king, Sigonio has conflated the two scenes into one.

201. Mark 12:41.

202. Luke 21:1.

203. Isaiah 22:15: *Go, get yourself to this treasurer, to Shebna, who is over the house...*

204. ταμίας τοῦ ἱεροῦ, "the treasurer of the sanctuary."

205. A Roman financial official.

206. Gk. *gazophylax.*

207. This is a paraphrase of Josephus *Jewish Antiquities* 18.4.3.

208. Josephus *Jewish War* 6.5.2. Sigonio's chapter headings for *War* are not those of modern editions but come from the *Halosis*, an ancient Latin translation of the part of the *War* that dealt with the capture of Jerusalem.

209. Josephus *Jewish War* 6.8.3.

210. Leviticus 7:16.

211. Leviticus 23:37–38.

212. Deuteronomy 23:21.

213. Philo *The Sacrifices of Cain and Abel* 13.53–54.

214. Judges 11:30–31.

215. 1 Samuel 1:11.

216. 2 Samuel 15:8.

217. Leviticus 22:18.

218. 2 Samuel 15:7.

219. Proverbs 7:14.

220. Numbers 30:2.

221. Firstborn sons were supposed to belong to God, but they could be redeemed one month after their birth; cf. Numbers 18:16.

222. I.e. it would have to be sacrificed or used by the Temple in some other way.

223. Heb. *shekel hakodesh.*

224. The *gera* of the Bible is equated here with the Athenian obol, a sub-unit of the silver drachma.

225. Jeremiah 33:11.

226. 2 Kings 12:4.

227. Ezra 1:4.

228. As he often does, Sigonio is suggesting that if the Bible makes one or more references to a particular practice, it follows that this practice was an established institution. In this case the evidence for fasting seems to be as follows. Seven days, in 1 Samuel 31:12–13: *All the valiant men arose, and went all night, and took the body of Saul and the bodies of his sons... and fasted seven days.* Three days, in Esther 4:16: *Go, gather together all the Jews who are present in Shushan, and fast for me, and neither eat nor drink three days, night or day.* Until evening, in Judges 20:26: *Then all the children of Israel, and all the people, went up, and came to the house of God, and wept, and sat there before the Lord, and fasted that day until evening;* in 1 Samuel 14:24: *And the men of Israel were distressed that day; for Saul had adjured the people,*

saying, Cursed be the man who eats any food until evening; and in 2 Samuel 1:12: *And they mourned, and wept, and fasted until evening, for Saul, and for Jonathan his son, and for the people of the Lord, and for the house of Israel.*

229. 2 Chronicles 20:3.

230. Jeremiah 36:9.

231. Ezra 8:21.

232. Judith 4:8–9, 11–12, 15–17.

233. Judges 20:26.

234. 1 Samuel 7:5–6.

235. 1 Maccabees 3:46–47.

236. 2 Maccabees 13:12.

237. Numbers 30:13. The Hebrew says only "to afflict the soul."

238. 2 Samuel 12:16.

239. 2 Samuel 12:22.

240. 1 Kings 21:27.

241. This is the Vulgate's name for the Book of Nehemiah; Sigonio uses both names indiscriminately.

242. Nehemiah 1:4.

243. 4 Esdras 5:13.

244. Judith 8:5–6.

245. Cf. Luke 18:12: *I fast twice in the week, I give tithes of all that I possess.*

246. According to Matthew (4:2) and Luke (4:2), Jesus fasted in the desert for forty days, just as Moses fasted on Mount Sinai for forty days (Deuteronomy 9:9) and Elijah did on Mount Horeb (1 Kings 19:8).

247. Matthew 6:16.

248. Isaiah 58:5–7.

249. Joel 2:12–13.

BOOK V

1. Psalms 25:5 and 22:22.

2. Sigonio is referring to the sectarian groups of the Second Temple period, including the Pharisees and Sadducees. He considers the scribes to be the source of these sects because they were the first (starting with Ezra) to interpret the Bible, which eventually led to the sort of unfounded beliefs and practices for which the scribes and Pharisees are constantly being criticized in the New Testament.

3. Cf. Numbers 3:12–13: *I have taken the Levites from among the people of Israel instead of every firstborn who opens the womb among the people of Israel. The Levites shall be mine, for all the firstborn are mine; on the day that I slew all the firstborn in the land of Egypt, I consecrated for my own all the firstborn in Israel, both of man and of beast; they shall be mine.*

4. Numbers 18:20–21.

5. I.e. *pontifex,* "bridge builder," considered the most prestigious priesthood of the later Roman republic. In the Torah, "priest" alone is generally used, though "high priest" (*kohen gadol*) appears in the law of the exile who must wait until the death of this priest to return to his city. "Great priest" (*sacerdos magnus*) is the Vulgate's translation of *kohen gadol.* "First priest" is very rare, and "chief of priests" appears only in the New Testament.

6. 2 Kings 23:4.

7. Judith 4:11.

8. Nehemiah 3:1.

9. 2 Kings 25:18.

10. Sigonio, following the Vulgate, calls this the "superhumeral," i.e. above the shoulders.

11. Heb. *hoshen.* Sigonio calls this the "rational."

12. Heb. *me'il.*

13. Heb. *k'tonet.*

14. Heb. *michnasaim.*

15. Heb. *avnet.*

16. Heb. *mitznefet.*

17. Heb. *tzitz.*

18. I.e. from outside the Pentateuch.

19. Exodus 28:6–7, 9–10.

20. Exodus 28:15–21, 29–30.

21. Exodus 28:31–35.

22. Exodus 28:39. In the text of the Bible, this verse actually comes at the end of the passage.

23. Exodus 28:36–38.

24. Exodus 28:42–43.

25. Leviticus 8:7–9.

26. Cf. Josephus *Jewish Antiquities* 3.7.1–7.

27. Jerome, Letter 64 (to Fabiola), 10–18.

28. I.e. it had legs that had to be sewn together down their sides, rather than being a flat piece of fabric. Josephus does not in fact say this.

29. The Greek term for a particularly valuable kind of flax and the linen garments made from it.

30. Heb. *bad*.

31. Unlike the loosely wrapped garments worn by Greeks and Romans.

32. A girdle worn by women.

33. Josephus (*Jewish Antiquities* 3.7.2) uses this simile to illustrate how loosely the girdle was wrapped around.

34. The mitre.

35. From the Latin for "head," it is described in medieval texts as a kind of hooded cloak.

36. A type of long cloak.

37. The Hebrew has *avnei shoham*.

38. The breastplate.

39. This could refer either to gold thread or to the gold settings of the jewels embedded in the breastplate.

40. The same stone has variously been called "opal" and "jacinth" (a kind of reddish zircon).

41. See previous note.

42. Josephus *Jewish Antiquities* 3.8.9.

43. 134–104 BCE.

44. Henbane. Josephus *Jewish Antiquities* 3.7.6.

45. Exodus 29:1, 4–7, 10.

46. Leviticus 8:4, 6–12. The reason for most of the omissions in this passage is that Sigonio has removed all the references to Aaron's sons; as he has told us, he wants to emphasize the distinction between Aaron, who was high priest, and his sons, and the fact that they were consecrated together might blur this distinction.

47. Leviticus 8:14–23, 25–34.

48. Philo *Life of Moses* 2.29.146–150; 30.152–153.

49. Leviticus 21:10, followed by a paraphrase of verses 18–20. Since the latter varies more than usual from the wording of the Vulgate, it seems to be Sigonio's own summary of the disfigurements that would disqualify a priest.

50. Philo *On the Special Laws* 16.80.

51. I.e. when a close relative has died.

52. Leviticus 21:10–15.

53. Philo *On the Special Laws* 1.101–102.

54. Leviticus 24:2–4.

55. 2 Chronicles 13:11.

56. 2 Maccabees 1:8.

57. 1 Samuel 2:28.

58. 1 Chronicles 6:49.

59. 1 Chronicles 23:13.

60. Leviticus 24:5–9.

61. 1 Samuel 21:4, 6.

62. Matthew 12:3–4.

63. 2 Maccabees 1:8.

64. 1 Chronicles 9:32.

65. Josephus *Jewish War* 5.5.7.

66. Leviticus 16:2–9.

67. Exodus 30:10.

68. Hebrews 9:6–7.

69. Philo *Embassy to Gaius* 38.306–39.308.

70. The title given by the manuscripts of Philo to *On the Special Laws* 1.13–65. This passage does not in fact come from here but is in the next section, "Of the Temple," i.e. *On the Special Laws* 1.72.

71. Josephus *Jewish War* 5.5.7.

72. I.e. on who could enter there.

73. The Latin text of Josephus has here "all the Jews."

74. I.e. they had been impure but immersed themselves in a ritual bath.

75. Josephus *Against Apion* 2.8.

76. This question, and Sigonio's analysis of it, was reexamined at length a few decades later by another Christian Hebraist, the Dutch scholar Petrus Cunaeus, in his own *Hebrew Republic* (Book 2, chapters 4–5).

77. Leviticus 16:17.

78. Exodus 28:42.

79. Exodus 29:29–30.

80. 1 Chronicles 23:13.

81. Numbers 25:13.

82. Sigonio is referring to the family of Eli. The Bible does not say that he was of the family of Ithamar, and neither he nor his descendants appear in the lists of high priests in 1 Chronicles and Ezra; instead there is a direct line of transmission from Eleazar to Zadok. But since the priests mentioned between Phinehas and Zadok do not appear in the biblical narrative, Josephus (*Jewish Antiquities* 5.11.5) assumes that they were passed over in favor of the only other legitimate family, that of Ithamar, and Sigonio follows his lead.

83. Sigonio seems to be being deliberately vague about when this happened, because the Bible itself is unclear. Zadok is the first descendant of Eleazar mentioned in the post-pentateuchal narrative who is clearly a high priest, but his father, Ahitub, is mentioned at 1 Samuel 14:3, where he is described as a grandson of Eli (who may therefore have been a descendant of Eleazar after all) but not explicitly as high priest. Josephus (see previous note) says that Eleazar's family returned "in the time of Solomon," which presumably refers to the fact that while David was king, Abiathar and Zadok served as priests together; but once Solomon had Abiathar killed, Zadok was the only official priest.

84. I.e. the Herodians.

85. Sigonio uses the term *principatus* because the first Hasmonean rulers used the biblical title *nasi*, sometimes translated "prince."

86. Hebrews 6:20.

87. Numbers 25:10, 12–13.

88. Judges 20:27–28.

89. 1 Maccabees 2:54.

90. While the biblical narrative does not mention them, they are included in the lists of high priests in 1 Chronicles 6:4–15, 50–53, and Ezra 7.

91. See note 82 above.

92. Josephus *Jewish Antiquities* 5.9–11.

93. Josephus *Jewish Antiquities* 6.6.5.

94. Josephus *Jewish Antiquities* 6.12.

95. Josephus *Jewish Antiquities* 6.12–8.1 and passim.

96. 1 Kings 2:27.

97. The priests cited as appearing in Book 10 of Josephus *Jewish Antiquities* are mentioned there only once, in a list of the successors of Zadok.

98. He is in fact called the son of Ahimaaz there.

99. 2 Chronicles 31:10. Though here Sigonio is interpreting the Latin *primus sacerdos* as "first priest," the Vulgate (and earlier in the chapter, Sigonio along with it) understands this as "high priest."

100. Possibly Joshua.

101. Possibly the Amariah of the Bible.

102. Possibly the Jehoiada of the Bible.

103. According to Josephus, the king in question was Joash (*Jewish Antiquities* 9.8.3).

104. Josephus does not actually equate the two men, and in fact mentions Azariah in the same list as Jotham, as being of an earlier generation.

105. Eusebius of Caesarea was a fourth-century scholar who, in addition to his history of the early Church, wrote the *Praeparatio Evangelica*, in which he supplied background information (drawn from earlier works about the Jews) about the people, places, and practices mentioned in the Gospels.

106. Josephus *Jewish Antiquities* 11.4.

107. Cf. Josephus *Jewish Antiquities* 11.7.1.

108. I.e. Ecclesiasticus.

109. Sigonio is referring to an episode reported in 2 Maccabees 4: Simon accused Onias of treason.

110. 2 Maccabees 4:23. Josephus, on the other hand, thinks he was the son of Onias III (*Jewish Antiquities* 12.5.1).

111. This Onias is different from the Onias IV whom Josephus equates with Menelaus. The latter may not in fact have been part of this family; if he were, then Onias III would have had two sons with the same name.

112. According to Josephus (*Jewish Antiquities* 15.9.3) Simon was the *son* of Boethus.

113. Josephus calls Joazar the son of Boethus (*Jewish Antiquities* 17.13.1). Although this would seem to make him the brother of the high priest Simon, Josephus otherwise identifies him only as the brother-in-law of the high priest Mattathias (*Jewish Antiquities* 17.6.4).

114. Nicephorus was a ninth-century patriarch of Constantinople.

115. 6–7 CE.

116. The form used in the New Testament.

117. 15–26 CE.

118. I.e. Simon son of Boethus, Herod's father-in-law. It is presumably because Josephus here calls him only "Boethus" that Sigonio thinks this was the surname of the elder Simon.

119. I.e. pure on the surface but filthy beneath.

120. Apparently not the Ishmael mentioned above.

121. Josephus does not call him this.

122. Luke 3:2.

123. Cf. *Jewish Antiquities* 18.2.2.

124. Cf. John 11:49: *And one of them, named Caiaphas, being the high priest that same year...*; and 18:12–13: *Then the band and the captain and officers of the Jews took Jesus, and bound him, and led him away to Annas first; for he was father-in-law to Caiaphas, who was the high priest that same year.*

125. Acts 4:6. Luke is generally considered to have been the author of the Acts of the Apostles. Sigonio's point is not clear, because the passage from Acts does not in fact deal with the same period as the John passages, but rather takes place after Jesus' death.

126. Augustine *On the Gospel of John* 49.27.

127. I.e. even though they no longer held the office for the rest of their lives. Sigonio seems to be thinking of the Roman practice of allowing former officials like consuls, whose office lasted for a year, to retain the dignity of their rank.

128. Emperor (41–54 CE). Cf. Josephus *Jewish War* 2.12.6: *Jonathan and Ananias the high priests.*

129. Josephus *Jewish War* 4.3.9.

130. Josephus *Jewish War* 4.3.7, 4.4.3.

131. Josephus *Jewish War* 4.3.9.

132. Cf. Josephus *Jewish War* 4.3.10.

133. Josephus *Jewish Antiquities* 20.8.8: *And such was the impudence and boldness that had seized on the high priests, that they resolved to send their servants to the threshing floors, to take away those tithes that were due to the priests.*

134. Josephus *Jewish Antiquities* 20.9.1.

135. Exodus 29:8–9.

136. Exodus 28:42–43.

137. Leviticus 8:13.

138. Ibid.

139. 1 Samuel 22:18.

140. This passage does not suggest that there was anything special about the way the priests were dressed, but since the Torah does not mention a linen ephod, Sigonio assumes that it was not part of their regular clothing.

141. Eucherius was a fifth-century bishop of Lyon. The passage comes from his *Instruction for His Son Salonius* 2.10.

142. Exodus 29:4–5, 9–10. Just as Sigonio omits Aaron's sons from the biblical passages that describe the high priest, so here he omits Aaron himself. This is made easier by the fact that in Latin, the singular and plural forms of the reflexive possessive adjective—"his (own)" and "their (own)"—are identical.

143. Leviticus 8:13.

144. Leviticus 10:8–9.

145. Leviticus 21:1–7, 9.

146. Josephus *Jewish War* 5.5.7.

147. Numbers 4:16.

148. 1 Chronicles 6:49.

149. 2 Chronicles 26:16–20.

150. This passage seems to be a version of 2 Chronicles 23:18, though its wording differs from that of the Vulgate to a much greater degree than is typical of Sigonio.

151. Luke 1:8–9.

152. Hebrews 7:27.

153. Sigonio adds the word "other" to the Vulgate, in order to make the passage refer explicitly to the regular priests rather than to the high priests. Paul himself is unclear about this—though the daily burnt offering to which he refers was commanded in Leviticus 6 of both Aaron and his sons, according to Leviticus 4 the sin offerings were performed by the high priest.

154. 2 Chronicles 29:22–24.

155. Leviticus 17:3–5, 7.

156. This is Sigonio's addition; Leviticus says that "he"—i.e. the man bringing the sacrifice—will kill it, and hand it over to the priests for sacrifice.

157. Leviticus 1:5–8.

158. 2 Chronicles 29:34.

159. Sigonio omits the phrase "the Levites" here, as he wants only the priests to be associated with this passage.

160. Ezekiel 44:15–22, 25–31.

161. 1 Chronicles 24:7–8.

162. Harim in both the Hebrew and Latin texts of Chronicles.

163. Mijamin in Chronicles.

164. Jeshebeab in Chronicles.

165. Hezir in Chronicles.

166. Gamul in Chronicles.

167. Maaziah in Chronicles.

168. Josephus *Jewish Antiquities* 12.6.1.

169. Josephus *Life* 1.1.

170. Luke 1:5.

171. The citizens of early Rome were organized into five divisions, called in Latin *classes*.

172. ἐφημερίαι, the term used in the New Testament; from *epi*="upon" and *hemera*="day."

173. An eleventh-century Bulgarian bishop who wrote a commentary on the Gospels.

174. 2 Chronicles 23:8.

175. This verse does not appear in 2 Chronicles 25; the closest verse to it seems to be 23:18, *the divisions (ephemeriae) of the priests and the Levites which David set up*, though the parallel in the Vulgate has none of the Latin terms for "division" which Sigonio mentions as equivalents of *ephemeria*.

176. The closest verse in the Septuagint is 2 Chronicles 5:11: *all the priests who were found were purified; they were not organized according to their divisions*.

177. 2 Chronicles 8:14.

178. Luke 1:8–9.

179. Fourth-century bishop of Milan. Among his writings was a commentary on Luke.

180. Luke 1:5.

181. Ezra 6:18.

182. I.e. *pontifices*, the same term with which Sigonio translates "high priest." As a plural it is found only in the New Testament.

183. Ezra 8:29.

184. Mark 14:53, 55. Sigonio adds here the word "Caiaphas" in order to remove any doubt that the "chief priest" of verse 53 is in fact the high priest, and not merely one of the "chief priests" of verse 55.

185. Though "chief priests" are frequently mentioned in the Gospels, they appear alongside the "high priest" in only two places—Mark 14:53, which Sigonio has just quoted, and Matthew 26:3.

186. In Ezra 8:24 and 10:5, the term "chiefs of the priests" (*sarei hakohanim*) is used to describe not Ezra but other men.

187. Even though Sigonio understands the phrase *princeps sacerdotum* as "chief of the priests," it is used everywhere else in the New Testament (and so presumably here as well) to mean "high priest."

188. Acts 4:6.

189. ἐκ γένους ἀρχιερατικοῦ, "from the high priestly class."

190. Since Sigonio has already pointed out that the term *archiereus* can mean "high priest," his assertion that it means something else here—in a verse which mentions the high priest himself—is unconvincing. His assertion that there was such a class of priests seems to stem from his difficulty in explaining the rank of people like Alexander and John, who are nowhere mentioned as actual high priests, and cannot therefore be placed in the same category as Annas and Caiaphas.

191. Acts 19:14.

192. By the same logic, Scaeva ought not to have been in charge of the priestly divisions of the Temple.

193. Hebrews 7:13–14.

194. Josephus has here "marry."

195. Josephus himself was a priest.

196. Josephus *Against Apion* 1.7.

197. Numbers 1:49–51.

198. Numbers 3:6–10, 12–13.

199. This is actually verse 32, which in the Bible comes between the descriptions of the families of Kohath and Merari. Sigonio has moved it to the end of the passage because it refers to the Levites in general.

200. Numbers 3:15–20, 23–26, 29–31, 35–37, 32, 38.

201. Numbers 8:24, 26. The passage reads, "shall do no service," because Sigonio has cut out the middle, in which the text moves from active Levites—between the ages of twenty-five and fifty—to those older than fifty, who do not perform sacred duties.

202. In the Vulgate at Joshua 3:3, it is the "priests of Levitical stock" who are to carry the ark across. This is an attempt to translate the Hebrew phrase *hakohanim halevi'im* as "the priests, the Levites."

203. The Bible has here thirty, but Sigonio has corrected it to agree with the figure twenty in verse 27.

204. 1 Chronicles 23:2–6.

205. 1 Chronicles 23:25–32.

206. 1 Chronicles 9:28–32.

207. Cf. 1 Chronicles 23:6: *And David divided them into courses among the sons of Levi, namely, Gershon, Kohath, and Merari.*

208. Sigonio is alluding to the fact that although the "chief men" whom Ezra brought back with him were priests, the narrative goes on to say (8:15) that there were no Levites among them.

209. 2 Chronicles 8:14.

210. 2 Chronicles 29:5, 11.

211. 2 Chronicles 29:12, 15–16, 33–34.

212. 2 Chronicles 31:2.

213. 2 Chronicles 35:3–6.

214. 2 Chronicles 35:10–11.

215. Ezekiel 44:11, 13.

216. I.e. as distinct from *organum*, the generic word for a musical instrument.

217. As in 1 Chronicles 16:34.

218. Only Heman seems to have been the son of Joel; cf. 1 Chronicles 15:17.

219. 1 Chronicles 24:31; 25:1–4, 6–8.

220. 1 Chronicles: Hashabiah.

221. 2 Chronicles 7:6.

222. 2 Chronicles 5:11–14.

223. 2 Chronicles 20:21.

224. Ezra 3:11.

225. Nehemiah 12:46.

226. Josephus *Jewish Antiquities* 8.3.8.

227. Josephus *Jewish Antiquities* 20.9.6.

228. Which held the money collected for repairs to the Temple.

229. 1 Chronicles 9:17–24, 26–27.

230. 1 Chronicles: Meshelemiah.

231. Sigonio has omitted one of the eight sons—Joah.

232. Chronicles does not say there were twenty-four divisions or explicitly link the first porters' names to them; and there are, in fact, twenty-five sons listed here.

233. 1 Chronicles 26:12–19.

234. It was actually Shelomoth, whom Sigonio has omitted, who with his brothers oversaw the treasury.

235. 1 Chronicles 26:20, 24, 26–27.

236. 2 Chronicles 23:19.

237. 2 Kings 22:4.

238. The manuscript heading for Philo, *On the Special Laws* 1.131–161.

239. Philo *On the Special Laws* 1.156.

240. 2 Chronicles 35:10–16.

241. 1 Chronicles 9:2.

242. Ezra 2:58.

243. Joshua 9:26–27.

244. Since *nethinim* is a generic title which means something like "subjects," it can tell us nothing about the ethnic origin of the members of the group.

245. Ezra 8:20.

246. Ezra 2:70. I.e. the cities set aside for the Levites.

247. The first group of scribes mentioned here consisted of interpreters like Ezra, whom the Bible (and therefore Sigonio) describes as leaders and teachers of the people. The second group were the "scribes" of the New Testament, who are—along with the Pharisees—consistently portrayed as the enemies and detractors of Jesus, and have therefore to be distinguished from their predecessors. These groups are "sects" because, as Jesus tells them, they have diverged from the true worship taught by the Bible.

248. Numbers 6:2–12.

249. Judges 13:4–5.

250. 1 Samuel 1:11.

251. An eastern writer of the second century who may have come from the Jewish Christian community of Palestine.

252. This passage comes from the *Ecclesiastical History* of Eusebius (2.23.3–6), who says it was originally from Hegesippus (whose work we no longer have). Clement was the source of the quotation immediately before this one.

253. Philo *On the Special Laws* 45.248–46.251.

254. 1 Samuel 9:9.

255. Perhaps Sigonio is thinking of God's promise to Moses that after his death, he would appoint Joshua as leader (cf. Deuteronomy 1:38).

256. Sigonio seems to mean that although the patriarchs did not write their own books of prophecy, they did give prophecy in the Torah. In Abraham's case this could be the "covenant between the pieces," where God tells him about the Exodus (Genesis 15:13–14); in Isaac's, when he tells Esau in Genesis 27:40 that he will rebel against his brother's authority; in Jacob's, when he blesses his sons and tells them about the "end of days" (Genesis 49); and in Joseph's, when he tells his family that it will eventually return to Canaan (Genesis 50:24).

257. Job is sometimes identified in rabbinic literature as a righteous gentile.

258. Numbers 12:6–8.

259. Deuteronomy 18:18–22.

260. Deuteronomy 18:15.

261. Deuteronomy 34:10.

262. Numbers 11:24–29.

263. He is not named.

264. Judges 6:7–8.

265. 1 Samuel 3:1.

266. 1 Samuel 3:9–11, 19–20.

267. 1 Samuel 28:6.

268. 1 Samuel 10:5–6.

269. 1 Samuel 10:10–11.

270. 1 Samuel 19:20–24.

271. 2 Kings 2:2–3.

272. 2 Kings 2:4–5.

273. 2 Kings 2:6–7.

274. I.e. to heaven.

275. 2 Kings 2:15.

276. This is the Zechariah son of Jehoiada mentioned in 2 Chronicles 24:20, rather than the Zechariah son of Berechiah whose prophecy is found in the Bible.

277. Gad: 1 Samuel 22:5 and passim; Nathan: 2 Samuel 7:2 and passim; Asaph: 2 Chronicles 29:30; Jeduthun: 2 Chronicles 35:15; Ahijah: 1 Kings 11:29–39 and passim; Shemaiah: 1 Kings 12:22–24 and passim; Iddo: 2 Chronicles 9:29 and passim; Azariah: 2 Chronicles 15:1–7; Hanani: 2 Chronicles 16:7–10; Jehu: 1 Kings 16:1–12;

Jahaziel: 2 Chronicles 20:14–17; Eliezer: 2 Chronicles 20:37; Zechariah: 2 Chronicles 24:20–21. Elijah is found in 1 Kings 17–21 and 2 Kings 1–2; Elisha in 1 Kings 19 and 2 Kings 2–9 and 13. Included in this list are the leaders of the Temple singers, who are described several times in the Bible as "prophesying" with their music, though not apparently in the same sense as the other prophets.

278. In the Hebrew Bible, the Book of Daniel is grouped not with the Prophets but with the Writings, because its prophecies are apocalyptic summaries of the future rather than exhortations to the people.

279. Malachi 3:1.

280. Exodus 25:22.

281. Numbers 7:89.

282. Though the Hebrew here has "with him," this is the Vulgate's reading, which supports Sigonio's argument that the mercy seat was an oracle.

283. Judges 1:1–2.

284. Judges 20:18.

285. Judges 20:23.

286. 1 Samuel 10:22.

287. 2 Samuel 21:1.

288. Sigonio quotes from Génébrard, *Chronographiae*, p. 94.

289. 1 Samuel 28:6.

290. 1 Samuel 30:7–8.

291. Judges 18:5–6.

292. Cf. Judges 18:20: *And the priest's heart was glad, and he took the ephod, and the teraphim, and the graven image, and went in the midst of the people.* This was not, however, the ephod of the Jerusalem cult, but one made by the priest's host for his family cult.

293. This is another term for the breastplate, which Sigonio normally calls *rationalis*; he may be borrowing it from whatever source he took this information from.

294. Sigonio quotes from Génébrard, *Chronographiae*, p. 94.

295. 1 Samuel 9:9.

296. 2 Kings 8:8.

297. 2 Chronicles 18:5, 22–24, 27.

298. This seems to mean that the practice (common in the classical world) of interpreting the symbolism of dreams was inappropriate, because when God communicates through them he says exactly what he means.

299. Deuteronomy 18:10–12.

300. Jeremiah 23:28.

301. Numbers 12:6-8.

302. Cf. Judges 7:13-15.

303. 1 Kings 3:5-6, 9, 15.

304. I.e. of the Bible.

305. Matthew 1:20.

306. Joel 2:28.

307. Genesis 15:1.

308. Genesis 22:11.

309. Matthew 2:13.

310. 1 Kings 13:17-18.

311. Basil of Caesarea *Homily on Psalm 28* 3.

312. Cf. Genesis 20:3: *But God came to Abimelech in a dream by night, and said to him, "Behold, you are a dead man, because of the woman whom you have taken; for she is a man's wife"*; and 31:24: *But God came to Laban the Aramean in a dream by night, and said to him, "Take heed that you say not a word to Jacob, either good or bad."*

313. Sigonio's description of prophecy draws a great deal on the classical tradition, in which oracles (the term he uses to describe the mercy seat and the high priest's breastplate) were consulted on pressing matters of public interest, and especially on the decision to go to war. He therefore tends to see prophecy as the prediction of future outcomes, even though it often appears in the Bible as a means of divine instruction or rebuke.

314. Philo *On Dreams* 1.191. Cf. Genesis 3:11: *He said, "Who told you that you were naked? Have you eaten of the tree of which I commanded you not to eat?"*

315. And therefore without the use of anthropomorphization.

316. Sigonio seems to be insinuating that his contemporaries see God the way Homer describes Zeus and the other Olympians in his epics.

317. Sigonio quotes from Génébrard, *Chronographiae*, pp. 37, 169. See the discussion in the introduction, pp. xxxiii-xxxiv.

318. Acts 6:14.

319. The passage in Acts (6:9) calls these men not elders, but "certain of the synagogue."

320. Judges 2:7.

321. Matthew 15:2-3; cf. Mark 7:5-8.

322. Mark 7:3.

323. Cf. Matthew 23:1–3: *Then spoke Jesus to the multitude, and to his disciples, saying, "The scribes and the Pharisees sit in Moses' seat; all therefore they bid you observe, that observe and do..."* The seat, then, was associated with the right to interpret the law.

324. Leviticus 10:8–11.

325. Josephus *Against Apion* 2.18.

326. Philo *Life of Moses* 2.39.215–216.

327. Philo has here a long list of these virtues.

328. Cf. Deuteronomy 31:10–13.

329. Cf. 1 Chronicles 23:4 (which gives the figure of six thousand) and 26:29.

330. I.e. 1 Chronicles 23:4.

331. γραμματεῖς and κριταὶ, "scribes" and "judges."

332. 1 Chronicles 26:29.

333. τὸ γραμματεύειν and διακρίνειν, "clerking" and "judging."

334. I.e. readers.

335. The lector's function was to read passages from the New Testament during the service.

336. Expert in the law.

337. Luke 10:25–26.

338. γραμματεῖς, νομικοὶ, and νομοδιδάσκαλοι, i.e. "scribes, lawyers, and teachers of law."

339. Sigonio seems to be saying that they are called "judges" not because they settled cases in court, but because they had to make fine distinctions in the course of their interpretation of the text.

340. Though it is not clear how well Sigonio understands this issue, the character of Hebrew conjugation means that two words that come from the same consonantal root, but are inflected differently, will have somewhat (and occasionally very) different meanings. And because the text of the Bible is written without vowels, which are often the only way to distinguish between two of these forms, part of the job of the interpreter is to decide which form he has before him.

341. Philo *That Every Good Man Is Free* 12.81–82.

342. 1 Corinthians 14:29.

343. διακρινέτωσαν, "judge" or "distinguish."

344. This seems to be a very rough paraphrase, with all the names of priests and Levites removed, of 2 Chronicles 17:7–9.

345. 2 Chronicles 17:7–9.

346. 2 Kings 23:2.

347. Both Jews and Christians of Sigonio's time believed that the Masoretic text, with its vocalization and phrasing, was produced after the Babylonian exile rather than in the early Middle Ages.

348. Ezra 7:10. While the Hebrew term translated here as "seek," *darash*, has the sense of "seek the meaning" or "interpret," Sigonio seems to be drawing on the experience of his own days—in which monasteries and libraries were scoured for classical manuscripts—for the idea that Ezra was actually doing the same for manuscripts of the Bible.

349. Nehemiah 8:13.

350. 3 Esdras 9:42–45.

351. 3 Esdras 9:49.

352. Sigonio quotes from Génébrard, *Chronographiae*, p. 94. As earlier in this chapter, Sigonio is identifying these "scribes" with the group called in rabbinic literature "the men of the great assembly," with whom a number of reforms of the early Second Temple period were associated.

353. Matthew 13:52. The "treasure" referred to here is a storehouse, from which one may take both older and fresher produce.

354. Matthew 17:10.

355. Mark 12:35.

356. Matthew 2:4.

357. Luke 20:1–2.

358. Cf. Matthew 5:21–22, 27–28, 31–33.

359. 1 Corinthians 1:20.

360. He actually calls Nicodemus a *master in Israel*. Cf. John 3:1–11.

361. Cf. Luke 2:42–46.

362. This passage is actually an amalgam of Matthew 22:35 and Acts 5:34.

363. James the son of Zebedee.

364. A quote from the thirteenth-century *Golden Legend*, a popular collection of lives of the saints.

365. John 18:20.

366. Acts 24:12.

367. Antiochus III, the father of Epiphanes (222–187 BCE).

368. Josephus *Jewish Antiquities* 12.3.3.

369. A paraphrase of 2 Chronicles 34:14–16.

370. 2 Kings 22:3-6.

371. Acts 15:21.

372. Matthew 4:23; Luke 4:16-17, 31-32.

373. Luke 13:10, 14.

374. Acts 9:1-2, 20.

375. Acts 13:5, 14-15, 43-44.

376. Acts 14:1.

377. Acts 17:1-2, 10, 13; 18:4, 7-8, 19.

378. Acts 19:8.

379. Cf. Acts 6:9.

380. As freed slaves, they received citizenship under Roman law.

381. As opposed to eating babies and committing incest, the sorts of things that Christians were accused of doing in their private gatherings.

382. Philo *Embassy to Gaius* 154-157.

383. I.e. of the Second Temple.

384. The name for the Essenes found in the account of Epiphanius, which Sigonio quotes at length below.

385. This is Abraham ibn Daud, the author of the eleventh-century *Sefer Hakabbala*, or "Book of Tradition." Sigonio has taken this information from Génébrard, *Chronographiae*, pp. 102-103. See the discussion in the introduction, pp. xxxii-xxxiv.

386. Cf. Josephus *Jewish Antiquities* 18.1.4; *Jewish War* 2.8.14.

387. Epiphanius *Panarion* 1.1.31.

388. Epiphanius *Panarion* 1.1.32-33.

389. This refers to Mark 7:3-8, where both the narrator and Jesus himself accuse the Pharisees and scribes of caring more for their traditions about how to wash themselves and their possessions than they do for the actual laws of the Torah.

390. This presumably refers to a ritual bath.

391. Cf. Matthew 23:5.

392. Though Matthew mentions phylacteries here, he does not describe them; it is Epiphanius who likens them to the Roman *latus clavus*, the broad, purple stripe woven into the toga of a senator.

393. Epiphanius seems to be thinking of the rabbinic practice of assigning traditions to the schools of various authorities like Rabbi Akiba and Rabbi Meir. There was also a category of teachings said to be *halacha l'Moshe miSinai*, "a law given to Moses at Sinai."

394. There seems to be some confusion here between Akiba and his follower Bar Kochba.

395. Perhaps Judah the Prince (*hanasi*), the editor of the Mishnah.

396. The Talmud does refer a number of times to laws passed by the "court of Hashmonai"; cf., for example, Sanhedrin 82a.

397. Except for the first phrase of the passage, which seems to have been borrowed from Josephus *Jewish War* 2.8.8, the rest comes from *Jewish Antiquities* 18.1.3 (though the final comment about reincarnation in cattle is not found in either).

398. I.e. the verb *parash*. Epiphanius *Panarion* 1.1.33–34.

399. Epiphanius *Panarion* 1.1.37.

400. *Hemera*="day."

401. Epiphanius *Panarion* 1.1.38.

402. Apparently a Hellenized form of *harei Elat*, the mountains of Eilat.

403. Epiphanius *Panarion* 1.1.40.

404. Josephus *Jewish War* 2.8.3–5, 7–11. The last comment is not strictly about the Essenes—Sigonio has omitted Josephus' description of their actual beliefs, but included the analogy he draws between these beliefs and those of the Greeks.

405. Josephus says that they *did* send offerings, even though they themselves were not allowed to attend. The problem here might be the term *anathema*, which Josephus uses in the sense of "offering" but which in Latin came to mean "forbidden." Since the Latin translation of Josephus simply transliterates the term, it may understand this phrase to mean something like "they prohibit forbidden things."

406. This is not intended as a criticism—Josephus was not an egalitarian.

407. Josephus *Jewish Antiquities* 18.1.5. The last phrase is not found in Josephus.

408. I.e. of the Dead Sea.

409. Pliny wrote this shortly after the destruction of Jerusalem in 70 CE.

410. Pliny *Natural History* 5.73.

411. Since Philo himself wrote in Greek, Sigonio has added this explanation.

412. I.e. those who deal with pure logic and physical phenomena.

413. This is Sigonio's encapsulation of a considerably longer list in Philo.

414. The following passage is, in Philo's book, a description of the virtues to be found in the Bible rather than of Essene practices as such. In Philo it follows the passage about the Essenes quoted in the last chapter (Sigonio has omitted that passage here), in which Philo says that they gathered on the Sabbath to learn about the laws.

415. Philo *That Every Good Man Is Free* 75–87.

416. Epiphanius *Panarion* 1.1.45.

417. A translation of Genesis 49:10, which, although (or because) its simple meaning has never been clear, has often been interpreted as a messianic prophecy.

418. Tertullian *On Rules* 45.

419. Sigonio uses the terms *populares* and *optimates*, which in Roman political culture represented leaders who drew their support from the people and its causes on one hand, and from the senatorial aristocracy on the other.

420. I.e. John Hyrcanus.

421. Cf. Josephus *Jewish Antiquities* 13.10.6. Sigonio uses the odd phrase "new traditions" because he wants to acknowledge Josephus' statement that the Pharisees' laws are traditions, and yet he cannot follow Josephus in accepting them for that reason as genuine and binding, because they are not part of the biblical text. Like other Christian scholars of his time, Sigonio rejects the validity of the oral law.

422. Alexander Jannaeus (103–76 BCE).

423. Cf. Josephus *Jewish Antiquities* 13.13.5–14.2. Josephus does not call them Pharisees here, but simply Jews.

424. Sigonio's dislike of the Pharisees is not based entirely on the New Testament—Josephus himself criticizes their influence over the later Hasmoneans. Given the difficulty of reconciling this critique with Josephus' general opinion of them, it is thought to have been taken from his main source for the period, a history written by a supporter of Herod named Nicolaus, who wanted to discredit the Hasmoneans by painting them as in thrall to the Pharisees.

425. According to Josephus *Jewish Antiquities* 13.16.2, Hyrcanus was under the control of the Pharisees, though he was not one of them as such. Josephus says nothing about the allegiance of Aristobulus.

426. Mark 3:6.

427. Mark 7:1–4.

428. Luke 11:39.

429. Matthew 15:1–6. The claim here is that the Pharisee, by vowing to the Temple the property he might otherwise have used to support his parents, acquires a legitimate reason not to support them.

430. δευτερώσεις, "recapitulations" (in the sense of the Heb. *mishna*).

431. I.e. the blood is the product of illicit sex.

432. Though there is nothing in rabbinic literature to affirm this claim, it may in fact be true.

433. Eucherius *Instruction for His Son Salonius* 2.1.

434. Acts 1:12.

435. The entire verse reads: *Then they returned to Jerusalem from the mount called Olives, which is from Jerusalem a Sabbath day's journey.*

436. Mark 8:15. Sigonio's point (which emerges from the next quote) is that "leaven" here means "the teaching of a school," and his version of the verse makes this point more clearly than the Vulgate, which has here "the leaven of the Pharisees and the leaven of Herod." Herod, after all, did not have a school.

437. Matthew 16:1, 6, 12. Sigonio has omitted a great deal here: the first verse introduces a debate between Jesus and his opponents, and the rest is part of a discussion with the apostles in which Jesus warns them about which leaven to accept—not because he was expecting them to buy bread for their journey (Jesus had already shown them he could provide bread by miraculous means), but because he was comparing the leaven to the teachings of the Pharisees and Sadducees.

438. Matthew 12:2. Sigonio apparently sees this as a case of a "tradition" not found in the Bible.

439. Matthew 12:38. Given Jesus' response—*it is an evil and adulterous generation that seeks after a sign*—the point may be that if they had truly followed God's teachings and not their own ways, they would not have looked for some kind of proof of Jesus' authority. On the other hand, over the course of this discussion Sigonio seems to be shifting his focus away from the teachings of the Jews and toward their efforts to trap Jesus. So perhaps he sees the request for a sign as a malicious attempt of this sort.

440. Matthew 22:23, 28. From the excised part of the passage: *If a man die, having no children, his brother shall marry his wife, and raise up seed unto his brother. Now there were with us seven brothers; and the first, when he had married a wife, died, and, having no issue, left his wife unto his brother. 22:26: Likewise the second also, and the third... And last of all the woman died also.*

441. Matthew 22:34–35.

442. Mark 12:13–14.

443. Matthew 23:3–7, 14–15, 23, 25, 27, 29.

444. Luke 20:46–47. This is a much shorter version.

445. This refers to the Roman practice of setting three couches at each wall of a dining room, and giving the couch at the head to the most honored guest.

446. Numbers 15:38–39.

447. Epiphanius *Panarion* 1.1.32–33. Sigonio has already used the same passage to describe the Pharisees, whom he regards as very much like the scribes.

448. Though this refers to the purple fringes mentioned in Numbers 15:38, the idea that they were "spread out" alludes to the Roman stripe of nobility, the *latus clavus.*

449. I.e. purple.

450. Cf. Numbers 15:39: *and it shall be to you a fringe to look upon and remember all the commandments of the Lord, to do them, not to follow after your own heart and your own eyes, which you are inclined to go after wantonly.*

451. Acts 4:1–2.

452. Acts 5:17.

453. Acts 23:6–8.

454. This is a constitutional issue: since Judea was a sovereign kingdom rather than (as it became later on) a Roman province, by what authority could Augustus collect a tribute?

455. Cf. Matthew 17:27.

456. Latin *sica*.

457. Luke 2:1; Matthew 17:24–27; Josephus *Jewish Antiquities* 18.1.1, 6; and *Jewish War* 2.8.1. The reference to Isidore is incorrect.

BOOK VI

1. A Roman theoretician and writer of the first century BCE.

2. As quoted by Augustine (*City of God* 6.4).

3. Ibid.

4. Sigonio, *De republica Atheniensium libri IIII*, first published in 1564.

5. Cf. Aristotle *Politics* 2.1.

6. Sigonio may be thinking here of a city like Athens, which had both juries and assemblies in which hundreds of people participated.

7. Sigonio uses the word *contio*, the Roman term for a meeting open to the entire people.

8. Psalms 111:1.

9. Though *ecclesia* became the standard word for "church," it was transliterated from the regular Greek term for an assembly.

10. Psalms 107:32.

11. Psalms 26:5.

12. Sigonio may again be thinking of Athens, where the council of the Areopagus was an older and even more august council that still retained some authority alongside the classical *boulē*.

13. Sigonio seems to be referring to the fact that though *ecclesia* is used generically in the Hebrew Bible to mean "congregation," in the New Testament (Acts and the Pauline letters) it almost always refers specifically to the new Christian community.

14. In Book I, chapter 5.

15. This second passage, Exodus 12:3, is in fact the only one in the Vulgate to use this specific wording. Though other passages (e.g. Leviticus 17:1, 22:18) do refer to "all the children of Israel," Sigonio may have chosen this one because it describes the Israelites as a *coetus*, "body" or "gathering."

16. Exodus 24:7.

17. Exodus 35:1.

18. The Vulgate has here *synagoga*.

19. Numbers 27:19–20.

20. Deuteronomy 9:10.

21. Sigonio uses the Roman term *summum imperium*, which was the authority held by the highest elected magistrates to conduct wars and administer the state.

22. Joshua 23:2.

23. Joshua 24:1.

24. 1 Samuel 7:5.

25. 2 Samuel 12:29.

26. 2 Chronicles 5:2.

27. 1 Kings 12:21.

28. I.e. *nasi*. Cf. Book IV, chapter 6.

29. 1 Maccabees 14:44.

30. Numbers 10:2–8.

31. I.e. at Mount Sinai.

32. Deuteronomy 4:10.

33. 1 Chronicles 29:1.

34. Judges 11:11.

35. 1 Maccabees 3:46–47.

36. 1 Samuel 7:5.

37. Judges 21:2.

38. 1 Samuel 11:15.

39. 1 Samuel 15:33.

40. 1 Samuel 7:17.

41. This is actually an amalgam of Judges 8:22 and 9:8.

42. 1 Samuel 10:17–19.

43. 1 Samuel 10:24.

44. 1 Maccabees 9:30.

45. Judges 10:17.

46. Judges 20:1–2, 7–9. These verses come from the story of the war that eleven of the tribes fought against Benjamin over one of its communities, Gibeah, whose citizens had raped to death the concubine of a Levite who was spending the night there on his way to Jerusalem.

47. Judges 21:1.

48. Judges 21:8.

49. 1 Samuel 7:5, 6, 11. These passages do not make an explicit connection between the gathering at Mizpeh and the decision to go to war.

50. Joshua 19:47.

51. Judges 12:1–4. Sigonio seems to be including Joshua 19 because it says that the inhabitants of Dan conducted their own war, i.e. they declared it on their own authority; while in Judges 12, the fact that the men of Ephraim were "called" is taken to mean that they were called together as a public assembly.

52. 2 Chronicles 30:2.

53. This verse does not seem to be in the Bible, but since the previous quote referred to the Passover sacrifice ordered by King Hezekiah, here Sigonio is presumably referring to the Passover of his successor, King Josiah.

54. 1 Kings 8:22.

55. Although ancient political theory groups states into democracies, aristocracies, and monarchies, it tends to put less stock in democracies than in the other two systems. Sigonio therefore means his comment as a compliment.

56. Latin *maiestas*, the Romans' term for the broad respect owed to them by other nations, beyond any specific treaty obligations those nations might have.

57. I.e. the style of a Greek state like Sparta, which had both kings and a council.

58. 2 Maccabees 1:10. This is "Greek" because there is a people (*demos*), a council (*gerousia*), and a leader.

59. 1 Maccabees 14:20.

60. Sigonio has left out the phrase "the priests," and changed "the rest of the people" to "the entire people," so as to preserve the same structure as before; here "elders"="council."

61. Josephus *Jewish Antiquities* 20.1.2.

62. This seems to be a paraphrase of Josephus' remarks in *Jewish Antiquities* 13.10.5.

63. Cicero *On Behalf of Flaccus* 67.

64. I.e. first under the republic, and then under the empire.

65. I.e. Asia Minor.

66. The proconsul was the chief Roman provincial official, and the assize was a traveling court that dealt throughout the province with cases that might require Roman legal procedures, such as disputes between Roman citizens and non-citizens.

67. Acts 19:28–30.

68. Acts 19:35, 38–39, 41.

69. An Athenian orator of the fourth century BCE.

70. Aeschines *On the False Embassy* 72. The "false embassy" was the delegation of Athenians sent to negotiate a treaty with the Macedonian king Philip, one of whose members, Aeschines, was accused by Demosthenes of having accepted a bribe in return for disregarding Athenian interests.

71. The third-century rhetorician Ulpian of Ashkelon wrote commentaries on a number of Demosthenes' speeches.

72. *Homilies on Acts* 42.2.

73. A Greek geographer of the Roman Empire.

74. Strabo *Geography* 13.4.12.

75. "Forum" in the sense of the center of a community or region.

76. Pliny *Natural History* 5.105–126.

77. Cicero is referring to freed slaves from Asia who have become Roman citizens.

78. Numbers 11:16–17.

79. The wording is awkward because Sigonio has cut out the transitive verb "sustain" that precedes the last phrase in the passage.

80. The term *senatus* and its Greek equivalent, *gerousia*, are both cognate with the Latin and Greek words for "old."

81. Josephus *Jewish Antiquities* 4.8.17. This idea does not appear in the text on which Josephus is basing himself (Deuteronomy 17:13–20), but he (like Sigonio) has been influenced by the classical idea that the best form of government is aristocracy. Since the king was not part of the classical conception of a city-state, Sigonio describes him here as merely a leader among other leaders, and he seems to understand the law to say that if there is to be a king, he should at least be advised by aristocrats like the Sanhedrin.

82. Deuteronomy 5:23.

83. Deuteronomy 27:1.

84. Joshua 23:2.

85. This is a summary of Judges 21:16–22.

86. 1 Kings 8:1.

87. 2 Chronicles 32:3.

88. This is the Septuagint; the Hebrew and the Vulgate have here "princes."

89. Ezekiel 8:11.

90. Sigonio is assuming that the system of choosing elders worked in the same way as, for example, the election of the council of democratic Athens, where each of ten tribes contributed fifty members.

91. Jeremiah 19:1.

92. Isaiah 1:26.

93. Ezra 10:8.

94. 1 Maccabees 12:6.

95. 2 Maccabees 1:10.

96. 2 Maccabees 11:27.

97. 1 Maccabees 15:1.

98. Luke 22:66.

99. *Presbuterion tou laou*, "the council of elders of the people."

100. Josephus *Jewish War* 2.15.6.

101. Josephus *Jewish War* 6.6.3.

102. In Greece and Rome, the council's authority was advisory rather than legislative.

103. Sigonio may be thinking of passages such as 2 Samuel 4:12 (David has killed and mutilated the men who murdered Saul's surviving son) and 11:14–17 (David has Uriah placed in the fiercest fighting in hopes of getting him killed); 1 Kings 2:46 (Solomon orders his father's enemy Shimei killed); 2 Kings 16:15 (Ahaz tells his priest to move the sacrificial altar and replace it with a copy of one he had seen in Damascus); and 2 Chronicles 16:10 (Asa has a prophet imprisoned) and 18:25 (Ahab has the prophet Micaiah imprisoned).

104. 2 Kings 23:1.

105. 1 Samuel 30:26.

106. Jeremiah 19:7.

107. Josephus *Jewish Antiquities* 11.8.2.

108. Judges 11:5–6.

109. Judges 8:14.

110. Ruth 4:2.

111. *Aequitas*, or fairness, is listed by Cicero as one of the components of justice.

112. κρίσις, "judgment."

113. δίκη, "justice."

114. "Empty," meant as an insult.

115. Matthew 5:22.

116. Psalms 1:5. Since restatement is such an important part of biblical poetry, this verse should if anything prove that the two institutions were one and the same.

117. γραμματοεισαγογεῖς, "instructors of reading" or perhaps "of the law." The sense of this term in the Septuagint is difficult to interpret, because despite its semantic roots it appears there several times as the equivalent of the Hebrew *shotrim*, which is usually translated as something like "officers."

118. The Greek terms are closer to the language of the Bible—"heads of thousands," "heads of hundreds," and so on. Sigonio, following the Vulgate, translates "heads of thousands" as "tribunes"; though this was a Roman military title that did not imply command of any specific number, the Vulgate may have chosen it because in the late Roman republic there were six tribunes to a legion, and the maximum size of a legion was six thousand men (though the tribunes commanded the entire legion in turn, rather than each commanding a sixth of it). As for "centurions," the century which they commanded was originally a unit of one hundred men.

119. In Book VII, chapter 7, Sigonio explains why he thinks this office had to do with bringing cases to the judges.

120. Exodus 18:25–26.

121. Deuteronomy 1:9, 12–17.

122. The Hebrew has here *shotrim l'shivteichem*, "officers for your tribes."

123. Deuteronomy 16:18–19. This is Sigonio's text. The standard Vulgate, like the Hebrew, has "you shall not wrest judgment" and "you shall not respect persons."

124. Josephus *Jewish Antiquities* 4.8.14.

125. 2 Chronicles 19:5–7.

126. Isaiah 1:26.

127. Ezra 7:25.

128. This is the Septuagint; the Vulgate has here not "scribes" but *praesides*, "magistrates."

129. Fourth-century bishop of Alexandria.

130. Gk. *eis krisin*.

131. Psalms 121:1–5.

132. This is unclear—the senate as such did not administer the courts. Perhaps Sigonio is thinking of the fact that while an elected official—the praetor—was in charge of trials, the judges for these trials were chosen ad hoc from among the senatorial aristocracy.

133. This verse does not exist in the Bible; it is reminiscent of the next passage, Deuteronomy 19:11–12, which discusses the intentional killer who tries to receive sanctuary.

134. Deuteronomy 19:11–12. Though we are meant to understand that they are fetching him for trial, the verse in fact says that they are to hand him over to the victim's family.

135. The Vulgate has "your elders and your judges."

136. Deuteronomy 21:1–2.

137. Ruth 4:2, 11.

138. Philo *On the Special Laws* 4.41–78.

139. The following is a selective paraphrase of *On the Special Laws* 4.59–78.

140. Exodus 23:1: *non suscipies vocem mendacii*.

141. Cf. Herodotus *Histories* 1.8.

142. Philo *On the Special Laws* 4.60.

143. Cf. Deuteronomy 16:19.

144. Exodus 23:3.

145. A reference to the fact that in antiquity, silver coinage was sometimes heavily debased with other metals that reduced its inherent value; or that, of the many coinages issued by various states, some were considered more reliable than others. In the same way, defendants should be judged not by their nominal social status but by their true character.

146. Deuteronomy 25:7.

147. The Vulgate has here "our son," since the boy's parents are speaking to the elders. Sigonio may have changed it to suggest that the elders were passing sentence on the boy themselves.

148. Deuteronomy 21:18–20.

149. Deuteronomy 22:15.

150. Deuteronomy 25:7. This is the same verse quoted above as part of Deuteronomy 21, though here it reads, "elders," as in the Vulgate, and "of that city" has been added.

151. Joshua 20:4.

152. Ruth 4:10–11.

153. Proverbs 22:22–23.

154. Proverbs 31:23.

155. Psalms 126:5.

156. See note 160 below on the reasons for this refusal.

157. Galatino was a sixteenth-century friar whose work *On the Mysteries of Catholic Truth* incorporated passages from rabbinic literature. Although he was educated by the Christian convert known as Paul de Heredia, the precision and detail with which he uses rabbinic sources is largely a result of his reliance on the *Pugio fidei* or *Dagger of Faith*, a work by the thirteenth-century Dominican Raymond Martin which quotes extensively from rabbinic literature and its later commentaries, and which was a very popular source of anti-Jewish polemic. There is therefore no explicit evidence for Sigonio's claim that Galatino was born a Jew. See the discussion in the introduction, pp. xxiii–xxv.

158. The following is, except for the beginning, a close translation of a passage in the Babylonian Talmud (Sanhedrin 88b), taken from Galatino *On the Mysteries of Catholic Truth* 4.5. Though Sigonio seems unaware of it, this passage has to do not with civil disputes between rival litigants, but with conflicts over the proper interpretation of the law. The confusion stems from the fact that in both the New Testament and Josephus, the Sanhedrin is portrayed as a conventional court, while in the rabbinic sources it is an academy that makes decisions on matters of law.

159. Sigonio's text—unlike Galatino's—differs considerably from the passage in the Talmud, which has: *At first there were no disputes in Israel, but the court of seventy-one judges sat in the Chamber of Hewn Stone, and there were two courts of twenty-three judges; one court met in the gate of the mountain of the House,* etc.

160. If, that is, they had heard a tradition about the point of law in question, they would inform the disputants of it. If not, they would send them to a higher court where the traditions were better known. Thus the rabbis avoided disputes, which, they believed, arose only because of ignorance. Because Galatino's translation is very literal here, and the Latin for "hear" (*audio*) does not have the sense of "receiving a tradition" found in rabbinic Hebrew, Sigonio may have been led to think that the judges were in fact refusing to listen to the plaintiffs.

161. I.e. the Chamber of Hewn Stone, in the Temple.

162. The Talmud has here *hel,* the name for a part of the grounds within the Temple walls.

163. Deuteronomy 17:6.

164. Deuteronomy 19:15.

165. Cf. Deuteronomy 19:16–19.

166. Josephus *Jewish Antiquities* 4.8.15.

167. John 7:51.

168. Deuteronomy 25:1–3.

169. The first part of this passage comes from Book 4, chapter 5, of Galatino's work, where it precedes the section already quoted above.

170. Deuteronomy 17:8.

171. A literal translation of *dinei nefashot*, the rabbinic term for capital cases.

172. The scepter of authority referred to in Jacob's prophecy in Genesis 49:10: *The scepter shall not depart from Judah, nor a lawgiver from between his feet, until Shiloh comes...* In both Hebrew and Latin, "scepter" has the broader sense of "sovereignty," which is how Sigonio uses it here.

173. This could refer to the judges, who were often military leaders.

174. Again a literal translation—the third method, beheading, is called in Hebrew *hereg*, from the root "to kill."

175. Maimonides (*Mishneh Torah*, Laws of the Sanhedrin 5:1) writes only that the Sanhedrin judged an entire tribe accused of idolatry; but since the word for tribe (*shevet*) is the same as that for "scepter," it seems that Galatino has confused them. (His source for this passage, the *Pugio fidei*, has here simply "tribe.")

176. I.e. extend the boundaries of Jerusalem.

177. Again, Maimonides does not mention this. But since he does say that only the court of seventy-one could expand the boundaries of the Temple, known as the *azarot*, Galatino may have thought he was referring to *ezrot* ("assistance," spelled the same way in Hebrew) given to the Temple.

178. Numbers 11:16.

179. What follows is Sigonio's paraphrase of sections of the next chapter of Galatino, whose theme is the decline of Jewish sovereignty and judicial authority.

180. Galatino says that this is one of two opinions.

181. John 18:31.

182. The Talmud (Rosh Hashana 31a) has here *hanut*, or "market." As this was within Jerusalem, the move must have happened before the destruction of the city.

183. Deuteronomy 17:10.

184. Deuteronomy 17:8.

185. Josephus tells us (*Jewish Antiquities* 14.9.4) that Herod also had the Sanhedrin of his day executed.

186. Sigonio is aware that the Sanhedrin's deliberative functions, which lead him to describe it as the council of state, are not found in connection with the judges of the Bible.

187. The Vulgate has here "leprous and leprous" for the Hebrew *nega lanega*. *Nega* is used in the Bible to refer either to the plague of leprosy, or to a blow or attack of some kind, and this phrase has been interpreted accordingly—as either a legal debate over the laws of leprosy, or a civil dispute between litigants who have injured one another. Sigonio seems to have changed it to "leprous and not leprous" because, as elsewhere in this chapter, he assumes that judges were concerned with civil issues rather than legal ones; but rather than change the Vulgate completely, he prefers to turn the two sides into litigants in a conflict involving leprosy.

188. Though this phrase and others like it very often follow on "the place which the Lord thy God shall choose" (cf., for example, Deuteronomy 16:6, 11), it does not appear in this passage.

189. Deuteronomy 17:8–12.

190. Josephus *Jewish Antiquities* 4.8.14.

191. Deuteronomy 19:16–17.

192. Josephus *Against Apion* 2.21.

193. Cf. Numbers 15:32.

194. Philo *Life of Moses* 2.39.214–40.218.

195. Respectively, *prostagma, entolē, dikaiōmata,* and *krimata.*

196. The Bible has here "Ishmael."

197. 2 Chronicles 19:8–11.

198. The scribes are mentioned as participants in the trial in each of the synoptic gospels; cf. Matthew 26:57; Mark 14:53; and Luke 22:66.

199. A "decurion" was, in the Roman Empire, a member of the council of a provincial town, and often a member of the local aristocracy. Cf. Mark 15:43; Luke 23:50. Sigonio is suggesting that Joseph served on both the council of Arimathea and the Sanhedrin.

200. Cf. Luke 23:51: *he had not consented to the counsel and deed of them.* The text says only that Joseph was a decurion, and it does not identify those with whom he did not agree.

201. Perhaps Sigonio is referring to *Against Apion* 1.6–8, where Josephus, while not actually calling the scribes prophets, does describe the prophets of the Bible as recorders of the events of their times.

202. I.e. those other than the monarchy.

203. Though the term "blood" appears only in the Septuagint text, it is presumably the reason Sigonio believes that this verse is referring to capital cases.

204. Ezekiel 44:23–24.

205. Presumably in Book I, chapter 4.

206. Athanasius, *Explanations of the Psalms*, on Psalm 121.

207. Psalms 121:5.

208. Sigonio seems to be basing this on one of the above passages, i.e. 2 Chronicles 19:11: *...Amariah the chief priest is over you in all matters of the Lord; and Zebadiah the son of Ishmael, the ruler of the house of Judah, for all the king's matters.* Although the idea that cases should be categorized according to the nature of the charge was part of Greek and Roman jurisprudence, there is no explicit evidence for it in the Bible. There is, for example, 1 Chronicles 26:32: *And his brothers, men of valor, were two thousand and seven hundred chief fathers, whom King David made rulers over the Reubenites, the Gadites, and the half tribe of Manasseh, for every matter pertaining to God and the affairs of the king.*

209. This exchange is based on the trial of the prophet Jeremiah, and in particular on Jeremiah 26:11–16, which Sigonio quotes below.

210. Cf. Matthew 26–27; Mark 14–15; Luke 22–23; and John 18–19.

211. Jeremiah 26:11, 16.

212. Matthew 26:65–66.

213. Mark 14:64.

214. Josephus *Jewish Antiquities* 14.9.3–5.

215. Judea did not become a province until after the rebellion of 70 CE. Until then it was associated with the province of Syria and run as an imperial possession by the procurators (who were personal representatives of the emperor) rather than by proconsuls, who since the days of the republic had been appointed by the senate to administer overseas provinces.

216. The Sanhedrin wanted to execute James, but his supporters asked the governor to forbid it. Cf. Josephus *Jewish Antiquities* 20.9.1.

217. See note 215.

218. Alexander, whose father had been king for a time, tried to seize power from his uncle Hyrcanus, who had the support of the local Roman administration.

219. Josephus *Jewish Antiquities* 14.5.4.

220. Matthew 10:17.

221. Josephus *Jewish Antiquities* 15.6.2.

222. Hyrcanus had written to the governor of Arabia asking him for sanctuary from Herod until he might find an opportunity to return to power.

223. This work is found in Joannes Annio da Viterbo's edition of the Babylonian history of Berossus (Lyon, 1554). For its use, see Guido Bartolucci, *La repubblica ebraica di Carlo Sigonio: modelli politici dell'età moderna* (Florence: Olschki, 2007), p. 187.

224. In France. This happened in 6 CE; cf. Josephus *Jewish Antiquities* 17.13.2.

225. During the early Roman Empire, many areas of the eastern Mediterranean were governed by tetrarchs appointed by the emperors. In principle these were sovereign rulers, but they were considered less powerful than the local kings. Their title alludes to the fact that it had originally been applied to the rulers of a nation divided into four districts.

226. Matthew 5:21–22.

227. The three penalties, therefore, are ordered from lightest to heaviest.

228. Augustine *On the Sermon on the Mount* 1.9.24.

229. I.e. he assumed that one court declared guilt and another decided punishments, while Sigonio—presumably guided by the biblical and talmudic passages he quotes in this book—believes that different courts handled different kinds of crimes.

230. Matthew 16:21.

231. Luke 20:1–2, 20–22.

232. John 11:46–50, 53.

233. John 11:57.

234. The following section of the narrative stays closest to the accounts of Matthew and Mark.

235. James and John.

236. I.e. to arrest him.

237. The term used in John 18:12, on which this sentence is based.

238. Bystanders asked Peter whether he was not in fact a disciple of Jesus, and he denied it every time.

239. The following is based on Luke.

240. The next part is based on John.

241. The next part is based on Luke.

242. Herod Antipas, the tetrarch of Galilee.

243. The next part is based on Matthew and Mark.

244. The next part is based on John.

245. The account continues from Matthew.

246. I.e. about noon.

247. Sigonio seems to be referring to the passage he quoted above from Galatino: *the Sanhedrin met from morning until evening.*

248. Acts 4:1–3, 5–7.

249. Acts 4:15.

250. In this chapter, a husband and wife who had tried to cheat the apostles suddenly collapse and die, sick people are healed, and after the apostles have been arrested an angel comes to lead them from the prison.

251. Acts 5:17–18, 21, 24, 26–27, 29, 34.

252. Acts 5:40.

253. Acts 6:11–13.

254. Acts 7:57.

255. Acts 22:29–30; 23:1–7.

256. The brother of Jesus, called "Younger" to distinguish him from James the son of Zebedee.

257. Josephus *Jewish Antiquities* 19.9.1. Josephus says that it was King Agrippa who removed him.

258. A literal translation of the Hebrew *mot yumat,* "he will surely die."

259. Cf. Leviticus 24:16.

260. Josephus *Jewish War* 4.5.4. Josephus is describing a kangaroo court set up by the Zealots to try a man whom they disliked because of his integrity and wealth.

261. This is the name given to Josephus in the *Yossipon,* the medieval Hebrew text which combines parts of both the *Jewish Antiquities* and the *Jewish War,* and which is the source of the following passage.

262. I.e. John of Gischala, the Zealot leader.

263. *Yossipon* 69.90 (ed. Flusser), which corresponds to Josephus *Jewish War* 4.5.4.

264. Exodus 22:1.

265. Exodus 21:22.

266. Exodus 21:23–25.

267. Deuteronomy 25:2–3.

268. Deuteronomy 22:3.

269. Deuteronomy 21:13.

270. In the Talmud, as in the above quote from Galatino, there are four deaths—burning, stoning, strangulation, and "killing," which the Talmud understands as beheading.

271. Leviticus 20:14.

272. Deuteronomy 21:22–23. In the rabbinic sources, crucifixion is not mentioned as a punishment, and these verses are taken to refer to hanging up a corpse after the victim has been executed (a presumption supported by some of the other verses Sigonio has quoted here). On the other hand, the idea that hanging or crucifixion was itself a punishment appears in the Dead Sea Scrolls, where betrayers are to be hanged *so that* they will die, and in Christian texts starting with Galatians 3:13.

273. Joshua 8:29.

274. Gk. *xylon didymon*.

275. Joshua 10:26–27. The beginning of this passage tells us that they were killed before they were hung up, which could also be true of the account in Joshua 8.

276. 2 Samuel 21:9.

277. Esther 7:9–10.

278. This was a decree of the Persian king Cyrus.

279. Ezra 6:11.

280. Acts 5:30. In this verse, which seems to allude to the Deuteronomy passage, the hanging again follows the execution.

281. Psalms 21:16–17.

282. Numbers 25:3–4.

283. Mark 15:12–13, 15, 26–27.

284. For Passover.

285. John 19:31–34.

286. There is an essay *De iudiciis* (*On the Courts*) included in Sigonio's *De antiquo iure populi Romani* (*On the Ancient Law of the Roman People*), first published in 1574.

287. *Maiestas*, the majesty of the Roman people, had been legally protected under the republic, and this protection had since been transferred to the person of the emperor. Any challenges to his authority or dignity (which were themselves called *maiestas*) could be prosecuted. See also note 56 above.

288. I.e. among the Romans.

289. An account of the attack on the Jewish community of Alexandria in 38 CE, and of the downfall of Flaccus, governor of Egypt, who allowed it to happen.

290. According to Philo, this was a celebration of the birthday of a member of the family of Augustus.

291. Philo *Against Flaccus* 83.

292. Leviticus 24:14–16.

293. Deuteronomy 13:8–10.

294. Deuteronomy 17:2-7.

295. Numbers 15:32-36.

296. Deuteronomy 22:23-24.

297. 1 Kings 21:13.

298. John 10:33.

299. Acts 6:11-13.

300. Acts 7:57-58. The witnesses did this to keep from soiling them.

301. John 8:3-5, 7.

302. Matthew 14:10.

303. Acts 1:18. Sigonio presumably thinks that strangulation was a punishment because it was one of the four types mentioned by the Talmud, but he has given its place in that scheme to crucifixion; while Judas, to whom the quote from Acts refers, was not punished at all, but rather hanged himself in despair.

BOOK VII

1. Sigonio seems to be referring to a specific use of the Latin *jubere* ("to command") which, when combined with *lex*, can mean "legislate."

2. Possibly a reference to 2 Chronicles 9:8: ...*therefore he made you king over them, to do judgment and justice*; or to Ezekiel 45:9: *Let it suffice you, O princes of Israel: remove violence and spoil, and execute judgment and justice.*

3. 1 Samuel 9:16.

4. 2 Samuel 5:2.

5. 1 Kings 1:35.

6. 1 Samuel 8:5.

7. 2 Samuel 8:15.

8. 2 Chronicles 9:8.

9. The speaker is the queen of Sheba.

10. Psalms 9:4. Despite Sigonio's interpretation of this verse, it is clear from the context in Psalms that it is God, rather than the king, who sits on the throne and does justice to his people.

11. See Book I, chapter 4.

12. Exodus 2:14.

13. Exodus 18:22–26 calls the cases to be reserved for Moses both "great" and "heavy" (*gravus*, the Vulgate's translation of the Hebrew *kashe*, "hard"). In Latin, "heavy" can mean either "grievous" or "weighty"; but Sigonio seems to have understood it as the latter, and to have associated it with religious issues, because Moses judges the case of the man found collecting wood on the Sabbath.

14. Deuteronomy 12:8–9.

15. The "princes and kings again" were the Hasmoneans, who were called first *nasi* and then king.

16. I.e. "rulers of tribes."

17. As he has before, Sigonio is envisioning a clear and comprehensive system of government akin to the Roman one, which by the Renaissance had come to seem perfect and unchanging (and which German scholarship would later try to explain in detail). Since, however, the Bible itself never offers a comprehensive "constitution" (or suggests that there ever was one), Sigonio is attempting to synthesize it out of the available sources.

18. κριτὴς and δικαστὴς, κρίνειν and δικάζειν, κρίσις and δικαίωσις; i.e. "judge and decider, to judge and to decide, judgment and decision."

19. ἐδίκαζε, "he judged."

20. δικασταὶ. It is not clear how this is meant to illustrate Sigonio's distinction between *dikastai*, who absolve, and *kritai*, who condemn—Deborah, Othniel, and Ehud are no more obviously associated with condemnations than is Samuel.

21. οἱ δικασταὶ οἱ δικάσαντες ἰσρὴλ, "The judges who judge Israel." Cf. Baruch 2:1.

22. I.e. once Jerusalem was made the capital, all the chief judges lived there.

23. Judges 4:4–5.

24. 1 Samuel 7:15–17.

25. Sigonio seems to be thinking of the various biblical incidents in which kings like David and Ahab personally ordered the execution of Israelites.

26. Even though Sigonio would like to suggest that the judges were conventional officials who held office one after another, in the first nine chapters of the Book of Judges there is no continuity from one judge to the next. In fact, there are no judges mentioned in the first two chapters, and when they do appear it is only at times of crisis. And while chapters 10 and 12 present the sort of sequence that could imply a fixed office, there the judges are not necessarily connected to any particular wars—they simply "judge" Israel. Sigonio's difficulty seems to be that he is accustomed to Greek and Roman historical sources that routinely name the holders of major magistracies whenever they entered office (such magistracies were even used as chronological markers), while the Book of Judges, like most biblical historiography, is not interested in providing a comprehensive record.

27. Judges 11:5–6.

28. Perhaps Sigonio is thinking of Deborah, whose leadership was acknowledged even by the general Barak.

29. This is not stated explicitly anywhere in the Book of Judges. Sigonio may be alluding to the fact that in most cases, the decision to go to war began with a divine pronouncement.

30. Cf. Judges 3:9, 15.

31. Judges 6:14, 16. Although the phrase "as one man" seems to mean that Gideon will easily defeat the Midianites, Sigonio is apparently taking it to refer to the people of Israel, who will be united in their support of Gideon.

32. Judges 11:6.

33. Othniel: Judges 3:9–11; Ehud: Judges 3:15–30; Deborah: Judges 4:4–14; Gideon: Judges 6:11–8:32.

34. Shechem. Cf. Judges 9.

35. Jephthah was from Gilead, the part of Manasseh which settled across the Jordan.

36. His name is Abdon in both the Hebrew and Latin Bibles, but he is called Labdon by the church fathers.

37. Tola: Judges 10:1–2; Jair: Judges 10:3–5; Jephthah: Judges 11:1–12:7; Ibzan: Judges 12:8–10; Elon: Judges 12:11–12; Abdon: Judges 12:13–15; Samson: Judges 13:1–16:31; Eli: 1 Samuel 1:9–4:18.

38. Cf. Aristotle *Politics* 3.16, where he places even absolute monarchy under the rule of law. Nor is the idea that the king was above the law found in the Bible—if anything, David and his successors are told to live by God's law, and punished when they do not. But Sigonio may be thinking of the kinds of constitutional restraints—such as term limits and the imposition of vetoes—that limited the power of many Greek and Roman officials, and of which the biblical narratives give no hint. See the discussion in the introduction, pp. xxiii–xxv.

39. 1 Samuel 15:17.

40. Deuteronomy 17:14–20.

41. *Superbia*, the quality with which Roman writers associated the kings who first ruled Rome but were expelled when the people decided to create a republic.

42. Josephus *Jewish Antiquities* 4.8.17.

43. This is Sigonio's interpretation of the phrase "like the other nations," guided as he is by the Greek idea that living under a king—and in particular the Persian king of kings—meant voluntary enslavement to the will of another.

44. 1 Samuel 8:5–7, 9–22.

45. The only power, both here and earlier in the chapter, that Sigonio seems to attribute to kings alone is the power to wage war, which the Bible in fact never explicitly denies to the judges.

46. The following passage, up to "*every man to his house*," is a paraphrase of 1 Samuel 10:1–25.

47. In both the Hebrew and Latin versions of 1 Samuel 11:15, Saul is "made king" at Gilgal, and there is no mention of anointment. Sigonio's text, which he quotes below, has "Samuel anointed King Saul," which is the reading found in the Septuagint.

48. Psalms 17:50.

49. 1 Samuel 24:6.

50. 1 Samuel 11:14–15.

51. ἐγκαινίζωμεν, "let us renew."

52. The Greek name for Hanukkah, the Festival of Dedication.

53. 1 Maccabees 4:53–54.

54. 1 Maccabees 4:56, 59.

55. Cf. 1 Samuel 13:8–14. The "priest" here is in fact Samuel, but Sigonio is suggesting that Saul's error was procedural: as a king he should not have usurped the prerogatives of a priest, which Samuel enjoyed as the successor of Eli.

56. Cf. 1 Samuel 16:1–13.

57. Cf. 2 Samuel 2:3–10.

58. 2 Samuel 5:1, 3–5.

59. 1 Kings 1:33–35.

60. Cf. 2 Chronicles 1–9.

61. Cf. 2 Chronicles 10:14: *My father made your yoke heavy, but I will add to it; my father chastised you with whips, but I will chastise you with scorpions.*

62. 1 Kings 12:1.

63. 2 Chronicles 22:1.

64. 2 Chronicles 23:11.

65. 2 Chronicles 36:1.

66. This phrase appears only in the Septuagint.

67. Cf. 2 Kings 18:9–11.

68. 2 Samuel 15:2, 6.

69. Psalms 72:1–2.

70. Psalms 96:2.

71. Psalms 98:4.

72. I.e. the Books of Samuel and Kings.

73. The Hellenistic dynasties of the Ptolemies and the Seleucids.

74. According to Josephus (*Jewish Antiquities* 12.5.1), Antiochus chose Jason to be high priest over his brother Menelaus, who then raised a rebellion against him. Perhaps Sigonio considers this an "internal conflict" because both men were legally eligible to be high priest. But since 2 Maccabees does not seem to consider Menelaus part of the high priestly family, this could in fact have been another case in which Antiochus gave the priesthood to an outsider.

75. 1 Maccabees 2:29. This verse is not explicitly connected in the text with Mattathias, whom the book does not describe as a public leader.

76. A Greek term for a civic leader.

77. Cf. Josephus *Jewish Antiquities* 12.10.6.

78. Josephus *Jewish Antiquities* 13.2.2–3; 1 Maccabees 10:20.

79. 1 Maccabees 9:30–31.

80. In 142 BCE.

81. 1 Maccabees 13:8–9.

82. 1 Maccabees 14:41–49.

83. 1 Maccabees 13:39–40.

84. 1 Maccabees 13:41–42.

85. 1 Maccabees 15:5–8.

86. In 135 BCE.

87. In 104 BCE.

88. Sigonio takes this from Josephus (*Jewish Antiquities* 13.10.11), who says it happened 481 years later. Since Aristobulus became king in 104 BCE, this would place the return from Babylonia in 585 BCE, fifty years earlier than the date assigned by modern scholarship.

89. 76–67 BCE.

90. In 67 BCE.

91. In 63 BCE.

92. According to Josephus (*Jewish Antiquities* 14.5.8), it was Julius Caesar who did this. Antipater's appointment did not, in any case, mean that Judea was now a Roman province—a "procurator" was anyone appointed to administer someone else's possessions, and as the commander of Rome's armies Caesar was in charge of its dealings overseas. Actual provinces were controlled by the senate, which appointed proconsuls to govern them. Judea, in fact, became a province only after the rebellion

of 68 CE; until then it had procurators like Pilate because it was under the emperor's direct control.

93. 41 BCE.

94. I.e. his new Temple and his other building projects throughout the country.

95. 4 BCE.

96. In 6 CE.

97. In 41 CE.

98. Caligula.

99. Greek and Roman tribes registered the children of their members when the children entered adulthood.

100. Numbers 1:44.

101. Numbers 4:34.

102. Numbers 31:13.

103. Joshua 22:13–14.

104. Numbers 7:2.

105. Philo *On Flight and Finding* 73.

106. Cf. 1 Chronicles 27:17–21. Manasseh was divided into two halves, each of whom had a chief; and Levi was not usually numbered among the twelve tribes; while one of Jacob's twelve sons, Joseph, was represented by his own two sons, Manasseh and Ephraim.

107. None of the following passages suggest that the chiefs of the tribes were being consulted in any way—they are given commands or information, they ask questions, or they are asked to do something; and several of the passages go on to mention people other than the chiefs to whom Sigonio's statement is meant to apply.

108. Numbers 30:1.

109. Deuteronomy 5:23.

110. Deuteronomy 31:28.

111. Deuteronomy 29:10.

112. ἀρχίφυλοι, i.e. "chiefs of tribes" instead of "your chiefs, your tribes."

113. 1 Chronicles 28:1.

114. 2 Chronicles 5:2.

115. 1 Kings 8:1.

116. Psalms 113:5–8.

117. For "chiefs" the Greek has *archontes*, which Sigonio has already described as a kind of political leader.

118. Psalms 121:4–5.

119. Isaiah 3:13–14.

120. Isaiah 32:1.

121. Matthew 19:28; cf. Luke 22:30.

122. 1 Kings 7:7–8.

123. *Place of judgment.* There is nothing in the verse to imply that this place was used by the chiefs of the tribes. Perhaps Sigonio sees such an implication in the fact that the Vulgate uses the word "tribunal," but if so it is a very weak one: in Rome, the tribunal was originally the place of the tribune, an official who was in turn originally linked to one of the Roman tribes.

124. Joshua 9:15.

125. Cf. ibid.

126. Ezra 6:17.

127. 3 Esdras 7:8, which also mentions the number twelve.

128. Ezra 8:24. This is the version in the Septuagint, where it is numbered as 8:54.

129. This is Sigonio's conflation of the passages from Psalms 121 and Matthew 19.

130. Cf. Book VI, chapter 7.

131. Numbers 1:2, 20, 21 (Septuagint).

132. Joshua 7:14, 16–17.

133. Joshua 18:11; 19:1.

134. Judges 17:7.

135. Which is not one of the families of Benjamin listed in Numbers.

136. 1 Samuel 10:19–21.

137. The genealogy of David at the end of the Book of Ruth extends several generations beyond the descendants of Judah listed in Numbers 26.

138. 1 Chronicles 28:4.

139. The third and fourth on the list of Greek terms, which Sigonio has not translated, mean "patriarchs" and "heads of families."

140. Numbers 1:4.

141. Numbers 7:2.

142. Numbers 36:1.

143. Joshua 14:1.

144. Joshua 19:51.

145. Joshua 21:1.

146. 1 Chronicles 24:4.

147. 1 Chronicles 8:28.

148. Cf. Ezra 1:5: *Then rose up the heads of fathers' houses of Judah and Benjamin, and the priests, and the Levites... to go up to build the house of the Lord, which is in Jerusalem.*

149. Ezra 3:12 mentions the "heads of fathers' houses," but does not tell us what if anything their responsibilities were.

150. I.e. *heads of tribes.*

151. Ezra 2:7 (according to the Septuagint enumeration).

152. Ezra 5:1 (Septuagint).

153. μεριδαρχία; Ezra 5:4 (Septuagint).

154. Cf., for example, Ezra 4:2, 3; 8:1, 29.

155. Nehemiah 8:13.

156. See below, chapter 11, where Sigonio equates the patriarchs with those heads of tribes who were also in command of troops.

157. 2 Chronicles 5:2. Here they are being asked not for advice, but to bring the ark to Jerusalem.

158. 2 Chronicles 19:8.

159. By "family" Sigonio seems to be thinking of something like the Roman *gens* (one of the kinds of groups he mentions at the beginning of chapter 6), a large body of people all of whom were believed to share the same primordial ancestor, and which could number in the thousands. The *gens* contained smaller units within it. Marcus Tullius Cicero, for example, was a member of the Cicero branch of the *gens Tullia.*

160. The Bible has here "Gaal son of Ebed."

161. Judges 9:30.

162. Judges 9:51.

163. 2 Kings 23:8.

164. There is no reason to assume that there were any others: the Hebrew *sar* can simply mean "governor." Sigonio, however, is envisioning a system like the Roman decurionate, a senate of local aristocrats.

165. Cf. Josephus *Jewish Antiquities* 4.8.14, where Josephus says in his summary of the laws of judges that each city had seven.

166. See Book VI, note 118.

167. Cf. Book VI, chapter 6.

168. Deuteronomy 1:12–15.

169. In his previous quotation from this passage, Sigonio bases himself on the Septuagint rather than the Vulgate.

170. I.e. they were like Roman judges, who were not public officials but senators who were sometimes asked to judge trials.

171. Exodus 18:25–26.

172. 1 Chronicles 28:1.

173. I.e. the priestly divisions.

174. Deuteronomy 16:18.

175. Deuteronomy 29:10.

176. Deuteronomy 31:28.

177. Joshua 23:2.

178. Joshua 24:1.

179. In Book 2, chapter 9. This commentary is actually the work of Hraban, a ninth-century bishop of Mainz.

180. I.e. in Exodus 18.

181. Because Jethro makes his suggestion already in chapter 18, while the Ten Commandments are given in chapter 20.

182. Sigonio has here *grammatici*, who in the Roman world were scholars of language.

183. I.e. of the passage in Deuteronomy 1.

184. Although there are no compelling reasons for such an interpretation, Sigonio's claim is not as arbitrary as it might seem: the word *graphe*, which is cognate with *gramma*, sometimes means in classical Greek "an indictment at court." Sigonio wants to suggest that this is true of *gramma* as well (though there are no actual cases of such a usage), in its compound with *eisagōgeis* ("those who lead in"). For his explanation, see below.

185. Josephus *Jewish Antiquities* 4.8.14. Sigonio's Latin text of Josephus has here "ministers," which usually has the sense of "assistant." The Greek, in fact, has for "officers" *hyperetai*, "underlings." Since, however, Sigonio wants to read Josephus as saying that these officers were the "superiors" of the judges, he has to take "minister" in

its more modern sense, i.e. someone who is the servant of the state but the governor of his fellow citizens.

186. Ezra 7:25.

187. Isaiah 1:23.

188. I.e. cases did not simply come to them, they had to accept them.

189. I.e. "*grammatoisagogue.*"

190. εἰσαγωγεῖς τῶν γραφῶν, "introducers of the writs."

191. γράμματα, "letters" or "documents" (though nowhere does it mean "writs").

192. Though Greek and Roman judges were not themselves officers of the state, there were systems of judicial administration.

193. Caesar *Civil War* 1.87. The verb used here, *introducere,* is the equivalent of the Greek *eisagogein,* "lead in."

194. Sigonio is assuming that, as in the Roman justice system, there were no court officers to compel the appearance of a defendant.

195. Luke 12:58–59. Because Sigonio assumes that both the Old and New Testaments are describing exactly the same legal system, he acknowledges that according to the latter there were also cases of imprisonment, though he does not try to incorporate them into the Old Testament scheme of punishments that he discussed above.

196. One of Sigonio's models was the Venetian republic. He may have in mind here the description of Venetian institutions offered by Contarini (*De republica Venetorum,* Lyon, 1626).

197. 2 Chronicles 1:2.

198. As in Sigonio's discussion of the grammatoisagogues' political role, these passages do not (with one exception) suggest that they were being consulted.

199. Deuteronomy 29:10.

200. Deuteronomy 31:28.

201. 1 Chronicles 13:1.

202. 1 Chronicles 28:1.

203. This seems to be based on the Septuagint, though there the text reads "divisions" rather than "tribes."

204. 2 Chronicles 1:2.

205. 2 Chronicles 29:20.

206. The following is a paraphrase of Jeremiah 36:11–25.

207. Jeremiah 37:14–15; 38:4–5.

208. A paraphrase of 2 Chronicles 18:25-26.

209. Luke 20:20.

210. *Principatus* in Latin.

211. Latin *praeses*.

212. The phrase in Luke—*principatui et potestati praesidis*—is usually interpreted as "to the power and authority of the governor," but Sigonio has separated the first of the two dative nouns from the genitive ("of the governor") that follows.

213. Micah 5:2.

214. The term used by the Septuagint.

215. In Book V, chapter 10.

216. γραμματεῖς, "scribes."

217. Psalms 44:1.

218. Not Baruch but the king's scribe.

219. Cf. Jeremiah 36:16-23. The razor was the tool used to scrape mistakes off the parchment.

220. Jeremiah 8:8.

221. Sigonio's problem is that scribes are mentioned in the Books of Kings as recorders only, while Ezra is described as both a scribe and an interpreter of the law, and the scribes of the New Testament also seem to perform both these functions.

222. Numbers 11:16.

223. This is the Septuagint. Scribes are not mentioned in either the Hebrew or Latin texts.

224. Deuteronomy 20:8. This is the Septuagint; the Vulgate has here *duces*, "commanders."

225. In the Bible they are called Elihoreph and Ahiah.

226. Cf. 2 Samuel 8:17; 1 Kings 4:3; 2 Kings 18:18.

227. 2 Kings 12:10.

228. I.e. that they were served by scribes.

229. Josephus *Jewish Antiquities* 4.8.14.

230. 2 Chronicles 34:13.

231. The context here is the refurbishing of the Temple, which was entirely in the hands of the Levites.

232. Deuteronomy 20:8 (Septuagint).

233. This is a paraphrase of Joshua 1:10–11 in the Septuagint; the Vulgate mentions not scribes but "chiefs of the people."

234. A paraphrase of the Septuagint for Joshua 3:2–3; the Hebrew has here "officers," and the Latin "heralds."

235. 1 Chronicles 27:1 according to the Septuagint. The Vulgate does not mention scribes or the people.

236. Cf. Josephus *Jewish War* 5.13.1.

237. Jeremiah 52:25.

238. Commanders, chiefs, and heralds.

239. Deuteronomy 20:1–20.

240. Philo *On the Special Laws* 4.224–226.

241. Chief of the army.

242. 2 Samuel 2:8.

243. This quote appears to be a conflation of two verses: 2 Samuel 20:23, where Joab is called "over all the army"; and 1 Kings 2:32, where Amasa is "the chief of the army of Judah."

244. This is a paraphrase of 2 Samuel 24:2, though the Bible has here "people" rather than "soldiers."

245. 2 Samuel 19:13.

246. Sigonio is quoting directly from the Vulgate, 2 Kings 25:19.

247. Because it is difficult to understand what a scribe would be doing in charge of soldiers (Heb. *hasofer sar hatzava*), the Vulgate assumes that the head of the army was a man named "Sopher," rather than the *sofer* mentioned in the Hebrew and translated in the Septuagint as "scribe."

248. The widow appears in the previous story about Elisha. The speaker here is the wealthy woman of Shunem, whom Elisha wants to thank for giving him a place to stay.

249. 2 Kings 4:13.

250. Latin *quinquagenarii*.

251. Latin *decani*.

252. Numbers 1:16 (Septuagint).

253. Sigonio seems to be thinking again of the Roman Empire, where local aristocrats might also serve as officials within the local Roman administration.

254. 1 Chronicles 12:19–20. In this passage and the next, Sigonio has substituted "chiliads" for "thousands."

255. 1 Chronicles 15:25.

256. By God.

257. Judges 6:15 (Septuagint).

258. Micah 5:20.

259. Cf. 1 Chronicles 28:1.

260. 2 Samuel 18:1–2.

261. A paraphrase of 2 Kings 11:4.

262. Which is the parallel version of this story.

263. In fact, both the heads of families and the heads of hundreds are mentioned here.

264. 2 Chronicles 25:5, according to the Septuagint.

265. Cf. 1 Maccabees 4:55.

266. Numbers 31:14.

267. 2 Samuel 24:4.

268. 2 Kings 1:9.

269. 1 Maccabees 3:55.

270. I.e. 2 Samuel 19:13: *God do so to me, and more also, if you are not captain of the host... continually...*

271. 1 Samuel 8:12.

272. 1 Samuel 18:13.

273. 2 Samuel 18:1.

274. 2 Samuel 18:4.

275. 1 Chronicles 11:6.

276. 2 Chronicles 25:5.

277. The Hebrew has here *rashei bet avot*, the "heads of fathers' houses."

278. The Hasmonean kings.

279. 1 Maccabees 4:60–61.

280. Josephus *Jewish Antiquities* 15.11.4.

281. Matthew 27:65.

282. The lictors attended senior Roman magistrates.

283. Of the two types of offenders who had to be brought in by soldiers, Jesus is obviously meant to be the sort whose power is so great that the authorities are afraid of him; but since he poses no concrete threat (a point made by the Gospels themselves), Sigonio is assuming it was his spiritual power that caused this reaction.

284. It is not clear if Sigonio is equating these officers with any of the other types of magistrates he has mentioned up till now.

285. I.e. at the trial of Jesus.

286. This quote is from Matthew 26:14–15; the passage in Mark (14:10–11) is worded differently.

287. Luke 22:4.

288. John 18:3.

289. John 18:12.

290. Luke 22:52.

291. στρατηγοὶ τοῦ ἱεροῦ, i.e. *commanders of the Temple*, the phrase Sigonio translates at the beginning of the chapter as "heads of the Temple forces."

292. Acts 4:1.

293. Acts 5:24, 26.

294. Although the king of Moab tries to place the Israelites under a curse, there is no battle; in fact, at Deuteronomy 2:9 the Israelites are told not to attack the Moabites, because they deserved their land as descendants of Abraham's nephew Lot.

295. Cf. Numbers 21:1, 21–24, 33–35; 31:1–20.

296. Cf. Joshua 24:11.

297. Mesopotamia: Judges 3:8–10; Canaanites: Judges 1:1–17; Midianites: Judges 6:2–8:28; Moabites: Judges 3:12–30; Ammonites: Judges 10:7–11:33; Philistines: Judges 13:1–16:31.

298. Nahash: 1 Samuel 11:1–11; Philistines: 1 Samuel 13:3–14:52; Agag: 1 Samuel 15:1–33.

299. Ishbosheth: 2 Samuel 2:10–4:12; Jebusites: 2 Samuel 5:6–8; Moabites: 2 Samuel 8:2; Ammonites: 2 Samuel 10:6–19; Absalom: 2 Samuel 16:15–19:4; Sheba: 2 Samuel 20:1–22; Philistines: 2 Samuel 5:17–25, 8:1, 21:15–22.

300. The expression used in 2 Samuel 8:6, where David places a garrison in Damascus.

301. David also placed garrisons there; cf. 2 Samuel 8:14.

302. In addition to the Assyrian and Babylonian invasions, Shishak king of Egypt invaded Jerusalem in the reign of Rehoboam (1 Kings 14:25–26); and Benhadad the king of Syria attacked the kingdom of Israel twice (1 Kings 15:18–20; 20:1–34).

303. The founders of the Seleucid and Ptolemaic dynasties were generals in Alexander's armies.

304. Idumeans: Josephus *Jewish Antiquities* 13.9.1; Samaritans: *Jewish Antiquities* 13.10.2; Itureans: *Jewish Antiquities* 13.11.3; Moabites and Gileadites: *Jewish Antiquities* 13.13.5.

305. Josephus *Jewish Antiquities* 14.4.1–4.

306. Josephus *Jewish Antiquities* 14.16.1–4; *Jewish War* 1.18.1–3.

307. Josephus *Jewish War*, Books 5–7.

308. Josephus, as Sigonio presumably was aware, does in fact mention several examples of Jews fighting for foreign armies.

309. In *Jewish Antiquities* 18.3.5, Josephus says that Tiberius expelled the Jews of Rome (in 19 CE), sent four thousand of them to Sardinia as soldiers, and punished a greater number who refused to serve for religious reasons.

310. Philo *Embassy to Gaius* 214–216.

311. In the Greek sense of a "mother city," which sends out colonists to found new communities.

312. Asia Minor.

313. I.e. the Black Sea coast.

314. I.e. European Greece.

315. Philo *Embassy to Gaius* 281–282.

316. Augustus' friend, general, and son-in-law.

317. Philo *Embassy to Gaius* 290–293.

318. In 186 BCE, the Roman senate—asserting that the worshipers of Bacchus in Italy were a secret society which threatened the state—outlawed the cult and punished a number of its members.

319. Philo *Embassy to Gaius* 311–313.

320. Philo *Embassy to Gaius* 210–212.

321. Rutilius Namatianus, a pagan Roman poet of the fifth century CE whose work *On His Return* criticizes both Judaism and Christianity.

322. Which was not part of the Catholic canon.

323. The authority of the Greek church fathers was open to question because of certain philosophical doctrines that the western Church came to regard as heretical.

324. Augustine *City of God* 444.

325. Psalms 48:8 and 84:4.

INDEX OF SOURCES

HEBREW BIBLE

Numbers

1:2, 20, 21	287 n.131
1:4	288 n.140
1:16	300 n.252
1:44	284 n.100
1:49	15 n.14
1:49–51	191 n.197
3	192 n.200
3:6–10, 12–13	191–192 n.198
3:12–13	163 n.3
4	45; 193
4:16	184 n.147
4:34	284 n.101
5:9–10	147 n.167
6:2–12	203 n.248
7:2	284 n.104; 288 n.141
7:89	208 n.281
8:24, 26	193 n.201
9:11	69 n.24
10:2–8	232 n.30
11:16	248 n.178; 295 n.222
11:16–17	237 n.78
11:24–29	206 n.262
12:6–8	205 n.258; 210 n.301
15:4, 9	122 n.35
15:20	333 n.6
15:32	249 n.193
15:32–36	262 n.295
15:38	362 n.448
15:38–39	225 n.446
15:39	363 n.450
18:11–14	147 n.168
18:15–18	147–148 n.170
18:16	341 n.221
18:20–21	163 n.4
18:26–29	148 n.175
20	176
21:1, 21–24, 33–35	390 n.295
25:3–4	260 n.282
25:10, 12–13	176 n.87
25:13	175 n.81
26	287; 383 n.137
27:19–20	231 n.19
28:3–8	74 n.59
28:9–10	76 n.71
28:11–14	73 n.53
28:26	329 n.116
29	85–86 n.131
29:39	146 n.161
30:1	284 n.108
30:2	156 n.220
30:13	158 n.237
31:1–20	305 n.295
31:13	284 n.102
31:14	301 n.266
36	15 n.16
36:1	288 n.142
36:3–4	91 n.156
36:6–7	91 n.157
36:8	15 n.17
36:13	21 n.41

Deuteronomy

	xxii; 14; 177; 215
1	291; 292 n.183
1:9, 12–17	241–242 n.121
1:12–15	290–291 n.168
1:38	354 n.255
2:9	390 n.294

JOSEPHUS

NEW TESTAMENT AND APOCRYPHA

CHRISTIAN SOURCES

RABBINIC SOURCES

GENERAL INDEX